D0205395

The New
Oxford Book of
Australian
Verse

THE NEW
OXFORD BOOK OF
AUSTRALIAN
VERSE

Chosen by Les A. Murray

Melbourne
OXFORD UNIVERSITY PRESS
Oxford   Auckland   New York

OXFORD UNIVERSITY PRESS

Oxford New York Toronto Delhi Bombay Calcutta Madras
Karachi Singapore Hong Kong Tokyo Nairobi
Dar es Salaam Cape Town Melbourne Auckland
and associates in
Beirut Berlin Ibadan Nicosia

© Les A. Murray 1986
First published 1986

National Library of Australia
Cataloguing-in-Publication data:
The New Oxford book of Australian verse.
ISBN 0 19 554618 0.
1. Australian poetry. I. Murray, Les A. (Leslie Allan),
1938—
A821'.008

Designed by Jan Schmoeger
Typeset by Asco Trade Typesetting Ltd., Hong Kong
Printed in Singapore by Singapore National Printers (Pte) Ltd.
Published by Oxford University Press, 7 Bowen Crescent, Melbourne
OXFORD is a trademark of Oxford University Press

CONTENTS

Foreword   xxi

Sam Woolagoodjah
Lalai (Dreamtime)   1

Barron Field (1786–1846)
The Kangaroo   6

Richard Whately (1787–1863)
There is a Place in Distant Seas   7

Anonymous
A Hot Day in Sydney   8
The Exile of Erin   11
Hey, Boys! Up Go We!   12
The Limejuice Tub   13

John Dunmore Lang (1799–1878)
Colonial Nomenclature   14

Anonymous
Van Diemen's Land   15
The Convicts' Rum Song   16
Hail South Australia!   16
The Female Transport   17
The Lass in the Female Factory   18

Francis MacNamara (Frank the Poet) (b. 1811?)
A petition from the chain gang   19
For the Company underground   22
A Convict's Tour to Hell   23

Robert Lowe (1811–1892)
Songs of the Squatters, I and II   28

Charles Harpur (1813–1868)
A Basket of Summer Fruit   31
Wellington   32
A Flight of Wild Ducks   33

Henry Parkes (1815–1896)
Our Coming Countrymen   34

Aboriginal Songs from the 1850s
Kilaben Bay song (Awabakal)   36

Women's rondo (Awabakal)   37
Two tongue-pointing (satirical) songs (Kamilaroi)   38
The drunk man (Wolaroi)   38

Anonymous
  Whaler's Rhyme   38
  The Diggins-oh   39

William W. Coxon (?)
  The Flash Colonial Barman   41

Charles R. Thatcher (1831–1882)
  Dick Briggs from Australia   42
  Taking the Census   45
  Moggy's Wedding   46

Anonymous
  The Banks of the Condamine   48
  The Stringybark Cockatoo   49

Henry Kendall (1839–1882)
  Bell-birds   50
  Beyond Kerguelen   51

Anonymous
  John Gilbert was a Bushranger   53

Jack McGuire (?)
  The Streets of Forbes   55

E. J. Overbury
  The Springtime it Brings On the Shearing   55

James Brunton Stephens (1835–1902)
  The Gentle Anarchist   56

Ada Cambridge (1844–1926)
  Fashion   57
  The Future Verdict   57
  The Virgin Martyr   58

Marcus Clarke (1846–1881)
  The Wail of the Waiter   59

Victor Daley (1858–1905)
  Mother Doorstep   60
  The Woman at the Washtub   61
  The Dove   63

J. A. Phelp
  The Duke of Buccleuch   63

Anonymous
The Wooyeo Ball 64

W. T. Goodge (1862–1909)
How We Drove the Trotter 65
A Bad Break! 66
Federation 67

Mary Gilmore (1863–1962)
The Harvesters 68
The Little Shoes that Died 68
The Saturday Tub 69

Andrew Barton Paterson ('The Banjo') (1864–1941)
The Travelling Post Office 70
Father Riley's Horse 71
Old Australian Ways 73

Bernard O'Dowd (1866–1953)
Cupid 75

Charles W. Hayward (1866–1950)
King George V 77

Barcroft Boake (1866–1892)
The Digger's Song 77

Louis Lavater (1867–1953)
The Barrier 78

Henry Lawson (1867–1922)
The English Queen 79
When Your Pants Begin to Go 81
The Men who Come Behind 82

Anonymous
The Bastard from the Bush 83

E. G. Murphy ('Dryblower') (1867–1939)
The Smiths 85

Mary Fullerton ('E') (1868–1946)
A Man's a Sliding Mood 86
Unit 86
Poetry 87

Anonymous
Shickered As He Could Be 87

E. J. Brady (1869–1952)
The Whaler's Pig 88

Christopher Brennan (1870–1932)
Sweet silence after bells! 91
Fire in the heavens 91

J. Le Gay Brereton (1871–1933)
Unborn 92

John Shaw Neilson (1872–1942)
May 92
Schoolgirls Hastening 93
To the Red Lory 93

Ngunaitponi (David Unaipon) (1873–1967)
The Song of Hungarrda 94

Anonymous (Narranyeri people, South Australia)
Song: The Railway Train 95

C. J. Dennis (1876–1938)
The Traveller 95

Hugh McCrae (1876–1958)
The Mimshi Maiden 96

Louis Esson (1879–1943)
The Shearer's Wife 98

P. J. Hartigan ('John O'Brien') (1879–1952)
The Field of the Cloth of Gold 99

Will Dyson (1880–1938)
The Trucker 99

'Furnley Maurice' (Frank Wilmot) (1881–1942)
Echoes of wheels... 101
Whenever I have... 102
The Victoria Markets Recollected in Tranquillity 102

'Brian Vrepont' (B. A. Trubridge) (1882–1955)
The Bomber 108

Frederic Manning (1882–1935)
The Trenches 109
Leaves 110

Anonymous
(From the diary of an Australian soldier) 110

Ethel Anderson (1883–1958)
Afternoon in the Garden 111

Charles Shaw
  The Search   112

W. J. Turner (1884–1946)
  Romance   113
  Marriage   114
  The Dancer   114

Vance Palmer (1885–1959)
  The Snake   115
  The Farmer Remembers the Somme   115

Dorothea Mackellar (1885–1968)
  Heritage   116
  Arms and the Woman   116
  Fancy Dress   117

Frederick Macartney (1887–1980)
  Kyrielle: Party Politics   118

Dunstan Shaw
  Retrospection   119

Lesbia Harford (1889–1925)
  Poems: XIV, XXII, LXIX   120

Anonymous
  Click go the Shears   122
  Dinky di   122

Harley Matthews (1889–1968)
  Women are not Gentlemen   123

James Devaney (1890–1976)
  Vision   130

Leon Gellert (1892–1977)
  House-Mates   131

Paul L. Grano (1894–1975)
  Headlined in Heaven   131
  In a Chain-store Cafeteria   132

Max Dunn (1895–1963)
  O, where were we before time was   133

W. E. Harney (1895–1962)
  West of Alice   134

Francis Letters (1897–1964)
  The Inglorious Milton   135

E. G. Moll (1900–1979)
The Bush Speaks 135
Clearing for the Plough 136
Beware the Cuckoo 137

Francis Brabazon
Victoria Market 137

Jack Lindsay (b. 1900)
Question Time 138
Angry Dusk 139
To my father Norman alone in the Blue Mountains 140

Kenneth Slessor (1901–1971)
A Bushranger 140
Metempsychosis 141
Five Bells 142

Robert D. FitzGerald (b. 1902)
Copernicus 145
Grace Before Meat 145
The Wind At Your Door 147

Mary Finnin (b. 1906)
The Man From Strathbogie 150

Arthur Davies
West Paddocks 151

A. D. Hope (b. 1907)
A Blason 153
Faustus 154
Parabola 155

Eve Langley (1908–1974)
This Year, Before It Ends 157

Harry Hooton (1908–1961)
A Sweet Disorder in the Dress 157

Ronald McCuaig (b. 1908)
Betty by the Sea 159
Recitative 160
Au tombeau de mon père 160

Elizabeth Riddell (b. 1909)
Wakeful in the Township 163
Suburban Song 163
The Letter 164

William Hart-Smith (b. 1911)
Boomerang 165
Golden Pheasant 165
The Inca Tupac Upanqui 166

Ian Mudie (1911–1976)
This Land 167

Anonymous
The Overlander 168

Hal Porter (1911–1984)
Four Winds 169
In a Bed-sitter 170
Hobart Town, Van Diemen's Land 171

J. J. Bray (b. 1912)
The Execution of Madame du Barry 172

Roland Robinson (b. 1912)
Deep Well 173
The Cradle 174
The Creek 175

Aboriginal Oral Traditions
Mapooram (related by Fred Biggs) 175
The Star-Tribes (related by Fred Biggs) 176
The Two Sisters (related by Manoowa) 176
The Platypus (related by Dick Donelly) 178
Captain Cook (related by Percy Mumbulla) 179

Central Australian Aboriginal Songs
Kangaroos 179
Song of the Progenitor-Hero Anakotarinja 180
The Brother Eagles 181
The Hollow at Ilbalintja Soak 182
Ringneck Parrots 183

Rex Ingamells (1913–1955)
Garchooka, the Cockatoo 183
From The Great South Land 183

Joyce Lee (b. 1913)
My Father's Country 185
Firebell for Peace 186

Kenneth Mackenzie (1913–1955)
Shall then another 187
Table-birds 188
Caesura 189

Douglas Stewart (1913–1985)
　Leopard Skin　　　　　　　　　　　　　189
　A Country Song　　　　　　　　　　　　190
　Terra Australis　　　　　　　　　　　　191

John Blight (b. 1913)
　The Coral Reef　　　　　　　　　　　　193
　The Oyster-Eaters　　　　　　　　　　　194
　Mangrove　　　　　　　　　　　　　　194

Joan Aronsten (b. 1914)
　Ad Infinitum　　　　　　　　　　　　　195

Judith Wright (b. 1915)
　Nigger's Leap, New England　　　　　　　195
　Legend　　　　　　　　　　　　　　196
　Wings　　　　　　　　　　　　　　197

David Campbell (1915–1978)
　Song for the Cattle　　　　　　　　　　198
　Hear the Bird of Day　　　　　　　　　199
　Duchesses　　　　　　　　　　　　　199

David Martin (Ludwig Detsinyi) (b. 1915)
　Dreams in German　　　　　　　　　　200

Dorothy Auchterlonie (b. 1915)
　The Tree　　　　　　　　　　　　　201

John Manifold (1915–1985)
　Fife Tune　　　　　　　　　　　　　202
　Makhno's Philosophers　　　　　　　　202

Harold Stewart (b. 1915)
　The Sage in Unison　　　　　　　　　　204

James McAuley (1917–1976)
　Terra Australis　　　　　　　　　　　205
　Liberal or Innocent by Definition　　　　　206
　Because　　　　　　　　　　　　　　206

Kath Walker (b. 1920)
　We Are Going　　　　　　　　　　　207

Aboriginal Women's Mourning Songs
　The blowflies buzz ...　　　　　　　　　208
　All you others, eat ...　　　　　　　　　209

Rosemary Dobson (b. 1920)
　Country Press　　　　　　　　　　　210

The Edge 211
Folding the Sheets 211

Colin Thiele (b. 1920)
Tom Farley 212
Radiation Victim 213

Gwen Harwood (b. 1920)
Homage to Ferd. Holthausen 214
Death Has No Features of His Own 214
A Simple Story 215

Max Harris (b. 1921)
Message from a Cross 216
Martin Buber in the Pub 217

Nan McDonald (1921–1973)
The Hatters 217
Burragorang 218

Lex Banning (1921–1965)
Epitaph for a Scientist 220
Apocalypse in Springtime 220

Aranda Native Cat Song Cycle
The Great Beam of the Milky Way 222

Geoffrey Dutton (b. 1922)
A Finished Gentleman 223
Burning Off 225
Fish Shop Windows 226

Dorothy Hewett (b. 1923)
In Moncur Street 227

Nancy Keesing (b. 1923)
A Queer Thing 228
Reverie of a Mum 229

Eric Rolls (b. 1923)
Bamboo 230
Rain Forest 231
Dog Fight 232

W. N. Scott (b. 1923)
Bundaberg Rum 233

David Rowbotham (b. 1924)
The Bus-stop on the Somme 234
The Cliff 234
Nebuchadnezzar's Kingdom-Come 235

John Rowland (b. 1925)
Canberra in April 235

Miidhu
War Dance 237

Pudjipangu
Aeroplane 238

Smiler Narautjarri
The Witch Doctor's Magic Flight 238

From the Dulngulg Song Cycle
Sunrise Sequence 239

Wonguri-Mandjigai People
Song Cycle of the Moon-Bone 239

Francis Webb (1925–1973)
End of the Picnic 246
Airliner 246
Wild Honey 247

Vincent Buckley (b. 1925)
Ghosts, Places, Stories, Questions 248

Alan Riddell (1927–1977)
At the Hammersmith Palais... 250

Grace Perry (b. 1927)
Time of Turtles 250

John Philip (b. 1927)
Manly Ferry 251

Robin Gurr
Creation 252

R. F. Brissenden (b. 1928)
Verandahs 252

Ray Mathew (b. 1929)
Seeing St. James's 253
Poem in Time of Winter 254
One Day 255

Bruce Beaver (b. 1929)
Letters to Live Poets V 255
The Entertainer 256

Peter Porter (b. 1929)
Soliloquy at Potsdam 258

What I Have Written I Have Written   259
On First Looking into Chapman's Hesiod   260

R. A. Simpson (b. 1929)
All Friends Together   262

Bruce Dawe (b. 1930)
At Shagger's Funeral   263
Suburban Lovers   264
Elegy For Drowned Children   265

Evan Jones (b. 1931)
Study in Blue   265
A Dream   266
The Point   266

Philip Martin (b. 1931)
Tongues   267

C. J. Koch (b. 1932)
The Boy who Dreamed the Country Night   268
Shelly Beach   269

Vivian Smith (b. 1933)
At an Exhibition of Historical Paintings, Hobart   269
Early Arrival: Sydney   270
Tasmania   271

Fay Zwicky (b. 1933)
Reckoning   271

Chris Wallace-Crabbe (b. 1934)
The Secular   272
Sporting the Plaid   272
The Shape-Changer   273

David Malouf (b. 1934)
The Year of the Foxes   274
Guide to the Perplexed   275

Margaret Scott (b. 1934)
Portrait of a Married Couple   275

Barry Humphries ('Edna Everage') (b. 1934)
Edna's Hymn   276

Rodney Hall (b. 1935)
Journey   277

Randolph Stow (b. 1935)
The Ghost at Anlaby   278
My Wish for My Land   279
The Enemy   280

Sam Mitchell
Thunderstorm   280

Thomas W. Shapcott (b. 1935)
June Fugue   281
The Litanies of Julia Pastrana (1832–1860)   282

Judith Rodriguez (b. 1936)
New York Sonnet   285
Eskimo Occasion   285
A Lifetime Devoted to Literature   286

Norman Talbot (b. 1936)
Ballad of Old Women   286

Graeme Hetherington (b. 1937)
The Man from Changi   287

Philip Hammial (b. 1937)
Russians Breathing   288

Les A. Murray (b. 1938)
Equanimity   289
The Smell of Coal Smoke   290

Peter Steele (b. 1939)
Marking Time   291

J. S. Harry (b. 1939)
Honesty-stones   292

Clive James (b. 1939)
Johnny Weissmuller dead in Acapulco   292

Jan Owen (b. 1940)
The Visitation   294

Kate Llewellyn (b. 1940)
Finished   295
Colonel   295

Tjinapirrgarri
Emu Shot   296

Gordon Mackay-Warna
Cattle Loading   297

Geoff Page (b. 1940)
  Grit 297
  Inscription at Villers-Bretonneux 299
  Premeditations 299

Geoffrey Lehmann (b. 1940)
  Pope Alexander VI 300
  Night Flower 301
  A Poem for Maurice O'Shea 302

Pambardu
  Windmill at Mandanthanunguna 303

Andrew Taylor (b. 1940)
  The Beast with Two Backs 304

Nigel Roberts (b. 1941)
  After/the Moratorium Reading 305
  The Gull's Flight 305

Alan Alexander (b. 1941)
  The Gathering Place 305
  For Raftery 306

Julian Croft (b. 1941)
  D-Zug 307
  Greenhalgh's Pub 307
  Graffiti 308

Allen Afterman (b. 1941)
  Their Thoughts Cling to Everything they See on the Way 309
  Van Diemen's Land 310
  Pietà 311

Jennifer Rankin (1941–1979)
  The Sea and other stories 312

Public Corroboree Songs, Nunggubuyu People
  Koel (Rainbird) and effigy 315
  Goanna 315
  Flood Water 315
  Mission Work Boat 316

R. R. Davidson
  The Gravy Train 316

Roger McDonald (b. 1941)
  1915 317
  The Blizzard 318
  Apis mellifica 319

Craig Powell (b. 1941)
  Nativity   320

Nicholas Hasluck (b. 1942)
  Islands   320
  From *Rottnest Island*   322

John Tranter (b. 1943)
  The Great Artist Reconsiders the Homeric Simile   323
  Lufthansa   324

David Foster (b. 1944)
  From *The Fleeing Atalanta: Poems 98, 104, 109*   325

Robert Adamson (b. 1944)
  Dead Horse Bay   326

Gumaitj People
  Songs from the Goulburn Island Song Cycle   327

Robert Gray (b. 1945)
  Flames and Dangling Wire   330
  Curriculum Vitae   331

Mark O'Connor (b. 1945)
  Turtles Hatching   335
  Fire   337
  The Sun-Hunters   337

Hal Colebatch (b. 1945)
  On the Death of Ludwig Erhard   340
  One Tourist's Cologne   340

Rhyll McMaster (b. 1947)
  Tanks   341
  Mutton Bird Man   342

Peter Kocan (b. 1947)
  Cows   343
  An Inmate   343
  The Mutineer's Ballad   344

Gary Catalano (b. 1947)
  The Jews Speak in Heaven   345
  Australia   346

Martin Johnston (b. 1947)
  In Memoriam   347

Dennis Haskell (b. 1947)
  The Call   349

Michael Dransfield (1948–1973)
That Which We Call a Rose 350
Fix 350
Pioneer Lane 351

Marion Alexopoulos (b. 1948)
Night Flight 352

Richard Tipping (b. 1949)
Men at Work 352
Mangoes 353

Susan Hampton (b. 1949)
The Crafty Butcher 353
The Fire Station's Delight 354

Alan Gould (b. 1949)
Ice 355
Galaxies 355
Pearls 356

Jamie Grant (b. 1949)
An Auditor Thinks about Female Nature 357
Planes Landing 358

Jennifer Maiden (b. 1949)
The Mother-in-law of the Marquis de Sade 359

John Forbes (b. 1950)
Malta 360
Up, Up, Home & Away 361
Angel 362

Philip Salom (b. 1950)
The Well 362
Winter 363
The World of Dreams 363

Andrew Sant (b. 1950)
Homage to the Canal People 365
Sound waves 366

Peter Goldsworthy (b. 1951)
Act Six 367
After Babel 367

Conal Fitzpatrick (b. 1951)
Discovering Lasseter 368

Robert Harris (b. 1951)
Sydney 369
Isaiah By Kerosene Lantern Light 369

John Foulcher (b. 1952)
  Wars of Imperialism   370
  After the Flood   370

Philip Mead (b. 1953)
  From A Republican Grave   371
  The Man and the Tree   373

Andrew Lansdown (b. 1954)
  Two Men   373
  Mercy   374
  Behind the Veil   374

Kevin Hart (b. 1954)
  The Members of the Orchestra   375
  The Horizon   376
  Flemington Racecourse   376

Philip Hodgins (b. 1959)
  Self-pity   377
  Making Hay   378

Linda Molony (b. 1960)
  Cat Washing   379

Richard Allen (b. 1960)
  Epitaph for the Western Intelligentsia   380

Acknowledgements   381
Index of First Lines   386
Index of Authors and Titles   394

FOREWORD

This anthology presents a conspectus of poetic activity in Australia from the early days of European settlement to the present. The principle of selection has been the poetic experience, the thing we mean when we ask how much poetry a text has in it. No poem has been included for purely historical reasons. The ancillary watchwords of the selection have been liveliness and readability; this anthology is not primarily intended for study, but for reading. Australia has always had a large number, larger than most Western countries to judge from book sales, of people prepared to read poetry for pleasure, rather than at the behest of the giant Curriculum. I have sought to encourage, perpetuate and supply this liberating tradition.

In order to survey something like the whole poetic topography of Australia, right out to its edges in humorous verse, folksong, popular rhymes and the like, it has been necessary to take a rather different viewpoint from that of many other anthologies of the last generation or so. I have turned away from a recent preoccupation with grading and weighting the representation of individual poets in accordance with some idea of their relative importance—if X has six poems, Y must be given eight, and on that scale Z is only worth four—and imposed a working limit of three poems on everyone. This has made it possible to present an oblique view of the poetic landscape, in which the peaks and larger hills do not obscure the smaller features. Or those remoter in time. The idea that there was little or no Australian poetry of value before the teens of this century, or specifically before *Vision* magazine in the early 1920s, was dominant for a few decades, but is now in full retreat. As is the class distinction it was based on, between vernacular and pukka verse; until recently, these were usually published in separate anthologies. The multitude of other Australian anthologies currently in print can be relied on to supply differing views of the poetic pecking order, as it changes from moment to moment under the pressure of groups and claims. In fact, the patterns of relative eminence in Australian poetry have proved fairly resilient, over time-spans of about thirty years each, but I have tried to mute this whole ranking-and-grading dimension as firmly as possible.

If reducing the relativities of fame allows a great many more poets to be represented, the same may be said of another feature of this book. Returning to the practice of most older anthologies, I have done away with biographical and critical notes on the poets represented. All that is given is their year of birth, and year of death if applicable. In a few cases, diligent research has failed to elicit the vital dates of less well-known authors, and this is regretted. The absence of notes and other prose apparatus is intended to focus attention solely on the poetry, and to leave room for more of it. A proliferation of prose around every occurrence of printed verse can suggest to the ordinary reader, perhaps only subliminally but still destructively, that poetry is somehow unnatural and precious, needing to be buffered or even legitimized by prose commentary. Educational values have subverted the normality of poetry as a literary form, shifting it towards the status of an exotic indulgence, or a declining but still faintly threatening primitive culture whose every move has to be explained by resident anthropologists. The potted commentaries which most anthologies provide are scholarly and innocuous enough, but in some collections of verse they approach the quality of a police dossier, implicitly inviting the reader to judge the poet at least partly on the basis of political, religious or artistic views he or she is alleged to hold. All this takes the matter far from considerations of poetic achievement, and is a development full of tyrannical potentials.

Most Australian anthologies come fitted with a condensed history of poetry in this country; for this reason, and once again in order to leave more room for poetry, I have felt free to omit a historical outline here. This book, after all, presents a very wide sampling of the primary data; I cannot help feeling that the synthesizing overview belongs in a different book. Of which many versions already exist. The only historical observation I would want to make concerns the fact that while most Australian poetry in the nineteenth and early twentieth centuries first saw the light of day in newspapers, since the 1920s or at the very latest the 1940s the small literary magazines and reviews have been by far the most usual venue of first publication here. The *Bulletin* long survived as a bridge between the two, being a newspaper with most of the features of a review, but having a very large popular circulation. This shift of poetry into the little magazines is a worldwide phenomenon and has effects which readers of this anthology may care to reflect on. A certain received 'modern' sensibility becomes dominant, and an older sprightliness and verve are at least heavily modified as we move into modern times. They become a somewhat elusive bloom most often to be found in writers considered faintly eccentric or peripheral, and in the 'odd' poems of otherwise mainstream poets.

Australian readers will notice that I have tended to steer clear of standard anthology pieces, and have even been sparing with the established classics. These latter did present problems, as some of them are so obviously their authors' best work and so clearly part of the nation's essential heritage, that to omit them even for the sake of freshness would have been merely perverse. You cannot easily leave Slessor's *Five Bells* out of an Australian anthology and retain credibility. In reading each poet, though, I have followed a consistent method: I have looked for quality, for their 'best' poems, which are often those in which their chief themes reached a culminating, transforming expression, and I have simultaneously scanned for *a* quality, for their untypical poem or poems. I have sought what I have elsewhere called their Strange poem; most poets have one or more of these. The two meanings of the word 'quality' very often coincide in such poems, and they will frequently yield glimpses into a wider, more timeless country of the spirit beyond the conditioning sensibility of any given period.

Some of the slight decline in idiosyncrasy—I mean the real kind, not the effortful originalities of modernism—that readers may notice in the latter parts of this anthology stems from the fact that ever-increasing numbers of mainstream poets, and perhaps the greater noise of collegial claims, made it harder and harder to fit in material from what we have come to think of as the fringe domains of poetry. The survey of folk material and hitherto neglected sources that enriched the nineteenth century segment could not be continued in any thoroughgoing way, without either bursting the bindings of a one-volume anthology or sentencing dozens of mainstream colleagues to undeserved relegation.

One tradition of Australian poetry which I was determined to represent in something like a decent proportion is Aboriginal verse, especially translations of song-texts collected from many parts of the continent. These usually come to us heavily swaddled in anthropological commentary. Useful as this may be in orienting non-Aboriginal and non-tribal readers, I believed that the texts could and should stand alone, to be read as poems in the way Western readers are accustomed to receive poetry. Even without their native accompaniments of music and sometimes of dance, I believed, they could pass the test. They would suffer the disadvantage of being translations—but this very fact meant that where the languages and traditions they came from were still alive, they had another and primary existence which no rendering into an alien form for strangers could damage. The Aranda song of the Milky Way is quite a separate thing in its tribal existence from the English-language text bearing that title and conveying perhaps a little of its essence out into the international literary world. Where a poem comes from a group which has lost its language, the ghost-form that a translation represents is at least a memorial, on which something may perhaps be rebuilt, or something new erected. Again, and not merely for liberal reasons, these texts have to be

present; without examples from the senior culture no picture of
poetry in Australia can be complete.

At times I have itched to rework halting literal versions concerned more with grammar than with poetic effect, but without a
profound knowledge of the source languages and the accompanying
culture the dangers of falsification were too great, and restrained
me. All but one of the translations are of texts originally composed
as songs. The exception is *Lalai* (Dreamtime), which is a sort of
found poem. It is actually the spoken commentary of a film made
by Michael Edols in 1973, in which the Worora elder Sam Woolagoodjah conducts his son Stanley and his granddaughter Kerry
around part of his old tribal territory in north-west Australia, in-
structing them in the meanings of the various sacred sites there. As
an introduction, for uninitiated people, to Aboriginal lore in its
pure pre-contact form, his words seemed to have great value for a
much wider audience, and the success of the film has borne this out.
It was in this spirit, too, that Andrew Huntley worked up the prose
translation originally made by Professor Michael Silverstein of Bos-
ton University. In all other translated Aboriginal texts the pre-
European traditions are assumed; in this one they are presented and
explained 'for all people'. It seemed a good way to bring to life,
right from the outset, a version of the native Australian culture
which existed at settlement and had existed for tens of thousands of
years before that. The short *tabi* songs translated by Dr Georg von
Brandenstein all come from the Pilbara region of north-west Australia; all the other texts are identified as to people, language and
region. So far as I can discover, David Unaipon's *Song of Hungarrda*, published in the 1920s, is the first Aboriginal poem ever written
in English. I am most grateful to Cliff Watego and Lawrence
Bourke for sending it to me.

Apart from the detailed copyright acknowledgements, there
are some personal debts of gratitude I wish to pay to people who
have helped me during the long job of compiling and editing this
book. My thanks go to Josie Hilliger, the keeper of Angus and
Robertson's house library, to Jill Tweedie of the Fisher Library at
Sydney University, to Catherine Santamaria of the National Library
in Canberra, to Jamie Grant and Alan Gould, who helped in all
sorts of ways, especially with dates of birth and death for various
poets, and to Vivian Smith for invaluable logistical assistance as
well as advice on nineteenth century poets. I thank the Fisher
Library and the English Department of Sydney University for kind-
nesses in the matter of photocopying; similar thanks must go to the
National Library and to my friend Wayne Hooper of the Department of Adult Education at Sydney University. I am also indebted
to the Institute of Aboriginal Studies in Canberra, and to Max

Richards of La Trobe University for some valuable tips and pieces of research while I was writer-in-residence in the English department. Despite my disagreements with many modern anthologists, I salute practically every one of them, and their publishers. In particular, I salute the pioneer anthologists who valued and sought to preserve Australian poetry in the long years before it became a respectable field of study, and the editors of the offbeat anthologies who have done so much to keep alive vernacular and extramural parts of our poetic tradition. Finally, I thank all those, colleagues and others, who patiently bore my enthusiastic monologues about this book during the time it was being compiled. Now at last I can shut up about it and let others speak.

Sam Woolagoodjah

Lalai (Dreamtime)

Dreamtime,
The first ones lived, those of long ago.
They were the Wandjinas—
Like this one here, Namaaraalee.
The first ones, those days,
shifted from place to place,
In dreamtime before the floods came.
   Bird Wandjinas, crab Wandjinas
Carried the big rocks.
They threw them into the deep water
They piled them on the land.
Other Wandjinas—
all kinds—
She the rock python,
He the kangaroo,
They changed it.
They struggled with the rocks,
They dug the rivers.
These were the Wandjinas. They talk with us
at some places they have marked.
Where the sun climbs, over the hill and the river
they came,
And they are with us in the land.
We remember how they fought each other
at those places they marked—
It is dreamtime there.

Some Wandjinas went under the land,
They came to stay in the caves
And there we can see them.
Grown men listen to their Wandjinas.
   Long ago, at another time,
these Wandjinas changed the bad ones
into the rocks
And the springs we always drink from.
These places hold our spirits,
These Wunger places of the Wandjinas.
There a man learns
who his child really is:
Its spirit comes when he is dreaming
and tells him its name.

Then the man has been given his child:
It has its own name
beside the landname of its father.

Wandjina children were playing:
Plucking out his feathers
They stuck in sharp, long blades of grass
To see him use his new wings.
They did this to the first owl,
Whose name is Dunbi.

They fooled with him
They fooled with him,
They bounced him up
They bounced him up,
They tossed him up again;

But then he went over the clouds.
Namaaraalee lifted him
And he became a Wunger
For all places.

Don't take.
'Wuduu, Wuduu':
At the fire I touch you—
I hand you the strength of Wuduu,
Don't let yourself be turned.
Here on your ankle
Here on your knee
Here on your thigh,
Stay strong.
Don't let your forehead swell
(wait, wait)
Don't say the words of the men,
Don't go begging, granddaughter.

Namaaraalee is highest, he made it all,
We must keep those ways he pointed out.
Now that I have told you
We are walking to the place his body was cradled.
He is in the sky.
This half moon we will go to him.

The children who fooled with Dunbi owl
were laughing;
Then they heard the roar.
The angry Wandjinas sent a flood
And the water reached them all.

But in the wave
One man, one woman,
grabbed the tail of a kangaroo.
They clung to its tail as it swam
And it reached the rocks.
Here, on this side, they climbed up,
So that we were born,
So we go on being born.

Now you see nothing is made up,
Each father has been told what happened:
How Wandjina Namaaraalee made it all
How he sent the flood
How he said no.
Then he showed us the Wuduu that we make
for the little boys and girls:
The men who know still touch them
So each day they learn to grow.

Her two thighs, her two legs, her fingers—
The words are put there
that the Wandjinas gave us.
They said to keep on
And until today those words have lived.
The Wuduu touching will not stop,
It is our strength.
They threw spears
They killed him.
Wunumbal, Ungarinyin, were fighting
Killing each other
Living no more.

All the spirits told me then: 'Do that':
I am going back
To the place the Wandjina made for me.
All ways, do not forget,
Give away, give away.
The first one, Namaaraalee, came from the Awawarii tribe.
He had been in many fights
before he came to this land.

Here he saw the woman he wanted to keep;
But the Wandjinas all looked, then each one tugged at her.
Backward, forward—hotter and hotter—
At last they flung spears that fell like rain—
And Namaaraalee felt one drop down his side.
Then they had killed him.

These rocks are Wandjinas
Marking the fight.
When they saw he was dead
They carried him over the creek.
'Djir'—for the first one
They made that dry sound on their tongues.
Then he was laid on a fork stick cradle
High off the ground;
Now, Namaaraalee lies
in his cave on top of the rocks.

They speared him in this water,
This water is Namaaraalee.
They carried him along here,
They laid him up there.
We belong to this place,
Strangers must stay away.

I am going there now.
We are coming to you—
To see you alone.
Are you listening?
That is what you wanted—
Namaaraalee, will you always lie down?

We have come to you,
He wanted to meet you.
We have always heard about you,
Even how you have destroyed.

That is what you wanted—
You even killed people far away.
You killed many people
When you chose to, Namaaraalee,
You have always done as you wanted to do.
And you chose to stay here:
You planned this as you planned your own death.

He showed us the Wuduu we make—
He said 'Wuduu, Wuduu'.
Not just for one person—
But for all the land, all the land.
Not only for us—
Wuduu is for everyone to make.
This one is the Wandjina.

Here is a man of the Aruluuli.
He was one of them

and they brought him here—
This place belongs to him.
Those who have died are brought to the caves,
They are carried in and stay here.
A man, like this, dies at last in his cave,
His spirit is free
To leave him and wait at its Wunger place.
All this cave belongs to the Aruluuli.
   We do the same when a man dies
As the Wandjinas did for Namaaraalee
When they had killed him.
That is the way he taught us what to do,
And the way he chose to teach all other people.
He started it for everyone.
We do the same as the Wandjinas—
And Namaaraalee made this way
For all kinds of men.

At its own Wunger place
A spirit waits for birth—
'Today, I saw who the child really is—'
That is how a man
Learns to know his child.

Namaaraalee made him,
No one else,
No one.
But not all things are straight
in this day.

As I looked at the water
Of Bundaalunaa
She appeared to me:
I understood suddenly
The life in our baby—
Her name is Dragon Fly.

Recounted by Sam Woolagoodjah, elder of the Worora people, north-west
Australia. Translated by Andrew Huntley from the prose version of
Michael Silverstein.

Barron Field

The Kangaroo

mixtumque genus, prolesque biformis.
—Virgil, *Aeneid VI*

Kangaroo, Kangaroo!
Thou Spirit of Australia,
That redeems from utter failure,
From perfect desolation,
And warrants the creation
Of this fifth part of the Earth,
Which should seem an after-birth,
Not conceiv'd in the Beginning
(For God bless'd His work at first,
And saw that it was good),
But emerg'd at the first sinning,
When the ground was therefore curst;—
And hence this barren wood!

Kangaroo, Kangaroo!
Tho' at first sight we should say,
In thy nature that there may
Contradiction be involv'd,
Yet, like discord well resolv'd,
It is quickly harmoniz'd.
Sphynx or mermaid realiz'd.
Or centaur unfabulous,
Would scarce be more prodigious,
Or Labyrinthine Minotaur,
With which great Theseus did war,
Or Pegasus poetical.
Or hippogriff—chimeras all!
But, what Nature would compile,
Nature knows to reconcile;
And Wisdom, ever at her side,
Of all her children's justified.

She had made the squirrel fragile;
She had made the bounding hart;
But a third so strong and agile
Was beyond ev'n Nature's art.
So she join'd the former two
    In thee, Kangaroo!

To describe thee, it is hard:
Converse of the camélopard,
Which beginneth camel-wise,
But endeth of the panther size,
Thy fore half, it would appear,
Had belong'd to some 'small deer',
Such as liveth in a tree;
By thy hinder, thou should'st be
A large animal of chace,
Bounding o'er the forest's space;—
Join'd by some divine mistake,
None but Nature's hand can make—
Nature, in her wisdom's play,
On Creation's holiday.

For howsoe'er anomalous,
Thou yet art not incongruous,
Repugnant or preposterous.
Better-proportion'd animal,
More graceful or ethereal,
Was never follow'd by the hound,
With fifty steps to thy one bound.
Thou can'st not be amended: no;
Be as thou art; thou best art so.

When sooty swans are once more rare,
And duck-moles the Museum's care,
Be still the glory of this land,
Happiest Work of finest Hand!

1819

Richard Whately

There is a Place in Distant Seas

There is a place in distant seas
Full of contrarieties:
There, beasts have mallards' bills and legs,
Have spurs like cocks, like hens lay eggs.
There parrots walk upon the ground,
And grass upon the trees is found;
On other trees, another wonder!
Leaves without upper sides or under.

There pears you'll scarce with hatchet cut;
Stones are outside the cherries put;
Swans are not white, but black as soot.
There neither leaf, nor root, nor fruit
Will any Christian palate suit,
Unless in desperate need you'd fill ye
With root of fern and stalk of lily.
There missiles to far distance sent
Come whizzing back from whence they went;
There quadrupeds go on two feet,
And yet few quadrupeds so fleet;
There birds, although they cannot fly,
In swiftness with your greyhound vie.
With equal wonder you may see
The foxes fly from tree to tree;
And what they value most, so wary,
These foxes in their pockets carry.
There the voracious ewe-sheep crams
Her paunch with flesh of tender lambs,
Instead of beef, and bread, and broth,
Men feast on many a roasted moth.
The north winds scorch, but when the breeze is
Full from the south, why then it freezes;
The sun when you to face him turn ye,
From right to left performs his journey.
Now of what place could such strange tales
Be told with truth save New South Wales?—

Anonymous

A Hot Day In Sydney

O this weather! this weather!
   It's more than a mortal can bear;
I fear we shall all melt together,
   So dreadfully hot is the air.

On rising from bed in the morning,
   You feel yourself thirsty and hot;
And while at the toilette adorning,
   You're helpless as though you'd been shot.

You get through the work with great trouble,—
   The shave, and the wash, and the dress;

And then comes your breakfast, to double
   The causes of former distress.

The coffee, the tea, and the butter,
   The smoking-hot muffin and bread—
Although you have put to the shutter—
   Invite you in vain to be fed.

The tea and the coffee are hissing,
   The butter is melting away,—
The flies in the milk-jug are kissing,
   The ants in the sugar-bowl play;—

You rise in disgust from the table,
   And, with your umbrella unfurl'd,
You toddle, as well as you're able,
   To the haunts of the mercantile world.

But whether you sit in your office,
   Or stroll to the market and shops,
To bargain for sugars or coffees,
   For snuff, or tobacco, or hops;—

You still are by no means forgetting
   The torments inflicted by heat—
For still you are puffing and sweating,
   And longing for some cool retreat.

You wash in Cologn's cooling water,—
   You swallow some brisk ginger-beer—
You say to some kind neighbour's daughter,
   'O give me some swizzle, my dear!'

You go to take luncheon at BAX's,
   And call for cool jellies and buns—
But hotter and hotter it waxes,—
   The jelly to liquid soon runs;—

His dainties are only a pester,
   And so you withdraw from his shop;—
Loud rages the fiery North-wester,
   As back to your office you pop.

The streets are with dust so beclouded,
   You cannot see over the way;
The town is so perfectly shrowded,
   You scarcely believe it is day.

At length comes the wish'd hour of dinner;
   Away to your dwelling you go—

But still you are far from a winner,
   The table displeases you so.

The poultry, the beef, and the mutton,
   The cabbage, potatoes, and peas,—
Though cook'd to delight e'en a glutton,
   Your palate in no degree please:—

The porter, the wine, and the brandy,
   Invite you to wet your parch'd lips,
And being so perfectly handy,
   You take a succession of sips:—

But then your blood burns into fever,
   And sets the whole system on fire,—
And finding the drink a deceiver,
   You soon from the table retire.

The drawing-room then you proceed to,
   And join in the ladies' discourse;
But the heat will not let you give heed to
   The topics their sweet lips enforce.

They offer you tea, bread, and butter,
   And other good things on the tray;
But while you your gratitude mutter,
   The tea-things you wish far away.

They press the piano, with fingers
   So graceful, so taper, so fair,
That while on the scene your heart lingers,
   At the heat you are tempted to swear.

And while they are busily fanning
   Their beautiful faces and necks,
To please them you fain would be planning,
   Did the heat not so cruelly vex.

At length you retire to your pillow,
   And hope for some comfort in sleep;—
But you toss like a tempest-wrought billow,
   And cannot in one posture keep.

The heat almost stops your respiring—
   The blanket and quilt you kick off;—
The peace you had hoped in retiring,
   You deplore in a yawn and a cough.

Mosquitos keep humming and stinging;
   Alighting all over your face;—

The cricket and locust are singing,
   And sleep flees your eyelids apace.

And there you be tossing and tumbling,
   So beated, and bitten, and stung,
So weary of puffing and grumbling,—
   You are ready to wish yourself hung.

And such are the pleasures of summer,
   In this Australasian land;—
How charming to every new-comer,
   If thus they can charm an old hand!

But still I would bear it with patience,
   And so I would recommend you—
Convinc'd that, of all the earth's nations,
   Not one would be *faultless* to

                        Q.

Sydney, 27 January 1829

The Exile of Erin

O! farewell, my country—my kindred—my lover;
Each morning and evening is sacred to you,
While I toil the long day, without shelter or cover,
And fell the tall gums, the black-butted and blue.
Full often I think of and talk of thee, Erin—
Thy heath-covered mountains are fresh in my view,
Thy glens, lakes, and rivers, Loch-Con and Kilkerran,
While chained to the soil on the Plains of Emu.

The ironbark, wattle, and gum-trees extending
Their shades, under which rests the shy kangaroo,
May be felled by the bless'd who have hope o'er them bending,
To cheer their rude toil, though far exiled from you.
But, alas! without hope, peace, or honour to grace me,
Each feeling was crushed in the bud as it grew,
Whilst 'never' is stamped on the chains that embrace me,
And endless my thrall on the Plains of Emu.

Hard, hard was my fate, far from thee to be driven,
Unstained, unconvicted, as sure was my due;
I loved to dispense of the freedom of Heaven,
But force gained the day, and I suffer for you.

For this land never broke what by promise was plighted,
Deep treason, this tongue to my country ne'er knew,
No base-earned coin in my coffer e'er lighted,
Yet enchained I remain on the Plains of Emu.

Dear mother, thy love from my bosom shall never
Depart, but shall flourish untainted and true;
Nor grieve that the base in their malice should ever
Upbraid thee, and none to give malice her due.
Spare, spare her the tear, and no charge lay upon her,
And weep not, my Norah, her griefs to renew,
But cherish her age till night closes on her,
And think of the swain who still thinks but of you.

But your names shall still live, though like writing in water,
When confined to the no es of the tame cockatoo,
Each wattle-scrub echo repeats to the other
Your names, and each breeze hears me sighing anew,
For dumb be my tongue, may my heart cease her motion,
If the Isle I forget where my first breath I drew!
Each affection is warmed with sincerest devotion,
For the tie is unbroken on the Plains of Emu.

'M', 1829

Hey, Boys! Up Go We!

When maize stands more than ten feet high,
And bursting cobs a yard or more,
On every rood ten bushels lie,
And each brings dollars three in store;
When pigs with dismal accents roar,
The sharpening steel and knife to see,
And pork keeps hunger from my door,
Why then, 'tis 'Hey, boys! up go we!'

When wheat is standing thick and strong,
On brushy hill, and flooded dale;
And yellow ridges wave along,
As swells or falls the alternate gale;
When bursting barns and stacks prevail,
From fresh or flood no harm can be,
When grass hides heifer's head and tail,
Why then, 'tis 'Hey, boys! up go we!'

When others hunt the kangaroo,
And seize the winged, or finny prey,
The plover—duck—and tall emu,
To them I still must answer nay.
Keen sport I love as much as they,
But sure, the keenest sport for me,
Are lowing herds at close of day,
For then, 'tis 'Hey, boys! up go we!'

When all my lads at Whitsuntide,
Are merry as every man should be,
Or drain the cup my care supplied,
Their mirth gives double mirth to me;
When forth they spurt the base Bengal,
If Austral gin perchance they see,
Why then, I think, each man should call,
As I, for 'Hey, boys! up go we!'

When peaches spread their rosy sides,
And bask in sun, and summer's ray,
And Hodge the falling heaps divides
For food, where sporting grunters play;
When pumpkins ripe salute the day,
And golden fruit loads every tree,
And grapes, 'Come eat me—eat me,' say,
Why then, 'tis 'Hey, boys! up go we!'

When woodmen cut their mazy wood,
And stately gums and cedars fall,
And groaning teams the fencers load,
And jocund herds their lambkins call;
When trees are split with wedge and maul,
And rising cots the settlers see,
And acres cleared give joy to all,
Why then, 'tis 'Hey, boys! up go we!'

Then long live George, our noble King,
And eke our Governor, long live he;
Let's stand around in double ring,
Each man of high and low degree;
Let's tune our pipes, to them we owe
Much peace—success—and harmony,
And sing to groaners high and low,
The dirge of 'Hey, boys! down go ye!'

1829

The Limejuice Tub

With a pint of flour and a sheet of bark,
We wallop up a damper in the dark,
With a ru-da-ma-rah, and a rub-a-dub-a-dub,
Drive me back to the lime-juice tub.

You cockatoos, you never need fret,
For to show you up I'll never forget,
But I'm a man that's game to bet,
That you're over your head, heels first in debt,
Over your head, your neck as well.
Your daughters wear no crinolines,
Nor are they troubled with boots or shoes,
For they're wild in the bush with the kangaroos,
With a ru-da-ma-rah, and a rub-a-dub-a-dub,
Drive me back to the lime-juice tub.

John Dunmore Lang

Colonial Nomenclature

'Twas said of Greece two thousand years ago,
    That every stone i' the land had got a name.
Of New South Wales too, men will soon say so too;
    But every stone there seems to get the same.
'Macquarie' for a name is all *the go*:
    The old Scotch Governor was fond of fame.
Macquarie Street, Place, Port, Fort, Town, Lake, River:
    'Lachlan Macquarie, Esquire, Governor', for ever!
I like the native names, as Parramatta,
    And Illawarra, and Woolloomoolloo;
Nandowra, Woogarora, Bulkomatta,
    Tomah, Toongabbie, Mittagong, Meroo;
Buckobble, Cumleroy, and Coolingatta.
    The Warragumby, Bargo, Burradoo;
Cookbundoon, Carrabaiga, Wingecarribbee,
The Wollondilly, Yurumbon, Bungarribbee.

I hate your Goulburn Downs and Goulburn Plains,
    And Goulburn River and the Goulburn Range,
And Mount Goulburn and Goulburn Vale! One's brains
    Are turned with Goulburns! Vile scorbutic mange

For immortality! Had I the reins
　　Of Government a fortnight, I would change
These Downing Street appellatives, and give
The country names that should deserve to live.

I'd have Mount Hampden and Mount Marvell, and
　　Mount Wallace and Mount Bruce at the old Bay.
I'd have them all the highest in the land,
　　That men might see them twenty leagues away.
I'd have the Plains of Marathon beyond
　　Some mountain pass yclept Thermopylae.
Such are th' immortal names that should be written
On all thy new discoveries, Great Britain!

Yes! let some badge of liberty appear
　　On every mountain and on every plain
Where Britain's power is known, or far or near,
　　That freedom there may have an endless reign!
Then though she die, in some revolving year,
　　A race may rise to make her live again!
The future slave may lisp the patriot's name
And his breast kindle with a kindred flame!

1824

Anonymous

Van Diemen's Land

Come all you gallant poachers, that ramble void of care
That walk out on moonlight night with your dog, gun and snare,
The lofty hare and pheasants you have at your command,
Not thinking of your last career upon Van Diemen's Land.

Poor Tom Browne, from Nottingham, Jack Williams, and Poor Joe,
We are three daring poachers, the country do well know.
At night we were trepann'd by the keepers hid in sand,
Who for fourteen years transported us into Van Diemen's Land.

The first day that we landed upon that fatal shore
The planters they came round us full twenty score or more,
They rank'd us up like horses, and sold us out of hand
Then yok'd us unto ploughs, my boys, to plow Van Diemen's
　　Land.

Our cottages that we live in were built of clod and clay,
And rotten straw for bedding, and we dare not say nay
Our cots were fenc'd with fire, we slumber when we can,
To drive away wolves and tigers upon Van Diemen's Land.

It's often when in slumber I have a pleasant dream
With my sweet girl a setting down by a purling stream,
Thro' England I've been roaming with her at command
Now I awaken broken-hearted upon Van Diemen's Land.

God bless our wives and families likewise the happy shore,
That isle of great contentment which we shall see no more
As for our wretched females, see them we seldom can,
There's twenty to one woman upon Van Diemen's Land.

There was a girl from Birmingham, Susan Summers was her name,
For fourteen years transported, we all well know the same
Our planter bought her freedom, and married her out of hand
She gave to us good usage upon Van Diemen's Land.

So all young gallant poachers give ear unto my song
It is a bit of good advice, although it is not long
Throw by your dogs and snare, for to you I speak plain,
For if you knew our hardships you'd never poach again.

The Convicts' Rum Song

Cut yer name across me backbone,
    Stretch me skin across a drum,
Iron me up on Pinchgut Island
    From to-day till Kingdom Come!

I will eat yer Norfolk dumpling
    Like a juicy Spanish plum,
Even dance the Newgate Hornpipe
    If ye'll only gimme RUM!

Hail South Australia!

Hail South Australia! blessed clime,
    Thou lovely land of my adoption;
(I never meant to see the spot
    If I had had the slightest option.)

Hail charming plains of bounteous growth!
    Where tufted vegetation smiles.
(Those dull, atrocious endless flats,
    And no plain less than thirteen miles.)

Hail far-famed Torrens, graceful stream!
  On whose sweet banks I often linger,
Soothed by the murmur of thy waves;
  (And plumb the bottom with my finger.)

Hail land! where all the wants of life
  Flow in cheap streams of milk and honey;
Where all are sure of daily bread
  (If they can fork out ready money.)

Hail *South Australia!* once more hail!
  That man indeed is surely rash
Who cannot live content in thee,
  Or wants for anything (but cash).

1843

The Female Transport

Come all young girls, both far and near, and listen unto me,
While unto you I do unfold what proved my destiny,
My mother died when I was young, it caused me to deplore,
And I did get my way too soon upon my native shore.

Sarah Collins is my name, most dreadful is my fate,
My father reared me tenderly, the truth I do relate,
Till enticed by bad company along with many more,
It led to my discovery upon my native shore.

My trial it approached fast, before the judge I stood,
And when the judge's sentence passed it fairly chilled my blood,
Crying, 'You must be transported for fourteen years or more,
And go from hence across the seas unto Van Diemen's shore.'

It hurt my heart when on a coach I my native town passed by;
To see so many I did know, it made me heave a sigh;
Then to a ship was sent with speed along with many more,
Whose aching hearts did grieve to go unto Van Diemen's shore.

The sea was rough, ran mountains high, with us poor girls 'twas
    hard,
No one but God to us came nigh, no one did us regard.
At length, alas! we reached the land, it grieved us ten times more,
That wretched place Van Diemen's Land, far from our native
    shore.

They chained us two by two, and whipped and lashed along,
They cut off our provisions if we did the least thing wrong;

They march us in the burning sun until our feet are sore,
So hard's our lot now we are got to Van Diemen's shore.

We labour hard from morn to night until our bones do ache,
Then every one they must obey, their mouldy beds must make;
We often wish when we lay down we ne'er may rise no more
To meet our savage Governor upon Van Diemen's shore.

Every night when I lay down I wet my straw with tears,
While wind upon that horrid shore did whistle in our ears,
Those dreadful beasts upon that land around our cots do roar,
Most dismal is our doom upon Van Diemen's shore.

Come all young men and maidens, do bad company forsake,
If tongue can tell our overthrow it will make your heart to ache;
Young girls I pray be ruled by me, your wicked ways give o'er,
For fear like us you spend your days upon Van Diemen's shore.

The Lass in the Female Factory

The Currency Lads may fill their glasses,
And drink the health of the Currency Lasses,
But the lass I adore, the lass for me,
Is the lass in the Female Factory.

O! Molly's her name, and her name is Molly,
Although she was tried by the name of Polly;
She was tried and sent for death at Newry,
But the judge was bribed and so were the jury.

She got 'death recorded' in Newry town
For stealing her mistress's watch and gown;
Her little boy Paddy can tell you the tale,
His father was turnkey at Newry jail.

The first time I saw the comely lass
Was at Parramatta, going to Mass;
Says I: 'I'll marry you now in an hour.'
Says she: 'Well, go and fetch Father Power.'

But I got into trouble that very same night!
Being drunk in the street I got into a fight;
A constable seized me—I gave him a box—
And was put in the watch-house and then in the stocks.

O! It's very unaisy as I remember,
To sit in the stocks in the month of December,

With the north wind so hot, and the hot sun right over.
O! sure, and it's no place at all for a lover!

'It's worse than the treadmill,' says I, 'Mr Dunn,
To sit here all day in the heat of the sun.'
'Either that or a dollar,' says he, 'for your folly'—
But if I had a dollar I'd drink it with Molly.

But now I am out again, early and late
I sigh and I cry at the Factory gate.
'O! Mrs Reordan, late Mrs Farson,
O! won't you let Molly out very soon?'

'Is it Molly McGuigan?' says she to me.
'Is it now?' says I, for I know'd it was she.
'Is it her you mean that was put in the stocks
For beating her mistress, Mrs Cox?'

'O! yes and it is, madam, pray let me in,
I have brought her a half-pint of Cooper's best gin.
She likes it as well as she likes her own mother,
O! now let me in, madam, I am her brother.'

So the Currency Lads may fill their glasses,
And drink the health of the Currency Lasses,
But the lass I adore, the lass for me,
Is the lass in the Female Factory.

Francis MacNamara

('Frank the poet')

A petition from the chain gang at Newcastle to Captain Furlong the superintendent praying him to dismiss a scourger named Duffy from the cookhouse and appoint a man in his room.

With reverence and submission due,
Kind sir those words are sent to you,
And with them a good wish too,
Long may you reign,
And like Wellington at Waterloo
Fresh laurels gain.

2nd

Your petitioners are under thy care,
In mercy therefore hear our prayer,
Nor let us wallow in despair,
      But soothe each pang,
But allow no flogger to prepare
      Food for your gang.

3rd

'Tis said that by your ordination
Our late cook lost his situation,
And Duffy is in nomination
      His berth to fill;
But has not got our approbation,
      Nor never will.

4th

Your judgement Sire, put to good use,
Nor burthen us with foul abuse,
Full long we've drunk the dregs and juice
      Of black despair,
Yet we can find another screw loose
      Or two somewhere.

5th

Our jaws now daily will grow thinner,
And stomachs weak, as I'm a sinner,
For Duffy is a human skinner,
      Most barbarous wretch.
Each day I'd rather have my dinner
      Cooked by Jack Ketch.

6th

It matters not whether salt or fresh,
Even his touch would spoil each dish.
His cooking we never can relish—
      We'd rather starve.
For be assured tis human flesh
      He best can carve.

7th

To any rational being I appeal,
Whether he's fit to cook a meal
For a vile caterpillar or snail,
     Or a beast of prey.
Men he has scoured in every gaol
     In Botany Bay.

8th

I know the damned devils when they sit
To dine, will long for a savoury bit.
Now Duffy's just the person fit
     To boil their kettles,
So send him to the Bottomless Pit
     To cook their victuals.

9th

But did he even touch our meat,
A furnace our coppers wouldn't heat,
And every knife, fork, spoon and plate
     Would cry out Shame,
And in the midst of our debate
     Would curse thy name.

10th

Or if Saints Matthew, Mark, John and Luke,
With Moses who wrote the Pentateuch
Consented to make this flogger our cook.
     I'd say 'tis foul;
If I wouldn't swear it on the Book,
     Hell seize my soul.

11th

Now sir, your petitioners great and small
On bended knees before you fall;
Nor let us in vain for redress call,
     Drive Duffy away,
And as in duty bound we all
     Will ever pray.

For the Company underground

Francis MacNamara of Newcastle to J. Crosdale Esq. greeting

> When Christ from Heaven comes down straightway,
> All His Father's laws to expound,
> MacNamara shall work that day
> For the Company underground.
>
> When the man in the moon to Moreton Bay
> Is sent in shackles bound,
> MacNamara shall work that day
> For the Company underground.
>
> When the Cape of Good Hope to Twofold Bay
> Comes for the change of a pound,
> MacNamara shall work that day
> For the Company underground.
>
> When cows in lieu of milk yield tea,
> And all lost treasures are found,
> MacNamara shall work that day
> For the Company underground.
>
> When the Australian Co.'s heaviest dray
> Is drawn 80 miles by a hound,
> MacNamara shall work that day
> For the Company underground.
>
> When a frog, a caterpillar and a flea
> Shall travel the globe all round,
> MacNamara shall work that day
> For the Company underground.
>
> When turkeycocks on Jews harps play
> And mountains dance at the sound,
> MacNamara shall work that day
> For the Company underground.
>
> When milestones go to church to pray
> And whales are put in the Pound,
> MacNamara shall work that day
> For the Company underground.
>
> When Christmas falls on the 1st of May
> And O'Connell's King of England crown'd,
> MacNamara shall work that day
> For the Company underground.

When thieves ever robbing on the highway
For their sanctity are renowned,
MacNamara shall work that day
For the Company underground.

When the quick and the dead shall stand in array
Cited at the trumpet's sound,
Even then, damn me if I'd work a day
For the Company underground.

                    Nor over ground.

A Convict's Tour to Hell

Composed at Stroud A.A. Co. Establishment Station
New South Wales

Nor can the foremost of the sons of men
Escape my ribald and licentious pen.
                    Swift

Composed and written
October 23rd day, Anno 1839

You prisoners of New South Wales,
Who frequent watchhouses and gaols
A story to you I will tell
'Tis of a convict's tour to hell.

Whose valour had for years been tried
On the highway before he died
At length he fell to death a prey
To him it proved a happy day
Downwards he bent his course I'm told
Like one destined for Satan's fold
And no refreshment would he take
'Till he approached the Stygian lake
A tent he then began to fix
Contiguous to the River Styx
Thinking that no one could molest him
He leaped when Charon thus addressed him
Stranger I say from whence art thou,
And thy own name, pray tell me now,
Kind sir I come from Sydney gaol
My name I don't mean to conceal
And since you seem anxious to know it

On earth I was called Frank the Poet.
Are you that person? Charon cried,
I'll carry you to the other side.
Five or sixpence I mostly charge
For the like passage in my barge
So stranger do not troubled be
For you shall have a passage free
Frank seeing no other succour nigh
With the invitation did comply
And having a fair wind and tide
They soon arrived at the other side
And leaving Charon at the ferry
Frank went in haste to Purgatory
And rapping loudly at the gate
Of Limbo, or the Middle State
Pope Pius the 7th soon appeared
With gown, beads, crucifix and beard
And gazing at the Poet the while
Accosts him in the following style
Stranger art thou a friend or foe
Your business here I fain would know
Quoth the Poet for Heaven I'm not fitted
And here I hope to be admitted
Pius rejoined, vain are your hopes
This place was made for Priests and Popes
Tis a world of our own invention
But friend I've not the least intention
To admit such a foolish elf
Who scarce knows how to bless himself
Quoth Frank were you mad or insane
When first you made this world of pain?
For I can see nought but fire
A share of which I can't desire
Here I see weeping wailing gnashing
And torments of the newest fashion
Therefore I call you silly elf
Who made a rod to whip yourself
And may you like all honest neighbours
Enjoy the fruit of all your labours
Frank then bid the Pope farewell
And hurried to that place called Hell
And having found the gloomy gate
Frank rapped aloud to know his fate
He louder knocked and louder still
When the Devil came, pray what's your will?

Alas cried the Poet I've come to dwell
With you and share your fate in Hell
Says Satan that can't be, I'm sure
For I detest and hate the poor
And none shall in my kingdom stand
Except the grandees of the land.
But Frank I think you are going astray
For convicts never come this way
But soar to Heaven in droves and legions
A place so called in the upper regions
So Frank I think with an empty purse
You shall go further and fare worse
Well cried the Poet since 'tis so
One thing of you I'd like to know
As I'm at present in no hurry
Have you one here called Captain Murray?
Yes Murray is within this place
Would you said Satan see his face?
May God forbid that I should view him
For on board the *Phoenix Hulk* I knew him
Who is that Sir in yonder blaze
Who on fire and brimstone seems to graze?
'Tis Captain Logan of Moreton Bay
And Williams who was killed the other day
He was overseer at Grosse Farm
And done poor convicts no little harm
Cook who discovered New South Wales
And he that first invented gaols
Are both tied to a fiery stake
Which stands in yonder boiling lake
Hark do you hear this dreadful yelling
It issues from Doctor Wardell's dwelling
And all those fiery seats and chairs
Are fitted up for Dukes and Mayors
And nobles of Judicial orders
Barristers Lawyers and Recorders
Here I beheld legions of traitors
Hangmen gaolers and flagellators
Commandants, Constables and Spies
Informers and Overseers likewise
In flames of brimstone they were toiling
And lakes of sulphur round them boiling
Hell did resound with their fierce yelling
Alas how dismal was their dwelling
Then Major Morriset I espied

And Captain Cluney by his side
With a fiery belt they were lashed together
As tight as soles to upper leather
Their situation was most horrid
For they were tyrants down at the Norrid
Prostrate I beheld a petitioner
It was the Company's Commissioner
Satan said he my days are ended
For many years I've superintended
The An. Company's affairs
And I punctually paid all arrears
Sir should you doubt the hopping Colonel
At Carrington you'll find my journal
Legibly penned in black and white
To prove that my accounts were right
And since I've done your will on earth
I hope you'll put me in a berth
Then I saw old Serjeant Flood
In Vulcan's hottest forge he stood
He gazed at me his eyes with ire
Appeared like burning coals of fire
In fiery garments he was arrayed
And like an Arabian horse he brayed
He on a bloody cutlass leaned
And to a lamp-post he was chained
He loudly called out for assistance
Or begged me to end his existence
Cheer up said I be not afraid
Remember No. Three Stockade
In the course of time you may do well
If you behave yourself in Hell
Your heart on earth was fraught with malice
Which oft drove convicts to the gallows
But you'll now atone for all the blood
Of prisoners shed by Serjeant Flood.
Then I beheld that well known Trapman
The Police Runner called Izzy Chapman
Here he was standing on his head
In a river of melted boiling lead.
Alas he cried behold me stranger
I've captured many a bold bushranger
And for the same I'm suffering here
But lo, now yonder snakes draw near
On turning round I saw slow worms
And snakes of various kinds and forms

All entering at his mouth and nose
To devour his entrails as I suppose
Then turning round to go away
Bold Lucifer bade me to stay
Saying Frank by no means go man
Till you see your old friend Dr. Bowman
Yonder he tumbles groans and gnashes
He gave you many a thousand lashes
And for the same he does bewail
For Osker with an iron flail
Thrashes him well you may depend
And will till the world comes to an end
Just as I spoke a coach and four
Came in full post haste to the door
And about six feet of mortal sin
Without leave or licence trudged in
At his arrival three cheers were given
Which rent I'm sure the highest Heaven
And all the inhabitants of Hell
With one consent rang the great bell
Which never was heard to sound or ring
Since Judas sold our Heavenly King
Drums were beating flags were hoisting
There never before was such rejoicing
Dancing singing joy or mirth
In Heaven above or on the earth
Straightway to Lucifer I went
To know what these rejoicings meant
Of sense cried Lucifer I'm deprived
Since Governor Darling has arrived
With fire and brimstone I've ordained him
And Vulcan has already chained him
And I'm going to fix an abode
For Captain Rossi, he's on the road
Frank don't go till you see the novice
The magistrate from the Police Office
Oh said the Poet I'm satisfied
To hear that he is to be tied
And burned in this world of fire
I think 'tis high time to retire
And having travelled many days
O'er fiery hills and boiling seas
At length I found that happy place
Where all the woes of mortals cease
And rapping loudly at the wicket

Cried Peter, where's your certificate
Or if you have not one to show
Pray who in Heaven do you know?
Well I know Brave Donohue
Young Troy and Jenkins too
And many others whom floggers mangled
And lastly were by Jack Ketch strangled
Peter, says Jesus, let Frank in
For he is thoroughly purged from sin
And although in convict's habit dressed
Here he shall be a welcome guest.
Isaiah go with him to Job
And put on him a scarlet robe
St Paul go to the flock straightway
And kill the fatted calf today
And go tell Abraham and Abel
In haste now to prepare the table
For we shall have a grand repast
Since Frank the Poet has come at last
Then came Moses and Elias
John the Baptist and Mathias
With many saints from foreign lands
And with the Poet they all join hands

Thro' Heaven's Concave their rejoicings rang
And hymns of praise to God they sang
And as they praised his glorious name
I woke and found 'twas but a dream.

Robert Lowe

(Viscount Sherbrooke)

Songs Of The Squatters I

The gum has no shade,
    And the wattle no fruit,
The parrot don't warble
    In trolls like the flute,
The cockatoo cooeth
    Not much like a dove,
Yet fear not to ride
    To my station, my love;

Four hundred miles off
  Is the goal of our way,
It is done in a week
  At but sixty a day;
The plains are all dusty,
  The creeks are all dried,
'Tis the fairest of weather
  To bring home my bride.
The blue vault of heaven
  Shall curtain thy form,
One side of a gum tree
  The moonbeam must warm;
The whizzing mosquito
  Shall dance o'er thy head,
And the guana shall squat
  At the foot of thy bed;
The brave laughing jackass
  Shall sing thee to sleep,
And the snake o'er thy slumbers
  His vigils shall keep.
Then sleep, lady, sleep,
  Without dreaming of pain,
Till the frost of the morning
  Shall wake thee again.
Our brave bridal bower
  I built not of stones,
Though, like old Doubting Castle,
  'Tis paved with bones,
The bones of the sheep
  On whose flesh I have fed,
Where thy thin satin slipper
  Unshrinking may tread,
For the dogs have all polished
  Them clean with their teeth,
And they're better, believe me,
  Than what lies beneath.
My door has no hinge,
  And the window no pane,
They let out the smoke,
  But they let in the rain;
The frying-pan serves us
  For table and dish,
And the tin pot of tea stands
  Still filled for your wish;

The sugar is brown,
   The milk is all done,
But the stick it is stirred with
   Is better than none.
The stockmen will swear,
   And the shepherds won't sing,
But a dog's a companion
   Enough for a king.
So fear not, fair lady,
   Your desolate way,
Your clothes will arrive
   In three months with my dray.
Then mount, lady, mount, to the wilderness fly,
My stores are laid in, and my shearing is nigh,
And our steeds, that through Sydney exultingly wheel,
Must graze in a week on the banks of the Peel.

Songs Of The Squatters II

The Commissioner bet me a pony—I won,
So he cut off exactly two-thirds of my run;
For he said I was making a fortune too fast,
And profit gained slower the longer would last.

He remarked, as devouring my mutton he sat,
That I suffered my sheep to grow sadly too fat;
That they wasted waste land, did prerogative brown,
And rebelliously nibbled the droits of the Crown.

That the creek that divided my station in two
Showed that Nature designed that two fees should be due.
Mr. Riddell assured me 'twas paid but for show,
But he kept it and spent it, that's all that I know.

The Commissioner fined me because I forgot
To return an old ewe that was ill of the rot,
And a poor wry-necked lamb that we kept for a pet:
And he said it was treason such things to forget.

The Commissioner pounded my cattle because
They had mumbled the scrub with their famishing jaws
On the part of the run he had taken away,
And he sold them by auction the costs to defray.

The border police they were out all the day
To look for some thieves who had ransacked my dray;
But the thieves they continued in quiet and peace,
For they'd robbed it themselves had the border police!

When the white thieves had left me the black thieves appeared,
My shepherds they waddied, my cattle they speared;
But for fear of my licence I said not a word,
For I knew it was gone if the Government heard.

The Commissioner's bosom with anger was filled
Against me, because my poor shepherd was killed;
So he straight took away the last third of my run,
And got it transferred to the name of his son.

The son had from Cambridge been lately expelled,
And his licence for preaching most justly withheld!
But this is no cause, the Commissioner says,
Why he should not be fit for my licence to graze.

The cattle that had not been sold at the pound,
He took with the run at five shillings all round;
And the sheep the blacks left me at sixpence a head;
'And a very good price!' the Commissioner said.

The Governor told me I justly was served,
That Commissioners never from duty had swerved;
But that if I'd fancy for any more land,
For one pound an acre he'd plenty on hand.

I'm not very proud; I can dig in a bog,
Feed pigs, or for firewood can split up a log,
Clean shoes, riddle cinders, or help to boil down—
Anything that you please, but graze lands of the Crown!

Charles Harpur

A Basket Of Summer Fruit

First see those ample melons—brindled o'er
With mingled green and brown is all the rind;
For they are ripe, and mealy at the core,
And saturate with the nectar of their kind.

And here their fellows of the marsh are set,
Covering their sweetness with a crumpled skin;
Pomegranates next, flame-red without, and yet
With vegetable crystals stored within.

Then mark these brilliant oranges, of which
A by-gone Poet fancifully said,

Their unplucked globes the orchard did enrich
Like golden lamps in a green night of shade.

With these are lemons that are even more
Golden than they, and which adorn our Rhyme,
As did rough pendants of barbaric ore
Some pillared temple of the olden time.

And here are peaches with their ruddy cheeks
And ripe transparency. Here nectarines bloom,
All mottled as with discontinuous streaks,
And spread a fruity fragrance through the room.

With these are cherries mellow to the stone;
Into such ripeness hath the summer nursed them,
The velvet pressure of the tongue alone
Against the palate were enough to burst them.

Here too are plums, like edible rubies glowing—
The language of lush summer's Eden theme:
Even through the skin how temptingly keeps showing
Their juicy comfort, a rich-clouded gleam!

Here too are figs, pears, apples (plucked in haste
Our summer treat judiciously to vary)
With apricots, so exquisite in taste,
And yellow as the breast of a canary.

And luscious strawberries all faceted
With glittering lobes—and all the lovelier seen
In contrast with the loquat's duller red,
And vulgar gooseberry's unlustrous green.

And lastly, bunches of rich blooded grapes
Whose vineyard bloom even yet about them clings,
Though ever in the handling it escapes
Like the fine down upon a moth's bright wings.

Each kind is piled in order in the Basket,
Which we might well imagine now to be
Transmuted into a great golden casket
Entreasuring Pomona's jewelry.

Wellington

Great captain if you will! great Duke! great Slave!
Great minion of the crown!—but a great man

He *was* not! He? the iron instrument
Of mere authority! the atheist
Of a conventional and most earthy duty!
To whom the powers that be were simply not
Of God—but in His stead! Shall we belie
All righteous instinct and profane all truth,
By calling *great* a man without a soul?
One who, apart from the despotic wills
Of crowned oppressors, knew no right, no wrong,
No faith, no country, and no brotherhood?
If such a man were *great*, may God most High
Spare henceforth to our universal race
All *greatness*, seeing it may sometimes be
A rigid, kindless battlement of Power
Self throned and sanctioned only by the sword.
And if, as Englishmen are proud to boast,
He was their greatest countryman—alas!
For England's national sterility!
But they who thus belaud him, *lie*, as all
True patriots most feelingly perceive.
Besides, he was not England's son at all:
He was an Irishman, with whom the name
Of Ireland was a scoff! An Irishman,
Who for a hireling's meed and ministry,
Could tear away from his inhuman heart
The pleading image of his native land.

A Flight of Wild Ducks

Far up the River—hark! 'tis the loud shock
Deadened by distance, of some Fowler's gun:
And as into the stillness of the scene
It wastes now with a dull vibratory boom,
Look where, fast widening up at either end
Out of the sinuous valley of the waters,
And o'er the intervenient forest,—up
Against the open heaven, a long dark *line*
Comes hitherward stretching—a vast Flight of Ducks!
Following the windings of the vale, and still
Enlarging lengthwise, and in places too
Oft breaking into solitary dots,
How swiftly onwards comes it—till at length,
The River, reaching through a group of hills,

Off leads it,—out of sight. But not for long:
For, wheeling ever with the water's course,
Here into sudden view it comes again
Sweeping and swarming round the nearest point!
And first now, a swift airy rush is heard
Approaching momently;—then all at once
There passes a keen-cutting, gusty tumult
Of strenuous pinions, with a streaming mass
Of instantaneous skiey streaks; each streak
Evolving with a lateral flirt, and thence
Entangling as it were,—so rapidly
A thousand wings outpointingly dispread
In passing tiers, seem, looked at from beneath,
With rushing intermixtures to involve
Each other as they beat. Thus seen o'erhead
Even while we speak—ere we have spoken,—lo!
The living cloud is onward many a rood,
Tracking as 'twere in the smooth stream below
The multifarious shadow of itself.
Far coming—present—and far gone at once!
The senses vainly struggle to retain
The impression of an Image (as the same)
So swift and manifold: For now again
A long dark *line* upon the utmost verge
Of the horizon, steeping still, it sinks
At length into the landscape; where yet seen
Though dimly, with a wide and scattering sweep
It fetches eastward, and in column so
Dapples along the steep face of the ridge
There banking the turned River. Now it drops
Below the fringing oaks—but to arise
Once more, with a quick circling gleam, as touched
By the slant sunshine, and then disappear
As instantaneously,—there settling down
Upon the reedy bosom of the water.

Henry Parkes

Our Coming Countrymen

England's poor who wanderers be
On her highway o'er the sea!

Trodden long in England's dust—
Out at last from England thrust!

Children of the former brave,
Who, on battle-field and wave,
Fought for England in the time,
Ere her poverty was crime.

Ye, whose labour and whose skill,
And whose scorn of every ill,
Save the woe ordain'd by state,
Made her greatest of the great!—

Whose intelligence and power,
(Though ye be old England's poor,)
Best support her mighty name
Of imperishable fame.

Ye who come—when statesmen say
That is left the only way
To appease lean Hunger's cries—
Out to England's colonies,

Know ye what fair masters wait—
Master both and magistrate—
Ye to give your sweat for bread,
When Australia's shores ye tread.

Know ye, gentlemen are they,
Who in open daylight say
England's convicts they prefer
To you pauper-scum from her!—

Convicts, for they cheaper are,
And more governable far;
Convicts, with no idle child
To be ration'd in the wild!—

In the wild, where go ye must,
And to these men's mercies trust;
And, arise what quarrels may,
Their adjudgment still obey!—

Where revenge and lust ne'er sleep,
Let wild nature smile or weep,
Unabash'd as unforgiven,
When the sun looks down from Heaven!

Where all British law is dead,
As our senators have said,

And the honest pay a price
For the sufferance of vice.

'Ample room for life' is there,
And it is a region fair,—
Ample room, but not for man
In the heaven-appointed plan.

Where the cedars fringe the river
In the summer light for ever,
And the plain and valley pine
For the plough and harrow's tine;

Not a single cottager,
Like the men your fathers were,
Is there through the sun-bright regions;
Only sheep in countless legions.

One man's flocks, for you to tend,
O'er a kingdom's space extend,—
You or isle-barbarian,
China's slave or cheaper man.

Though the factory's crowded floor
Hold you not as heretofore;
Though ye tread the fragrant ground,
With the free pure air all round;

Though no workhouse mandate now
May your suffering spirits bow;
Though ye feel, and justly may,
Ye have won your bread each day:

Ye all Christian faith will need,
Not to curse your lot indeed,
Still pursued by wretchedness,
New and different, but not less.

Aboriginal Songs from the 1850s

Kilaben Bay song

(Awabakal language, Lake Macquarie, New South Wales)

Ela! Ngorokan-ta killi-bin-bin katan
Pannal-la bulliko kul-kulin

Tokoi-ro oowalin
Kore-la ngarabin
Wonnai-baran korien korun yikora
Ngu-koong-baran kullai tirriki kotillin
Tibbin-tara wiyalin
Boot-ikiang korien berekabin yikora
Kolbee kio-yoong koba kowaul
Kore-baran koroong kolang oowalin
Ngu-koong baran bahto boa-malin
Wonnai baran koppiri yantin kaibaillin
Ngu-koong bahto boa-mah
Kore baran tura makero-lo mankullan
Kuri yantin takillin
Katan ta-ba koi-yoong wi wi

Hail! Dawn is shining glory doing
The sun shining (blazing with warmth)
Night moving
Man stirring
Children restless
Women fire-wood thinking
Birds singing
Animals awakening (sleeping not)
Camp noise grows
Men bush towards moving
Women water gathering
Children they hungry, all shouting
Women water collected
Men spear fish, return
People all eating
Camp quiet again

Literal translation by Perce Haslam

Women's rondo

Awabakal language, New South Wales

Nga ba ya!	Ah, it is so!
Kore wonnung ke?	Where is the man?
Kore yo!	Man is away!
Kore wonnung ke?	Where is the man?
Nga ba ya!	Ah, it is so!

Two tongue-pointing (satirical) songs

Kamilaroi language, New South Wales

1.
Ngandu-nga?
Tirree Ghilbana
Bungoon mulli-ago
Ngaigh-heen bular

Ngai murreen?
Ngai-ah warram-bria
ngirri go-mah

Toh dirral dia

1.
Who comes?
Large head of hair
Arms crooked
Like two cockle shells

One of my people?
One road he is
(visible but useless)

like smoke from a fire

2.
Murri goriah
Yerar-man booraldi
Wi Wi kurral -ah
Millim-brai kakullah

Kira-wah!

2.
Blackfellow very fat
Horses driving
Firewood sawing
Milking cows crying out
(off he goes)
Looking for them!

The drunk man

Wolaroi language, New South Wales

Publika-or wiri thea
Djea-mellia meer meer
Ngum-milde-ago
Karni -wee—andi
Drunk-gilla
Ti-unal a doonee

Public house screaming
Seizing hips
He appears,
tripped by stick
Drunken
Stricken with fists

Anonymous

Whaler's Rhyme

When shearing comes, lay down your drums,
Step on to the board, you brand-new-chums,
And when you cross the briny deep
To gammon you can shear a sheep.

Chorus With a ra-dum, a rub, a dub, a dub,
      Drive him back to the tar-boy's tub.

There's brand-new-chums and cockies' sons,
They fancy that they are great guns;
They think that they can shear the wool,
But the beggars only tear and pull.

They tar the sheep—they're nearly black—
Roll up! roll up! and get the sack.
Once more, once more on the wallaby track:
Once more to look for shearing.

The very next thing they undertake
Is to press the wool—they make a mistake.
They press the wool without a bale,
When the joker sings out jam his tail.

And when they meet upon the road
From off their backs throw down their load
Then at the sun they'll take a look
Saying it's nearly time to breast the cook.

We camp in huts without any door,
And sleep upon the dirty floor;
A pannikin of flour and a sheet of bark
To wallop up a damper in the dark.

Three little johnny-cakes, looking nicely cooked;
A nice little codfish hanging on a hook;
Tea and sugar-bag looking very plump,
And the blessed old flour-bag lying on the stump.

It's Home, it's Home I'd like to be—
Not humping my drum in this country;
Sixteen thousand miles I've come,
To march along with a blanket drum.

The Diggins-oh

I've come back all skin and bone
From the diggins-oh.
And I wish I'd never gone
To the diggins-oh.
Believe me, 'tis no fun,
I once weighed fifteen stone,
But they brought me down to one
At the diggins-oh!

I thought a good home could be found
At the diggins-oh.
But soon I found I got aground
At the diggins-oh.
The natives came one day,
Burnt my cottage down like hay,
With my wife they ran away
To the diggins-oh.

I built a hut with mud
At the diggins-oh.
That got washed away by flood
At the diggins-oh.
I used to dig, and cry
It wouldn't do to die,
Undertakers charge too high
At the diggins-oh.

I paid for victuals with a frown,
At the diggins-oh.
Three potatoes half a crown,
At the diggins-oh.
Sprats five shillings a dish
If for Dutch plaice you wish,
Two dollards buys that fish
At the diggins-oh.

A crown a pound for steaks,
At the diggins-oh.
Ditto chops, and no great shakes,
At the diggins-oh.
Five 'hog' a small pig's cheek;
If a herring red you'd seek,
One will keep you dry a week,
At the diggins-oh.

Table beer two bob a quart,
At the diggins-oh.
Get your eyes gouged out for nought,
At the diggins-oh.
Five shillings a four-pound brick,
Butter a shilling a lick,
They never give no tick
At the diggins-oh.

They tied me to a tree,
At the diggins-oh.

With my nuggets they made free,
At the diggins-oh.
I escaped from bodily hurt,
Though they stole my very shirt,
I had to paint myself with dirt,
At the diggins-oh.

I felt quite a ruined man,
At the diggins-oh.
Thinks I, I'll get home, if I can,
From the diggins-oh.
I was always catching cold,
And I've been both bought and sold
Like many more, for gold,
At the diggins-oh.

But now I'm safe returned
From the diggins-oh.
Never more I mean to roam
To the diggins-oh.
It some peoples' fortune mends.
Much on the man depends—
I'd sooner be here with my friends
Than at the diggins-oh.

William W. Coxon (?)

The Flash Colonial Barman

(Air—'The Old English Gentleman')

Since I've been in this colony I've written many a song
Of the peculiarities which to each class belong,
But if my memory serves me right I never yet have told
Of the flash colonial barman of this glorious land of gold.
These flash colonial barmen who do 'the thing' so fine;
The fine flash Yankee barmen you see this side the line.

At home, if in a bar you stray to have a glass or so,
The barman doesn't look as if he stood there just for show;
His apron's on, his waistcoat too, his sleeves turned up as well,
And as he serves you, on my word, he doesn't cut the swell

Of these flash colonial barmen you see this side the line;
These fine flash Yankee barmen who once cut such a shine.

But here, in these large Yankee bars, behind the counter stands
A gentleman with fierce moustache, and rings upon his hands;
His patent boots are faultless; his shirts without a splash;
Got braceless pants, and round his waist he wears a crimson sash—
The flash colonial barman you see this side the line;
The fine flash Yankee barman who once cut such a shine.

While ordering your nobbler he up a tumbler throws
And catches it—though sometimes smash upon the floor it goes.
No matter, another quick, is taken from the shelf,
The bottle's pushed towards you and you're told to 'help yourself'
By these flash colonial barmen you see this side the line;
Those fine flash Yankee barmen who once cut such a shine.

He's fine on *fences*, sweet on *slings*—at *juleps* too he's great,
And you'll very often find, he *hails* from 'New York State';
At *spiders* too he's clever, and to notice do not fail
His scientific *see-saw* when he mixes a *cocktail*—
The flash colonial barman you see this side the line;
The fine flash Yankee barmen who once cut such a shine.

Of course he has his *weakness,* and when you see him out,
By his side you'll find his lady, and then, my word won't he *shout;*
He's certain to be *all the go* where he *attention* pays,
For with the fair sex he has most insinuating ways—
The flash colonial barman you see this side the line;
The fine flash Yankee barman who once cut such a shine.

One day a rush breaks out, and then he goes off *right away.*
Puts up a place—*chances the ducks*—whether it'll pay;
If it does, he makes *a pile;* if not, 'twon't cause him pain,
For he'll *burst up* and go to the colonial bar again,
And become again a barman you see this side the line—
A fine flash Yankee barman, and once more cut a shine.

Charles R. Thatcher

Dick Briggs from Australia

(Air—'King of the Cannibal Islands')

Dick Briggs a wealthy farmer's son
To England lately took a run

To see his friends and have some fun;
     He'd been five years in Australia.
Arrived in London off he went
To his native village down in Kent
For in that pleasant spot he meant
That lots of his rhino should be spent.
No splendid fine clothes on had he
But a jumper and boots up to the knee
With a dirty hat of cabbage-tree,
     The costume of Australia.

Chorus So if you ever take a run
       To England for a bit of fun
       You're safe to astonish everyone
       With the queer ways of Australia.

To the farm he went in this array
And his sister came out and did say,
'We don't want anything today'
     To her brother from Australia.
Says he, 'What, don't you know poor Dick?'
She recognized him pretty quick
And the family all rushed out slick
And his dad embraced him like a brick.
There was joy and feasting there that night,
Dick was quite a welcome sight
For of course they hailed with great delight
     The wanderer from Australia.

Now instead of a glass of home-brewed ale
Every morning he'd not fail
To sing out for a gin cocktail,
     A favourite drink in Australia.
He talked away at a fearful rate
Of nobblers and of brandy straight;
On spiders too he would dilate
And astonish his poor sister Kate.
He kissed the buxom servant maid,
Nice pranks I tell you he played—
Says he, 'My dear don't be afraid,
     It's a way we've got in Australia.'

The blessed cattle on the farm
Regarded him with great alarm,
His swearing acted like a charm—
     He gave 'em a touch of Australia.
He talked bullock and 'no flies'

And when he blessed poor Strawberry's eyes
They regarded him with great surprise
For out of them he took a rise.
'Fie, fie' his mother cried one day,
'What dreadful wicked words you say!'
Says he, 'Lor', mother, that's the way
    We wake 'em up in Australia.'

To a great fox-hunt he went one day
And on horseback made a grand display
And in his red coat looked so gay,
    So different to Australia.
The huntsman said with a joyous brow,
'There's music for you, listen now!'
Says Dick, 'I hear no music, I vow,
For those dashed dogs make such a row.
Fox-hunting's pretty sport it's true,
But I'd sooner, I declare to you,
Run down an old-man kangaroo
    Or a flying doe in Australia.'

The winter he found dreadful cold;
And instead of rising early, I'm told,
Till ten o'clock in the blankets rolled,
    And wished himself in Australia.
He couldn't stand the frost and snow,
My word it made him shiver so,
Out of doors he wouldn't go
But sit at the fire to get in a glow.
The summer came and his blood was thinned
But he couldn't exist without a hot wind
And he grumbled because his nose wasn't skinned
    By the glaring sun (Like it used to be) of Australia.

Dick went to London for a spree,
And got drunk there most gloriously;
He gave them a touch of 'Coo-oo-ee!'
    The bush cry of Australia.
He took two ladies to the play,
Both so serene, in dresses gay;
He had champagne brought on a tray
And said, 'Now girls, come fire away.'
They drank till they could drink no more,
And then they both fell on the floor.
Cried Dick, as he surveyed them o'er,
    'You wouldn't do for Australia.'

Taking the Census

*A New Original Song, as written and sung by Thatcher, with
deafening applause, at the 'Shamrock'.*

(Air—'Miser's Man')

When the census is taken, of course,
    All the elderly females are furious,
They don't like to tell their real age,
    For gov'ment they say is too curious:
I got hold of a chap that went round,
    For I wanted to twig their rum capers,
So I tipped him a crown on the sly
    To let me look over his papers.

There's that elderly dame, Mother Baggs,
    Has marked down her age twenty-seven,
Although she's possessed of five kids,
    The eldest of which is eleven;
Miss Fluffen says she's thirty-two,
    But to tell such a story is naughty,
She's a regular frumpish old maid,
    And if she's a year old she's forty.

There's another thing struck me as queer,
    As the papers I sat overhauling,
Beneath occupation, thinks I,
    I'll soon find out each person's calling;
But the first I looked at made me grin,
    My wash'woman, old Mother Archer,
Beneath occupation I found
    Had described herself as a clear starcher.

The chemist's assistant up here,
    When his paper I happened to see, sirs,
'Pon my honour had had the vile cheek
    To mark after his name M.D., sirs,
And Bolus, that wretched old quack,
    Whom folks here regard with suspicion,
When his paper I looked at, I found
    He'd put himself down a physician!

Here's a *barberous* custom you'll say,
    No less than three diff'rent hairdressers,
In the papers which they have filled up
    Have described themselves all as *professors*;

In Heidelberg district I find
   My bounceable friend, Harry Potter,
In the paper that he has sent in,
   Tries to make us believe he's a squatter.

My friend said he called on two girls,
   Who are noted for cutting rum capers,
They live in an elegant crib,
   And he knocked at the door for their papers;
They handed him what he required,
   He read, but exclaimed with vexation,
'The instructions you haven't fulfilled—
   'You've not put down your occupation.'

'Well, Poll, that's a good 'un,' says one,
   And both of them burst out a-laughing,
But the young man exclaimed precious quick
   'I can't stay all day while you're chaffing;'
'Occupation' says she, with a scream,
   (Her laughter was pretty near killing her),
'Poll, I'm blowed if I knows what you are,
   But, young man, shove me down as a milliner.'

Moggy's Wedding

(Tune—'Joe Buggins')

Jemmy Ball, a lucky digger,
   Who on Ballarat had been some while,
Resolved that he would cut a figure,
   Acos he had just made his pile.
He stuck up to a gal named Moggy—
   A big stout lass from t'other side;
And though at times she got quite groggy,
   He determined she should be his bride.

To ask his mates all to the wedding,
   Round the diggings he did pop;
And then to purchase clothes and bedding
   He took his Moggy to a shop;
And she, resolved to 'shew her muscle,'
   Bought satin, lace, and bombazine,
A Tuscan bonnet and a bustle,
   And any quantity of crinoline.

On the bridal morn the sun shone brightly,
  The guests began then to arrive;
And Jim sang out to Mog so sprightly,
  'Come on, old woman, look alive.'
Jim was dressed up like a dandy,
  With rings his fingers they were full;
And Mog uncorked a case of brandy,
  And took a most tremendous pull.

The guests into the tent kept dropping,
  And they then prepared to start,
And Jemmy up the lush kept mopping,
  And then went for an old spring cart.
Up got Moggy, and her bonnet
  With orange blossoms round was lined;
But the seat broke slap ven she sat on it,
  And pitched her right whop out behind.

Next came a dray, and Sydney Polly
  With Jack Johnson up did pop,
And Tony Cheeks, with Adelaide Dolly,
  Who kept a little sly-grog shop.
Bill Grummet said then, 'Let's be going,'
  A black belltopper he did wear;
And when some coves began their joeing,
  Crikey! oh, how he did swear.

If you had seen them all alighting,
  You would have laughed, upon my life;
But it regularly licked dog fighting,
  When asked if she would be his wife:
This produced a vacant stare from Moggy—
  To ask this question is the rule;
'Of course I will' says she, half groggy,
  'I comed on purpose, you old fool.'

They all then went home rather merry,
  Resolved that they'd get drunk that day,
And lots of brandy, port, and sherry,
  They managed soon to stow away:
Mog to do her share was able,
  And she soon got precious tight;
And stretch'd blind drunk beneath the table
  Was how she spent her wedding night.

Anonymous

The Banks of the Condamine

Oh, hark the dogs are barking, love,
I can no longer stay,
The men are all gone mustering
And it is nearly day.
And I must off by the morning light
Before the sun doth shine,
To meet the Sydney shearers
On the banks of the Condamine.

Oh Willie, dearest Willie,
I'll go along with you,
I'll cut off all my auburn fringe
And be a shearer, too,
I'll cook and count your tally, love,
While ringer-o you shine,
And I'll wash your greasy moleskins
On the banks of the Condamine.

Oh, Nancy, dearest Nancy,
With me you cannot go,
The squatters have given orders, love,
No woman should do so;
Your delicate constitution
Is not equal unto mine,
To stand the constant tigering
On the banks of the Condamine.

Oh Willie, dearest Willie,
Then stay back home with me,
We'll take up a selection
And a farmer's wife I'll be:
I'll help you husk the corn, love,
And cook your meals so fine
You'll forget the ram-stag mutton
On the banks of the Condamine.

Oh, Nancy, dearest Nancy,
Please do not hold me back,
Down there the boys are waiting,
And I must be on the track;

So here's a good-bye kiss, love,
Back home here I'll incline
When we've shore the last of the jumbucks
On the banks of the Condamine.

The Stringybark Cockatoo

I'm a broken-hearted miner, who loves his cup to drain,
Which often times has caused me to lie in frost and rain.
Roaming about the country, looking for some work to do.
I got a job of reaping off a stringybark cockatoo.

Chorus Oh, the stringybark cockatoo,
      Oh, the stringybark cockatoo,
      I got a job of reaping off a stringybark cockatoo.

Ten bob an acre was his price—with promise of fairish board.
He said his crops were very light, 'twas all he could afford.
He drove me out in a bullock dray, and his piggery met my view.
Oh, the pigs and geese were in the wheat of the stringybark
   cockatoo.

The hut was made of the surface mud, the roof of a reedy thatch,
The doors and windows open flew without a bolt or latch.
The pigs and geese were in the hut, the hen on the table flew,
And she laid an egg in the old tin plate for the stringybark cockatoo.

For breakfast we had pollard, boys, it tasted like cobbler's paste,
To help it down we had to eat brown bread with vinegar taste.
The tea was made of the native hops which out on the ranges grew;
'Twas sweetened with honey bees and wax for the stringybark
   cockatoo.

For dinner we had goanna hash, we thought it mighty hard;
They wouldn't give us butter, so we forced down bread and lard.
Quondong duff, paddymelon pie, and wallaby Irish stew
We used to eat while reaping for the stringybark cockatoo.

When we started to cut, the rust and smut was just beginning to
   shed,
And all we had to sleep on was a dog and a sheepskin bed.
The bugs and fleas tormented me, they made me scratch and screw;
I lost my rest while reaping for the stringybark cockatoo.

At night when work was over I'd nurse the youngest child,
And when I'd say a joking word, the mother would laugh and smile.
The old cocky, he grew jealous, and he thumped me black and blue,
And he drove me off without a rap—the stringybark cockatoo.

Henry Kendall

Bell-birds

By channels of coolness the echoes are calling,
And down the dim gorges I hear the creek falling:
It lives in the mountain where moss and the sedges
Touch with their beauty the banks and the ledges.
Through breaks of the cedar and sycamore bowers
Struggles the light that is love to the flowers;
And, softer than slumber, and sweeter than singing,
The notes of the bell-birds are running and ringing.

The silver-voiced bell-birds, the darlings of daytime!
They sing in September their songs of the May-time;
When shadows wax strong, and the thunder-bolts hurtle,
They hide with their fear in the leaves of the myrtle;
When rain and the sunbeams shine mingled together,
They start up like fairies that follow fair weather;
And straightway the hues of their feathers unfolden
Are the green and the purple, the blue and the golden.

October, the maiden of bright yellow tresses,
Loiters for love in these cool wildernesses;
Loiters, knee-deep, in the grasses, to listen,
Where dripping rocks gleam and the leafy pools glisten:
Then is the time when the water-moons splendid
Break with their gold, and are scattered or blended
Over the creeks, till the woodlands have warning
Of songs of the bell-bird and wings of the Morning.

Welcome as waters unkissed by the summers
Are the voices of bell-birds to thirsty far-comers.
When fiery December sets foot in the forest,
And the need of the wayfarer presses the sorest,
Pent in the ridges for ever and ever
The bell-birds direct him to spring and to river,
With ring and with ripple, like runnels whose torrents
Are toned by the pebbles and leaves in the currents.

Often I sit, looking back to a childhood,
Mixt with the sights and the sounds of the wildwood,
Longing for power and the sweetness to fashion,
Lyrics with beats like the heart-beats of Passion;—
Songs interwoven of lights and of laughters
Borrowed from bell-birds in far forest-rafters;

So I might keep in the city and alleys
The beauty and strength of the deep mountain valleys:
Charming to slumber the pain of my losses
With glimpses of creeks and a vision of mosses.

Beyond Kerguelen

Down in the South, by the waste without sail on it—
    Far from the zone of the blossom and tree—
Lieth, with winter and whirlwind and wail on it,
    Ghost of a land by the ghost of a sea.
Weird is the mist from the summit to base of it;
    Sun of its heaven is wizened and grey;
Phantom of light is the light on the face of it—
    Never is night on it, never is day!
Here is the shore without flower or bird on it—
    Here is no litany sweet of the springs:
Only the haughty, harsh thunder is heard on it—
    Only the storm with a roar in its wings!

Shadow of moon is the moon in the sky of it—
    Wan as the face of a wizard, and far!
Never there shines from the firmament high of it
    Grace of the planet or glory of star.
All the year round, in the place of white days on it—
    All the year round, where there never is night—
Lies a great sinister, bitter, blind haze on it:
    Growth that is neither of darkness nor light!
Wild is the cry of the sea in the caves by it—
    Sea that is smitten by spears of the snow.
Desolate songs are the songs of the waves by it—
    Down in the South where the ships never go.

Storm from the Pole is the singer that sings to it
    Hymns of the land at the planet's grey verge.
Thunder discloses dark wonderful things to it—
    Thunder, and rain, and the dolorous surge.
Hills, with no hope of a wing or a leaf on them,
    Scarred with the chronicles written by flame,
Stare, through the gloom of inscrutable grief on them,
    Down on the horns of the gulfs without name.
Cliffs, with the records of fierce flying fires on them—
    Loom over perilous pits of eclipse:

Alps, with anathema stamped in the spires on them—
    Out by the wave with a curse on its lips.

Never is sign of soft beautiful green on it—
    Never the colour, the glory of rose!
Neither the fountain nor river is seen on it:
    Naked its crags are, and barren its snows!
Blue as the face of the drowned is the shore of it—
    Shore, with the capes of indefinite cave.
Strange is the voice of its wind, and the roar of it
    Startles the mountain and hushes the wave.
Out to the south, and away to the north of it,
    Spectral and sad are the spaces untold!
All the year round a great cry goeth forth of it—
    Sob of this leper of lands in the cold.

No man hath stood all its bleak bitter years on it—
    Fall of a foot on its wastes is unknown:
Only the sound of the hurricane's spears on it,
    Breaks, with the shout from the uttermost zone.
Blind are its bays with the shadow of bale on them;
    Storms of the nadir their rocks have uphurled;
Earthquake hath registered deeply its tale on them—
    Tale of distress from the dawn of the world!
There are the gaps with the surges that seethe in them—
    Gaps in whose jaws is a menace that glares!
There, the wan reefs with the merciless teeth in them
    Gleam on a chaos that startles and scares!

Back in the dawn of this beautiful sphere, on it—
    Land of the dolorous, desolate face—
Beamed the blue day; and the bountiful year on it
    Fostered the leaf and the blossom of grace,
Grand were the lights of its midsummer noon on it—
    Mornings of majesty shone on its seas:
Glitter of star and the glory of moon on it
    Fell, in the march of the musical breeze.
Valleys and hills, with the whisper of wing in them,
    Dells of the daffodil—spaces impearled,
Flowered and flashed with the splendour of Spring in them—
    Back in the morn of this wonderful world.

Soft were the words that the thunder then said to it—
    Said to this lustre of emerald plain:
Sun brought the yellow, the green, and the red to it—
    Sweet were the songs of its silvery rain.

Voices of water and wind in the bays of it
    Lingered, and lulled like the psalm of a dream.
Fair were the nights, and effulgent the days, of it—
    Moon was in shadow and shade in the beam.
Summer's chief throne was the marvellous coast of it,
    Home of the Spring was its luminous lea!
Garden of glitter! but only the ghost of it
    Moans in the South by the ghost of a sea.

Anonymous

John Gilbert was a Bushranger

John Gilbert was a bushranger
    Of terrible renown
For sticking lots of people up
    And shooting others down.

John Gilbert said unto his pals,
    'Although they make a bobbery
About our tricks, we've never done
    A tip-top thing in robbery.

'We've all of us a fancy for
    Experiments in pillage;
But never have we seized a town,
    Or even sacked a village.'

John Gilbert stated to his mates,
    'Though partners we have been
In all rascality, yet we
    No festal day have seen.'

John Gilbert said he thought he saw
    No obstacle to hinder a
Piratical descent upon
    The town of Canowindra.

So into Canowindra town
    Rode Gilbert and his men,
And all the Canowindra folk
    Subsided there and then.

The Canowindra populace
    Cried, 'Here's a lot of strangers,'

But suddenly recovered when
    They found they were bushrangers.

John Gilbert with his partisans
    Said, 'Don't you be afraid—
We are but old companions whom
    Rank outlaws you have made.'

So Johnny Gilbert says, says he,
    'We'll never hurt a hair
Of men who bravely recognise
    That we are just and fair.'

The New South Welshmen said at once,
    Not making any fuss,
That Johnny Gilbert, after all,
    Was 'just but one of us'.

So Johnny Gilbert took the town
    And all the public houses,
And treated all the cockatoos
    And shouted for their spouses.

And Miss O'Flanagan performed
    In manner quite 'ginteely'
Upon the grand piano for
    The bushranger O'Meally.

And every stranger passing by
    They took, and when they'd got him,
They robbed him of his money, and
    Occasionally shot him.

And Johnny's enigmatic freak
    Admits of this solution,
Bushranging is in New South Wales
    A favoured institution.

So Johnny Gilbert ne'er allows
    An anxious thought to fetch him,
Because he knows the Government
    Don't really want to catch him.

And if such practices should be
    To New South Welshmen dear,
With not the least demurring word
    Ought we to interfere?

Jack McGuire (?)

The Streets of Forbes

Come all you Lachlan men, and a sorrowful tale I'll tell
Concerning of a hero bold who through misfortune fell.
His name it was Ben Hall, a man of good renown
Who was hunted from his station, and like a dog shot down.

Three years he roamed the roads, and he showed the traps some fun;
A thousand pound was on his head, with Gilbert and John Dunn.
Ben parted from his comrades, the outlaws did agree
To give away bushranging and to cross the briny sea.

Ben went to Goobang Creek, and that was his downfall;
For riddled like a sieve was valiant Ben Hall.
'Twas early in the morning upon the fifth of May
When the seven police surrounded him as fast asleep he lay.

Bill Dargin he was chosen to shoot the outlaw dead;
The troopers then fired madly, and filled him full of lead.
They rolled him in a blanket, and strapped him to his prad,
And led him through the streets of Forbes to show the prize they
   had.

E. J. Overbury

The Springtime it Brings On the Shearing

The springtime it brings on the shearing,
And it's then you will see them in droves,
To the west-country stations all steering,
A-seeking a job off the coves.

Chorus:
With my raggedy old swag on my shoulder
And a billy quart-pot in my hand,
I tell you we'll 'stonish the new chums,
When they see how we travel the land.

From Boonabri up to the border,
Then it's over to Bourke; there and back.
On the hills and the plains you will see them,
The men on the Wallaby Track.

And after the shearing is over
And the wool season's all at an end,
It is then you will see the flash shearers
Making johnny-cakes round in the bend.

James Brunton Stephens

The Gentle Anarchist

I am a gentle Anarchist,
  I couldn't kick a dog,
Nor ever would for sport assist
  To pelt the helpless frog.
I'd shoot a Czar, or wreck a train,
  Blow Parliament sky-high,
But none could call me inhumane;
  I wouldn't hurt a fly.
    I wouldn't hurt a fly,
    And why indeed should I?
  . It has neither land nor pelf
    That I covet for myself,
    Then wherefore should I hurt a fly?

I am a gentle Anarchist,
  I live on herbs and fruits;
It don't become a communist
  To eat his fellow-brutes.
I'd fire a town, upset a State,
  Make countless widows weep,
Yet I am so compassionate
  I wouldn't kill a sheep.
    I wouldn't hurt a fly;
    And why indeed should I?
    If it doesn't interfere
    With my personal career,
    Why the dickens should I hurt a fly?

I'm such a gentle Anarchist
  I hate all hunting men;
I couldn't hook a fish, or twist
  The neck of cock or hen.
I'd level gaols, let scoundrels loose,
  Blow priests and churches up—
But, oh, my pity's so profuse

I couldn't drown a pup.
   I wouldn't hurt a fly;
   And why indeed should I?
    Unless, that is to say,
    I found it in my way,
And then it's all up with the fly.

Ada Cambridge

Fashion

See those resplendent creatures, as they glide
   O'er scarlet carpet, between footmen tall,
   From sumptuous carriage to effulgent hall—
A dazzling vision in their pomp and pride!
See that choice supper—needless—cast aside—
   Though worth a thousand fortunes, counting all,
   To them for whom no crumb of it will fall—
The starved and homeless in the street outside.

Some day the little great god will decree
   That overmuch connotes the underbred,
   That pampered body means an empty head,
And wealth displayed the last vulgarity.
When selfish greed becomes a social sin
The world's regeneration may begin.

The Future Verdict

How will our unborn children scoff at us
    In the good years to come,
    The happier years to come,
Because, like driven sheep, we yielded thus,
    Before the shearers dumb.

What are the words their wiser lips will say?
    'These men had gained the light;
    'These women knew the right;
'They had their chance, and let it slip away.
    'They did not, when they might.

'They were the first to hear the gospel preached,
    'And to believe therein;
    'Yet they remained in sin.

'They saw the promised land they might have reached,
    'And dared not enter in.

'They might have won their freedom, had they tried;
    'No savage laws forbade;
    'For them the way was made.
'They might have had the joys for which they cried
    'And yet they shrank, afraid.

'Afraid to face—the martyr's rack and flame?
    'The traitor's dungeon? Nay—
    'Of what their world would say—
'The smile, the joke, the thinnest ghost of blame!
    'Lord! Lord! What fools were they!'

And we—no longer actors of the stage
    We cumber now—maybe
    With other eyes shall see
This wasted chance, and with celestial rage
    Cry 'O what fools were we!'

The Virgin Martyr

Every wild she-bird has nest and mate in the warm April weather,
But a captive woman, made for love—no mate, no nest has she.
In the spring of young desire, young men and maids are wed
    together,
And the happy mothers flaunt their bliss for all the world to see:
Nature's sacramental feast for these—an empty board for me.

I, a young maid once, an old maid now, deposed, despised,
    forgotten—
I, like them have thrilled with passion and have dreamed of nuptial
    rest,
Of the trembling life within me of my children unbegotten,
Of a breathing new-born body to my yearning bosom prest,
Of the rapture of a little soft mouth drinking at my breast.

Time, that heals so many sorrows, keeps mine ever freshly aching;
Though my face is growing furrowed and my brown hair turning
    white,
Still I mourn my irremediable loss, asleep or waking—
Still I hear my son's voice calling 'mother' in the dead of night,
And am haunted by my girl's eyes that will never see the light.

O my children that I might have had! my children, lost for ever!
O the goodly years that might have been—now desolate and bare!

O malignant God or Fate, what have I done that I should never
Take my birthright like the others, take the crown that women wear,
And possess the common heritage to which all flesh is heir?

Marcus Clarke

The Wail of the Waiter

(A Tavern Catch)

All day long, at Scott's or Menzies', I await the gorging crowd,
Panting, penned within a pantry, with the blowflies humming loud.
There at seven in the morning do I count my daily cash,
While the home-returning reveller calls for 'soda and a dash'.
And the weary hansom-cabbies set the blinking squatters down,
Who, all night, in savage freedom, have been 'knocking round the
    town'.
Soon the breakfast gong resounding bids the festive meal begin,
And, with appetites like demons, come the gentle public in.
'Toast and butter!' 'Eggs and coffee!' 'Waiter, mutton chops for
    four!'
'Flatheads!' 'Ham!' 'Beef!' 'Where's the mustard?' 'Steak and
    onions!' 'Shut the door!'
Here sits Bandicoot, the broker, eating in a desperate hurry,
Scowling at his left-hand neighbour, Cornstalk from the Upper
    Murray,
Who with brandy-nose empurpled, and with blue lips cracked and
    dry,
In incipient delirium shoves the eggspoon in his eye.
'Bloater paste!' 'Some *tender* steak, sir?' 'Here, *confound* you,
    where's my chop?'
'Waiter!' 'Yessir!' '*Waiter!*' 'Yessir!!'—running till I'm fit to drop.
Then at lunch time—fearful crisis! In by shoals the gorgers pour,
Gobbling, crunching, swilling, munching—ten times hungrier than
    before.
'Glass of porter!' '*Ale* for me, John!' 'Where's my stick?' 'And
    where's my *hat!*'
'Oxtail soup!' '*I* asked for curry!' 'Cold boiled beef, and cut it fat!'
'Irish stew!' 'Some pickled cabbage!' 'What, no *beans*?' 'Bring *me*
    some pork!'
'Soup, sir?' 'Yes. You grinning idiot, can I eat it with a FORK?'
'Take care, waiter!' 'Beg your pardon.' 'Curse you, have you two
    left legs?'

'I asked for *bread* an hour ago, sir!' 'Now then, have you *laid* those
    eggs?'
'Sherry!' 'No, I called for *beer*—of all the fools I ever saw!'
'Waiter!' 'Yessir!' 'WAITER!!' 'Here, sir!' 'Damme, sir, this steak is
    RAW!'

Thus amid this hideous Babel do I live the livelong day,
While my memory is going, and my hair is turning grey.
All my soul is slowly melting, all my brain is softening fast,
And I know that I'll be taken to the Yarra Bend at last.
For at night from fitful slumbers I awaken with a start,
Mumuring of steak and onions, babbling of apple-tart.
While to me the Poet's cloudland a gigantic kitchen seems,
And those mislaid table-napkins haunt me even in my dreams
Is this right?—Ye sages tell me!—Does a man live but to eat?
Is there nothing worth enjoying but one's miserable meat?
Is the mightiest task of Genius but to swallow buttered beans,
And has Man but been created to demolish pork and greens?
Is there no *unfed* Hereafter, where the round of chewing stops?
Is the atmosphere of heaven clammy with perpetual chops?
Do the friends of Mr Naylor sup on spirit-reared cow-heel?
Can the great Alexis Soyer really say 'Soyez tranquille?'
Or must I bring spirit beefsteak grilled in spirit regions hotter
For the spirit delectation of some spiritual squatter?
Shall I in a spirit kitchen hear the spirit blowflies humming,
Calming spiritual stomachs with a spiritual 'Coming!'?
Shall—but this is idle chatter, I have got my work to do.
'WAITER!!' 'Yessir.' 'Wake up, stupid! Biled calves' feet for
    Number Two!'

Victor Daley

Mother Doorstep

'Wanted Kind Person to take charge of Baby Boy (or Girl),' etc.
         —Any newspaper, any day.
'Early this morning the body of an infant was found on a doorstep
        in — Street,' etc.
         —Any newspaper, every other day.

Unto the Person Kind there came
A young girl bearing her fruit of shame:

She fell and *it* had to pay the price—
Innocent Lamb of Sacrifice!

Lovingly then the Person smiled,
Gazing upon the face of the child;
Smiled like an ogress—'Don't despond!—
I am of children all too fond.'

Then said the mother, speaking low,
Kissing the babe she had born in woe:
'Treat him tenderly—nurse him well.'
Hotly the tears on the baby fell.

Taking the mother's coin with a leer
Ogress remarked: 'Don't cry, my dear,
Motherly persons to me are known,
One is named Wood and another Stone.

'Either of them will your baby keep
Hushing him into a soft, long sleep,
Crooning a lonesome lullaby song;
They have been used to children long.'

. . . .

Cold and yet kind was the nurse's breast;
Cold fell the rain on the babe at rest;
Pale was his face as an immortelle,
Old Mother Doorstep had nursed him well.

The Woman at the Washtub

The Woman at the Washtub,
    She works till fall of night;
With soap and suds and soda
    Her hands are wrinkled white.
Her diamonds are the sparkles
    The copper-fire supplies;
Her opals are the bubbles
    That from the suds arise.

The Woman at the Washtub
    Has lost the charm of youth;
Her hair is rough and homely,
    Her figure is uncouth;
Her temper is like thunder,
    With no one she agrees—

The children of the alley
   They cling around her knees.

The Woman at the Washtub,
   She too had her romance;
There was a time when lightly
   Her feet flew in the dance.
Her feet were silver swallows,
   Her lips were flowers of fire;
Then she was Bright and Early,
   The Blossom of Desire.

O Woman at the Washtub,
   And do you ever dream
Of all your days gone by in
   Your aureole of steam?
From birth till we are dying
   You wash our sordid duds,
O Woman of the Washtub!
   O Sister of the Suds!

One night I saw a vision
   That filled my soul with dread,
I saw a Woman washing
   The grave-clothes of the dead;
The dead were all the living,
   And dry were lakes and meres,
The Woman at the Washtub
   She washed them with her tears.

I saw a line with banners
   Hung forth in proud array—
The banners of all battles
   From Cain to Judgment Day.
And they were stiff with slaughter
   And blood, from hem to hem,
And they were red with glory,
   And she was washing them.

'Who comes forth to the Judgment,
   And who will doubt my plan?'
'I come forth to the Judgment
   And for the Race of Man.
I rocked him in his cradle,
   I washed him for his tomb,
I claim his soul and body,
   And I will share his doom.'

The Dove

Within his office, smiling,
　　Sat JOSEPH CHAMBERLAIN,
But all the screws of Birmingham
　　Were working in his brain.

The heart within his bosom
　　Was as a millstone hard;
His eye was cold and cruel,
　　His face was frozen lard.

He had the map of Africa
　　Upon his table spread:
He took a brush, and with the same
　　He painted it blood-red.

He heard no moan of widows,
　　But only the hurrah
Of charging lines and squadrons
　　And 'Rule Britannia.'

A white dove to his window
　　With branch of olive sped—
He took a ruler in his hand,
　　And struck the white dove dead.

J. A. Phelp

The Duke Of Buccleuch

There once was a bull named the Duke of Buccleuch
Whose hide it was shiny, whose blood it was blue,
He was shipped to Australia, stud-duty to do,
Was this highly-priced bovine, the Duke of Buccleuch.

And a lord-loving cableman sent out a line
To announce to Australia its visitor fine,
But if it was human, or if it was kine,
Was left quite in doubt—merely 'Duke of Buccleuch'.

And Sydney lickspittledom went off its head
As the news round the club-room like lightning did spread;

A jook, a live jook, and perhaps he ain't wed!
Let us hasten to welcome the Duke of Buccleuch!

When the steamer arrived, the crowd it was great,
And Circular Quay seemed to be quite en fête;
And the Gov. he was there in vice-regal state
To receive his old pal the Duke of Buccleuch.

And the Mayor was there too with a speech in his hand,
To read to the Duke as he stepped on the land
And spruce Dan O'Connor, a-smiling so bland,
All ready to cheer for the Duke of Buccleuch.

And Railway-Commissioner Eddy was there,
All properly clobbered, with nicely-brushed hair
And he had in his pocket—oh, courtesy rare—
A gilt-edged free pass for the Duke of Buccleuch.

    .   .   .   .

There was horror, confusion, a frightful to-do—
How the larrikins laughed—and the jeers from the crew!
And the maidens and matrons shamefacedly flew
When they learned 'twas a bull—the great Duke of Buccleuch!

Anonymous

The Wooyeo Ball

Also known as 'The Euabalong Ball'

Oh, who has not heard of the Wooyeo Ball
Where the clans of the Lachlan, the great and the small,
Come bent on diversion from far and from near,
To shake off dull care, at least once a year.

The lairds of fat wethers assembled in force
And with them their dames, as a matter of course,
While here may be seen the spruce manager, too,
And the best of good fellows, the gay jackeroo.

There were maidens in plenty, some two or three score,
Some weaners, some two-tooths, it may be some more,
And their fleeces so puffy, so fluffy and clean
Hid the daintiest creatures that ever were seen.

The bachelors seemed to be frisky and stout,
But the old fellows suffered immensely from drought.
If the water was scarce, sure the whisky was there,
And the way they tucked in was a caution, I'll swear.

There was music and dancing, and going the pace,
Some went at a canter, some went at a race.
There was bobbing and sliding, and twisting and gliding,
And to vary the measure, some couples colliding.

Much hugging and squeezing—of course on the sly—
And tender emotions when bidding good-bye.
The men swore they were all as right as a trivet
As they gulped down their twentieth nip of 'Glenlivet'.

Oh, the Wooyeo Ball was a wonderful sight,
And the dancing went on through the whole blessed night,
And many there were who may blush to recall
The polkas they danced at the Wooyeo Ball.

1888

W. T. Goodge

How We Drove the Trotter

Oh, he was a handsome trotter, and he couldn't be completer,
He had such a splendid action and he trotted to this metre,
Such a pace and such a courage, such a record-killing power,
That he did his mile in two-fifteen, his twenty in the hour.
When he trotted on the Bathurst road the pace it was a panter,
But he broke the poet's rhythm when he broke out in a canter—

As we were remarking the pace was a panter,
But just as we liked it he broke in a canter,
And rattled along with a motion terrific,
And scattered the sparks with a freedom prolific;
He tugged at the bit and he jerked at the bridle,
We pulled like a demon, the effort was idle,
The bit in his teeth and the rein in the crupper,
We didn't much care to get home to our supper.

              Then we went
              Like the wind,
              And our hands
              They were skinned,

> And we thought
> With a dread
> To go over his head,
> And we tugged
> And we strove,
> Couldn't say
> That we drove
> Till we found
> It had stopped
> And the gallop was dropped!

Then he dropped into a trot again as steady as a pacer,
And we thought we had a dandy that was sure to make a racer
That would rival all the Yankees and was bound to beat the British,
Not a bit of vice about him though he was a trifle skittish;
Past the buggies and the sulkies on the road we went a-flying,
For the pace it was a clinker, and they had no chance of trying,
But for fear he'd start a canter we were going to stop his caper
When he bolted like a bullet at a flying piece of paper—

> Helter skelter,
> What a pelter!
> Such a pace to win a welter!
> > Rush,
> > Race,
> > Tear!
> > Flying through the air!
> Wind a-humming,
> Fears benumbing,
> Here's another trap a-coming!
> > Shouts!
> > Bash!
> > Crash!
> Moses, what a smash!

A Bad Break!

> The preacher quoted, and the cranks
>   Among his congregation smiled,
> 'How sharper than a serpent's thanks
>   It is to have a toothless child.'
>
> He saw he erred, his eye grew wild,
>   He frowned upon the mirthful ranks:

'How toothless than a serpent's child
It is to have a sharper's thanks!'

Federation

Let us sing of Federation
    ('T is the theme of every cult)
And the joyful expectation
    Of its ultimate result.
'T will confirm the jubilation
Of protection's expectation,
And the quick consolidation
Of freetrade with every nation;
And teetotal legislation
Will achieve its consummation
And increase our concentration
On the art of bibulation.
We shall drink to desperation,
And be quite the soberest nation
We'll be desperately loyal
Unto everything that's royal,
And be ultra-democratic
In a matter most emphatic.
We'll be prosperous and easeful,
And pre-eminently peaceful,
And we'll take our proper station
As a military nation!
We shall show the throne affection,
Also sever the connection,
And the bonds will get no fainter
And we'll also cut the painter.
We'll proclaim with lute and tabor
The millennium of labour,
And we'll bow before the gammon
Of plutocracy and Mammon.
We'll adopt all fads and fictions
And their mass of contradictions
If all hopes are consummated
When Australia's federated;
For the Federation speeches
This one solid moral teach us—
That a pile of paradoxes are expected to result!

Mary Gilmore

The Harvesters

In from the fields they come
To stand about the well, and, drinking, say,
'The tin gives taste!' taking in turn
The dipper from each other's hands,
The dregs out-flung as each one finishes;
Then as the water in the oil-drum bucket lowers,
They tip that out, to draw a fresher, cooler draught.

And as the windlass slowly turns they talk of other days,
Of quaichs and noggins made of oak; of oak
Grown black with age, and on through generations
And old houses handed down to children's children,
Till at last, in scattered families, they are lost to ken.
'Yet even so the dipper tastes the best!' they say.
Then having drunk, and sluiced their hands and faces,
Talk veers to fields and folk in childhood known,
And names are heard of men and women long since dead,
Or gone because the spirit of adventure
Lured them from familiar scenes to strange and far.
Of these old names, some will have been so long unheard
Not all remember them. And yet a word its vision brings,
And memory, wakened and eager, lifts anew
The fallen thread, until it seems the past is all about them
Where they group, and in two worlds they stand—
A world that was, a world in making now.

Then in sudden hush the voices cease,
The supper horn blows clear, and, from community
Where all were one, each man withdraws his mind
As men will drop a rope in haulage held,
And, individuals in a sea of time,
In separateness they turn, and to the cook-house go.

The Little Shoes that Died

These are the little shoes that died.
We could not keep her still,
But all day long her busy feet
Danced to her eager will.

Leaving the body's loving warmth,
　The spirit ran outside;
Then from the shoes they slipped her feet,
　And the little shoes died.

The Saturday Tub

Dreaming I sat by the fire last night,
And all at once I jumped in a fright,
For I really thought, as the embers burned,
That somehow or other the years had turned,
And I was back where I used to be,
In eighteen hundred and something three,
Still in my place for the old bath tub,
Flannel and soap, and rub-a-dub-dub!

All in a line by the fire we stood—
'Johnny, keep still!' and, 'Hughie, be good!'
And as, one by one, we took it in turn
To stand in a tub the size of a churn,
It was, 'Where's the flannel?' and, 'Mind the soap!'
Slither and slide, and scuffle and grope,
Soap and flannel, and rub-a-dub-dub,
Each in his turn in the old bath tub!

On Saturday nights we stood in a row,
Spotlessly clean and white as the snow,
Except that the little round knees stayed brown,
Though the soap had smothered us toes to crown;
The firelight flickered on breast and brow
(I loved it then, and I love it now!)
Lathered and flannelled, scrub-a-dub-dub,
Each in his turn from the old bath tub!

When each little shirt went over each head,
'Gentle Jesus' and 'Our Father' said,
It was 'Quick with a kiss!' and 'Now then, run!
And off into bed with you, every one!'
Ah, would we had kept, in these later days,
To the kind old path and the simple ways,
When nation by nation, rub-a-dub-dub,
The world fell into a blood-bath tub!

Andrew Barton Paterson

('The Banjo')

The Travelling Post Office

The roving breezes come and go, the reed beds sweep and sway,
The sleepy river murmurs low, and loiters on its way,
It is the land of lots o'time along the Castlereagh.

     . . . .

The old man's son had left the farm, he found it dull and slow,
He drifted to the great North-west where all the rovers go.
'He's gone so long,' the old man said, 'he's dropped right out of
     mind,
'But if you'd write a line to him I'd take it very kind;
'He's shearing here and fencing there, a kind of waif and stray,
'He's droving now with Conroy's sheep along the Castlereagh.
'The sheep are travelling for the grass, and travelling very slow;
'They may be at Mundooran now, or past the Overflow,
'Or tramping down the black soil flats across by Waddiwong,
'But all those little country towns would send the letter wrong,
'The mailman, if he's extra tired, would pass them in his sleep,
'It's safest to address the note to "Care of Conroy's sheep,"
'For five and twenty thousand head can scarcely go astray,
'You write to "Care of Conroy's sheep along the Castlereagh."'

By rock and ridge and riverside the western mail has gone,
Across the great Blue Mountain Range to take that letter on.
A moment on the topmost grade while open fire doors glare,
She pauses like a living thing to breathe the mountain air,
Then launches down the other side across the plains away
To bear that note to 'Conroy's sheep along the Castlereagh.'

And now by coach and mailman's bag it goes from town to town,
And Conroy's Gap and Conroy's Creek have marked it 'further
     down.'
Beneath a sky of deepest blue where never cloud abides,
A speck upon the waste of plain the lonely mailman rides.
Where fierce hot winds have set the pine and myall boughs asweep
He hails the shearers passing by for news of Conroy's sheep.
By big lagoons where wildfowl play and crested pigeons flock
By camp fires where the drovers ride around their restless stock,
And past the teamster toiling down to fetch the wool away
My letter chases Conroy's sheep along the Castlereagh.

Father Riley's Horse

'Twas the horse thief, Andy Regan, that was hunted like a dog
  By the troopers of the Upper Murray side;
They had searched in every gully, they had looked in every log
  But never sight or track of him they spied,
Till the priest at Kiley's Crossing heard a knocking very late
  And a whisper 'Father Riley—come across!'
So his Reverence, in pyjamas, trotted softly to the gate
  And admitted Andy Regan—and a horse!

'Now, it's listen, Father Riley, to the words I've got to say,
  For it's close upon my death I am tonight.
With the troopers hard behind me I've been hiding all the day
  In the gullies keeping close and out of sight.
But they're watching all the ranges till there's not a bird could fly,
  And I'm fairly worn to pieces with the strife,
So I'm taking no more trouble, but I'm going home to die,
  'Tis the only way I see to save my life.

'Yes, I'm making home to mother's, and I'll die o'Tuesday next
  An' buried on the Thursday—and, of course,
I'm prepared to do my penance; but with one thing I'm perplexed
  And it's—Father, it's this jewel of a horse!
He was never bought nor paid for, and there's not a man can swear
  To his owner or his breeder, but I know
That his sire was by Pedantic from the Old Pretender mare,
  And his dam was close related to The Roe.

'And there's nothing in the district that can race him for a step—
  He could canter while they're going at their top:
He's the king of all the leppers that was ever seen to lep;
  A five-foot fence—he'd clear it in a hop!
So I'll leave him with you, Father, till the dead shall rise again,
  'Tis yourself that knows a good un; and, of course,
You can say he's got by Moonlight out of Paddy Murphy's plain
  If you're ever asked the breeding of the horse!

'But it's getting on to daylight, and it's time to say good-bye,
  For the stars above the East are growing pale.
And I'm making home to mother—and it's hard for me to die!
  But it's harder still, is keeping out of gaol!
You can ride the old horse over to my grave across the dip,
  Where the wattle-bloom is waving overhead.
Sure he'll jump them fences easy—you must never raise the whip
  Or he'll rush 'em!—now, good-bye!' and he had fled!

So they buried Andy Regan, and they buried him to rights,
    In the graveyard at the back of Kiley's Hill;
There were five-and-twenty mourners who had five-and-twenty
    fights
    Till the very boldest fighters had their fill.
There were fifty horses racing from the graveyard to the pub,
    And the riders flogged each other all the while—
And the lashins of the liquor! And the lavins of the grub!
    Oh, poor Andy went to rest in proper style.

Then the races came to Kiley's—with a steeple chase and all,
    For the folk were mostly Irish round about,
And it takes an Irish rider to be fearless of a fall;
    They were training morning in and morning out.
But they never started training, till the sun was on the course,
    For a superstitious story kept 'em back.
That the ghost of Andy Regan on a slashing chestnut horse
    Had been training by the starlight on the track.

And they read the nominations for the races with surprise
    And amusement at the Father's little joke,
For a novice had been entered for the steeplechasing prize,
    And they found that it was Father Riley's moke!
He was neat enough to gallop, he was strong enough to stay!
    But his owner's views of training were immense,
For the Reverend Father Riley used to ride him every day,
    And he never saw a hurdle nor a fence.

And the priest would join the laughter; 'Oh,' said he, 'I put him in,
    For there's five-and-twenty sovereigns to be won;
And the poor would find it useful if the chestnut chanced to win,
    As he'll maybe do when all is said and done!'
He had called him Faugh-a-ballagh (which is French for 'Clear the
    course'),
    And his colours were a vivid shade of green:
All the Dooleys and O'Donnells were on Father Riley's horse,
    While the Orangemen were backing Mandarin!

It was Hogan, the dog-poisoner—aged man and very wise,
    Who was camping in the racecourse with his swag,
And who ventured the opinion, to the township's great surprise,
    That the race would go to Father Riley's nag.
'You can talk about your riders—and the horse has not been
    schooled,
    And the fences is terrific, and the rest!
When the field is fairly going, then ye'll see ye've all been fooled.
    And the chestnut horse will battle with the best.

'For there's some has got condition, and they think the race is sure,
　And the chestnut horse will fall beneath the weight;
But the hopes of all the helpless, and the prayers of all the poor,
　Will be running by his side to keep him straight.
And it's what the need of schoolin' or of workin' on the track,
　Whin the Saints are there to guide him round the course!
I've prayed him over every fence—I've prayed him out and back!
　And I'll bet my cash on Father Riley's horse!'

　　　　　•　•　•　•

Oh, the steeple was a caution! They went tearin' round and round.
　And the fences rang and rattled where they struck.
There was some that cleared the water—there was more fell in and
　　drowned—
　Some blamed the men and others blamed the luck!
But the whips were flying freely when the field came into view
　For the finish down the long green stretch of course,
And in front of all the flyers, jumpin' like a kangaroo,
　Came the rank outsider—Father Riley's horse!

Oh, the shouting and the cheering as he rattled past the post!
　For he left the others standing, in the straight;
And the rider—well, they reckoned it was Andy Regan's ghost,
　And it beat 'em how a ghost would draw the weight!
But he weighed in, nine stone seven; then he laughed and disappeared,
　　Like a Banshee (which is Spanish for an elf),
And old Hogan muttered sagely, 'If it wasn't for the beard
　They'd be thinking it was Andy Regan's self!'

And the poor at Kiley's Crossing drank the health at Christmastide
　Of the chestnut and his rider dressed in green.
There was never such a rider, not since Andy Regan died,
　And they wondered who on earth he could have been,
But they settled it among 'em, for the story got about,
　'Mongst the bushmen and the people on the course,
That the Devil had been ordered to let Andy Regan out
　For the steeplechase on Father Riley's horse!

Old Australian Ways

The London lights are far abeam
　　Behind a bank of cloud,
Along the shore the gaslights gleam,
　　The gale is piping loud;

And down the Channel, groping blind,
　　We drive her through the haze
Towards the land we left behind—
The good old land of 'never mind',
　　And old Australian ways.

The narrow ways of English folk
　　Are not for such as we;
They bear the long-accustomed yoke
　　Of staid conservancy:
But all our roads are new and strange,
　　And through our blood there runs
The vagabonding love of change
That drove us westward of the range
　　And westward of the suns.

The city folk go to and fro
　　Behind a prison's bars,
They never feel the breezes blow
　　And never see the stars;
They never hear in blossomed trees
　　The music low and sweet
Of wild birds making melodies,
Nor catch the little laughing breeze
　　That whispers in the wheat.

Our fathers came of roving stock
　　That could not fixed abide:
And we have followed field and flock
　　Since e'er we learnt to ride;
By miner's camp and shearing shed,
　　In land of heat and drought,
We followed where our fortunes led,
With fortune always on ahead
　　And always farther out.

The wind is in the barley-grass,
　　The wattles are in bloom;
The breezes greet us as they pass
　　With honey-sweet perfume;
The parakeets go screaming by
　　With flash of golden wing,
And from the swamp the wild-ducks cry
Their long-drawn note of revelry,
　　Rejoicing at the Spring.

So throw the weary pen aside
  And let the papers rest,
For we must saddle up and ride
  Towards the blue hill's breast:
And we must travel far and fast
  Across their rugged maze,
To find the Spring of Youth at last,
And call back from the buried past
  The old Australian ways.

When Clancy took the drover's track
  In years of long ago,
He drifted to the outer back
  Beyond the Overflow;
By rolling plain and rocky shelf,
  With stockwhip in his hand,
He reached at last (oh, lucky elf!)
The Town of Come-and-Help-Yourself
  In Rough-and-Ready Land.

And if it be that you would know
  The tracks he used to ride,
Then you must saddle up and go
  Beyond the Queensland side,
Beyond the reach of rule or law,
  To ride the long day through,
In Nature's homestead—filled with awe,
You then might see what Clancy saw
  And know what Clancy knew.

Bernard O'Dowd

Cupid

To get recruits for Pain, I use
  The bait of Pleasure's lips:
I crimp from soft oblivion crews
  For planet coffin-ships.

Lest Father Chaos' rule should cease
  I mingle Near with Far;
Afflict alternate years of peace
  With progeny of war:

In years of fat increase select
   The victims for the lean,
And into choicer veins inject
   Infusions of the mean.

In democratic tyranny
   I cleanse the human face
Of tattoo-marks of low and high,
   The black and white of race:

So mate I handmaid of the vale
   With baron of the height,
The sable ogre or the pale
   With angel brown or white;

Yet unity they scarce attain
   When, as your Science knows,
I rend them into castes again
   And fertile racial woes.

At times I urge to noble ways,
   At times for evil strive:
But reckless aye for good or base
   If but the race survive.

My only care is that blind Life
   Shall man the world-ship's deck
In spite of peace, in spite of strife,
   Until its day of wreck.

So that it may I weave as charm
   Protean loveliness.
The little prides of face and form,
   The alchemies of dress,

Repute's hypnotic pageantry,
   The hope of ended strife,
The vision, that is vanity,
   Of nobler types of life.

The fruitful kisses of the trees
   Wind-wafted to their mates,
The maiden-mother aphides.
   The alternating fates

Of jelly-fish, or fluke, or moss,
   In higher skies I set
Than wifeless Christ upon His cross,
   Or childless Juliet.

So that it live—The Germ ! The Germ !
   It matters not to me
If sheep or tiger, man or worm
   Earth's victor-captain be.

Charles W. Hayward

('T. the R.')

King George V

He did his duty both by peers and peasants
In council chambers, gilded halls and camps;
And in his leisure moments potted pheasants
And perseveringly collected stamps.

Barcroft Boake

The Digger's Song

Scrape the bottom of the hole: gather up the stuff!
   Fossick in the crannies, lest you leave a grain behind!
Just another shovelful and that'll be enough—
   Now we'll take it to the bank and see what we can find...
      Give the dish a twirl around!
      Let the water swirl around!
Gently let it circulate—there's music in the swish
      And the tinkle of the gravel,
      As the pebbles quickly travel
Around in merry circles on the bottom of the dish.

Ah, if man could wash his life—if he only could!
   Panning off the evil deeds, keeping but the good:
What a mighty lot of diggers' dishes would be sold!
   Though I fear the heap of tailings would be greater than the
      gold...
      Give the dish a twirl around!
      Let the water swirl around!
Man's the sport of circumstance however he may wish.
      Fortune! are you there now?
      Answer to my prayer now—
Drop a half-ounce nugget in the bottom of the dish.

Gently let the water lap! Keep the corners dry!
    That's about the place the gold will generally stay.
What was the bright particle that just then caught my eye?
    I fear me by the look of things 'twas only yellow clay...
        Just another twirl around!
        Let the water swirl around!
That's the way we rob the river of its golden fish...
        What's that? ... Can't we snare a one?
        Don't say that there's ne'er a one!...
Bah! there's not a colour in the bottom of the dish.

Louis Lavater

The Barrier

I lay face-downward on the grass
Listening for the Earth's heart-beats;
And I heard
The broken echoes of my own—
And, in my own, of all men's.

I came upon a water-pool
At the foot of a leaning gum-tree;
The sky was in it,
And the motionless branches of the gum-tree.

With steadying hand upon the bole
I, too, leaned over;
And there in the still water I saw
The hates and loves of the unquiet souls
Of all men,
And the pool was become unrestful,
Though not a whiff of air had ruffled it.

I drew back shamefastly,
And, from a little distance, saw
The mother-quiet nestle down again.
And so it is—always!
The consciousness of being
Is like a barrier round about us,
A barrier we may neither breach nor overpass.

Henry Lawson

The English Queen

A Birthday Ode

There's an ordinary woman whom the English call 'the Queen':
They keep her in a palace, and they worship her, I ween;
She's served as one to whom is owed a nation's gratitude;
(May angels keep the sainted sire of her angelic brood!)
The people must be blind, I think, or else they're very green,
To keep that dull old woman whom the English call 'the Queen,'
     Whom the English call 'the Queen',
     Whom the English call 'the Queen'—
That ordinary woman whom the English call 'the Queen'.

The Queen has reigned for fifty years, for fifty years and five,
And scarcely done a kindly turn to anyone alive;
It can be said, and it is said, and it is said in scorn,
That the poor are starved the same as on the day when she was born.
Yet she is praised and worshipped more than God has ever been—
That ordinary woman whom the English call 'the Queen',
     Whom the English call 'the Queen',
     Whom the English call 'the Queen'—
That cold and selfish woman whom the English call 'the Queen'.

The Queen has lived for seventy years, for seventy years and three;
And few have lived a flatter life, more useless life than she;
She never said a clever thing or wrote a clever line,
She never did a noble deed, in coming times to shine;
And yet we read, and still we read, in every magazine,
The praises of that woman whom the English call 'the Queen',
     Whom the English call 'the Queen',
     Whom the English call 'the Queen'—
That dull and brainless woman whom the English call 'the Queen'.

They say that she is 'Gracious', and that she's inspired with love,
They also say that she's inspired with wisdom from above.
They say that she's a noble Queen, and can do nothing wrong,
They call on God to bless her, and they hope she'll reign for
  long;
And where her foot has never trod, her heart has never been,
There's many a statue raised to her whom English call 'the Queen',
     Whom the English call 'the Queen',

Whom the English call 'the Queen'—
That ordinary woman whom the English call 'the Queen'.

They magnify her sorrow, too (it goes beyond belief),
She lost her husband and was called 'Pre-eminent in Grief';
And now she's more pre-eminent because her son is dead,
Though pauper widows starve and hear their children cry for bread.
The cares of those who starve and freeze—the hungry-eyed and
    lean—
Are nothing to the grief of one, whom people call 'the Queen',
    Whom the English call 'the Queen',
    Whom the English call 'the Queen'—
That fat and selfish person, whom the English call 'the Queen'.

She's lived a 'virtuous life', 'tis true, but then there's nothing in
The useless life of one who ne'er had heart enough to sin.
She's lived a blameless life, they say—she thinks it not a crime
To take her thousands while the poor are starving half the time.
And when they blow the final trump, we rather think Faustine
Will stand as good a show as she whom English call 'the Queen',
    Whom the English call 'the Queen',
    Whom the English call 'the Queen'—
That pure and selfish woman whom the English call 'the Queen'.

The Prince of Wales is worshipped next (it is a funny thing)
For he will be the loafer whom the fools will call 'the King'.
They keep the children of 'the Queen', and they are not a few;
The children of 'the Queen' and all her children's children too.
The little great-grandchild is great because the nation's green
And Grandmama's the person whom the English call 'the Queen',
    Whom the English call 'the Queen',
    Whom the English call 'the Queen'—
The dull, yet gilded dummy whom the English call 'the Queen'.

And yearly, on 'the Queen's' birthday they praise her and rejoice,
And even far across the sea is heard the toady's voice.
They gammon Christianity, they go to church and pray,
Yet thrust HER in the sight of God, an idol of to-day,
And she is praised and worshipped more than God has ever been—
That ordinary woman whom the English call 'the Queen',
    Whom the English call 'the Queen',
    Whom the English call 'the Queen'—
That selfish, callous woman whom the English call 'the Queen'.

When Your Pants Begin to Go

When you wear a cloudy collar and a shirt that isn't white,
And you cannot sleep for thinking how you'll reach to-morrow
    night,
You may be a man of sorrows, and on speaking terms with Care,
But as yet you're unacquainted with the Demon of Despair;
For I rather think that nothing heaps the trouble on your mind
Like the knowledge that your trousers badly need a patch behind.

I have noticed when misfortune strikes the hero of the play
That his clothes are worn and tattered in a most unlikely way;
And the gods applaud and cheer him while he whines and loafs
    around,
And they never seem to notice that his pants are mostly sound;
But, of course, he cannot help it, for our mirth would mock his care,
If the ceiling of his trousers showed the patches of repair.

You are none the less a hero if you elevate your chin
When you feel the pavement wearing through the leather, sock, and
    skin;
You are rather more heroic than are ordinary folk
If you scorn to fish for pity under cover for a joke;
You will face the doubtful glances of the people that you know;
But—of course, you're bound to face them when your pants begin
    to go.

If, when flush, you took your pleasures—failed to make a god of
    Pelf,
Some will say that for your troubles you can only thank yourself;
Some will swear you'll die a beggar, but you only laugh at that
While your garments hang together and you wear a decent hat;
You may laugh at their predictions while your soles are wearing
    through,
But—a man's an awful coward when his pants are going too.

Though the present and the future may be anything but bright,
It is best to tell the fellows that you're getting on all right.
And a man prefers to say it—'tis a manly lie to tell,
For the folks may be persuaded that you're doing very well;
But it's hard to be a hero, and it's hard to wear a grin,
When your most important garment is in places very thin.

Get some sympathy and comfort from the chum who knows you
    best,
That your sorrows won't run over in the presence of the rest;

There's a chum that you can go to when you feel inclined to whine;
He'll declare your coat is tidy, and he'll say: 'Just look at mine!'
Though you may be patched all over he will say it doesn't show,
And he'll swear it can't be noticed when your pants begin to go.

Brother mine, and of misfortune! times are hard, but do not fret,
Keep your courage up and struggle, and we'll laugh at these things
    yet.
Though there is no corn in Egypt, surely Africa has some—
Keep your smile in working order for the better days to come!
We shall often laugh together at the hard times that we know,
And get measured by the tailor when our pants begin to go.

Now the lady of refinement, in the lap of comfort rocked,
Chancing on these rugged verses, will pretend that she is shocked.
Leave her to her smelling-bottle; 'tis the wealthy who decide
That the world should hide its patches 'neath the cruel cloak of
    pride;
And I think there's something noble, and I'll swear there's nothing
    low,
In the pride of Human Nature when its pants begin to go.

The Men who Come Behind

There's a class of men (and women) who are always on their
    guard—
Cunning, treacherous, suspicious—feeling softly—grasping hard—
Brainy, yet without the courage to forsake the beaten track—
Cautiously they feel their way behind a bolder spirit's back.

If you save a bit of money, and you start a little store—
Say, an oyster-shop, for instance, where there wasn't one before—
When the shop begins to pay you, and the rent is off your mind,
You will see another started by a chap that comes behind.

So it is, and so it might have been, my friend, with me and you—
When a friend of both and neither interferes between the two;
They will fight like fiends, forgetting in their passion mad and blind,
That the row is mostly started by the folk who come behind.

They will stick to you like sin will, while your money comes and
    goes,
But they'll leave you when you haven't got a shilling in your
    clothes.
You may get some help above you, but you'll nearly always find
That you cannot get assistance from the men who come behind.

There are many, far too many, in the world of prose and rhyme,
Always looking for another's 'footsteps on the sands of time'.
Journalistic imitators are the meanest of mankind;
And the grandest themes are hackneyed by the pens that come
 behind.

If you strike a novel subject, write it up, and do not fail,
They will rhyme and prose about it till your very own is stale,
As they raved about the region that the wattle-boughs perfume
Till the reader cursed the bushman and the stink of wattle-bloom.

They will follow in your footsteps while you're groping for the
 light;
But they'll run to get before you when they see you're going right;
And they'll trip you up and baulk you in their blind and greedy
 heat,
Like a stupid pup that hasn't learned to trail behind your feet.

Take your loads of sin and sorrow on more energetic backs!
Go and strike across the country where there are not any tracks!
And—we fancy that the subject could be further treated here,
But we'll leave it to be hackneyed by the fellows in the rear.

Anonymous

(Attributed in part to Henry Lawson)

The Bastard from the Bush

As night was falling slowly on city, town and bush,
from a slum in Jones's Alley came the Captain of the Push,
and his whistle, loud and piercing, woke the echoes of the Rocks,
and a dozen ghouls came slouching round the corners of the blocks.

Then the Captain jerked a finger at a stranger by the kerb,
whom he qualified politely with an adjective and verb.
Then he made the introduction: 'Here's a covey from the bush;
fuck me blind, he wants to join us, be a member of the Push!'

Then the stranger made this answer to the Captain of the Push:
'Why, fuck me dead, I'm Foreskin Fred, the Bastard from the Bush!
I've been in every two-up school from Darwin to the Loo;
I've ridden colts and blackgins; what more can a bugger do?'

'Are you game to break a window?' said the Captain of the Push.
'I'd knock a fucking house down!' said the Bastard from the Bush.

'Would you out a man and rob him?' said the Captain of the Push.
'I'd knock him down and fuck him!' said the Bastard from the Bush.

'Would you dong a bloody copper if you caught the cunt alone?
Would you stoush a swell or Chinkie, split his garret with a stone?
Would you have a moll to keep you; would you swear off work for
     good?'
Said the Bastard: 'My colonial silver-mounted oath I would!'

'Would you care to have a gasper?' said the Captain of the Push.
'I'll take that bloody packet!' said the Bastard from the Bush.
Then the Pushites all took council, saying, 'Fuck me, but he's game!
Let's make him our star basher; he'll live up to his name.'

So they took him to their hideout, that Bastard from the Bush,
and granted him all privileges appertaining to the Push.
But soon they found his little ways were more than they could
     stand,
and finally their Captain addressed the members of his band:

'Now listen here, you buggers, we've caught a fucking Tartar.
At every kind of bludging, that Bastard is a starter.
At poker and at two-up he's shook our fucking rolls;
he swipes our fucking likker and he robs our bloody molls!'

So down in Jones's Alley all the members of the Push
laid a dark and dirty ambush for that Bastard from the Bush.
But against the wall of Riley's pub the Bastard made a stand,
a nasty grin upon his dial; a bike-chain in each hand.

They sprang upon him in a bunch, but one by one they fell,
with crack of bone, unearthly groan, and agonising yell,
till the sorely battered Captain, spitting teeth and gouts of blood,
held an ear all torn and bleeding in a hand bedaubed with mud.

'You low polluted Bastard!' snarled the Captain of the Push,
'Get back where your sort belongs—that's somewhere in the bush.
And I hope heaps of misfortunes may soon tumble down on you;
may some lousy harlot dose you till your ballocks turn sky-blue!

'May the itching piles torment you; may corns grow on your feet!
May crabs as big as spiders attack your balls a treat!
And when you're down and outed, to a hopeless bloody wreck,
may you slip back through your arsehole and break your fucking
     neck!'

E. G. Murphy

('Dryblower')

The Smiths

We had many problems set us when Coolgardie was a camp,
When the journey to the goldfields meant a coach-fare or a tramp;
We had water questions, tucker ditto, also that of gold,
How to clothe ourselves in summer, how to dress to dodge the cold.
We marvelled how the reefs occurred in most unlikely spots,
For the topsy-turvy strata tied geologists in knots;
But though we plumbed the depths of many mysteries and myths,
The worst we had to fathom was the prevalence of Smiths.

To say they swarmed Coolgardie was to say the very least,
For they over-ran the district like the rabbits in the East;
The name predominated in the underlay and drive,
The open-cut and costeen seemed to be with Smiths alive;
Where the dishes tossed the gravel they had gathered from afar,
They clustered at the two-up school and at the shanty bar;
And while Jones and Brown were just as thick as herrings in a frith,
If you threw a stone at random you were sure to hit a Smith.

There were Smiths from every region where the Smiths are known
    to grow,
There were cornstalk Smiths, Victorian Smiths, and Smiths who eat
    the crow;
There were Maori Smiths, Tasmanian Smiths, and parched-up
    Smiths from Cairns;
Bachelor Smiths and widower Smiths and Smiths with wives and
    bairns.
Some assumed the names for reasons that to them were known the
    best
When silently they packed their ports and flitted to the West,
Till every second man you met to yarn or argue with
Was either a legitimate or else a bogus Smith.

It really mattered little till the days the big mails came,
And then began the trouble with that far too frequent name;
For the Smiths rolled up in regiments when the letter 'S' was called,
To drive the post-officials mad and prematurely bald.
Shoals of Smiths demanded letters that were never to them sent,
Wrong Smiths got correspondence which for them was never meant:
And many a Smith, whose facial calm shamed Egypt's monolith,
Bought jim-jams with the boodle sent to quite a different Smith.

The climax came one Christmas Eve, the mail was on its way,
And the post-officials yearned to block the Smiths on Christmas day;
So they faked an Eastern telegram by methods justified,
Upon it put no Christian name and tacked it up outside;
It was from a Melbourne lawyer, and addressed to 'Smith, Esquire',
It was stamped 'prepaid and urgent', so 'twould confidence inspire,
And when Coolgardie sighted it and marked its pungent pith,
There was pallid consternation in the habitat of Smith.

'Our client has informed us you are over in the West,'
Ran the message, 'and she threatens your immediate arrest;
She hears you're known as Smith, but says you needn't be afraid
If you'll come and face the music and redeem the promise made.'
The population read it, and before the daylight came
A swarm of Smiths rolled up their swags and took a different name,
They declined to 'face the music' and return to kin and kith,
And the maidens who were promised still await the absent Smith.

Mary Fullerton

('E')

A Man's a Sliding Mood

Ardent in love and cold in charity,
Loud in the market, timid in debate:
Scornful of foe unbuckled in the dust,
At whimper of a child compassionate,

A man's a sliding mood from hour to hour,
Rage, and a singing forest of bright birds,
Laughter with lovely friends, and loneliness,
Woe with her heavy horn of unspoke words.

What is he then this heir of heart and mind?
Is this the man with his conflicting moods,
Or is there in a deeper dwelling place
Some stilly shaping thing that bides and broods?

Unit

Had Life remained one whole,
Compact of attributes,

Balanced without excess:
Nor men had been, nor brutes.

Had nought been chipped apart,
The fragments found no shapes,
Achieved not temperament:
Men had not been, nor apes.

Undo the forms and lines,
And see the units fall
With prisoned attributes
Back to the primal All.

Oh, gone the tiger's fire,
The blue snake's poison sting,
Each nevermore himself,
But part of everything.

Rob rose of breath and hue,
Diana's limbs unform:
Up, down, and bad and good
Lapped in a pointless norm.

Hope, and desire, and dread,
The mara, and the grapes
Unfeatured, and annulled!
God keep us struggling shapes.

Poetry

Ecstatic thought's the thing:
Its nature lifts it from the sod.
The father of its soul is God,
And in God's house are many scansions.

Anonymous

Shickered As He Could Be

A bloke I know came rolling home as shickered as he could be,
He saw a horse tied in the yard, where his horse ought to be;
He said, *Oh wife, my darling wife, now come and tell to me*
Whose is that horse tied in the yard where my horse ought to be?

She said, You damn fool, you are a fool, you're shickered and
　　cannot see;
That horse it is a milking cow my mumma gave to me.
For all the miles I've travelled, ten million miles, or more,
A saddle on a milking cow I never saw before.

A bloke I know came rolling home as shickered as he could be,
He saw a coat behind the door, where his coat ought to be;
He said, *Oh wife, my darling wife, now come and tell to me*
Whose is that coat behind the door where my coat ought to be?
She said, You damn fool, you are a fool, you're shickered and
　　cannot see;
That coat, it is a blanket which my mumma gave to me.
For all the miles I've travelled, ten million miles, or more,
Buttons on a blanket, well, I never saw before.

A bloke I know came rolling home as shickered as he could be,
He saw a head right in the bed, where his head ought to be;
He said, *Oh wife, my darling wife, now come and tell to me*
Whose is that head right in the bed, where my head ought to be?
She said, You damn fool, you are a fool, you're shickered and
　　cannot see;
That head, it is a cabbage which my mumma gave to me.
For all the miles I've travelled, ten million miles, or more,
Whiskers on a cabbage, well, I never saw before.

A bloke I know came rolling home as shickered as he could be,
He saw two boots beneath the bed, where his boots ought to be;
He said, *Oh wife, my darling wife, now come and tell to me*
Whose are those boots beneath the bed, where my boots ought to be?
She said, You damn fool, you are a fool, you're shickered and
　　cannot see;
That only is a chamber-pot my mumma gave to me.
For all the miles I've travelled, ten million miles, or more,
Spurs upon a chamber-pot I never saw before.

E. J. Brady

The Whaler's Pig

We shipped him at the Sandwich Isles
　　'Fore God, he's mostly nose—
We've fetched him full eight thousand miles
　　To fatten in the floes.

The Arctic wind may whistle down
    The ice-strewn Baffin Sea,
Our 'passenger' don't care a darn—
    A whaler's pig is he.

The blubber which the brute devours—
    Hard fruit of our harpoon—
He merely holds in trust; 'tis ours,
    Fresh pork! God send it soon!

Now, when her sloppy deck's amuck
    With stale cetacean spoil,
The glutton wallows in the ruck,
    His paunch a-drip with oil.

When from the crow's-nest rings the shout,
    Clean-echoed, 'There she blows!'
'Jeff Davis' lifts his grizzled snout
    To let us know *he* knows.

The white ash blades drop down and rise,
    The royal chase begins,
He watches with his wicked eyes,
    And multiplies his sins.

With critic squint he stands beside,
The harpooner prepares,
And, if the erring steel goes wide
In swinish tongue he swears.
(Great Heavens! how he swears!)

But when we strike her good and fair,
    Before the line runs hot,
He'll lift a hoarse hog cheer out there
    With all the strength he's got.

And when he sees the steerer take
    The bold boat-header's place,
A gourmand smile will slowly break
    Like sunrise round his face.

Around the loggerhead that line
    Grows taut as taut may be—
Three turns to hang your life and mine
    High o'er Eternity!

Who thinks of that? Not I, not you,
    Not he who most complains;
When like hell's fire the blood swirls through
    Our thumping hearts and veins,

'Tis 'Fast she is'—'Now! Let her go.'
    Our college stroke-oar yells;
This hour is worth a life to know;
    'Tis now the *savage* tells.

They maybe shared (ere progress rose)
    Who sired first earls and dukes,
A kindred ecstasy with those
    Who dodge a 'fighter's' flukes.

So felt our simian sires who tied
    Their sheet-o'-bark canoes
To some mosasaur's slimy hide
    With only life to lose.

But this Kanaka hog will see
    The whetted lance succeed;
Glad epicure, he grunts in glee,
    Fore-knowledged of his feed.

Thus will his belly teach his tongue
    What eloquence it may
(Some noble songs by poets sung
    Have been inspired that way).

So will he squeal approval when
    Our six-hour fight is done,
And lord it bravely in his pen
    O'er quarry chased and won.

So will he join the chanty free
    That echoes as she tows,
To add his porcine jubilee
    And glad his adipose.

It is not clean or nice of taste,
    This episode of trade,
That lurches with indecent haste
    Towards the blubber spade.

But still it goes that man made sail,
    Invented rig on rig,
And God Almighty made the whale
    That feeds the whaler's pig.

This sorry beast which might have drowned,
    As hogs and human can,
He also made, so runs the round,
    To feed the whaler-man.

The whaler-man will get his 'lay',
   The whaler's pig his share—
First whale, then pig, then man, some day
   The worm will make it square.

Christopher Brennan

Sweet silence after bells!

Sweet silence after bells!
deep in the enamour'd ear
soft incantation dwells.

Filling the rapt still sphere
a liquid crystal swims,
precarious yet clear.

Those metal quiring hymns
shaped ether so succinct:
a while, or it dislimns,

the silence, wanly prinkt
with forms of lingering notes,
inhabits, close, distinct;

and night, the angel, floats
on wings of blessing spread
o'er all the gather'd cotes

where meditation, wed
with love, in gold-lit cells,
absorbs the heaven that shed

sweet silence after bells.

Fire in the heavens

Fire in the heavens, and fire along the hills,
and fire made solid in the flinty stone,
thick-mass'd or scatter'd pebble, fire that fills
the breathless hour that lives in fire alone.

This valley, long ago the patient bed
of floods that carv'd its antient amplitude,
in stillness of the Egyptian crypt outspread,
endures to drown in noon-day's tyrant mood.

Behind the veil of burning silence bound,
vast life's innumerous busy littleness
is hush'd in vague-conjectured blur of sound
that dulls the brain with slumbrous weight, unless

some dazzling puncture let the stridence throng
in the cicada's torture-point of song.

J. Le Gay Brereton

Unborn

O wistful eyes that haunt the gloom of sleep,
Are you my own remembered from the night
I sat before my glass in dumb affright
And saw my cowering soul afraid to weep?
Perhaps you are his, foreshadowed, when I creep
Behind him and confess the hopeless blight
That wilts the bloom of our supreme delight
—The breath of horror from the unknown deep.

Eyes that have never seen a mother's face,
Have you no mercy that you stare and stare,
Although I never felt the hope I slew?

Wide eyes, but when I kneel to God for grace,
Your steadfast pity deepens my despair;
The darkness I desire is full of you.

John Shaw Neilson

May

Shyly the silver-hatted mushrooms make
    Soft entrance through,
And undelivered lovers, half awake,
    Hear noises in the dew.

Yellow in all the earth and in the skies,
    The world would seem
Faint as a widow mourning with soft eyes
    And falling into dream.

Up the long hill I see the slow plough leave
   Furrows of brown;
Dim is the day and beautiful; I grieve
   To see the sun go down.

But there are suns a many for mine eyes
   Day after day:
Delightsome in grave greenery they rise,
   Red oranges in May.

Schoolgirls Hastening

Fear it has faded and the night:
   The bells all peal the hour of nine:
The schoolgirls hastening through the light
   Touch the unknowable Divine.

What leavening in my heart would bide!
   Full dreams a thousand deep are there:
All luminants succumb beside
   The unbound melody of hair.

Joy the long timorous takes the flute:
   Valiant with colour songs are born:
Love the impatient absolute
   Lives as a Saviour in the morn.

Get thou behind me Shadow-Death!
   Oh ye Eternities delay!
Morning is with me and the breath
   Of schoolgirls hastening down the way.

To the Red Lory

At the full face of the forest lies our little town:
Do thou from thy lookout to heaven, O lory, come down!

Come, charge with thy challenge of colour our thoughts cool and
   thin;
Descend with the blood of the sunlight—O lory, come in!

The clouds are away, 'tis October, the glees have begun;
Thy breast has the valour of music, O passionate one!

The rhythm is thine, the beloved, the unreason of Spring.
How royal thy raiment! No sorrow is under thy wing.

O thou of intrepid apparel, thy song is thy gown;
Translate thy proud speech of the sunlight—O lory, come down!

Ngunaitponi

(David Unaipon)

The Song of Hungarrda

Bright, consuming Spirit. No power on earth so great as Thee,
First-born child of the Goddess of Birth and Light,
Thy habitation betwixt heaven and earth within a veil of clouds
    dark as night.
Accompanied by furious wind and lashing rain and hail. Riding
majestically upon the storm, flashing at intervals, illumining the
abode of man.
Thine anger and thy power thou revealest to us. Sometimes in a
streak of light, which leaps upon a great towering rock, which stood
impregnable and unchallenged in its birth-place when the earth was
formed, and hurls it in fragments down the mountain-side, striking
terror into man and beast alike.
Thus in wonder I am lost. No mortal mind can conceive. No
mortal tongue express in language intelligible. Heaven-born Spark,
I cannot see nor feel thee. Thou art concealed mysteriously wrapped
within the fibre and bark of tree and bush and shrubs.
Why dost thou condescend to dwell within a piece of stick?
As I roam from place to place for enjoyment or search of food,
My soul is filled with gratitude and love for thee.
And conscious, too, of thine all pervading spirit presence.
It seems so strange that thou wilt not hear or reveal thyself nor
bestow a blessing unless I pray.
But to plead is not enough to bring thee forth and cause thy
glowing smiles to flicker over my frame.
But must strive and wrestle with this piece of stick—pressing and
twirling into another stick with all the power I possess, to release
the bonds that bind thee fast.
Then shall thy living spark leap forth in contact with grass and
twig.
Thy flame leaps upward like waves that press and roll.
Radiant sister of the Day, I cannot live without thee. For when at
twilight and in the depth of midnight; before the morning dawns,
the mist hangs over the valley like death's cold shroud, And

dewdrops chill the atmosphere. Ingee Too Ma.
   Then like thy bright Mother shining from afar,
   Thy beaming smiles and glowing energy radiates into this frail
      body.
   Transfusing life, health, comfort, and happiness too.

Anonymous

Narranyeri people, South Australia

Song: The Railway Train

You see the smoke at Kapunda
The steam puffs regularly,
Showing quickly, it looks like frost,
It runs like running water,
It blows like a spouting whale.

Translated by George Taplin, 1897

C. J. Dennis

The Traveller

As I rode in to Burrumbeet,
I met a man with funny feet;
And, when I paused to ask him why
His feet were strange, he rolled his eye
And said the rain would spoil the wheat;
So I rode on to Burrumbeet.

As I rode in to Beetaloo,
I met a man whose nose was blue;
And, when I asked him how he got
A nose like that, he answered, 'What
Do bullocks mean when they say 'Moo'?'
So I rode on to Beetaloo.

As I rode in to Ballarat,
I met a man who wore no hat;
And, when I said he might take cold,
He cried, 'The hills are quite as old

As yonder plains, but not so flat.'
So I rode on to Ballarat.

As I rode in to Gundagai,
I met a man and passed him by
Without a nod, without a word.
He turned, and said he'd never heard
Or seen a man so wise as I.
But I rode on to Gundagai.

As I rode homeward, full of doubt,
I met a stranger riding out:
A foolish man he seemed to me;
But, 'Nay, I am yourself,' said he,
'Just as you were when you rode out.'
So I rode homeward, free of doubt.

Hugh McCrae

The Mimshi Maiden

Round the island of Zipangu,
Crowned with lilies, silver-sandal'd,
Through the amber bending bamboo,
In a rickshaw, many-candled,
Rode a tiny Mimshi maiden,
Mimshi, princess of Zipangu,
To the temple where she prayed in...
Drums and trumpets! (Such a bang, you
Never heard in all creation—)
Stunned the moonlight! And they sang too,
With one voice, the Mimshi nation!

Through the thickets strolled a yellow
Onyx-taloned, whisker-curling,
Evil-omened tiger-fellow.
Ribs and muscles! Tail up-twirling!
Starved and thirsty, hardly pleasant,
Crouching on his twenty pincers,
Grinned he down o'er lord and peasant,
Baring top and bottom mincers,
Growled, and swore he'd have their princess!
Not a soul but leapt to cover...
Priest and boy, two-handed sworder;
All except one rickshaw-shover,

Victim of some queer disorder
Which became a (such his cunning)
Proof of valour, in that he did
Stand his ground, instead of running,
While the bigwigs yet receded:
Worse than any—Mishu-Mishu,
He the princess pledged to marry,
Climbed a loquat, dodged the issue,
Almost scared to *hara-kari*;
Never grew a man so soon white—
Still the tiger did a toe-trot,
Elegantly striped with moonlight,
Round poor Mishu, up his loquat.

Strange that, of the whole procession,
Not a Zoomi pulled an arrow;
Truth to tell, through intercession
June the seventh (signed Ko Tahro,
Mimshi Monarch), every marksman
Had, in honour, as was rightful,
Left his ticklers with a craftsman
Who could make them doubly frightful,
Hence it happened, all the forces
Stood like shadows, inorganic,
Save the buglers, who, on horses,
Spurred to ... nowhere ... in a panic.

Gaily pranced the princely tiger,
Past the rickshaw, merely saying
'None so nice or sweet as I ... Gurr!
Let us two—Gurr! ... go a-Maying.'
Then he turned him to the coolie;
Stuck him in the rearward haulers,
Showed his teeth, said 'Pully-Pully!'
Took the front ones in his maulers ...

Far away, across Zipangu,
Fled he with the Mimshi maiden
Through the amber bending bamboo
Past the temple where she prayed in,
Past the Forty Singing-Fountains
Where the ring-throats fly in millions,
Golden, from the Golden Mountains,
Through the Seventeen Pavilions.
Thenceforth upward, tracing alleys
Where the dead men, drunk with knowledge,

Stuffed in classes, burst the valleys
With the laughter of their college.

Under falling blooms of Pomo,
Dimly anthered, like the moon,
Eyed like women dear old Homer,
Child of Smyrna, sang the rune,
Came the tiger to the river—
Stones across the splashing water
Took him safely, without quiver,
Took him—and Ko Tahro's daughter,
While he whispered, 'I can kiss you
Ninety kisses to the minute;
You won't miss your Mishu-Mishu—
Mishu-Mishu isn't in it.'

Mimshi felt she must adore him,
(Such things sometimes do grow fixtures),
Loved the tiger; and she bore him
Little Mimshi-tiger mixtures.

Louis Esson

The Shearer's Wife

Before the glare o'dawn I rise
To milk the sleepy cows, an' shake
The droving dust from tired eyes.
I set the rabbit traps, then bake
The children's bread.
There's hay to stook, an' beans to hoe,
Ferns to cut in the scrub below.
Women must work, when men must go
Shearing from shed to shed.

I patch an' darn, now evening comes,
An' tired I am with labour sore,
Tired o' the bush, the cows, the gums,
Tired, but must dree for long months more
What no tongue tells.
The moon is lonely in the sky,
The bush is lonely, an' lonely I
Stare down the track no horse draws nigh
An' start ... at the cattle bells.

P. J. Hartigan

('John O'Brien')

The Field of the Cloth of Gold

Oh, the hireling sun in a slipshod way
   Is a-slant on the city street,
But the heart of him's back in the bush today
   And a-tune to the galloping feet,
Where the school-kids ride to the rigadoon
   By the scampering hoof-beats trolled,
And the flower-decked sward 'neath the sun a-swoon
   In the clear white light of the afternoon
Is a Field of the Cloth of Gold.

So, put him astride of a sober hack
   With a length of rope for a rein,
And the hands of the clock turn back, turn back
   And make him a boy again.
Let him rise to the pomp and circumstance
   That were his in the days of old,
When he rode like a Knight of the old Romance—
   With a chaff-bag under his Sunday pants,
On the Field of the Cloth of Gold.

Will Dyson

The Trucker

If you want a game to tame you and to take your measure in,
Try a week or two of trucking in a mine
Where the rails are never level for a half-a-minute's spin,
And the curves are short and sharp along the line.

Try the feverish bottom level, down five hundred feet of shaft,
Where the atmosphere is like a second suit,
When the wash is full of water, and you've got to run the graft,
For there's forty ton of gravel in the shoot.

'Want a job o' truckin', dost tha?' says the boss, old Geordie Rist,
'Shift's a trucker short, ma lad, but aw don' know—

Can'st tha do th' work, though, think'st tha? Art a pretty decent
    fist?
Eh, well, damme! thoo can try it; go below.'

So the cage is manned, the knocker clangs and clatters on the brace,
The engine draws a deep, defiant breath
To inflate her lungs of iron; and in silence, face to face,
We drop into the darkness deep as death.

Then a fairy sense of lightness and of floating on the night,
A sudden glare, and Number Three is passed;
Soon a sound of warring waters and another rush of light—
'All clear!' The up-trip never seems so fast.

It is rough upon the tyro, that first tussle with the trucks—
The wretched four with worn, three-cornered wheels
That are sure to fall to his lot and to floor him if his pluck's
Not true when mates are grinding at his heels.

Then the struggle at the incline, and the deucéd ticklish squeeze
At the curves where strength alone not all avails,
And the floundering in the mullock, and the badly-broken knees
Before he learns to run upon the rails.

But it's like all other grafting, and the man that has the grit
Won't tucker out with one back-racking shift;
When he's sweated to condition, with his muscles firm and fit,
He'll disdain to stick at seven trucks of drift.

He can swarm around the pinches with a scramble and a dash,
And negotiate the inclines just as pat;
And the sheets of iron rattle and the waters surge and splash
As he shoots the 'full 'uns' in along the plat.

When the empties wind and clatter down the drive and through the
    dark—
As 'blowing' spells those backward journeys serve—
On before, deep set in darkness, glints and glows a feeble spark,
The candle burning dimly at the curve.

After cribs are polished off, and when the smoke begins to rise
And cling about the caps and in the cracks,
There's a passing satisfaction in the patriarchal lies
Of the Geordie pioneers and Cousin Jacks—

Lanky Steve's unwritten stories of the fun of Fifty-two,
Or the dashing days at Donkey Woman's Flat,
Of traps, and beaks, and heavy yields, and pugilists put through,
And lifting up the flag at Ballarat.

Yes, the truckers' toil is rather heavy grafting as a rule—
Much heavier than the wages, well I know;
But the life's not full of trouble, and the fellow is a fool
Who cannot find some pleasure down below.

'Furnley Maurice'

(Frank Wilmot)

Echoes of wheels ...

Echoes of wheels and singing lashes
    Wake on the morning air;
Out of the kitchen a youngster dashes,
    Giving the ducks a scare.
Three jiffs from house to gully,
    And over the bridge to the gate;
And then a panting little boy
    Climbs on the rails to wait.

For there is long-whipped cursing Bill
    With four enormous logs,
Behind a team with the white-nosed leader's
    Feet in the sucking bogs.
Oh it was great to see them stuck,
    And grand to see them strain,
Until the magical language of Bill
    Had got them out again!

I foxed them to the shoulder turn,
    I saw him work them round,
And die into the secret bush,
    Leaving only sound.

And it isn't bullocks I recall,
    Nor waggons my memory sees;
But in the scented bush a track
    Turning among the trees.

Not forests of lean towering gums,
    Nor notes of birds and bees,
Do I remember so well as a track
    Turning among the trees.

Oh track where the brown leaves fall
    In dust to our very knees!

And it isn't the wattle that I recall,
Nor the sound of the bullocky's singing lash,
When the cloven hoofs in the puddles splash;
But the rumble of an unseen load,
Swallowed along the hidden road
    Turning among the trees!

Whenever I have ...

Whenever I have, in all humility, moved
Amid dire forests of fact, unproved and overproved,
Then only the incomprehensible thing has vividness of hue
And only the unutterable is true.

There's weariness in the columned and tabular shame
Of elaborate amplification of law half-discerned
Which from their thrones of authority the hooded doctors declaim.
So I light my path with a candle lit from the altar that burned
In the deep arbours of vision, remote and untended.
And there I return for solace to things only apprehended,
The uncapturable, the indefinable thing, the unlearned.

The Victoria Markets Recollected in Tranquillity

I

Winds are bleak, stars are bright,
Loads lumber along the night:
Looming, ghastly white,
A towering truck of cauliflowers sways
Out of the dark, roped over and packed tight
Like faces of a crowd of football jays.

The roads come in, roads dark and long,
To the knock of hubs and a sleepy song.
Heidelberg, Point Nepean, White Horse,
Flemington, Keilor, Dandenong,
Into the centre from the source.

Rocking in their seats
The worn-out drivers droop
When dawn stirs in the streets
And the moon's a silver hoop;
Come rumbling into the silent mart,

To put their treasure at its heart,
Waggons, lorries, a lame Ford bus,
Like ants along the arms of an octopus
Whose body is all one mouth; that pays them hard
And drives them back with less than a slave's reward.

When Batman first at Heaven's command
Said, 'This is the place for a peanut-stand.'
It must have been grand!

II

'Cheap to-day, lady; cheap to-day!'
Jostling water-melons roll
From fountains of Earth's mothering soul.
Tumbling from box and tray
Rosy, cascading apples play
Each with a glowing aureole
Caught from a split sun-ray.
'Cheap to-day, lady, cheap to-day.'
Hook the carcases from the dray!
(*Where the dun bees hunt in droves*
Apples ripen in the groves.)

An old horse broods in a Chinaman's cart
While from the throbbing mart
Go cheese and celery, pears and jam
In barrow, basket, bag or pram
To the last dram the purse affords—
Food, food for the hordes.

Shuffling in the driven crush
The souls and the bodies cry,
Rich and poor, skimped and flush,
'Spend or perish, buy or die!'

Food, food for the hordes!
Turksheads tumble on the boards.

There's honey at the dairy produce stall
Where the strung saveloys festooning fall;
Yielding and yellow, the beautiful butter blocks
Confront the poultryman's plucked Plymouth Rocks.
The butcher is gladly selling,
Chopping and slaughtering, madly yelling.
A bull-like bellow for captured sales;
A great crowd surges around his scales.

Slap down the joint!
The finger point
Wobbles and comes alive,
Springs round to twenty and back to five.

No gracious burbling, nor arts to please,
No hypocritical felicities.
Buy and be damned to you! Sell and be damned also!
Decry the goods, he'll tell you where to go!

To him Creation's total aim
Is selling chops to a doubting dame.
And what will matter his steaks and joints,
The underdone and the overdone,
On the day when the old Earth jumps the points
And swings into the sun?

Along the shadows furtive, lone,
The unwashed terrier carries his week-end bone.
An old horse with a pointed hip
And dangling disillusioned under-lip
Stands in a harvest-home of cabbage leaves
And grieves.
A lady by a petrol case,
With a far-off wounded look in her face
Says, in a voice of uncertain pitch,
'Muffins' or 'crumpets,' I'm not sure which.
A pavement battler whines with half a sob,
'Ain't anybody got a bloody bob?'
Haunted by mortgages and overdrafts
The old horse droops between the shafts.
A smiling Chinaman upends a bag
And spills upon the bench with thunder-thud
(A nearby urchin trilling the newest rag)
Potatoes caked with loamy native mud.

Andean pinnacles of labelled jam.
The melting succulence of two-toothed lamb.
The little bands of hemp that truss
The succulent asparagus
That stands like tiny sheaves of purple wheat
Ready to eat!
Huge and alluring hams and rashered swine
In circular repetitive design.
Gobbling turkeys and ducks in crates,
Pups in baskets and trays of eggs;
A birdman turns and gloomily relates
His woes to a girl with impossible legs.

When Batman first at Heaven's command
Stuck flag-staffs in this sacred strand...
We'll leave all that to the local band.

Rabbits skinned in a pink nude row,
Little brown kidneys out on show;
'Ready for the pot, mum, ready to bake!'
Buy them, devour them for pity's sake—
(*Trapped, 'neath the moon in a field of dream,*
Did anyone hear a bunny scream?)

'Cheap to-day, lady, cheap to-day.'
Slimy fish slide off the tray.
Women pondering with a sigh—
'Spend or perish, buy or die!'
Packed with babies and Brussels sprouts,
It's a ricketty pram for a woman to shove—
But tell me, lady, whereabouts
Is the long leisure of love?

Flattened out on a trestle board
Somebody's trousers await their lord.

The populace takes a sidelong view
Of a coolie from one of the Orient boats,
With the help of the bo's'n and half the crew,
Trying on all of the sick-bob coats.
'Will these fit, Willie?' 'No, they're fours.'
'Oh, don't be silly, they're bigger than yours.'

'Midst iron and kitchenware,
In shameful, hidden nooks,
'Twixt wrenches and rakes and brackets at fourpence a pair,
Some dirty little crumpled books.
Pitiful they are—
'Dred' and 'A Mother's Recompense'
So pitiful and drab and far
From use or influence.
Dead gilt lettering in faded banners,
Dead laws, dead names, dead manners.
And yet I dare not touch
Their gritty spines, remembering, vaguely moved,
So many of their dear cousins that I have known and loved,
Possibly, at times, too much.
'Lost Gyp' and 'Garnered Sheaves'
Their curled and withered leaves
Stir in the faint draught of a passing dame;
Lift, fall, and again lift,

Till, parted, some pages drift
'Without a home,' without a name,
Far down the dusty aisle
Beyond the stocking stall and the man that's a bargain suit
And the girl with a loud, loud smile.
Alas! These pages originally
Were stolen from a Sunday School library,
Now 'tis their dismal fate to be
Crushed in the crimson saw-dust under a butcher's boot!

When Batman first at Heaven's command
Set foot on this square mile of land...
Ah, no, he never would understand...

III

Apples ripen in the groves
Where the dun bees hunt in droves
And the dainty blossom slips
Honey fetters on their lips.
            Tumble down
            Thistledown
Where the strawberries are sown.

Snowdrop pulls back from the bail.
Now the sickle's on the nail.
Now the plough is in the shed
And old Nugget paws his bed.
            Steal away,
            Gentle day;
Apples, ripen for the dray!

IV

Shuffling in the driven tide
The huddled people press,
Hoarding and gloating, having defied
Hunger, cold and nakedness
For a few days more—or less.
Is it nothing to you that pass?
Will you not pity their need?
Store beef fattens on stolen grass,
Brows grow dark with covetous greed.
Storm or manacle, cringe or pray,
There is no way but the money way.

Pouring sun, pouring heavens, pouring earth,
And the life-giving seas:
Treasure eternally flowing forth,
None greater than these!
Richness, colour and form,
Ripe flavours and juices rare!

Within men's hearts rises a deathless prayer
Deep as a spirit storm,
Giving thanks that earth has offered such
(So grateful to the eye, so rich to touch)
Miraculous varieties of fare.

And yet that lamb with the gentle eye
She had to die...
There have been foolish dreams
Of fishes pulled from reedy streams
Of delicate earthly fruits
Being torn up by the roots—
But only the Mandragora screams.

Gentle curates and slaughtermen
Murder the cattle in the pen:
Body, Spirit, the Word, the Breath
Only survive by so much death.
The old horse with the pointed hip
And disillusioned under-lip
Stands in a drift of cabbage leaves
And grieves.

V

There is no wile to capture
Rugged and massive things
In all their fervent rapture
Soaring without wings.
No high vision can fashion
Bowed body, groping hand
Urged by a frenzy of passion
Difficult to understand;
Stripped of affected aversions
And muffling mannerliness
Which, like the laws of the Medes and Persians,
Cramp and oppress.

Grace is the power:
Only vision can flower

Into immortal song.
Art is mannered, pure and long—
These folk, accursed, can have no vital part
In schooled philosophies or templed art.
A force that throngs the by-ways and the streets
A dark, enormous influence that pours
Its passion through the light and vainly beats
On spired churches and closed college doors.
In love—the jealous pistol and the 'jug,'
In hate—the bottle-swinger and the thug,
In peace—some rows of figures and a graph,
In war—a motto on a cenotaph.
Now the plough is in the shed,
And old Nugget paws his bed.
Steal away,
Gentle day;
Apples, ripen for the dray!

'Brian Vrepont'

(B.A. Trubridge)

The Bomber

In a hollow of the forest
They were beyond neighbours;
He said to her, in a lift of peace
After their ecstasy—'Can it be?'
After a silence, when only the forest spoke,
He said, 'It is all roses,'
But she, more secretly listening,
Said, 'No! blue-cool cornflowers,'
But the forest, profound in nature's truth, said,
'No! It is lilies.'

There was a host about
Absorbed in secrecies,
Shut off and imprisoned in selves
Beyond good neighbourhood,
Beyond touch of friendliness,
Oneness, each separate,
Beyond dark, beyond light—
Insular insects in armour safe

Only pretending death;
Prisoned by fear.

There was no love about,
Neither in shape, sound, nor movement,
Only the protoplasm of love;
Thing ate thing, prowled and preyed,
In life foredoomed to dung;
But deaf, the man said,
'No! It is roses!'
She, with the ear of earth, said,
'It is blue-cool cornflowers.'
The forest said, 'It is
Funereal lilies!'

The lovers rose; pregnant with love,
Deaf to the moment, he cupped
A hand over her breast and they went
Home slowly in a sun
Descending over the purple hills;
The bomber roared over their dream.

Frederic Manning

The Trenches

Endless lanes sunken in the clay,
Bays, and traverses, fringed with wasted herbage,
Seed-pods of blue scabious, and some lingering blooms;
And the sky, seen as from a well,
Brilliant with frosty stars.
We stumble, cursing, on the slippery duck-boards,
Goaded like the damned by some invisible wrath,
A will stronger than weariness, stronger than animal fear,
Implacable and monotonous.

Here a shaft, slanting, and below
A dusty and flickering light from one feeble candle
And prone figures sleeping uneasily,
Murmuring,
And men who cannot sleep,
With faces impassive as masks,
Bright, feverish eyes, and drawn lips,
Sad, pitiless, terrible faces,
Each an incarnate curse.

Here in a bay, a helmeted sentry
Silent and motionless, watching while two sleep,
And he sees before him
With indifferent eyes the blasted and torn land
Peopled with stiff prone forms, stupidly rigid,
As tho' they had not been men.

Dead are the lips where love laughed or sang,
The hands of youth eager to lay hold of life,
Eyes that have laughed to eyes,
And these were begotten,
O love, and lived lightly, and burnt
With the lust of a man's first strength: ere they were rent.
Almost at unawares, savagely; and strewn
In bloody fragments, to be the carrion
Of rats and crows.

And the sentry moves not, searching
Night for menace with weary eyes.

Leaves

A frail and tenuous mist lingers on baffled and intricate
    branches;
Little gilt leaves are still, for quietness holds every bough;
Pools in the muddy road slumber, reflecting indifferent stars;
Steeped in the loveliness of moonlight is earth, and the valleys,
Brimmed up with quiet shadow, with a mist of sleep.

But afar on the horizon rise great pulses of light,
The hammering of guns, wrestling, locked in conflict
Like brute, stone gods of old struggling confusedly;
Then overhead purrs a shell, and our heavies
Answer, with sudden clapping bruits of sound,
Loosening our shells that stream whining and whimpering
    precipitately,
Hounding through air athirst for blood.

And the little gilt leaves
Flicker in falling, like waifs and flakes of flame.

Anonymous

Adieu, the years are a broken song,
And the right grows weak in the strife with wrong,

The lilies of love have a crimson stain
And the old days never will come again.

From the diary of an Australian soldier, September 1917

Ethel Anderson

Afternoon in the Garden

Put the sun a thought below his prime
Shake the light across the apple-tree.
Let the shadow lengthen on the lawn.

Dent a dimple in a passing cloud.
Show a flight of field-fares on the wing.
Fling a wedge-tailed swallow in the height.

Run an azure ribbon through the wheat.
Where the willows linger by the stream
Dip their weeping tendrils in the blue.

Right beyond the hazy rim of sight
Swathe the amber grasses on the plain.
Lie the folded mountains in a ring.

Hark! The happy tap of bat and ball!
Beat of flitting feet across the court.
Laughter in the precincts of the sun.

See! bright figures flit between the trees!
One picks apples. Someone pats a horse.
Eight play tennis. (Let the Navy win.)

Time, you rogue, be still a little while,
Space, be kind, a moment keep your place,
Call King Joshua, let the sun stand still.

Good King Joshua's dead and turned to clay.
I, evoking pictures from the past,
Do again what lordly Joshua did.

Charles Shaw

The Search

I've dropped me swag in many camps
From Queensland west to Boulder,
An' struck all sorts of outback champs
An' many a title-holder.
But though I've heard the episode
Be drover told, an' dogger,
I've still to meet the bloke who rode
The big white bull through Wagga.

I struck the hero out at Hay
Who beat the red-back spider
In fourteen rounds one burnin' day;
An' up along the Gwydir
There lives the man outslept the toad—
A champeen blanket-flogger—
But he is not the bloke who rode
The big white bull through Wagga.

The cove that hung up Bogan Gate
Once called me in a hurry
To buy drinks for his 'China plate',
The bloke that dug the Murray.
An' though down south of Beechworth road
I met Big Bob the Frogger,
I've still to meet the bloke who rode
The big white bull through Wagga.

The man who steered the kangaroo
From Cue to Daly Waters;
The cove who raced the emu, too,
To win three squatters' daughters;
I know the fellow moved the load
That stopped the Richmond logger;
But still I want the bloke who rode
The big white bull through Wagga.

But some fine day I'll run him down,
An' stop his flamin' skitin'.
I'll punch him on his lyin' crown,
Or go down gamely fightin'.

For *I'm* the bloke to whom is owed
What's paid that limelight-hogger.
I'd *love* to meet that bloke who rode
The big white bull through Wagga.

W.J. Turner

Romance

When I was but thirteen or so
  I went into a golden land,
Chimborazo, Cotopaxi
  Took me by the hand.

My father died, my brother too,
  They passed like fleeting dreams,
I stood where Popocatapetl
  In the sunlight gleams.

I dimly heard the master's voice
  And boys' far-off at play,
Chimborazo, Cotopaxi
  Had stolen me away.

I walked in a great golden dream
  To and fro from school—
Shining Popocatapetl
  The dusty streets did rule.

I walked home with a gold dark boy
  And never a word I'd say
Chimborazo, Cotopaxi
  Had taken my speech away:

I gazed entranced upon his face
  Fairer than any flower—
O shining Popocatapetl
  It was thy magic hour:

The houses, people, traffic seemed
  Thin fading dreams by day,
Chimborazo, Cotopaxi
  They had stolen my soul away.

Marriage

The Sun sank in the thunderous sky of the town,
And I rose in the glittering hall and strode through the people
And went to my room, and laid me down with a Spirit—
There was lightning out in the land beyond my window.

Black was the night where lay that shining Spirit,
That slim, white, glimmering body, my soul's companion
And the trees and rocks and waters and hills around me
Stood black and mournful in flashes about my bed.

The trees that were drooping around, the rocks and waters,
The gloom-hung hills, the carven and frenzied silences
Then worshipped that glimmering body, that white cascade
That shone in my dark-hung cavern dug out of the sky.

And I wondered how long ere the bolt should fall and destroy us,
Ere we should go out like the spurt of a match in the darkness
Having one glimpse of that wild and passionate country,
Those woods and ravines dark-graven by summer lightning;

And I stared at the wall and the little distant window,
The world shrivelled up to a low and far horizon,
To a few bare hills in a sudden flash of lightning,
And the glimmering Spirit I kissed in the gloom beside me.

The Dancer

The young girl dancing lifts her face
    Passive among the drooping flowers;
The jazz band clatters sticks and bones
    In a bright rhythm through the hours.

The men in black conduct her round;
    With small sensations they are blind:
Thus Saturn's Moons revolve embraced
    And through the cosmos wind.

But Saturn has not that strange look
    Unhappy, still, and far away,
As though upon the face of Night
    Lay the bright wreck of day.

Vance Palmer

The Snake

I killed a snake this morning in the grass,
   A lovely, sinister thing of gleaming jet:
    I see it yet!
Gliding across the place my feet would pass,
In effortless motion, fluid as molten glass,
Yet live as fire, and evilly aware
Of all the magic in its jewelled stare,
   The founts of poison in its being set.

I struck with savage force, and now it lies
   With small ants swarming round its mangled head,
    Surely it's dead!
Yet in the sunlight myriad shapes arise
And flow in rhythm before my dazzled eyes;
Each black stick melts in curves, each tussock holds
Its crimson belly and its shining folds,
   Till mind and sense recoil in nameless dread.

Who dragged this creature from the nether streams
   And on an innocent world its presence thrust?
    Its eyes hold lust
And evil will beyond man's darkest dreams;
Yet when it moves a baleful beauty gleams,
The shy birds flutter and shriek, each lyric note
Turned to bat's cry in the quivering throat
   By this insidious dragon of the dust.

O slender vial filled with poisoned wine!
   If all the subtle alchemy you hold
    To turn men cold
Had been denied you in that first design,
Would harmonies of form, and colour, and line
Fill all my being now with life intense?
Or would I pass with unawakened sense
   A coloured worm that wriggled in the mould?

The Farmer Remembers the Somme

Will they never fade or pass!
The mud, and the misty figures endlessly coming

In file through the foul morass,
And the grey flood-water lipping the reeds and grass,
And the steel wings drumming.

The hills are bright in the sun:
There's nothing changed or marred in the well-known places;
When work for the day is done
There's talk, and quiet laughter, and gleams of fun
On the old folks' faces.

I have returned to these:
The farm, and the kindly Bush, and the young calves lowing;
But all that my mind sees
Is a quaking bog in a mist—stark, snapped trees,
And the dark Somme flowing.

Dorothea Mackellar

Heritage

Though on the day your hard blue eyes met mine
    I did not know I had a heart to keep,
All the dead women in my soul
    Stirred in their shrouded sleep.

There were strange pulses beating in my throat,
    I had no thought of love: I was a child:
But the dead lovers in my soul
    Awoke and flushed and smiled;

And it was years before I understood
    Why I had been so happy at your side
With the dead woman in my soul
    Teaching me what to hide.

For it was not the springtime that had come,
    Only one strong flower thrusting through the snows,
But the dead women in my soul
    Knew all that summer knows.

Arms and the Woman

What if I do go armed? she said.
    Where's the law that you say I've broken?

Firearms, yes—but my weapon's steel,
   A two-edged dagger, and more by token
Its supple keenness that seldom slips
Is mostly quiet behind my lips.

Life's not often a peaceful job,
   Enemies lurk or else attack you,
Horns well down in a daunting way—
   There's not always a friend to back you.
I am peaceable *sans* pretence:
That's not always enough defence.

Though the ewe be a gentle beast,
   Supercilious and yet a-tremble,
Deprecating and obstinate,
   She's not one that I would resemble.
Rather I'd be a tiger-cat,
Even an outlaw thing like that.

Friends or honour or self-respect—
   There are times when a weapon ready
(Often readiness is enough)
   Can defend them or keep them steady;
One may walk in a zone of charmed
Peace and courtesy, being armed.

Who can say that I struck him first?
   Many might think I love the quarrel,
Though it sickens me—yet at worst
   This pet folly may point a moral,
Women should lead a guarded life—
God be thanked, I carry a knife.

Fancy Dress

'Last night the moon had a golden ring—'

She smiled behind a lawny cloud,
   A Tudor lady in a ruff,
A chubby Holbein, douce and proud.
   Starchy, but genial enough.
Wide ring on ring of lawn and lace
Spread around her inexpressive face,
Which yet was deeply memorable—
Lady, the Holbein type wears well!

Frederick Macartney

Kyrielle: Party Politics

In the multitude of counsellors
There is safety—also many bores.
The proverb nevertheless is wise:
Society has to organize.

Policy, a big name for the small
Belief that one's good is the best for all,
Is a tactful sort of compromise
Society has to organize.

As for our Parties, glance at these
In a political strip-tease—
All the Jack Horners who poke at the pies
Society has to organize.

The Liberal skates as near as he dare
To the very thin ice of laissez-faire:
For protection of private enterprise
Society has to organize;

But why should the noise of lathe and hammer
Interfere with the people's grammar?—
Unless free speech disdains this guise
Society has to organize!

The Country member has his say
(Nymphs and shepherds, come away!).
Earth has its bounties—a new device
Society has to organize!

The Independent weakens the grip
Of the hand that holds the Party whip.
It disturbs the mob when a brumby shies:
Society has to organize.

The fellow may be a Communist
Saluting the world with a menacing fist,
For even the rebel who defies
Society has to organize;

And he has the help of the stalwarts who
Attend opponents' meetings and boo
For freedom, which (their creed implies)
Society has to organize.

Or he may be a preacher of Douglas Credit,
Which painlessly bites the hand that fed it:
Money's a myth—just one of those lies
Society has to organize.

Yet we must admit that the Public Schools
Put a decent varnish on their fools,
With loyalty knotted in those old ties
Society has to organize.

The key to Labour in our nation
Is the peaceful resort to arbitration,
Which (with strikes to synthesize)
Society has to organize;

Each one, when a Cabinet colleague goes,
Has a bag-snatcher's eye for portfolios,
At a funeral of impressive size
Society has to organize.

The axe or rope or guillotine
Might be a suitable go-between
When they help themselves to another rise
Society has to organize.

Dunstan Shaw

Retrospection

Oh, tell me why you make the school
    So like a prison drear?
The one thing in it beautiful
    You vilify with fear.

And further, tell me why you make
    The child to leave his play.
And all for what? That you may take
    His fairy tales away!

'Tis well to lead man from the mist,
    'Tis well to give him truth,
But better is it far, I wist,
    To leave him with his youth.

His youth is short-lived, and, indeed,
    A charity of God;

The sail will leave the cotton seed
   When carried to the sod.

And youth is but a silken sail,
   To break the fall of man;
And every quill a fairy tale,
   Within that silken van.

Then tell me why the child you raid
   Of youth. I know not why:
Unless it be that men must trade,
   And there are men to buy.

Lesbia Harford

Poems

XIV

I'm like all lovers, wanting love to be
A very mighty thing for you and me.

In certain moods your love should be a fire
That burnt your very life up in desire.

The only kind of love, then, to my mind
Would make you kiss my shadow on the blind.

And walk seven miles each night to see it there,
Myself within serene and unaware.

But you're as bad. You'd have me watch the clock
And count your coming while I mend your sock.

You'd have my mind devoted day and night
To you, and care for you and your delight.

Poor fools, who each would have the other give
What spirit must withhold if it would live.

You're not my slave; I wish you not to be,
I love yourself and not your love for me,

The self that goes ten thousand miles away
And loses thought of me for many a day.

And you love me for loving much beside,
But now you want a woman for your bride.

Oh, make no woman of me, you who can,
Or I will make a husband of a man!

By my unwomanly love that sets you free
Love all myself, but least the woman in me.

XXII

Sometimes I wish that I were Helen-fair
And wise as Pallas,
That I might have most royal gifts to pour
In love's sweet chalice.

Then I reflect my dear love is no god
But mortal only
And in this heavenly wife might deem himself
Not blest, but lonely.

LXIX

When I was still a child
I thought my love would be
Noble, truthful, brave,
And very kind to me.

Then,—all the novels said
That if my lover prove
No such man as this
He had to forfeit love.

Now I know life holds
Harder tasks in store,
If my lover fail
I must love him more.

Should he prove unkind,
What am I, that he
Squander soul and strength
Smoothing life for me!

Weak or false or cruel
Love must still be strong:
All my life I'll learn
How to love as long.

Anonymous

Click go the Shears

Out on the board the old shearer stands,
Grasping his shears in his thin bony hands;
Fixed is his gaze on a bare-bellied yoe
Glory if he gets her, won't he make the ringer go.

Chorus:
Click go the shears boys, click, click, click,
Wide is his blow and his hands move quick,
The ringer looks around and is beaten by a blow,
And curses the old snagger with the bare-bellied yoe.

In the middle of the floor in his cane-bottomed chair
Sits the boss of the board with his eyes everywhere,
Notes well each fleece as it comes to the screen,
Paying strict attention that it's taken off clean.

The colonial experience man, he is there of course,
With his shiny leggin's on, just got off his horse,
Gazes all around him like a real connoisseur,
Scented soap, and brilliantine and smelling like a whore.

The tar-boy is there waiting in demand
With his blackened tar-pot, in his tarry hand,
Spies one old sheep with a cut upon its back,
Hears what he's waiting for it's 'Tar here, Jack!'

Now the shearing is all over, we've all got our cheques
So roll up your swags and it's off down the track.
The first pub we come to it's there we'll have a spree,
And everyone that comes along it's 'Have a drink with me.'

There we leave him standing shouting for all hands,
Whilst all around him every 'shouter' stands,
His eye is on the keg which now is lowering fast,
He works hard, he drinks hard, and goes to hell at last!

Dinky di

He came over to London and straight away strode,
To army headquarters in Horseferry Road,
To see all the bludgers who dodge all the strafe,
By getting soft jobs on the headquarters staff.

Dinky di, dinky di,
By getting soft jobs on the headquarters staff.

A lousy lance-corporal said, 'Pardon me, please,
You've mud on your tunic and blood on your sleeve,
You look so disgraceful the people will laugh,'
Said the lousy lance-corporal on the headquarters staff.
Dinky di, dinky di,
Said the lousy lance-corporal on the headquarters staff.

The digger then shot him a murderous glance;
He said: 'We're just back from the balls-up in France,
Where bullets are flying and comforts are few,
And brave men are dying for bastards like you;
Dinky di, dinky di,
And brave men are dying for bastards like you.'

'We're shelled on the left and we're shelled on the right,
We're bombed all the day and we're bombed all the night,
And if something don't happen, and that pretty soon,
There'll be nobody left in the bloody platoon;
Dinky di, dinky di,
There'll be nobody left in the bloody platoon.'

This story soon got to the ears of Lord Gort,
Who gave the whole matter a great deal of thought,
He awarded the digger a VC and two bars,
For giving that corporal a kick up the arse;
Dinky di, dinky di,
For giving that corporal a kick up the arse.

Now when this war's over and we're out of here,
We'll see him in Sydney town begging for beer.
He'll ask for a deener to buy a small glass,
But all he'll get is a kick in the arse.
Dinky di, dinky di,
All he'll get is a kick in the arse.

Harley Matthews

Women are not Gentlemen

They said there was a woman in the hills
Behind us. All day long she watched for when
A man's head showed.

        Some knew that she was young
And beautiful. And some that she was old,
Mad with a hate of men.
'Each shot she fires she kills,'
They said. 'She never misses. Then at night
She comes and takes their money from the dead.'
She would not even leave them with their names.
Her hiding place was hung
With paper, silver, gold;
Her neck with all the things that would have told
Who a man was when we must bury him.
'Here lies an unknown soldier,' we would write.
Oh, we'd be bitter when we turned and left
Him pushed out of men's sight, and mind. Bereft
Of body and of name. For all time more,
In the one world we knew, nothing. And all
Through an old woman's spite,
Or young girl's whim.

  Those weeks we moved in fear of her all day.
Up in the trenches we crouched low. 'Stand-to!'
The word would come. 'They're forming to attack.
UP! Watch!' And there again the dead men lay,
Sharing the sunlight and the flowers that grew
In the old places. Often nothing stirred
Beyond. Then in the trench a man would fall,
Shot in the back.
'Down! Quick!' There, kneeling on that gritty floor,
We'd watch him sob his life out. Some men swore
From her had come the word,
Sent through a spy amongst us—'And I'll bet
The bastard sleeps with her.
One night I'll find her burrow. He'll die first.'
None laughed at the old soldier's boasting now.

  But sometimes there would gleam a bayonet
Then others. On the left firing. Bombs burst.
In front the ground heaves men up, up, and out
Into the open. On they come. The shout
To see at last these men set on to kill
Us. 'Fire!' Still they come running. 'Get out, boys,
And meet them.' I am up here. My legs take
Me forward. Faces rush in. And hurt eyes.
Steel flashes. Impacts. Bodies struggle, strive
In big gasps. A red darkness. Thrust. I break
Up through it. I see men's backs running. Cries:

Cheers all around. A dry mouth. My own voice
At last cheering. Sunlight. I am alive.
                          A whistle blows: 'Retire.
Get back before they open fire.'
Run. Run. Here is our trench. Breathless we drop
Into it safe. 'We're coming through the wire,'
A voice calls. 'Help me down with him. Take care.'
Two feet show first, feeling the air. They stop.
That shot was from behind.
Down! 'There! She fires again.' No voice on top
Calls for help now. Past help, those feet hang there—
'She's got them both.' We know they both are dead.

　　Machine guns stutter. Rifles start up. Lead
Weighs down the air above.
'They're coming soon, again,' a man cries. 'No,
You fool, they think that we'll attack instead.
Hear how afraid of us they are.' High, low,
The bullets come and go.
We lie back, glad to know that there is dread
Out there, too. With that woman still in mind,
Pity, almost a love.
We feel for those men in the trench ahead.

　　Then someone would want water. There'd not be
A drop in any bottle. Straightway thirst
Came into every mouth.
Water—It was behind our talk of guns.
Guns—Why we heard guns drumming in the south?
Slaughter by battleships—
Mines blowing up advancing battalions—
Of generals' new schemes to have more killed.
Through it all we would see
A corner of the valley road. There lay
Water—a muddied pool where tins were filled.
But no one dared start down. We sat and cursed
That woman with set lips.

　　We did not watch the sun, those evenings, sink
Behind the ships, the day
Plunge from the headlands. There would come a star
Into our strip of sky. Then could we stand
And see the lights afloat off-shore, afar.
Along the paths they laid,
Homeward we wandered from the gloomy land—
'Go down, you two, to fill them. Come
Back quick.'

            'It is like home. Off for a drink
While she's not looking.'
                     The old soldier laughed.

You know that you are near it by the hum
Of talk. But not a word
You hear until you drink that long, first draught.
'They got into our trench to-day. We had
To bomb them out of it.' You break the scum.
There is your form beneath you in the pool,
Deep down. Dipping and filling, it grows blurred.
'Who says the navy is no help? The fool.'
'I do. And our artillery is as bad.
They've killed more of our own than Turks.' By some
Fresh fit of firing stirred
Your form down there is breaking
Into strange shapes. 'I say, that's near Lone Pine.
Hear the destroyer on our right join in?'
Shadows, not of your making,
Trouble the water. Fires into it come
And pass, and go. 'Our colonel has gone mad;
They're taking him away.'
'I wish they'd take ours, too. He's drunk all day.
Fewer of us get killed. But it's our rum.'
'A soldier, you? To talk
Of officers like that. Why, ours all say
We'll be across to Maidos in a week.'
'Yes, if the battleships go overland.'
More men crowd in. Lights shine.
The pool mirrors it all, not right, not wrong.
'She shot my mate to-day.' 'Here, that's my tin.'
'I tell you it is mine.'
'Clean out behind his eyes the bullet came—'
'Stop fighting, there. No war's down here. Get back,
You two, where you belong.'
New faces show as matches flame.
The cigarettes glow and the pool turns black.
'We buried him just now.'

    All the way back it seemed the earth were waking
To a new life from some day-dream of Death's.
The slopes were deafening with fiery flowers,
Winds of all colours blew.
Forests of smoke rode by on unfelt breaths.
Lights crashed. Flames strode along the ridges, making
A world where nought was fixed, but all was true:

A time that had no hours,
No days, nor years;
A world where, a time when
Height called to height and kindred ears,
And, without speaking, men could speak to men.
Pallor bloomed dim as shapes came, carried by,
Towards ease at last. No moan was heard, no cry
Of pity. Pain was here an ecstasy
That held lips mute, made eyes too wide for tears.
And figures passed, heads high,
Walking as men should walk the earth,
Proud, without pride of birth,
Gentle, though unbeset by fears.

   And in the morning still was Beauty there.
We lived. We could stand up and watch the sea,
Telling its dream. Then how
The wind would have it told another way:
See how the first light found
A new cape, a fresh tree;
The mist still hid a hollow, until now
Unguessed at.
           We would hear again the sound
Of silence settling in from everywhere:
Then voices floating strangely in. Far-off
In front behind their lines the same cock crew.
And still his brother lived beneath the hill
To answer. Closer in the dog barked still.
We'd listen, straining towards the trench out there
To catch the same man's laugh, his comrade's cough.
We'd call good morning, then. And they'd call, too.

   Deep in the hush somewhere
A rifle whispers, a spent bullet whirs
Past us. 'That is not hers.
It is too early for her yet. She knows
We'd see her rifle smoking in this light.'
The left is waking. As it stretches, stirs
Its limbs, things crash. It mutters now in fear
Of the time coming—'That is where the fight
Will be to-day. There—' Its full roar we hear
Of rifle, bomb, rifle. 'Look!
It's our men attacking. See the way
They're going over?' 'Here, let me
Up! Why, you'd think they're walking out to play
A game of football.' The rifle fire rushes

All to one spot, to one noise. In the trench
We crowd together, clambering up to see.
'Get down, men. It will be
Her time, soon.' Arms, heads, bodies drop to stay
Down. Every voice hushes.

And still the battle shouts. The hill behind
Mimics it shrilly. 'They are never done,
Women, spoiling our fun,'
The old soldier mutters. 'I came here to get
Away from one.
For King and country, I told her. She swore
I went because I was a coward. True,
That was, truer than she knew.
Now here is this one saying the same thing yet:
"Sneak! Liar! Coward! You won't see the war."'
A youngster down the trench says: 'And I am here
Because a girl said I'm a coward, too.
She never even came to wave good-bye.'
The firing stops for breath. Only the shout,
Shout from men's throats, strikes on that other ear
Of ours. 'You have an eye for women, son,
I have a way with them. Point this one out
And I'll soon show her it is not
Her war.' Bombs. Up there rifles snarl.
Leashes are slipped. New packs give tongue. 'They've got
Our fellows on the run.'

And then, one morning, the young soldier raised
His rifle up. He cried: 'I've got her. Look!
There is her rifle lying beneath that bush.
I saw the sun shine on it when she took
Aim at somebody.' 'Get down. Quick!
You young fool. You shoot her? It's just a trick
Of hers.'
Still he stood there and no shot came.
Then men began to push
Hats up on bayonets. Their arms grew tired
And let them fall while we looked on amazed.
A man stood up, and then another. Soon
We were all standing, and no rifle fired
At us. 'There, see it lying shining there.'
There was a wrinkled smile upon the sea.
The leaves across the valley gleamed. Below,
Uncringing, men went on their ways, as though
They knew already. 'It makes a man feel

The War is almost over.' 'God! For me
It is all over,' the old soldier said.
'What is there now to be afraid of?' 'Her!'
Our sergeant told him, 'We are going across
To-night to see if she is really dead.'
'What for? If she stays quiet I don't care.'
'The sergeant wants to get that money. Share
And share alike, I say.'
'But it's the boys' here.'
                              'God! I wouldn't touch
The bloody stuff. Yes, yes, there's too much
Blood on it.'
                  'We can play
For it, then.'
                  Someone found
Two pennies. 'Let the sergeant toss.'
'Heads! Tails!' It went. 'Heads!'
                  The old soldier won.

   We felt our way down; up. Our best guide was
To keep the uproar of the fight
Behind us. Bushes clutched, leaves felt our faces,
Then whispered us to pass.
Eyes told but little, blind with all the light
Of one bright instant, then the sudden dark.
Like that for hours we went. Our whispers grew
To mutterings—'We've long lost our landmark,
Sergeant. Let us go back.'
                              'Come on! The place is
Somewhere between that hump there and that star.'
We crept behind him still, sick of it all,
Cold, tired. 'We can't be far
From it now. This way!'
                              Then we heard him fall,
Snapping wood, cursing. 'Help me out of this.
Stop laughing up there. God, there's something soft
Under my foot. It's her.
Give me that torch. Yes, here she is.'
We leaned over. Then a man laughed. He coughed
With laughing, still—
                              'Sergeant, she grew a strong
Beard, did that woman there.'
                              'God,' a voice gasped,
'It was a man, poor bastard, all the time.'

'What,' the old soldier cried. 'But what about
My money? Turn the pockets out.'
'Here you are. Look!' There were
Some copper coins, a charm, a crust of bread.

Nobody spoke till we began the climb
Back to the trench. Then the old soldier said,
'My luck with women never lasted long.'
Another laughed: 'Well, anyway, she's dead.'
Someone was humming to himself a song:
'And my thoughts back there fly,
To where I said good-bye.
To my land, my own land, where the sky
Is always blue,
And blue her eyes are, too.
Oh, I love her true,
And she loves—'
The young soldier's tawdry song
Told us that she would never die.

James Devaney

Vision

I rose from daylong desk at last
And out under the evening passed.

And lo, a wonder-while 'twas plain,
The secret world long sought in vain.

I looked along the ridge and knew
I gazed on trees that never grew.

And no one ever saw but I
That flaming, dreamt, incredible sky.

The house I left was never there
Before I turned and saw it flare.

I knew the hill now stared upon
Next hour would be for ever gone.

Oh, say not all was bright pretence,
A fancy-lit inconsequence.

The ever-imminent gleamed a space
Through the dull wear of commonplace.

Leon Gellert

House-Mates

Because his soup was cold, he needs must sulk
From dusk till dark, and never speak to her;
And all the time she heard his heavy bulk
Blunder about the house, making a stir
In this room and in that. She heard him mutter
His foolish breathless noises, snarling and thick.
She knew the very words he first would utter;
He always said them, and they made her sick—
Those awkward efforts at a gracious peace
And kindly patronage of high-forgiving
She knew these quarrelling calms would never cease
As long as she could keep his body living;
And so she lay and felt the hours creep by,
Wondering lazily upon her bed,
How cold the world would be if he should die
And leave her weeping for her stupid dead.

Paul L. Grano

Headlined in Heaven

ON THE OCCASION OF THE PEACE OF MUNICH

God our fathers formerly knew,
Lord who always held our line,
many things both strange and true
you know of us 'neath palm and pine—
Cromwell, Limerick and the Boer,
a headless king, an opium war,
each perfumed by the purest virtue,
all for your honour and none to hurt you;
a queen whose lovers despite her urging
managed to leave her still a virgin,
an empire that like Topsy grew—
a friendly gesture that from you;
and many other things you wot—
the Baldwin-Eden-Canterbury lot

who, strong with virtue, put the crimps on
King Edward and his Mrs. Simpson,
whom they showed the gate of course
because *we're* sound upon divorce,—
and other things both strange and true
there is no need to mention to you.
Yet there's something stranger still
that will your royal household thrill:

Gather your saints about you, Lord—
Michael with the flaming sword,
Peter with his master-key,
Thomas, slain at Canterbury,
Fisher and More, especially these,
Katharine, the Aragonese,
Alfred, King who socked the Dane,
Clitheroe we squashed in vain,
and all and others both near and far
with whom we're possibly popular
(many there be who owe their quarters
to us who made them holy martyrs);
and, Sir, since this my news I bring
will likely make all angels sing,
lest it happen there may be some
who cannot for good reason come,
have Gabriel at the microphone
to trumpet forth the news when known.
God of our fathers known of old,
Lord who direct in flurry and calm,
strange things you know but I make bold
here's one that surely will take the palm:

When yester eve War failed to break,
there happened a thing most strange of strange:
I know not why or for whose sake,
THEY WEPT UPON THE STOCK EXCHANGE.

In a Chain-store Cafeteria

This is where the People take tea—
Salmon rissoles, two, and chips for sevenpence,
Meat pie, potato mash, a penny less—
This is where the People take tea.
Fat clenk of cheap china clashing,
Clap of metal tray and rattlecade of cutlery,
And chatter ... much chatter.

This is a secret place where all is hidden
Save the appetite that sevenpence assuages.
Here may we sit and plot a murder,
Or write a poem, and none be wiser,
Screened as we are by walls of clatter,
Or merely talk of weather or the bargains
We have purchased at the finger-tempting counters.
'Such a bargain, dear! Elastic step-ins, one and threepence ...'
'Yes, dear, I always come to town to do my shopping ...'
'You know, dear, those suburban shops ...' 'It's such a saving ...'
'But Mr Morgan of our corner grocery ...'

This is where the People take tea,
With buttered crumpets two for sixpence,
And dine upon the body of old Morgan,
Of Morgan of the local corner grocery,
'The Beehive, established 1890',
Who yesterday gave up a ghost and filed his schedule.
Yes, this is where the People take tea.

Max Dunn

O, *where were we before time was*

O, where were we before time was,
and where was death before we breathed?
And what were we before love came—
sea without stars, land without leaves?

Were we one in the dark nowhere
before the world was cut in two,
and was our joy on the first dawn
the exaltation of the dew?

Where now is the country we called
our own before joy fell to shame?
Who spoke the unnaked tongue first?
Was the voice in the tree to blame?

Or was there no voice but our fear?
And was the fruit of the tree doubt?
And was it doubt that made our mind
an unlocked room with no way out?

And did we have to love to learn
how lonely is the room of I
and that whoever seeks to know
all of the loved will see love die?

W. E. Harney

West of Alice

We are travelling west of Alice Springs, and Sam is at the wheel;
Riding the diesel-grader I am watching its blade of steel
Roll back the dark-red sandy loam or grind the limestones grey,
And the wheels whirl in a red-dust swirl along the new highway.

We pass where Sturt-peas clothe the earth with a scarlet sweep of
    flowers,
And burst through green acacia-trees that send down golden
    showers;
The parakeelia's purple blooms are crushed in the dry, red sand
When the bright blade sweeps as the grader creeps over the stern,
    strange land.

The mulga, mallee, desert-oaks fall prostrate as we pass,
The lizards, pigeons, porcupines crouch low in stone and grass;
We brush the spinifex aside; tear down the bush-rat's shade,
And the desert mole in its sandhill hole digs faster from our blade.

The honey-ants are rooted out to roll upon the sand,
But ever the ramping, stamping fiend goes roaring through the land;
The tyres grind and the steel blade cuts the pads where camels trod
And claws at the ground of a stony mound where tribesmen praised
    their God.

We cross the desert rivers, formed when the world was new,
And churn to dust the fossil-bones of the giant kangaroo;
I wave to naked native kids upon Erldunda's plain,
And we fill our tank where the black men drank from rock-holes
    filled by rain.

We camp in Kulgera's weathered hills, scarred core of an ancient
    range,
Where the camp-fire flame throws out its light on a scene that is
    ever strange
As a dingo wails by the painted wall of a sacred cave near by
And the stars shine bright as we lie at night beneath a frosty sky.

We rise as mulga-parakeets go whirling through the dawn,
We see old star-man Manbuk rise from depths of midnight drawn;
We hear the grader's engine roar with Sam behind the wheel,
And I sing my song as we plunge along to the chatter of wheel and
    steel.

Francis Letters

The Inglorious Milton

North of our science, east of the hashish dream
The retina of his here-there fantasy
Mingles the Boreal lights and painted heat
Of desert air; from decks of thought he leans
Watching, in darkened trance, the sealine show
No lands but the golden coasts of the half-risen moon;
From flushed snowcaps of wind-piled Everests
Beholds the glorious world, with heart that swings,
A bell of gladness; but his lips are still;
From Sinais of fulgurant evening clouds
Descends aglow, but with no carven phrase:
The Muses gave him everything but song.
Time-space's strangest crannies he explores,
Hears the last moonquake still, already sees
Earth's lunar dotage, at a glance takes in
Australia's central forest glooms and gleams,
And space, uncurved upon the Absolute Day,
Merging within the straight-grained Infinite;
But never can do more than hint his dream.
I have seen him in the company of eloquent poets
Wistful and unsatisfied amid their epigrams,
Like a stockrider in a crowded restaurant
Homesick for a mirage.

E. G. Moll

The Bush Speaks

I will be your lover
If you keep my ways.
All delights I'll give you:

Gum-tree scented days,
Skies where kestrels hover,
Nights with stars ablaze.

But if you diminish
Care and think me won,
Other gifts I'll give you
Edged with thorn and sun,
And the crows will finish
What I have begun.

Clearing for the Plough

Through tranquil years they watched the changes
Creep over hill and plain; they saw
The kangaroo go from his ranges,
The clucking emu come no more.

And then the Blacks, with startled faces
Broke off the dance where laughter sprang
Naked and free; and the old places
Forgot the spear and boomerang.

And over plain and hill there drifted
Sheep numberless and meek and brown
That grazed all day in peace and lifted
Low bleatings when the sun went down.

But the great gums watched on, unknowing
What time was saying, could they hear:
'The end has come of bloom and growing,
The blade and the red fire are near.

The round of change is sure and steady:
The kangaroo, the sheep, the plough.
The axe is ground and bright and ready
The sleeve rolled—and it's your turn now!'
              ·   ·   ·
The stars, when the long nights close over,
Will miss them in the accustomed spot,
And the great sun who was their lover
Will come each day and find them not.

And winds that laughed to see them shaken
To mighty song, will pause and pass
Half loath, for sorrow, to awaken
The lesser music of the grass.

Beware the Cuckoo

Beware the cuckoo, though she bring
Authentic tidings of the spring.
And though her voice among the trees
Transport you to the Hebrides!

I saw her come one sunny day,
And pause awhile and fly away,
And I knew where she took her rest
There was a honeyeater's nest.

Later I came again and found
Three dead fledglings on the ground,
And red ants busy in a throng
At throats that had been made for song.

But in the low nest in the tree
The cuckoo chick sat cosily,
And seemed to my unhappy sight
A grey and monstrous appetite.

Beware the cuckoo! By what name
You call her, she is still the same.
And, if you must admire her art,
Keep a wing over your heart.

Francis Brabazon

Victoria Market

I said to my companion, this is walking
I said to my companion, how my heart goes
   out to all lovers.

The darkness was still warm
but the fields were freshening beautifully
   in the winter rain;
the market was full of little lights
and I remarked the ear of a sack
sleeping on top of a tyre like a cat
   on the kerbstone

I said to my friend stop falling on your knees
I have to keep pulling you on to your feet again—

then the dawn came down silently between
   the rows of vegetables
and we passed out into the white star
rejoicing companionless in our love

As I crossed the square on my way home
the highest spires were ablaze with the movement of feet.

Jack Lindsay

Question Time

'Who made God, daddy?'
The amoeba and no other.
'Who made the amoeba, daddy?'
Go and ask your mother.

'Who kept the first pet, daddy?'
Prometheus was his name,
he kept a sharp-beaked birdie
and tried to make it tame.
Perched on his loins, it tore
the liver from his back,
but he, a true birdlover,
let it have its peck.

'Why do we eat meat, daddy?'
Fire makes it holy food.
Someone has died for us.
Blood, though disguised, is good.
Cooked lumps of decaying bull
declare the civilised man,
but meals of apple and lettuce
are pure barbarian.

'What's a human being?'
Somebody endowed
with glorious powers of reason,
and that's why we are proud.

'But why are aeroplanes?
and why are motorcars?'
To move around the earth
like the god-speck stars.

Though arrival and departure
are both the same, you see,

the motion throws the earth away
and makes us heavenly.
Since we're on earth to live
we count that man as blest
who variously can die
. more often than the rest.

'But what is death for, daddy?'
That's going to heaven too.
'Then why don't men just die
instead of trying to fly?'
They do, my son, they do.
'Who was the first flyer?'
Ixion was his name.
'What did he do, daddy?'
He whirled on a wheel of flame.
'Why did he do that, daddy?'
He did what isn't allowed.
He thought he could ride forever
straddling a pleasure-cloud.

'But why do you and mother—'
Enough now, I forbid—
'Who started the Great War?'
I did, I did, I did.

Angry Dusk

See them sprawl with earth for bed
gulping beef and tea;
and if they've a word for their dead
a joking word it will be,
a triviality
that earthily clings.

See them sprawl and curse;
and if they've a rhyme for their rage
it will be a latrine-verse
you'd blush to read on this page,
this bloody libellous page
where truth sings.

O if we can only hold
the love that fills them then,
we shall break the distorting mould,
we shall have a world of men
treating men only as men,
not as things.

To my father Norman alone in the Blue Mountains

Though you in your hermitage
of cold and scornful stone,
of tranquil and ruthless light,
refuse to accept these pages,
what other name can I write
over the arch of the ruin
made my sole monument?
Your rejecting word I ignore
and call up your name once more,
though you will pay no heed
though you will never read
these words in your mountain-lair.

So long for you alone
I wrote, all my thoughts I bent
on you as friend and foe
so long, no name I know
but yours for this empty space
now Ray and Phil are both gone
and the spiralling fury of Time
bores remorselessly on.

As a bitter tribute then take
these pages that strip me bare
in death's thin bleakening ray.
Turn for a moment I say
turn from your obdurate place
in that clarity of stone,
that terrible folly of light,
turn for a moment this way
your abstracted face.

Kenneth Slessor

A Bushranger

Jackey Jackey gallops on a horse like a swallow
Where the carbines bark and the blackboys hollo.
When the traps give chase (may the Devil take his power!)
He can ride ten miles in a quarter of an hour.

Take a horse and follow, and you'll hurt no feelings;
He can fly down waterfalls and jump through ceilings,
He can shoot off hats, for to have a bit of fun,
With a bulldog bigger than a buffalo-gun.

Honeyed and profound in his conversation
When he bails up Mails on Long Tom Station,
In a flyaway coat with a black cravat,
A snow-white collar and a cabbage-tree hat.

Flowers in his button-hole and pearls in his pocket,
He comes like a ghost and he goes like a rocket
With a lightfoot heel on a blood-mare's flank
And a bagful of notes from the Joint Stock Bank.

Many pretty ladies he could witch out of marriage,
Though he prig but a kiss in a bigwig's carriage;
For the cock of an eye or the lift of his reins,
They would run barefoot through Patrick's Plains.

Metempsychosis

Suddenly to become John Benbow, walking down William Street
With a tin trunk and a five-pound note, looking for a place to eat,
And a peajacket the colour of a shark's behind
That a Jew might buy in the morning....

To fry potatoes (God save us!) if you feel inclined,
Or to kiss the landlady's daughter, and no one mind,
In a peel-papered bedroom with a whistling jet
And a picture of the Holy Virgin....

Wake in a shaggy bale of blankets with a fished-up cigarette,
Picking over 'Turfbird's Tattle' for a Saturday morning bet,
With a bottle in the wardrobe easy to reach
And a blast of onions from the landing....

Tattooed with foreign ladies' tokens, a heart and dagger each,
In places that make the delicate female inquirer screech,
And over a chest smoky with gunpowder-blue—
Behold!—a mermaid piping through a coach-horn!

Banjo-playing, firing off guns, and other momentous things to do,
Such as blowing through peashooters at hawkers to improve the
    view—

Suddenly paid-off and forgotten in Woolloomooloo....

Suddenly to become John Benbow....

Five Bells

Time that is moved by little fidget wheels
Is not my Time, the flood that does not flow.
Between the double and the single bell
Of a ship's hour, between a round of bells
From the dark warship riding there below,
I have lived many lives, and this one life
Of Joe, long dead, who lives between five bells.

Deep and dissolving verticals of light
Ferry the falls of moonshine down. Five bells
Coldly rung out in a machine's voice. Night and water
Pour to one rip of darkness, the Harbour floats
In air, the Cross hangs upside-down in water.

Why do I think of you, dead man, why thieve
These profitless lodgings from the flukes of thought
Anchored in Time? You have gone from earth,
Gone even from the meaning of a name;
Yet something's there, yet something forms its lips
And hits and cries against the ports of space,
Beating their sides to make its fury heard.

Are you shouting at me, dead man, squeezing your face
In agonies of speech on speechless panes?
Cry louder, beat the windows, bawl your name!

But I hear nothing, nothing ... only bells,
Five bells, the bumpkin calculus of Time.
Your echoes die, your voice is dowsed by Life,
There's not a mouth can fly the pygmy strait—
Nothing except the memory of some bones
Long shoved away, and sucked away, in mud;
And unimportant things you might have done,
Or once I thought you did; but you forgot,
And all have now forgotten—looks and words
And slops of beer; your coat with buttons off,
Your gaunt chin and pricked eye, and raging tales
Of Irish kings and English perfidy,
And dirtier perfidy of publicans
Groaning to God from Darlinghurst.

Five bells.

Then I saw the road, I heard the thunder
Tumble, and felt the talons of the rain

The night we came to Moorebank in slab-dark,
So dark you bore no body, had no face,
But a sheer voice that rattled out of air
(As now you'd cry if I could break the glass),
A voice that spoke beside me in the bush,
Loud for a breath or bitten off by wind,
Of Milton, melons, and the Rights of Man,
And blowing flutes, and how Tahitian girls
Are brown and angry-tongued, and Sydney girls
Are white and angry-tongued, or so you'd found.
But all I heard was words that didn't join
So Milton became melons, melons girls,
And fifty mouths, it seemed, were out that night,
And in each tree an Ear was bending down,
Or something had just run, gone behind grass,
When, blank and bone-white, like a maniac's thought,
The naphtha-flash of lightning slit the sky,
Knifing the dark with deathly photographs.
There's not so many with so poor a purse
Or fierce a need, must fare by night like that,
Five miles in darkness on a country track,
But when you do, that's what you think.

Five bells.

In Melbourne, your appetite had gone,
Your angers too; they had been leeched away
By the soft archery of summer rains
And the sponge-paws of wetness, the slow damp
That stuck the leaves of living, snailed the mind,
And showed your bones, that had been sharp with rage,
The sodden ecstasies of rectitude.
I thought of what you'd written in faint ink,
Your journal with the sawn-off lock, that stayed behind
With other things you left, all without use,
All without meaning now, except a sign
That someone had been living who now was dead:
'At Labassa. Room 6 × 8
On top of the tower; because of this, very dark
And cold in winter. Everything has been stowed
Into this room—500 books all shapes
And colours, dealt across the floor
And over sills and on the laps of chairs;
Guns, photoes of many differant things
And differant curioes that I obtained....'

In Sydney, by the spent aquarium-flare
Of penny gaslight on pink wallpaper,
We argued about blowing up the world,
But you were living backward, so each night
You crept a moment closer to the breast,
And they were living, all of them, those frames
And shapes of flesh that had perplexed your youth,
And most your father, the old man gone blind,
With fingers always round a fiddle's neck,
That graveyard mason whose fair monuments
And tablets cut with dreams of piety
Rest on the bosoms of a thousand men
Staked bone by bone, in quiet astonishment
At cargoes they had never thought to bear,
These funeral-cakes of sweet and sculptured stone.

Where have you gone? The tide is over you,
The turn of midnight water's over you,
As Time is over you, and mystery,
And memory, the flood that does not flow.
You have no suburb, like those easier dead
In private berths of dissolution laid—
The tide goes over, the waves ride over you
And let their shadows down like shining hair,
But they are Water; and the sea-pinks bend
Like lilies in your teeth, but they are Weed;
And you are only part of an Idea.
I felt the wet push its black thumb-balls in,
The night you died, I felt your eardrums crack,
And the short agony, the longer dream
The Nothing that was neither long nor short;
But I was bound, and could not go that way,
But I was blind, and could not feel your hand.
If I could find an answer, could only find
Your meaning, or could say why you were here
Who now are gone, what purpose gave you breath
Or seized it back, might I not hear your voice?

I looked out of my window in the dark
At waves with diamond quills and combs of light
That arched their mackerel-backs and smacked the sand
In the moon's drench, that straight enormous glaze,
And ships far off asleep, and Harbour-buoys
Tossing their fireballs wearily each to each,
And tried to hear your voice, but all I heard
Was a boat's whistle, and the scraping squeal

Of seabirds' voices far away, and bells,
Five bells. Five bells coldly ringing out.

Five bells.

Robert D. FitzGerald

Copernicus

The cock that crowed this dawn up, heard
along the east an earlier call
as through sunk acres bird by bird
till imminent upon sleep's coast
day-urgent messages were tossed,
forerunners of the flaring ball;

and reckoned thus: 'Let one voice fail
our sacred task, then drowns the sun;
nor could the parted chain avail
to fish him forth or in the least
appease that Rooster of the East
by whom first daylight is begun.

'So, stern like destinies, we bear
the signals westward without bound;
and always heralds waiting there
will stretch and flap and pass the shout,
and still no last ... whence—reason it out—
last is new first: the world's egg-round!

'Boast across morning each to each
this toil has made our proud estate
far other than old fables teach
which call us puppets jerked for sport;
cry, every bird is in some sort
that leader clamouring at dawngate.'

Grace Before Meat

Life is in the rice-field, wealth in the wheat—
pray that our children continue to have meat,
know best their needs and take what they require:
food of the stronger of body and of desire.

While—true—there's merit in the meal of fruit or fish,
as in piled potatoes and butter with the dish,
sweet health in honey, stamina in cheese,
meat has other virtue, a far thing from these.

This is not of nurture. Appetite was meant
less to fill hunger than to kill content.
Not the pinched belly nor the spread girth
but the hand reaching climbs above earth.

Milk's a sounder diet than the bled beast.
Men eat unwisely; there's famine at the feast;
yet the mouth's greed mirrors that behind
star-devouring fever and foraging of mind.

Never to be despised are the tillers of the plain
labouring tireless on a handful of grain.
Think, though, what ravagers have overrun their soil,
eyes fixed on cattle, the best part of spoil.

Those too who built, where dawns of time strike,
Parthenon and Pyramid on onions and the like,
all had behind them the ganger with the lash,
craftsmen and designers, feeders upon flesh.

Beggars' fare may bring you that peace in the soul
too akin to nothingness for men born whole.
Let the pilgrim seek it on his thin shanks.
Spare him his morsel and yourself give thanks.

Chopsticks and tin bowl—never come at that,
fingers in the common plate, cross-legged on the mat.
Though men are brothers and all share the meal
your share is eaten with fork and bright steel.

Abel was the hunter and keeper of the herd,
gentle with his great hands, friend of beast and bird,
lover of the game he killed for the flesh and hides,
given man for man's use like all else besides.

Generous and trusting ... so he came, one
clean as his sacrifice, straight from air and sun.
Cain the vegetarian had dark thoughts in his head:
envy and evil of the ill-fed.

All the world's goodness is theirs who most live;
strong hands taking it are warm hands to give.
Health is in the orchard, vision in the vine....
So! then be their masters your son and mine.

The Wind at Your Door

(To Mary Gilmore)

My ancestor was called on to go out—
a medical man, and one such must by law
wait in attendance on the pampered knout
and lend his countenance to what he saw,
lest the pet, patting with too bared a claw,
be judged a clumsy pussy. Bitter and hard,
see, as I see him, in that jailhouse yard.

Or see my thought of him: though time may keep
elsewhere tradition or a portrait still,
I would not feel under his cloak of sleep
if beard there or smooth chin, just to fulfil
some canon of precision. Good or ill
his blood's my own; and scratching in his grave
could find me more than I might wish to have.

Let him then be much of the middle style
of height and colouring; let his hair be dark
and his eyes green; and for that slit, the smile
that seemed inhuman, have it cruel and stark,
but grant it could be too the ironic mark
of all caught in the system—who the most,
the doctor or the flesh twined round that post?

There was a high wind blowing on that day;
for one who would not watch, but looked aside,
said that when twice he turned it blew his way
splashes of blood and strips of human hide
shaken out from the lashes that were plied
by one right-handed, one left-handed tough,
sweating at this paid task, and skilled enough.

That wind blows to your door down all these years.
Have you not known it when some breath you drew
tasted of blood? Your comfort is in arrears
of just thanks to a savagery tamed in you
only as subtler fears may serve in lieu
of thong and noose—old savagery which has built
your world and laws out of the lives it spilt.

For what was jailyard widens and takes in
my country. Fifty paces of stamped earth
stretch; and grey walls retreat and grow so thin

that towns show through and clearings—new raw birth
which burst from handcuffs—and free hands go forth
to win tomorrow's harvest from a vast
ploughland—the fifty paces of that past.

But see it through a window barred across,
from cells this side, facing the outer gate
which shuts on freedom, opens on its loss
in a flat wall. Look left now through the grate
at buildings like more walls, roofed with grey slate
or hollowed in the thickness of laid stone
each side the court where the crowd stands this noon.

One there with the officials, thick of build,
not stout, say burly (so this obstinate man
ghosts in the eyes) is he whom enemies killed
(as I was taught) because the monopolist clan
found him a grit in their smooth-turning plan,
too loyally active on behalf of Bligh.
So he got lost; and history passed him by.

But now he buttons his long coat against
the biting gusts, or as a gesture of mind,
habitual; as if to keep him fenced
from stabs of slander sticking him from behind,
sped by the schemers never far to find
in faction, where approval from one source
damns in another clubroom as of course.

This man had Hunter's confidence, King's praise;
and settlers on the starving Hawkesbury banks
recalled through twilight drifting across their days
the doctor's fee of little more than thanks
so often; and how sent by their squeezed ranks
he put their case in London. I find I lack
the hateful paint to daub him wholly black.

Perhaps my life replies to his too much
through veiling generations dropped between.
My weakness here, resentments there, may touch
old motives and explain them, till I lean
to the forgiveness I must hope may clean
my own shortcomings; since no man can live
in his own sight if it will not forgive.

Certainly I must own him whether or not
it be my will. I was made understand
this much when once, marking a freehold lot,

my papers suddenly told me it was land
granted to Martin Mason. I felt his hand
heavily on my shoulder, and knew what coil
binds life to life through bodies, and soul to soil.

There, over to one corner, a bony group
of prisoners waits; and each shall be in turn
tied by his own arms in a human loop
about the post, with his back bared to learn
the price of seeking freedom. So they earn
three hundred rippling stripes apiece, as set
by the law's mathematics against the debt.

These are the Irish batch of Castle Hill,
rebels and mutineers, my countrymen
twice over: first, because of those to till
my birthplace first, hack roads, raise roofs; and then
because their older land time and again
enrolls me through my forbears; and I claim
as origin that threshold whence we came.

One sufferer had my surname, and thereto
'Maurice', which added up to history once;
an ignorant dolt, no doubt, for all that crew
was tenantry. The breed of clod and dunce
makes patriots and true men: could I announce
that Maurice as my kin I say aloud
I'd take his irons as heraldry, and be proud.

Maurice is at the post. Its music lulls,
one hundred lashes done. If backbone shows
then play the tune on buttocks! But feel his pulse;
that's what a doctor's for; and if it goes
lamely, then dose it with these purging blows—
which have not made him moan; though, writhing there,
'Let my neck be,' he says, 'and flog me fair.'

One hundred lashes more, then rest the flail.
What says the doctor now? 'This dog won't yelp;
he'll tire you out before you'll see him fail;
here's strength to spare; go on!' Ay, pound to pulp;
yet when you've done he'll walk without your help,
and knock down guards who'd carry him being bid,
and sing no song of where the pikes are hid.

It would be well if I could find, removed
through generations back—who knows how far?—
more than a surname's thickness as a proved

bridge with that man's foundations. I need some star
of courage from his firmament, a bar
against surrenders: faith. All trials are less
than rain-blacked wind tells of that old distress.

Yet I can live with Mason. What is told
and what my heart knows of his heart, can sort
much truth from falsehood, much there that I hold
good clearly or good clouded by report;
and for things bad, ill grows where ills resort:
they were bad times. None know what in his place
they might have done. I've my own faults to face.

Mary Finnin

The Man from Strathbogie

Kelly on a mountain
Beating on a drum
Thundering down Strathbogie
Bringing brumbies home.

Kelly is the clouded night,
The white face in the rain
Seeking a late candle
Set to window pane.
The stranger in the shadow
Of the last camp fire,
Silent as a snow gum,
Burdened with desire.

Kelly is the wild man
In the heart of all,
Running short on conscience,
Holding law in thrall;
The apocalyptic horseman
'Twixt moonlight and the day
Who rides through gold to murder,
To quicklime and to clay.

Arthur Davies

West Paddocks

Peter broke the ragged branch to push his nostrils closer.
    Yellow, plump like chicken down, it led him by the nose.
Then he wanted the west paddocks bitterly; and louder
    Barked the dog and bellowed the black creek that always flows.

Grandmother needs no spectacles. She took the wattle from him.
    The night came down. The boundary creek screamed louder and
        bled blacker.
    And other things came out of it   His knees went slack and
        slacker.
She lifted up the branch and dragged him downward to the edge.

They crossed it in a battered box that creaked like any staircase.
    They crossed it nine times over to reach the western bank,
For the creek and all its billabongs made hairpin bends in duplicate.
    But north and south the mangrove swamps for ever sucked and
        stank.

Through slats of fog, in mustard streaks, dilapidated homesteads
    Hung over them, decaying. The dog crawled out and growled.
Sundowners must have made that swishing, never showing heads,
    And on the wide verandahs covered children wailed and howled.

The watchdog shot his prickles up and, open like a crocodile,
    Strained back, steaming for a thunderbolt. He is the ace of dogs.
Grandmother, turning sideways, fished a moment in her reticule,
    Tossed bait he gulped that headlong struck him snoring with the
        logs.

They stepped on whining floorboards, through cobwebs, through
        the spaces.
    Fog overhead was ceiling and they never felt the walls.
(Like creeping through a hill of caves—with gentle people
        whispering
    You never see when they flap past—and squelches, and footfalls).

'This is the house,' Grandmother said. 'This is the home, the fold.
    When I have brushed this window clean, you press your face
        against it
And you will see the whole estate before you people fenced it.'
    So Peter stared. He saw a younger Peter, drowned with gold.

Then, gripping on the window ledge, his hours and years raced
　　backward.
　　He forgot he was a father. He forgot his sons and gains.
Watching his soft primeval self new risen up against him,
　　His armoured nerves were wrung again by its confiding pains.

It was the spice of downy gold young Peter smelt that morning,
　　The flavour of a holiday: the spread of light, the drums
When frosting waves surrender to the blistered sandy furnaces;
　　But hunger made him shut his nose and battle for his crumbs.

'And now, the rest,' said Peter. Grandmother said, 'There is no rest.
　　That's all your people's history, as ever written out.'
'But Persia, Egypt, Babylon?' 'Same words, new punctuation.'
　　'Read me the preface, Grandmother.' The picture swirled about.

Before the flood young Peter raced, one in a gang of Indians,
　　With catapults and pocket knives to raid Stonehenge again.
Stung with shot peas he bit and kicked. The outlaws took him
　　prisoner.
　　They pricked his nose with grass. He had to serve their men.

'This was the longest time of all,' Grandmother said to Peter.
　　'Whole ages longer than your years of quarrelling in bulk.
So totems, hunting, sacrifice, magic, god-kings and eloquence
　　Crowd commonsense to corners in the cabins of your hulk.'

'Show me west paddocks.' Out they crept, spread full before them
　　West paddocks, wattle tumbling, unsnaked, for holidays,
Damp scents of morning in the air and many men and women
　　With no leisure to be busy under summer's holy blaze.

In pairs, in groups or solitude they moved and lay and idled,
　　Unlike as crystals, purposeless, intent and occupied.
Some built, some pried, some tested. Many sang and played
　　together.
　　There were goodbyes and welcomes for the restless on their ride.

'Who gets the meals?' 'They all must take it turn about by plan.'
　　'Don't they have rows?' 'Most certainly. They never scrap for
　　long.'
'But is there such a place?' 'There is not. Never has been.'
　　'But will there be?' 'What answer could be wrong?'

'I want to build it.' 'No you don't,' said Grandmother most firmly.
　　'You want some fun, you want a break, you want a fatter screw.
These children play to no routine, they're satisfied with fooling.
　　Just talk a bit with anyone. They'll never do for you.

'You're still afraid some buffalo may miss your club and arrow.
   You shudder from a sabretooth may jump on you at dark.
You know all hands must work all day to stuff the bellies silent,
   Since Grandad broke the council's regulation in the park.'

A.D. Hope

A Blason

My foundling, my fondling, my frolic first-footer,
My circler, my sidler, shy-sayer yes-and-no,
Live-levin, light-looker, darter and doubter,
Pause of perhaps in my turvey of touch-and-go;

My music, my mandrake, merrythought to my marrow-bone,
Tropic to my true-pole and ripe to my rich,
Wonderer, wanderer, walker-in-wood-alone,
Eye-asker, acher, angel-with-an-itch;

My tittup, my tansy, tease-tuft in tumble-toil,
My frisker, my fettler, trickster and trier,
Knick-knacker, knee-knocker, cleaver in kindle-coil,
My handler, my honeysuckler, phoenix-on-fire;

My cunny, my cracker-jack, my cantrip, my kissing-crust,
Rock-rump and wring-rib in wrestle of randy-bout,
Lithe-lier, limber-leg, column of counter-thrust,
My heave-horn, my hyphener, dew-dealer in-and-out;

My, ah, my rough-rider now; my, oh, my deep-driver,
Burly-bags, bramble-ball, brace-belly, bruise-bud,
Shuttle-cock, slow-shagger, sweet-slugger, swift-swiver,
My, YES now and yes NOW—rip, river and flood!

My breacher, my broacher, my burst-boy, my bubblyjock,
My soberer, slacken-soon, numb-nub and narrower,
My wrinkler, my rumplet, prim-purse of poppycock,
Slither-slot, shrivel-shaft, shrinker and sorrower;

My soft-sigher, snuggle-snake, sleeper and slaker,
My dandler, my deft-dear, dreamer of double-deal,
And, oh, my wry-writher, my worker and waker,
Stirrer and stander now, fledge to my feel;

My prodigy, prodigal, palindrome of pleasure,
Rise-ripe and rive-rose, rod of replevin,
Now furrow my fallow, now trench to my treasure,
Harvester, harbinger, harrow my heaven.

Faustus

Laying the pen aside, when he had signed,
'I might repent, might yet find grace,' he said,
'What could you do?' The Devil shook his head,
'You're not the first, my friend: we know your kind.

'Logic, not justice, in this case prevails:
This bond can't be enforced in any court.
You might prove false as hell, but have you thought
The fraud may damn you, though the promise fails?'

'Suppose I use these powers, as well I may,'
Said Faustus then, 'to serve the cause of good!
Should Christ at last redeem me with his blood
You must admit there'd be the devil to pay.'

The Devil laughed and conjured from the air
A feast, a fortune and a naked bed.
'Suppose you find these powers use you instead!
But pun your way to heaven, for all I care.

'We could have had your soul without this fuss.
You could have used your wits and saved your breath,
Do what you like, but we at least keep faith.
You cheated God, of course; you won't cheat us.'

Faustus unclasped the Book: when that first hour
Struck on his heart, a fragment broke away.
What odds? With four and twenty years to pay
And every wish of man within his power!

He asked to know: before the words were said
Riddles that baffled Kepler all lay bare;
For wealth, an argosy walled in his chair;
For love and there lay Helen in his bed.

Years passed in these enchantments. Yet, in fact
He wondered sometimes at so little done,
So few of all his projects even begun.
He did not note his will, his power to act

Wither, since a mere wish would serve as well,
His reason atrophy from day to day
Unexercised by problems, Love decay
Untried by passion, desire itself grow stale,

Till he, who bought the power to command
The whole world and all wisdom, sank to be

A petty conjurer in a princeling's fee
Juggling with spells he did not understand

And when, at last, his last year came, and shrank
To a bare month and dwindled to an hour,
Faustus sat shuddering in his lamp-lit tower
Telling the time by seconds till time went blank.

Midnight had come: the fiend did not appear;
And still he waited. When the dawn began
Scarce crediting his luck he rose and ran
And reached the street. The Devil met him there.

It was too much. His knees gave way. He fell.
'The bond?... My soul?' Quite affable the fiend
Helped him to rise: 'Don't fret yourself my friend;
We have your soul already, quite safe, in Hell.

'Hell is more up-to-date than men suppose.
Reorganized on the hire-purchase plan,
We take souls by instalment now and can
Thus save the fuss and bother to foreclose.

'And since our customers prefer, you know,
Amortized interest, at these higher rates,
Most debts are paid in full before their dates.
We took your final payment months ago.

'But, as I say, why fret? You've had your fun.
You're no worse off without a soul you'll find
Than the majority of human kind,
Better adjusted, too, in the long run.'

Back in his tower Faustus found all bare.
Nothing was left. He called: the walls were dumb,
Drawing his knife, he stalked from room to room
And in the last he found her, waiting there,

That fabulous Helen his magic art had won.
Riches and power, she was their sum and prize;
Ten thousand years of knowledge were in her eyes
As first he cut her throat and then his own.

Parabola

Year after year the princess lies asleep
Until the hundred years foretold are done,
Easily drawing her enchanted breath.

Caught on the monstrous thorns around the keep,
Bones of the youths who sought her, one by one
Rot loose and rattle to the ground beneath.

But when the Destined Lover at last shall come,
For whom alone Fortune reserves the prize,
The thorns give way; he mounts the cobwebbed stair;
Unerring he finds the tower, the door, the room,
The bed where, waking at his kiss she lies
Smiling in the loose fragrance of her hair.

That night, embracing on the bed of state,
He ravishes her century of sleep
And she repays the debt of that long dream;
Future and Past compose their vast debate;
His seed now sown, her harvest ripe to reap
Enact a variation on the theme.

For in her womb another princess waits,
A sleeping cell, a globule of bright dew.
Jostling their way up that mysterious stair,
A horde of lovers bursts between the gates,
All doomed but one, the destined suitor, who
By luck first reaches her and takes her there.

A parable of all we are or do!
The life of Nature is a formal dance
In which each step is ruled by what has been
And yet the pattern emerges always new
The marriage of linked cause and random chance
Gives birth perpetually to the unforeseen.

One parable for the body and the mind:
With science and heredity to thank,
The heart is quite predictable as a pump,
But, let love change its beat, the choice is blind.
'Now' is a cross-roads where all maps prove blank,
And no one knows which way the cat will jump.

So here stand I, by birth a cross between
Determined pattern and incredible chance,
Each with an equal share in what I am.
Though I should read the code stored in the gene,
Yet the blind lottery of circumstance
Mocks all solutions to its cryptogram.

As in my flesh, so in my spirit stand I
When does *this* hundred years draw to its close?

The hedge of thorns before me gives no clue.
My predecessor's carcass, shrunk and dry,
Stares at me through the spikes. Oh well, here goes!
I have this thing, and only this, to do.

Eve Langley

This Year, Before It Ends

This year, before it ends, holds out time as a weight to us,
We that are met in the streets as the streets are met in us,
And light is a weight, too; men shake it mightily off.
A youth, kicking the self-starter of a motor-bike, sends
A vast vibration out to the sun, and it returns his shadow in rain.
Out from the sun startles the line of things, and the flying cars
Set their undertones in a dark and silver note upon the line.
Even the weeds, ground weeds, can in their green brains sing that
    song.
This year, before it ends, is the imploring city—ageing before us.
Raising the delicate dust from the streets as a veil that will
Set million-branched forests sibilant before its eyes ... Faint
    darkness,
And the desolate set of the tides, hidden: only the shadowed face
Dust-powdered, stone-calm, set to us, and the sad cry of the
    pilgrims
In the slow patch of moonlight under the nameless trees, crying
'Our god was night-hour, and the white path before us;
We, the homeless; and the shuddering branches ours and the great
    moan,
Rising out of agony, and the going, form on form of the dead;
And the façade that we are; this year before it ends.'

Harry Hooton

A Sweet Disorder in the Dress

You exquisite girl, dressed absurdly deliciously artificially,
Scented, manicured, fondling beautifully manufactured thrills to
    escape the outworn human frame—
Written about, painted, sculptured, worshipped for far too long—
    you

Waste your hours on dress, cheeky and unashamed.
You are right to be unashamed! I give you your due.

You little girl—you do not know
(You should not know—what an awful world would be a world of
    knowers)
That your petty, pretty inessential fripperies are the eternal
Upsurge of art and love out of you.
In the sweet innovations of clothes
Art and the spirit will out.
Your passion for clothes is the artistic love
And that is the love for what is new
And in the warm walks of common life
Clothes are new.

What are these fashions charming changing,
Precarious hats pert perching,
All these different flower-frocks flirting,
But the yielding to the sweeter loves of art,
For whatever is new?
What are the petals assumed and shed at will—
Or even the woad and shells of yore
(For the body died with the advent of tools)—
But attempts to transcend the flesh?
Flesh is for animals.

Whence this desire to cover if not from shame—
And girlie you should be ashamed,
The body is finished.
It is finished in economics
We have the machine.
It is finished for painters
We have cameras,
For sculptors we have Madame Tussauds.
It is finished for psychology, we have its behaviour, the soul.

It is finished for love—we have matter.
Things. Velvet and silk, ersatzes, gauze ...
For the things of matter are for their own sakes beautiful.
The sculptor's stones are for their own sake,
Colours, techniques, ciphers, words are notes in new musics for
    their own sakes;
And to touch or see velvet silk, nail lacquer, high heeled shoe-
    leather is thrilling for its own sake—
Shapes, morphologies, superficial behaviours, clothes are divine.

Whence dress but the desire to improve—
Let the nude hairy bestial neolithic be bare!

Let the backters—back to nature, back to nuts and primitive
    barbarians—
Preach the human form divine:
Nothing is too good for the living, the lovers,
Nothing—no not man—is good enough for the fighters—
We will preach the human aurora,
The extended ego around us,
The exquisite loves before us,
Heaven outside us....

The human body is ten thousand years beneath us.

Who is afraid of civilization?
In the names of effeminacy, pornography, civilised virility is
    crushed
By poets giving strawberries to pigs,
Dressing elephants in negligee,
Painting nudes.
Stripped of clothes man is the weakest animal in the jungle
By a tigress the beautifullest bare woman is crude.

I say I am rapt in Dian
She trips through faint oceans of scent.
She revolves through an ether of art.
Her attire is redolent of heaven,
Her body perfumes apparel—
But then I am not a lion.
I am a man.

The lust of the spirit is fighting the flesh—but is blind,
The poet alone can see
High heels are to heighten your low behind, are artistry;
Nudes are not new enough; clothes, sweet mystery.
Art, beauty, spirit will out—if only in dress.
Dear little shop-girl, *you* sense that your body's worn out
Save for the body's caress. Poets! it's time *you* found out
The exit of body from soul....
New things for the word's caress.

Ronald McCuaig

Betty by the Sea

Her drooping flowers dabble upon
Drooping breasts of crisp cretonne;

The thirsty sun has drained her breasts
Of milk of human interests
In babies, chatting, recipes,
Husband's pleasing lewderies
And gossip over the kitchen fence,
And left this earthy innocence;
The kindly sun has drained away
Her life, like suds on washing day,
And left her in this chair on the sands,
Clasping her flowers with laundered hands:
As though a storm of breeding-pains
And work and worry, which scoured her veins,
Had passed, she opens her tired eyes,
Like still seas, to vacant skies.

Recitative

The farmer's son is good and mad
Apologizing to his dad,
For where his horses wheeled and crossed
An axle shook a paddock post:
'I should have took a wider turn.'
'Well, all right, son; you've got to learn.'
And onward plough and ploughmen go
Into the field where farmers grow.

Au tombeau de mon père

I went on Friday afternoons
Among the knives and forks and spoons
Where mounted grindstones flanked the floor
To my father's office door.

So serious a man was he,
The Buyer for the Cutlery…
I found him sketching lamps from stock
In his big stock-records book,

And when he turned the page to me:
'Not bad for an old codger, eh?'
I thought this frivolous in him,
Preferring what he said to them:

They wanted reparations paid
In German gold and not in trade,

But he rebuked such attitudes:
'You'll have to take it out in goods.'

And what they did in time was just,
He said, what he had said they must:
If Time had any end in sight
It was, to prove my father right.

The evening came, and changed him coats,
Produced a rag and rubbed his boots,
And then a mirror and a brush
And smoothed his beard and his moustache;

A sign for blinds outside to fall
On shelves and showcases, and all
Their hammers, chisels, planes and spades,
And pocket-knives with seven blades.

Then, in the lift, the patted back:
'He's growing like you, Mr Mac!'
(The hearty voices thus implied
A reason for our mutual pride.)

And so the front-door roundabout
Gathered us in and swept us out
To sausage, tea in separate pots,
And jellies crowned with creamy clots.

And once he took me on to a
Recital, to hear Seidel play,
And Hutchens spanked the piano-bass,
Never looking where it was.

When I got home I practised this,
But somehow always seemed to miss,
And my cigar-box violin,
After Seidel's, sounded thin.

And once he took me to a bill
Of sporadic vaudeville.
A man and woman held the stage;
She sneered in simulated rage,

And when he made a shrewd reply
He'd lift his oval shirt-front high
And slap his bare and hairy chest
To celebrate his raucous jest.

Then, as the shout of joy ensued,
Uniting mime and multitude,

And mine rang out an octave higher,
A boy-soprano's in that choir,

My father's smile was half unease,
Half pleasure in his power to please:
'Try not to laugh so loudly, Ron;
Those women think you're catching on.'

But far more often it was to
The School of Arts we used to go;
Up the dusty stairway's gloom,
Through the musty reading-room

And out to a veranda-seat
Overlooking Hunter Street.
There in the dark my father sat,
Pipe in mouth, to meditate.

A cake-shop glowed across the way
With a rainbow-cake display;
I never saw its keeper there,
And never saw a customer,

And yet there was activity
High in the south-western sky:
A bottle flashing on a sign
Advertising someone's wine.

So, as my father thought and thought
(Considering lines of saws he'd bought,
Or, silence both his church and club,
Feeling close to Nature's hub,

Or maybe merely practising
Never saying anything,
Since he could go, when deeply stirred,
Months, at home, without a word,

Or pondering the indignity
Of having to put up with me),
I contemplated, half awake,
The flashing wine, the glowing cake:

The wine that no one can decant,
And the cake we didn't want:
As Mr Blake's Redeemer said,
'This the wine, and this the bread.'

Elizabeth Riddell

Wakeful in the Township

Barks the melancholy dog,
Swims in the stream the shadowy fish.
Who would live in a country town
If they had their wish?

When the sun comes hurrying up
I will take the circus train
That cries, cries once in the night
And then not again.

In the stream the shadowy fish
Sleeps below the sleeping fly.
Many around me straitly sleep
But not I.

Near my window a drowsy bird
Flickers its feathers against the thorn.
Around the township's single light
My people die and are born.

I will join the circus train
For mangy leopard and tinsel girl
And the trotting horses' great white haunches
Whiter than a pearl.

When to the dark blue mountains
My captive pigeons flew
I'd no heart to lure them back
With wheat upon the dew.

When the dog at morning
Whines upon the frost
I shall be in another place.
Lost, lost, lost.

Suburban Song

Now all the dogs with folded paws
Stare at the lowering sky.
This is the hour when women hear
Their lives go ticking by.

The baker's horse with rattling hooves
Upon the windy hill
Mocks the thunder in the heart
Of women sitting still.

The poppies in the garden turn
Their faces to the sand
And tears upon the sewing fall
And on the stranger's hand.

Flap flap the washing flies
To meet the starting hail.
Close the door on love and hang
The key upon the nail.

The Letter

I take my pen in hand
               there was a meadow
Beside a field of oats, beside a wood,
Beside a road, beside a day spread out
Green at the edges, yellow at the heart.
The dust lifted a little, a finger's breadth,
The word of the wood pigeon travelled slow,
A slow half pace behind the tick of time.

To tell you I am well, and thinking of you
And of the walk through the meadow, and of another walk
Along the neat piled ruin of the town
Under a pale heaven, empty of all but death
And rain beginning. The river ran beside.

It has been a long time since I wrote. I have no news.
I put my head between my hands and hope
My heart will choke me. I put out my hand
To touch you and touch air. I turn to sleep
And find a nightmare, hollowness and fear.

And by the way, I have had no letter now
For eight weeks, it must be
               a long eight weeks,
Because you have nothing to say, nothing at all,
Not even to record your emptiness
Or guess what's to become of you, without love.

I know that you have cares,
Ashes to shovel, broken glass to mend
And many a cloth to patch before the sunset.

Write to me soon, and tell me how you are.
If you still tremble, sweat and glower, still stretch
A hand for me at dusk, play me the tune,
Show me the leaves and towers, the lamb, the rose.

Because I always wish to hear of you
And feel my heart swell, and the blood run out
At the ungraceful syllable of your name
Said through the scent of stocks, the little snore of fire,
The shoreless waves of symphony, the murmuring night.

I will end this letter now. I am yours with love.
Always with love, with love.

William Hart-Smith

Boomerang

Behold! wood into bird and bird to wood again.
A brown-winged bird from the hand of a brown man.

Elbow of wood from flexed elbow of bone
to a swift hawk has amazingly grown

that mounts the sky, sun in its wings,
up, up, over the far tree fluttering

where it turns as if seized with doubt in the air.
Looks back down to the man carved there

and, afraid of the gift of sudden blood,
beats back to his hand and melts once more to wood.

Golden Pheasant

Golden Pheasant. Mating Pair.
First Prize. Pity the poor hen!
Fancy putting her in there
all day alone

with Him!
There is simply nowhere
for her to go, to hide, to get away
from his relentless mating dance.

There is a bird-tear
fixed permanently in her glance
when she looks at me.
I am overcome with helpless sympathy.

He runs, he swoops, he struts,
he jumps over her tail,
always to confront her with his golden ruff, saying:
Admire my profile!

She is as drab and dull as he is gorgeous.
While her tail-feathers trace
weary arcs in the wood-shavings,
his tail gives her a swipe across the face.

She is doomed to perpetually evade
a sex-vain lunatic.
When she stops, stops running,
he gives her a kick.

The Inca Tupac Upanqui

The Inca Tupac Upanqui,
suffering from a surfeit of idleness,
amuses his scalp with a golden comb.

For the sun does not stand still, the Sun,
embracing nightly the fairheaded
daughters of the Sun, rises,

arms himself and goes forth.
But the Inca Tupac Upanqui, Son of the Sun,
is hidden. He dreams on his couch,

drowns in the sweat of his body, dreams
the rugs are pleated reeds,
his bed a raft of thong-bound balsa logs

groaning and complaining on the sea.
The curtain of his bed bends like a sail
marked with his regal emblem.

                              … All his wives,
a fleet of sails attending.

He has taken the look of the condor now
he has shaken off sleep, has bound
his hair in a loop of wire. His ears

enclose twin suns in their thin-stretched lobes.
He has taken a comb
of ships and set it lightly on the sea

to comb the sea for islands and for gold.
Four hundred ships,
each one in sight of two,

each two in sight of four ...
drifting in a line across the main.
They look like shepherds moving on a plain.

Ian Mudie

This Land

Give me a harsh land to wring music from,
brown hills, and dust, with dead grass
straw to my bricks.

Give me words that are cutting-harsh
as wattle-bird notes in dusty gums
crying at noon.

Give me a harsh land, a land that
swings, like heart and blood,
from heat to mist.

Give me a land that like my heart
scorches its flowers of spring,
then floods upon its summer ardour.

Give me a land where rain
is rain that would beat high heads low.
Where wind howls at the windows

and patters dust on tin roofs
while it hides the summer sun
in a mud-red shirt.

Give my words sun and rain,
desert and heat and mist,
spring flowers, and dead grass,
blue sea and dusty sky,

song-birds and harsh cries,
strength and austerity
that this land has.

Anonymous

The Overlander

There's a trade you all know well,
It's bringing cattle over.
On every track, to the Gulf and back,
Men know the Queensland drover.

Chorus:
Pass the billy round, my boys!
Don't let the pint-pot stand there!
For tonight we drink the health
Of every overlander.

I come from the northern plains
Where the girls and grass are scanty;
Where the creeks run dry or ten foot high
And it's either drought or plenty.

There are men from every land,
From Spain and France and Flanders;
They're a well-mixed pack, both white and black,
The Queensland overlanders.

When we've earned a spree in town
We live like pigs in clover;
And the whole year's cheque pours down the neck
Of many a Queensland drover.

As I pass along the roads,
The children raise my dander
Crying 'Mother dear, take in the clothes,
Here comes an overlander!'

Now I'm bound for home once more,
On a prad that's quite a goer;
I can find a job with a crawling mob
On the banks of the Maranoa.

Hal Porter

Four Winds

WEST

A Gentle Annie, willow wind, the West
holds hope and snowdrops on her snowdrop breast,
and wears mild keys of milk-rain at her waist.

Through shallow maize and wheat's September sea
she swallow-sweeps in green obliquity;
her fallow tongue has sweetness yet to say.

She is the maid of madrigal and myth
who breathes Spring buds awake with half-a-crith,
and Botticelli weeds for aftermath.

In back-street plots suburban petals wince
on sonless plum and peach and flowering quince:
all nunned as she, though country matrons once.

Her love approves no love of flesh. Her dew
is holy water, and her retinue
cloud-virgins in sky's nave madonna-blue.

NORTH

Drought's kiln of cabaret serves playboy fare:
crop, farm, nag, man or faith, North gnaws them bare,
drains heeltap creeks, and picks his teeth of fire

while dancing sluts of dust on fever toes
like corkscrews twist, gyrating to disclose
through sleazy gauze their nautch obscenities.

To stun the tribes of crows as thick as flies
he puffs sunset's cigar until it dies,
and nigger night-soot brims all heaven's flues.

He tears out parrots from the windbreak pine,
then rounds up red-field sand to kalsomine
tomorrow's miles-off privet, peace and pane.

As Caliban and larrikin, his mark
is ruby-scratched on dadoes of the dark:
the bushfire's lit and lustrous Luna Park.

EAST

Neurotic spinster East darts dingo-eyed
to fig-leaf leaves on Summer's shameless hide,
to tear to tears the heart's contented ode.

She jerks her tines in anger's sleeping cyst;
the curled smiles straighten; the white lies untwist:
from the gutter blows hate's palimpsest.

In splitting heads the doors like gunshots slam—
and slam of guns. Her vicious epigram:
'I cleanse with torment the tormented slum.'

On lovers' dartboard hearts sharp lovers throw
more bitter-better totals than they know;
cannot deny her nagging follow-through.

All undecided suicides she'll free—
her last unsubtle straw of misery
breaks Hamlets' backs to bone with, 'Not to be.'

SOUTH

Is South the Nimrod, nude and lad and loud,
who steers the jostling prides of pregnant cloud,
his egg in each great lotus belly laid?

or amazon in Atalanta flight,
lithe arrow through the annuli of light
that sizzling spin, and hoopla-fly and -float?

Electric eyes seem his or hers. They break
tree's globe to passion, and wave's fluke to flake,
and charge to blazing silvers all they broke.

The grass-plains race ahead to sea's laned land,
to wilder, wider wonders both expand,
run fresh as South who chases but to lend.

A rural wind that scythes the weather clean,
and doubles lustres and redoubles sheen,
how wisely wanton is this epicene!

In a Bed-sitter

Lust's too genteel to let the weather in:
nor sun nor common sense the drawn blinds pass.
He rides her through a fug of fags and gin
across the cracked and grimy looking-glass

wherein, pig-nude and used, she rakes her hair,
picks at the pimples of her soul and face
and from the mirror-room, the Here that's there,
sneers at him prone and sweaty from the race.
She shrills, rehashing from a There not here,
past paramours and gods. Unjealous, mum,
he yawns as on her sour breath they rear
and, grinning, turns on them a placid bum.
He snores. He knows her heroes dead or cheap,
the gods defrocked, and Troy a rubbish heap.

Hobart Town, Van Diemen's Land (11th June, 1837)

Sir John Franklin, Governor of V.D.L., 1834–43, perished on
11th June 1847 in attempting the north-west passage

Mike Howe's head with frozen frown
Is on display in Hobart Town.

By Wapping Stairs the alley whale-oils blaze;
The tap-room skittle-grounds are stews of din
Where tripeman, shepherd, fence and whitesmith daze
Pock-pitted doxies with the Sky Blue gin.

Now, knuckle-bashers soak chapped fists in brine;
The cockpit curs lick bloody-feathered paws;
The chandler, sinking Bengal Rum like wine,
Brags at the Cornstalks and the Johnny Raws.

The gibbet chandeliers sag down—
Glass-frosted thieves of Hobart Town.

On night-tubs, water-butts and cobbled mud
Ice knits its mica-spiked and bitter wheels;
By the Jew's slop-shop pot-boy barks out blood;
The chill-struck tollgate-keeper dreams hot eels.

Through Russia tweed and kerseymere and smock
And red shell jackets and Valencia vests
Cold, like a watchman's cutlass, drives its shock;
The apple-woman shawls her stony breasts.

In Geneva-stinking gown
Venus paces Hobart Town.

By his last lucifer the forger's fooled,
His jackal stumbles cursing in the mire.
Governor Franklin shuts his *Birds* by Gould,
Says, 'Far too hot!' and leaves the cedar fire.

Return, and ring for extra logs, Sir John;
Refill the Monteith with a burning brew:
The final decade left ticks freezing on
And North-west icebergs inch upon your view.

Watchman Death—eternal clown—
Crows the hour through Hobart Town.

J.J. Bray

The Execution of Madame du Barry

Keen as the blade of the guillotine, grey as its steel,
Schematic as school-texts, angular as asterisks, lean as the lamp-
posts,
Is death's republic: profile without feature, blue-print without
dwelling, line without depth,
Axioms for arteries, logic for life-blood, hydrometer for heart.
No colour in the country of silhouettes but the drops from the
slivered necks,
And Robespierre's jacket, green as a grasshopper: jerky in his
courtship
Of that grimy Gorgon, the Revolution, grinning through her
elf-locks
At her prim wooer, presenting her a posy
Of severed heads. Actors and audience stiffen in her glare.
Click go the needles, creak go the scaffold-steps, clang goes the
knife-blade, clap go the hands.
So, too, the lead parts role-play on the platform:
Roman rhetoric, elegant insouciance, pride of patrician:
Charm or composure: scorn or stoicism: Watteau or Canova.
But she was different: shop-girl turned call-girl, courtesan turned
countess.
Too late ennobled to marble more than manners,
Pleasure she proffered for many men's provender,
Pain she gave no one; but once a king's congealing lust
Melted, and spattered spuming diamonds round her breasts.

See her now, standing before that stage tribunal,
Soft, a little silly. Spreading in their forties,

Her swelling contours confute their diagrams.
Hardly she comprehends all the canting clichés
Pounded by the prosecutor—'Enemy of the People',
'Toy of the Tyrant', 'Infamous Harlot', 'Modern Messalina'—
Amiably assured no real harm could assail her,
Till with tied hands, tumbled in the tumbrel
Clattering on the cobbles, spattered with snow-flakes,
At last she comprehends, crying to her convoy,
'You're going to hurt me. Oh, please, don't hurt me. I can't stand
                                        being hurt.'
Then as they shoved her, stumbling up the scaffold-steps,
One prolonged deep animal bellow broke out of her breast,
Life's manifesto, denouncing the title-deeds
Of death's dark dominion: like a wounded sheep-dog,
Or like a cow whose calf is carted to the butcher:
Nightlong she mourns and lows her lamentable wrong.

And yet, they say, that mammalian cry cracked that frozen façade,
Soon, in sweltering Thermidor, comes the consummation
Of Robespierre's mantis match. The Revolution
Receives and rends him. The spell is shattered, the executioner
Confined to normal clients: conventional criminals.
The prisons open. Life explodes in opulence.
Girls in see-through gauzes, preposterous neck gear,
Coups on the Stock Exchange, cafés and cabarets.
Spanking in his curricle, bowling to his counting-house,
Drives Ouvrard, the banker, past Barras, the Director,
Charging with champagne the chemise of Josephine.
The temple of reason totters down in rubble.
The goddess gainsays it, glides home to the academy.
Balls and nude bathing, rackets and rockets. Medusa sleeps once
                                        more.

Roland Robinson

Deep Well

I am at Deep Well where the spirit trees
writhe in cool white limbs and budgerigar
green hair along the watercourse carved out
in deep red earth, a red dry course that goes
past the deep well, past the ruined stone
homestead where the wandering blacks make camp

(their campfire burning like a star at rest
among dark ruins of the fallen stone)
to find the spinifex and ochre red
sandhills of a land inhabited by those
tall dark tribesmen with long hair and voices
thin and far and, deepening, like a sea.
I am at Deep Well where the fettlers' car
travels towards the cool blue rising wave
that is the Ooraminna Range, and starts
those pure birds screaming from the scrub to swerve,
reveal their pristine blush in wings and breasts,
to scatter, settle and flower the desert-oak.
Here I have chosen to be a fettler, work
to lay the red-gum sleepers, line and spike
the rails with adze and hammer, shovel and bar,
to straighten up and find my mates, myself
lost in the spinifex flowing down in waves
to meet the shadow sharpened range and know
myself grown lean and hard again with toil.
Here, in the valley camp where hills increase
in dark blue depths, the desert hakea stands
holding the restless finches and a single star.

The Cradle

A corrugated iron shack. One room.
Tree-posts its uprights, saplings, axe-
trimmed, its beams and rafters. It stands
fast, no matter how the huge hands
of mountain winds grasp it. Rain
is tumult, deafening peace on the roof.

Rain-forest rises behind it, a maze
of cicada-sound. Tonight you will hear
the creek like rain as, just on dark,
the cat-bird meows and yowls from the edge
of the jungle-forest. Your eyes will daze,
close in lamplight over your book.

The kettle sings on the 'Waratah' stove.
Pots and pans gleam on their ledge
above. You will wish dawn not to come.
You will sleep, a child, as the hoarse wind
cradles you in the trees, as the arm
of the mountain holds the light of the farm.

The Creek

You are one of those clear cold creeks
I found in my solitary, impetuous youth.
You are those innocent sonatinas running
from rock-shelf to pool to rock-shelf.
I make my camp beside you, a dove-grey
deep pool fretting its fronds and tangled
flowers. Waratahs burn above you. You
give me billyfuls of rainwater wine, a
bright wing-case, a boronia petal, a white
rose tinted tea-tree star. I thought all
my creeks were spent, shrivelled at their
source, that time had stamped out my last
campfire, that never again should I kindle
ritual incense, my prayers, psalms. Now
by your plashing pool, needle sharp near,
rings the rain wrought round of the wren.
You are that image which had never died
in me, Eve, of my primavera, personified.

Aboriginal Oral Traditions

Collected by Roland Robinson

Mapooram

Related by FRED BIGGS

Go out and camp somewhere. You're lying down.
A wind comes, and you hear this 'Mapooram'.
'What's that?' you say. Why, that's a Mapooram.
You go and find that tree rubbing itself.
It makes all sorts of noises in the wind.
It might be like a sheep, or like a cat,
or like a baby crying, or someone calling,
a sort of whistling-calling when the wind
comes and swings and rubs two boughs like that.

A Wirreengun, a clever-feller, sings
that tree. He hums a song, a Mapooram:
A song to bring things out, or close things up,
a song to bring a girl, a woman from that tree.

She's got long hair, it falls right down her back.
He's got her for himself. He'll keep her now.

One evening it was sort of rainy-dark.
They built a mia-mia, stripping bark.
You've been out in the bush sometime and seen
them old dry pines with loose bark coming off.
You get a lot of bark from them dry pines,
before they rot and go too far, you know.
That woman from the tree, she pulled that bark.
It tore off, up and up the tree. It pulled
her up into the tree, up, up into the sky.
Well, she was gone. That was the end of it.
No more that Wirreengun could call her back.

'Mapooram. Mapooram.' 'What's that?' you say.
Why, that's two tree boughs rubbing in the wind.

The Star-Tribes

Related by FRED BIGGS

Look, among the boughs. Those stars are men.
There's Ngintu, with his dogs, who guards the skins
of Everlasting Water in the sky.
And there's the Crow-man, carrying on his back
the wounded Hawk-man. There's the Serpent, Thurroo,
glistening in the leaves. There's Kapeetah,
the Moon-man, sitting in his mia-mia.

And there's those Seven Sisters, travelling
across the sky. They make the real cold frost.
You hear them when you're camped out on the plains.
They look down from the sky and see your fire
and, 'Mai, mai, mai!' they sing out as they run
across the sky. And, when you wake, you find
your swag, the camp, the plains all white with frost.

The Two Sisters

Related by MANOOWA

On the Island of the Spirits of the Dead,
one of two sisters talks.
'We must make a canoe and follow the way
the sun walks.'

They've filled the canoe with sacred
rannga things,
and paddled away into the night
singing ritual songs.

'Sister, look back!' the first sister calls.
'Do you see the morning star?'
Her sister looks out along their wake.
'Nothing. Nothing's there.'

The little sister has fallen asleep.
Again her sister calls,
'Sister, look back for the morning star.'
'Nothing. Nothing at all.'

A spear of light is thrown across
the sea and lies far
ahead upon the sister's course.
'Sister, the morning star.'

The sun comes up and walks the sky.
A fish with whiskers swims
ahead, and leaps out of the sea,
while the sisters sing.

Day and night, and day and night,
the sisters are gone
with the morning star and the leaping fish
and the sky-walking sun.

The sisters, hoar with dried salt spray,
the semen of the sea,
make landfall where parrots scream
from paperbark trees.

The sisters beach the bark canoe,
unload the *rannga* things.
They thrust one in the earth. From there
the first goanna comes.

They've gone inland. Their digging sticks
make sacred springs.
They leave behind them *rannga* forms
for all living things.

Out gathering food, the sisters have hung
their dilly-bags in a tree.
While they're away, men come and steal
their sacred ceremonies.

The sisters hear men singing and
song-sticks' 'tjong-tjong'.
'Cover your ears. We cannot hear
the sacred song.'

'O, all our sacred ceremonies
belong now to the men.
We must gather food, and bear
and rear children.'

The Platypus

Related by DICK DONELLY

Djanbun's the platypus. He was a man one time.
He came out of Washpool Creek, the old people said.
Djanbun's travelling, a firestick in his hand,
across the big mountains to the Clarence River.
He's blowing on the firestick to make it flame.
But it won't flame, and wherever the sparks
fall down from the firestick they turn to gold.

This platypus man's mouth starts to get wide
from blowing on the firestick. We used to blow
on the firestick when we were young. My mother
used to say to us, 'Don't blow on the firestick
like that, or you'll be like Djanbun the platypus.'

When Djanbun gets down to the Clarence River,
he's got a big mouth from blowing on the firestick.
He starts to wonder, 'What am I going to do now?'
He'd got tired of trying to make the firestick flame.
So he throws the firestick down, and he thinks,
'I'll jump into the water.' As soon as he jumps
in the water, he turns into a platypus. That's him,
that's Djanbun now. He was a man one time.

Now Billy Charlie, he found this nugget of gold
at the place where Djanbun jumped into the water.
When I heard about this, I thought, 'Well now,
that's the firestick he found.' Because he found
that gold where the firestick was thrown down.

The old people told me this story. They showed me
the way Djanbun went across the mountain range.

Captain Cook

Related by PERCY MUMBULLA

Tungeei, that was her native name.
She was a terrible tall woman
who lived at Ulladulla.
She had six husbands,
an' buried the lot.

She was over a hundred, easy,
when she died.
She was tellin' my father,
they were sittin' on the point
that was all wild scrub.

The big ship came and anchored
out at Snapper Island.
He put down a boat
an' rowed up the river
into Bateman's Bay.

He landed on the shore of the river,
the other side from where the
church is now.
When he landed he gave the Kurris clothes,
an' those big sea-biscuits.
Terrible hard biscuits they was.

When they were pullin' away to go back
to the ship, these wild Kurris
were runnin' out of the scrub.
They'd stripped right off again.
They were throwin' the clothes an' biscuits
back at Captain Cook
as his men were pullin' away in the boat.

Central Australian Aboriginal Songs

(Aranda and Loritja languages)

Kangaroos

Crunching their food in their mouths,—
While feeding they smack their lips noisily.

Grinding their food in their mouths,—
While feeding they smack their lips noisily.

The white-whiskered ones
While feeding smack their lips noisily.

The black-mouthed ones
While feeding smack their lips noisily.

Through their fodder stands of *tnelja* vines
They drag themselves along leisurely, leaving their tail prints
    behind.

In a thick plot of everlastings
They are forever playfully fighting with each other.

In a thick plot of everlastings
They are forever sportively fighting with each other.

In a thick plot of everlastings
They are forever resting with faces turned upwards.

Their foreheads darkened with down
They are sitting around glowing like fires.

The white sand crunches under them, the white sand crunches
    loudly under them;
The white sand echoes under them, the white sand echoes loudly
    under them.

The night parrots are speaking, the night parrots are speaking
    merrily;
In the tree tops they are speaking, in the tree tops they are speaking
    merrily.

With their ears pricked up
The broad-eared ones are looking about intently.

With their ears pricked up
The red-faced ones are looking about intently.

Song of the Progenitor-Hero Anakotarinja

Red is the down which is covering me;
Red I am as though I was burning in a fire.

Red I am as though I was burning in a fire,
Bright red gleams the ochre with which I have rubbed my body.

Red I am as though I was burning in a fire,
Red, too, is the hollow in which I am lying.

Red I am like the heart of a flame of fire,
Red, too, is the hollow in which I am lying.

The red tjurunga is resting upon my head,
Red, too, is the hollow in which I am lying.

Like a whirlwind it is towering to the sky,
Like a pillar of red sand it is towering to the sky.

The tnatantja is towering to the sky,
Like a pillar of red sand it is towering to the sky.

A mass of red pebbles covers the plains,
Little white sand-rills cover the plains.

Lines of red pebbles streak the plains,
Lines of white sand-rills streak the plains.

An underground pathway lies open before me,
Leading straight west, it lies open before me.

A cavernous pathway lies open before me,
Leading straight west, it lies open before me.

He is sucking his beard into his mouth in anger,
Like a dog he follows the trail by scent.

He hurries on swiftly, like a keen dog;
Like a dog he follows the trail by scent.

Irresistible and foaming with rage,—
Like a whirlwind he rakes them together.

Out yonder, not far from me, lies Ankota;
The underground hollow is gaping open before me.

A straight track is gaping open before me,
An underground hollow is gaping open before me.

A cavernous pathway is gaping open before me,
An underground pathway is gaping open before me.

Red I am, like the heart of a flame of fire,
Red, too, is the hollow in which I am resting.

The Brother Eagles

Splinters of the sky.   In the air they float:
In each other's shade   In the air they float.

In each other's shade   In the air they float:
All but lost to view.   In the air they float.

Shrunk to hazy specks.   In the air they float:
Splinters of the sky.   In the air they float.

Facing Pmoierka.   In the air they float:
Splinters of the sky.   In the air they float.

In the sky's [blue] flesh   In the air they float:
Shrunk to hazy specks.   In the air they float.

In the sky's [blue] flesh   In the air they float:
Pause on folded wings.   Shatterers of shrubs!

Breast-plumes gleaming black.   In the air they float:
In the sky's [blue] flesh   In the air they float.

'You and I at once   In the air now float:
You and I as mates   In the air now float.'

'With wind-ruffled plumes   In the air we float:
You and I at once   In the air now float.'

'Eagles newly-winged.   In the air they float:
Veiled by smoky haze.   In the air they float.'

'Eagles newly-winged.   In the air they float:
Pause on folded wings.   Shatterers of shrubs!'

Off the fissured face   In the air they float:
All but lost to view.   In the air they float.

'Near the shadowed cliff   In the air we float:
You and I as mates   In the air now float.'

Near the shadowed cliff   In the air they float:
Off the fissured face   In the air they float.

In bald rocky crests   His trail let him lay!
In sweeping bare slopes   His trail let him lay!

In polished bare cliffs   His trail let him lay!
In shining quartz seams   His trail let him lay!

The Hollow at Ilbalintja Soak

White creek sand!
Impenetrable hollow!

White limestone band!
Impenetrable hollow!

Rich yellow soil!
Impenetrable hollow!

Red and orange soil!
Impenetrable hollow!

Ringneck Parrots

The ringneck parrots, in scattered flocks,—
The ringneck parrots are screaming in their upward flight.

The ringneck parrots are a cloud of wings;
The shell parrots are a cloud of wings.

Let the shell parrots come down to rest,—
Let them come down to rest on the ground!

Let the caps fly off the scented blossoms!
Let the blooms descend to the ground in a shower!

The clustering bloodwood blooms are falling down,—
The clustering bloodwood blossoms, nipped by birds.

The clustering bloodwood blooms are falling down,—
The clustering bloodwood blossoms, one by one.

Translated by T.G.H. Strehlow

Rex Ingamells

Garchooka, the Cockatoo

Though the waters, wind-stirred and red-glowing,
shadowed by the evening-gloom of gums,
bend in their banks the way the day is going,
while a dusk-gold haze of insects comes
over the ripples in their coloured flowing,
Garchooka, beating from high branches, screeches
discord up and down the river-reaches.

From *The Great South Land*

Cook admired the native courage, made
observations on the native life:

'They balance their lances on pieces of wood
of fore-arm length,
from which they gather force in throwing them...

'Their canoes are the poorest that I ever saw;
their houses are primitive and not much used,
the people being content to lie on grass,
with simple breaks of bark against the wind....

'Clothing and houses they easily do without,
in their warm and clement weather....

'They live a simple life, all un-acquainted
with Civilization's superficial modes,
the earth and the sea providing
the things they need....

'They did not covet anything we had,
would pass our heaps of equipment—left
by our wooders and waterers lying on the beach—
not seeming to notice it;
and they despised our gifts,
spurning our advances,
desiring nothing but for us to go.'

To Joseph Banks,
more interested in plants than savages,
New Holland natives were of small account.

The botany of this Land
brought a light to his eyes,
and caused his heart to pound in ecstasy.

Devoted to his Science,
he did good work, and carried back to England
a marvellous store of specimens—new knowledge,
but a cursory, thin opinion of the natives.

'These people,' he said, 'are cowards. They run away
whenever they see us. They even run from Tupia.

'Solander and myself, we wander freely.

'Myself in the woods,' wrote Joseph, 'botanizing,
and quite devoid of fear.'

                        But the Kurin-gai
observed him carefully, and mimicked him,
long after, in their play-corroborees.

[*The Corroboree about Banka Banka*]
'*I am Banka Banka.*
I am the Hunter of grasses and flowers.
I dig up anything that grows in the ground.
I pick as many leaves as I can hold from the trees,
I move about on my knees.

'*Awkward I am, and clumsy, like a dying kangaroo,*
with my head drooping to the ground.

'*Suddenly I drop down.*
No, I am not a dying kangaroo: I have found something.
Look, it is a blade of grass!

'*Now I carry all these victims of my morning's hunting—*
these yams and berries and leaves and bunches of grass;
I carry all these victims down to the beach.

'*Now I spread them out, very carefully I spread them out,*
very carefully I spread them out on my great rugs under the Sun.

'*Come and help me get more leaves and grass, more flowers.*
There are more than I can carry, in the Country of the Kurin-gai.
Help me carry as many as possible of the victims of my hunting,
so that I can spread them out on my great rugs under the Sun.

'*Come, my brothers, help me. I am Banka Banka,*
I am the Hunter of grasses and flowers.'

Joyce Lee

My Father's Country

I can close my eyes one heartbeat
and smell the Wimmera summers of the twenties,
call up cloud continents
through incredible blue gateways,
breaking stubbled plains on Grampians rock.

This is my father's country. Manager of the flour mill,
he belongs in a crowded picture. His friends
and busy, flour-dusted ghosts
lumping wheat from Rainbow, Patchewollock, Brim.
Even on Sundays he spars with a string of stationmasters,
pleading for trucks to feed Manila, Mauritius, Hong Kong.

Upstaging him, especially on Sundays, is George Freeman
polishing his darling the steam engine,

lighting her fires with Mallee wood. A new mill
four storey brick and diesel,
retires him from the corrugated-iron shed
too soon. He spends the extra time
popping his red bright face over the fence to chat with anyone.

At first light, I can smell hot dust from wagons creaking past
my sleepout. In slow procession to the weighbridge,
each farmer bolstered by a sewn-up harvest, gentles
six outsize horses with a flick
of sunblackened hands. An old felt hat
scalloped by seasons of sweaty tides, crowns the load.

Eventually, I find my engine under a mountain
where timbercutters left her
the last day. Saplings dance on the dappled body
buried to the knees in wildflowers. Far
from my father's niche at the Necropolis,
George Freeman lies, cellar cool in Wimmera clay.
Safe from death, I keep them in endless summer.

Firebell for Peace

The war to end them all
rang the firebell at midnight.
'It's only peace' my father's
flamboyant red hair
shone in a brilliant lamplit circle
beside my bed.

Through hessian-paper walls
mild argument, my mother
in her strong singer's voice
'How can you be sure?'
I didn't need to see his unwillingness,
sliding stove-pipe pants
over pyjamas. Two minutes
he confirmed stale news:
'Peace just as I said
we expected it
go back to sleep.'

My hardheaded father
died long ago. Committee friends
at the funeral
spoke of him as visionary.
'It's only peace'
he prophesies across my years.

Kenneth Mackenzie

Shall then another

'C'est vous perdre une seconde fois, que de croire qu'un autre vous possède ...' —Villarceaux à Ninon de Lenclos

Shall then another do what I have done—
be with those legs and arms and breasts at one?
Shall the warm silken skin, that I alone knew,
be for another's couching, and shall he own new
gestures of hers—some subtle modification
of that loose drop of the head, of that dilation
amorous yet brutal of her pupils' caverns?
Shall he bait beasts and halt at the white taverns
and scale those purple climaxes, half-sleeping,
knowing not what he's accomplished? Shall the weeping
of that warm womb, the sobbing of its throat
be music to him till by note by note
it's lost and wasted, as he grows there—too
used and occasion-hardened, and the brew
of love sours in his belly?
How can I think that he between her knees
shall at length find time to think, or hawk, or sneeze,
go over the day's events, yet up and down,
plan for tomorrow, cool above her frown
and tighter arms, as in the pleasure-pain
she parts from beauty, and becomes huge and plain
and draws him deeper—a Demeter's sigh
sealing the spasm. Tell me—how shall I,
who always knew these monstrous movements of her,
dream and know now she has let another love her?
How shall I bear or dare to bring to mind
memory's cheap coin, finding it unrefined
by the heat of mental passions and sharp fires?
Or how, in her importunate desires
being somehow re-embraced, shall I go on,
saying, 'These contacts have been, but are gone
into the void of all such', and not fling
back to her, roused to frenzy by the sting
of knowing my own demise was not my end?
There are some women who would have a friend
out of a vanquished lover; but not she—

'Get off,' she said; 'you are an enemy.'
And so the gate of returning was left unlocked
though closed; however called against and mocked,
the enemy can return, but the friend's bound
by welcome's pleasant-coloured chains, and ground
under the heel of mighty unsuspicion.

This is a murderous and foul condition!
I love the woman. Let me forget my fear
and find a courage such as harlots wear
who stultify the mind till the body looms
merry and dominating in their rooms
and fills out space and squashes memory
by frequent repetition. Let me be
all body, and mindless.

How warm and dry her skin was! It outglowed
the single candle flame whose colour flowed
up to her overleaning face like a flower.
She never made one move to test her power,
but, with a smile as happy as a child's,
blew out the golden light.

Table-birds

The match-bark of the younger dog sets fire to
an indignation of turkeys under the olives.
Scurf-wigged like senescent judges, drum-puffing desire,
they bloat their wattles, and the chorus gives
a purple biased judgment on the pup:
Trouble enough, pup, bloody trouble enough!

So much for morning and the sun's generous
flattery of the metal of their feathers.
Noon makes them somnolent, dusty, glad to drowse
the fly-slurred hours of midday August weather
in scooped hollows under the ripe trees
whose fruit sweetens them for the Christmas season.

The tilted sun, the craw's shrunk emptiness
wake them to stir their lice and strut again,
head back, tail spread, and dangling crest
and greedy, angered eye.... The spinsterly hen
blinks the lewd fan and frets among the grains,
knife-grey and sleek, hungrier, less restrained

by stifling turkey pride beneath the red
slap of the leering comb. But they submit.
The fan snaps to; head doubles over head—
and day's escape delineates them fitfully
like darkness clotted into nervous shapes
under the olives, in whose night they sleep.

Caesura

Sometimes at night when the heart stumbles and stops
a full second endless the endless steps
that lead me on through this time terrain
without edges and beautiful terrible
are gone never to proceed again.

Here is a moment of enormous trouble
when the kaleidoscope sets unalterable
and at once without meaning without motion
like a stalled aeroplane in the middle sky
ready to fall down into a waiting ocean.

Blackness rises. Am I now to die
and feel the steps no more and not see day
break out its answering smile of hail all's well
from east full round to east and hear the bird
whistle all creatures that on earth do dwell?

Not now. Old heart has stopped to think of a word
as someone in a dream by far too weird
to be unlikely feels a kiss and stops
to praise all heaven stumbling in all his senses ...
and suddenly hears again the endless steps.

Douglas Stewart

Leopard Skin

Seven pairs of leopard-skin underpants
Flying on the rotary clothes-line! Oh, look, look, virgins,
How with the shirts and pyjamas they whirl and dance.
And think no more, trembling in your own emergence

Like butterflies into the light, that tall soft boy
Who nightly over his radio crooned and capered
Alone in his room in weird adolescent joy
Is mother's boy, softy: has he not slain a leopard?

But more than that: does he not wear its skin,
Secretly, daily, superbly? Oh, girls, adore him,
For dreaming on velvet feet to slay and to sin
He prowls the suburb, the wild things flee before him,
He miaous at the leopardesses, and they stop:
He *is* a leopard—he bought himself in a shop.

A Country Song

Schute, Bell, Badgery, Lumby,
How's your dad and how'd your mum be?
What's the news, oh, far from here
Under the blue sky burning clear
Where your beautiful business runs
Wild as a dingo, fresh as a brumby?

Lumby, Badgery, Bell, Schute,
Pipe me a song, for I am mute,
Of red earth growing you hides and tallow,
Rivers wandering brown and shallow
And old grey gum-trees never dead
While magpies play them like a flute.

Bell, Lumby, Schute, Badgery,
How's the world in your menagerie?—
Hennessey's stallion and Hogan's bull
Sheds at Yass crammed full with wool
Heifers and vealers, rams and lambs,
From Nimmitabel to Wantabadgery.

Badgery, Schute, Lumby, Bell,
How's the world? The world goes well.
The auctioneer, that merry man,
Out in the sleet at Queanbeyan
Swigged his whisky neat from the bottle
And up went prices while buyers fell.

Schute, Bell, Badgery, Lumby,
Town's all stone and stone so dumb be.
Past Wee Jasper I remember
The ewes drew out through the green timber ...

Oh what's your price for all that country
Wild as a dingo, fresh as a brumby?

Terra Australis

1

Captain Quiros and Mr William Lane,
Sailing some highway shunned by trading traffic
Where in the world's skull like a moonlit brain
Flashing and crinkling rolls the vast Pacific,

Approached each other zigzag, in confusion,
Lane from the west, the Spaniard from the east,
Their flickering canvas breaking the horizon
That shuts the dead off in a wall of mist.

'Three hundred years since I set out from Lima
And off Espiritu Santo lay down and wept
Because no faith in men, no truth in islands
And still unfound the shining continent slept;

'And swore upon the Cross to come again
Though fever, thirst and mutiny stalked the seas
And poison spiders spun their webs in Spain,
And did return, and sailed three centuries,

'Staring to see the golden headlands wade
And saw no sun, no land, but this wide circle
Where moonlight clots the waves with coils of weed
And hangs like silver moss on sail and tackle,

'Until I thought to trudge till time was done
With all except my purpose run to waste;
And now upon this ocean of the moon,
A shape, a shade, a ship, and from the west!'

2

'What ship?' 'The *Royal Tar*!' 'And whither bent?'
'I seek the new Australia.' 'I, too, stranger;
Terra Australis, the great continent
That I have sought three centuries and longer;

'And westward still it lies, God knows how far,
Like a great golden cloud, unknown, untouched,

Where men shall walk at last like spirits of fire
No more by oppression chained, by sin besmirched.'

'Westward there lies a desert where the crow
Feeds upon poor men's hearts and picks their eyes;
Eastward we flee from all that wrath and woe
And Paraguay shall yet be Paradise.'

'Eastward,' said Quiros, as *San Pedro* rolled,
High-pooped and round in the belly like a barrel,
'Men tear each other's entrails out for gold;
And even here I find that men will quarrel.'

'If you are Captain Quiros you are dead.'
'The report has reached me; so is William Lane.'
The dark ships rocked together in the weed
And Quiros stroked the beard upon his chin:

'We two have run this ocean through a sieve
And though our death is scarce to be believed
Seagulls and flying-fish were all it gave
And it may be we both have been deceived.'

3

'Alas, alas, I do remember now;
In Paradise I built a house of mud
And there were fools who could not milk a cow
And idle men who would not though they could.

'There were two hundred brothers sailed this ocean
To build a New Australia in the east
And trifles of money caused the first commotion
And one small cask of liquor caused the last.

'Some had strange insects bite them, some had lust,
For wifeless men will turn to native women,
Yet who could think a world would fall in dust
And old age dream of smoke and blood and cannon

'Because three men got drunk?' 'With Indian blood
And Spanish hate that jungle reeked to Heaven;
And yet I too came once, or thought I did,
To Terra Australis, my dear western haven,

'And broke my gallows up in scorn of violence,
Gave land and honours, each man had his wish,
Flew saints upon the rigging, played the clarions:
Yet many there were poisoned by a fish

'And more by doubt; and so deserted Torres
And sailed, my seamen's prisoner, back to Spain.'
There was a certain likeness in the stories
And Captain Quiros stared at William Lane.

4

Then 'Hoist the mainsail!' both the voyagers cried,
Recoiling each from each as from the devil;
'How do we know that we are truly dead
Or that the tales we tell may not be fable?

'Surely I only dreamed that one small bottle
Could blow up New Australia like a bomb?
A mutinous pilot I forebore to throttle
From Terra Australis send me demented home?

'The devil throws me up this Captain Quiros,
This William Lane, a phantom not yet born,
This Captain Quiros dead three hundred years,
To tempt me to disaster for his scorn—

'As if a blast of bony breath could wither
The trees and fountains shining in my mind,
Some traveller's tale, puffed out in moonlit weather,
Divert me from the land that I must find!

'Somewhere on earth that land of love and faith
In Labour's hands—the Virgin's—must exist,
And cannot lie behind, for there is death,
So where but in the west—but in the east?'

At that the sea of light began to dance
And plunged in sparkling brine each giddy brain;
The wind from Heaven blew both ways at once
And west went Captain Quiros, east went Lane.

John Blight

The Coral Reef

In the baroque style of coral, India,
Java, your conglomerate gods assemble.
Having just walked the reef at low water,
I have a fear of their numbers, a psychic tremble,

a mental numbness at my failure to describe
their Nirvana, their inscrutable jungle of peace
—a peace that is death in stone. As though a rib
were stolen from every mortal, each piece
cemented in place a monument to mankind—a reef?

I walked it—walked on the faces of its gods,
on their many visages ... on my own belief,
I fear; exhausted my many moods,
my paucity of words—a failure at expression
by this mass of death; unable to follow its vast progression.

The Oyster-Eaters

I had heard the bird's name, and searched with intent
The oyster banks; and a bird with a red bill
And a hingeing, unoiled note gave a high call
In a flat treble. Whatever the bird-voice meant,
It sounded ajar; a door protestingly forced;
A bivalve opening, shell from shell divorced.

I saw the oyster-bird with red cockade-like beak;
White, blue-black, like a tricolour; plump as a chef—
And it could well prepare banquets to last a week:
Oysters, hors-d'oeuvres. Somewhere around a cliff
A door's answering squeak, and two birds fed together,
At turn of the tide, with wind blowing us salty weather.

Mangrove

I saw its periscope in the tide;
its torpedo-seed seeking the soft side
of the island, the grey mud-bank.
And, where it touched, it seemed the land sank
with its trees exploding from water; the green
mangroves' fountainhead of leaves bursting, seen
like a mushroom-top of detritus and spray.
Today, in my boat, at the close end of the bay,
I saw its dark devastations; islet and spit
sunk in the flat high tide. Where these war-seeds hit,
gaps of horizon and sea; then trees ... gaps ... trees
... like men on a flushed foredeck. No ease:
the drab olive-green swarming everywhere;
troops of the mangroves, uniform, everywhere.

Joan Aronsten

Ad Infinitum

A trickle of sand on the grave's edge
moves with limitless momentum.
The mass follows and hurries downhill into the pit
as time, with its last thrust
has rushed through the body
ravaging all but the spirit.

The walls close in
and the bereaved shout within their walls of grief—
Stay! But the sand pours over the remains
in time with the tears
that at this terrible moment
cannot be contained.

The flowers lie in hopeful profusion,
but there is no end to the sand
that is moving towards them.
Already it is creeping towards the shadows
of those who turn away.
They turn to tread the impetus
that moves about their feet.

Judith Wright

Nigger's Leap, New England

The eastward spurs tip backward from the sun.
Night runs an obscure tide round cape and bay
and beats with boats of cloud up from the sea
against this sheer and limelit granite head.
Swallow the spine of range; be dark, O lonely air.
Make a cold quilt across the bone and skull
that screamed falling in flesh from the lipped cliff
and then were silent, waiting for the flies.

Here is the symbol, and the climbing dark
a time for synthesis. Night buoys no warning
over the rocks that wait our keels; no bells
sound for her mariners. Now must we measure

our days by nights, our tropics by their poles,
love by its end and all our speech by silence.
See in these gulfs, how small the light of home.

Did we not know their blood channelled our rivers,
and the black dust our crops ate was their dust?
O all men are one man at last. We should have known
the night that tided up the cliffs and hid them
had the same question on its tongue for us.
And there they lie that were ourselves writ strange.

Never from earth again the coolamon
or thin black children dancing like the shadows
of saplings in the wind. Night lips the harsh
scarp of the tableland and cools its granite.
Night floods us suddenly as history
that has sunk many islands in its good time.

Legend

The blacksmith's boy went out with a rifle
and a black dog running behind.
Cobwebs snatched at his feet,
rivers hindered him,
thorn-branches caught at his eyes to make him blind
and the sky turned into an unlucky opal,
but he didn't mind,
I can break branches, I can swim rivers, I can stare out any spider
    I meet,
said he to his dog and his rifle.

The blacksmith's boy went over the paddocks
with his old black hat on his head.
Mountains jumped in his way,
rocks rolled down on him,
and the old crow cried, 'You'll soon be dead.'
And the rain came down like mattocks.
But he only said
I can climb mountains, I can dodge rocks, I can shoot an old crow
    any day,
and he went on over the paddocks.

When he came to the end of the day the sun began falling.
Up came the night ready to swallow him,
like the barrel of a gun,
like an old black hat,

like a black dog hungry to follow him.
Then the pigeon, the magpie and the dove began wailing
and the grass lay down to pillow him.
His rifle broke, his hat blew away and his dog was gone
and the sun was falling.

But in front of the night the rainbow stood on the mountain,
just as his heart foretold.
He ran like a hare,
he climbed like a fox;
he caught it in his hands, the colours and the cold—
like a bar of ice, like the column of a fountain,
like a ring of gold.
The pigeon, the magpie and the dove flew up to stare,
and the grass stood up again on the mountain.

The blacksmith's boy hung the rainbow on his shoulder
instead of his broken gun.
Lizards ran out to see,
snakes made way for him,
and the rainbow shone as brightly as the sun.
All the world said, Nobody is braver, nobody is bolder,
nobody else has done
anything to equal it. He went home as bold as he could be
with the swinging rainbow on his shoulder.

Wings

Between great coloured vanes the butterflies
drift to the sea with fixed bewildered eyes.

Once all their world was food; then sleep took over,
dressed them in cloaks and furs for some great lover—

some Juan, some Helen. Lifted by air and dream
they rose and circled into heaven's slipstream

to seek each other over fields of blue.
Impassioned unions waited—can't-come-true

images. Blown, a message or a kiss,
earth sent them to the sun's tremendous Yes.

Once met and joined, they sank; complete and brief
their sign was fastened back upon the leaf;

empty of future now, the wind turned cold,
their rich furs worn, they thin to membraned gold.

Poor Rimbauds never able to return
out of the searing rainbows they put on,

their wings have trapped them. Staring helplessly
they blow beyond the headland, to the sea.

David Campbell

Song for the Cattle

Down the red stock route
Hock-deep in mirage
Rode the three black drovers
Singing to the cattle.

And with them a young woman,
Perhaps some squatter's daughter
From homestead or township,
Who turned her horse easily.

To my mind she was as beautiful
As the barmaid in Brewarrina
Who works at the Royal. Men
Ride all day to see her.

Fine-boned as a brigalow
Yet ample as a granary,
She has teeth good for laughing
Or biting an apple.

I'm thinking of quitting
My mountain selection,
The milking at morning
And the lonely axe-echoes;

Of swapping my slab hut
For a rolled-up blanket
And heading north-westward
For a life in the saddle—

For the big mobs trailing
Down the empty stock routes,
A horned moon at evening
And songs round the campfire.

Yes, I'll soon be drinking
At the Royal in Brewarrina

And ambling through mirage
With the squatter's daughter.

Hear the Bird of Day

Hear, the bird of day
Stirs in his blue tree,
Fumbles for words to say
The things a bird may learn
From brooding half the night,
What's matter but a hardening of the light?

Out of this seed of song
Discoursing with the dark,
Now in a clear tongue
Rises his lonely voice,
And all the east is bright.
What's matter but a hardening of the light?

Mountain and brilliant bird,
The ram and the wren,
For each there is a word;
In every grain of sand
Stands a singer in white.
What's matter but a hardening of the light?

Duchesses

A mob of dressing-tables is grazing
The pile of the plain
Under paper blue mountains.

Now and then one will pause
And raise its mirror
Reflecting the white sunlight.

Little cupboards
Hop in and out of the drawers
And suck at the crockery knobs.

The only sounds are the snip, snip,
Of grazing furniture
And the rattle of wooden droppings.

A truck is hurrying over the plain.
The mob raises its mirrors,
Little cupboards hop back in the drawers.

The dressing-tables head for the paper hills,
But the truck is upon them.
Pom pom! Corks fly from swivel guns.

Pomeranians snap
At the heels of wheeling dressing-tables.
They snarl in mirrors, savaging the doilies.

The furniture is surrounded.
Men rope the younger pieces
And load them squealing onto the truck.

Now solitary in bedrooms
Dressing-tables look back at women
Who question them with rouge lips.

Sometimes through windows
They glimpse the paper blue mountains,
And the tears of the women fall on the doilies.

David Martin

(Ludwig Detsinyi)

Dreams in German

Undated dreams: the sea of Heringsdorf,
The Brocken behind Schierke and the snow
That falls like sugar on the Christmas trees
They're selling in the square. It's hard to know
This land in English. What is Grunewald,
And what is Weissensee and what the name
I seek for her who lies there? All my keys
Are lost. Die Schlüssel sind verloren. Do I still,
As I return to Brandenburg at night,
Declare my landmarks in the tongue I knew,
Say Deutscher Wald when I'm with Rosenrot
Deep in the forest? No, for life went ill
With all my fairies, and in nightmares only
I call by name the giant Schlagetot
Who killed my people and stays close to me
Wherever I may sleep. Yes, not until
He dies shall I go home to childhood. Say it now:
Say Rosenrot, Schneeweisschen, how they came
Tief aus dem Walde, and how Schlagetot
Schlug alle tot and took my book away ...

Snow White and Rose Red, they are not the same.
Stretch out your hand and gather what is left:
The frieze upon the nursery wall, a light
Kept covered on the landing, or the face
Of Lotte in Charlottenburg that day;
But in translation, like a gazetteer.
Du liebes Land! To call my country dear
Still burns the mouth. But Buchenwald flows right
From German lips into my English ear.

Dorothy Auchterlonie

The Tree

He watched them as they walked towards the tree,
Through the green garden when the leaves stood still,
He saw his scarlet fruit hang tremulously:
He whispered. 'Eat it if you will.'

Knowing as yet they had no will but his,
Were as his hand, his foot, his braided hair.
His own face mocked him from his own abyss:
He whispered, 'Eat it if you dare!'

Without him they could neither will nor dare;
Courage and will yet slumbered in the fruit,
Desire forbore, they still were unaware
That doubt was set to feed the root.

God held his breath: If they should miss it now,
Standing within the shadow of the tree ...
Always the I, never to know the Thou
Imprisoned in my own eternity.

'Death sits within the fruit, you'll surely die!'
He scarcely formed the words upon a breath;
'O liberating seed! Eat, then, and I
For this release will die your every death.

'Thus time shall be confounded till you come
Full-circle to this garden where we stand,
From the dark maze of knowledge, with the sum
Of good and evil in your hand.

'Then you will shed the journey you have made,
See millenniums fall about your feet,

Behold the light that flares within each blade
Of grass, the visible paraclete.'

The harsh Word stirred the leaves, the fruit glowed red,
Adam's foot struck against the root;
He saw his naked doubt and raised his head:
Eve stretched her hand and plucked the fruit.

John Manifold

Fife Tune

For Sixth Platoon, 308th I.T.C.

One morning in spring
We marched from Devizes
All shapes and all sizes
Like beads on a string,
But yet with a swing
We trod the bluemetal
And full of high fettle
We started to sing.

She ran down the stair
A twelve-year-old darling
And laughing and calling
She tossed her bright hair;
Then silent to stare
At the men flowing past her—
There were all she could master
Adoring her there.

It's seldom I'll see
A sweeter or prettier;
I doubt we'll forget her
In two years or three,
And lucky he'll be
She takes for a lover
While we are far over
The treacherous sea.

Makhno's Philosophers

Back in *tachanka* days, when Red and Green
Pursued in turn each other and the White,

Out on the steppe, I'm told, there could be seen
A novel sight.

Professors of philosophy, whom war
From some provincial faculty dismissed
To seek new pasture on the Black Sea shore,
Fell in with Makhno—anarchist,

Terrorist, bandit, call him what you will—
Who spared their lives and, either for a laugh
Or from some vague respect for mental skill,
Attached them to his staff.

Their duties were not hard. For months or years,
Lacking a porch in which to hold debate,
These peripatetics, ringed by Cossack spears,
Had leisure to discuss The State.

With flashing pince-nez, while the sabres flashed,
They sat berugged in carts and deep dispute,
Or in some plundered village hashed and thrashed
The nature of The Absolute.

Bergsonians quite enjoyed it: from the first
They'd known Duration to depend on Space.
But Nietzscheans found their values arsy-versed
By Supermen of unfamiliar race.

And, whereas Platonists got mulligrubs,
Cynics were cheerful—though I'll not deny
They grumbled when obliged to share their tubs
With hogs from Epicurus' sty.

On quiet nights, bandits would form a ring
And listen with amazed guffaws
As syllogisms flew, and pillaging
Was reconciled with Universal Laws.

Symposia were held, whereat the host
(Taught by Hegelians of the Left)
In stolen vodka would propose a toast
To Proudhon's dictum: Property is Theft!

How did this idyll end? There's some confusion.
Makhno, I fear, was caught—
Perhaps he let his native resolution
Get sicklied o'er with other people's thought.

But what of his philosophers? I feel
Certain they reached an Academe at last

Where each in his own manner might conceal
His briefly bandit past.

To fool the OGPU or the C.I.A.
Would not be hard for any skilled expounder
Of Substance and Illusion, growing grey
But ever metaphysically sounder.

Yet each might feel at times old memories stir,
And know himself, as ever, set apart:
Once, among bandits, a philosopher;
Now, among academics, Green at heart.

In fact—I've wondered—take Professor X—
Mightn't his arid manner be a blind?
Are those lack-lustre eyes, behind those specs,
Truly the mirror of his mind?

Or is the real man, far away
From Kantian imperatives, once more
Roaming the steppe, not as a waif and stray
But waging revolutionary war?

Although his tongue belabours
The stony boundaries of a bloodless creed,
His soul is back again among the sabres
Yelling, 'The Deed! The Deed!'

Harold Stewart

The Sage in Unison

(For James Bayley)

When a disciple asked of Lu Chü how
To demonstrate Man's true accord with Tao;
The master placed two cithers, which his skill
And ear for pitch had perfectly attuned,
In neighbouring studios where all was still.
Whichever string he strummed on one alone,
The other hummed the corresponding tone,
As though by Taoist magic they communed.
And while his elegantly slender nails,
Pointed like plectra, plucked a school of scales;
'Finger this instrument,' he said, 'until

Its vibrant rings concentrically fill
The pool of quiet with their tingling boom:
Its twin, untouched in the adjoining room,
Faintly with fairy music now resounds.'
Thus Chuang-tzŭ in a parable expounds
The Sage's temperament, which is attained
Neither too slack, nor tautly overstrained.
For if a single interval is changed
From its due place within the octave's bounds,
The stars' celestial ratios are deranged.
Let discord once invade the five-tone scale,
The rites for Earth's fertility will fail,
And order in the State no more prevail:
Their key-note's rule deposed, the other four
And twenty jangling wires are set at war.

James McAuley

Terra Australis

Voyage within you, on the fabled ocean,
And you will find that Southern Continent,
Quiros' vision—his hidalgo heart
And mythical Australia, where reside
All things in their imagined counterpart.

It is your land of similes: the wattle
Scatters its pollen on the doubting heart;
The flowers are wide-awake; the air gives ease.
There you come home; the magpies call you Jack
And whistle like larrikins at you from the trees.

There too the angophora preaches on the hillsides
With the gestures of Moses; and the white cockatoo,
Perched on his limbs, screams with demoniac pain;
And who shall say on what errand the insolent emu
Walks between morning and night on the edge of the plain?

But northward in valleys of the fiery Goat
Where the sun like a centaur vertically shoots
His raging arrows with unerring aim,
Stand the ecstatic solitary pyres
Of unknown lovers, featureless with flame.

Liberal
or
Innocent by Definition

This is the solid-looking quagmire
The bright-green ground that tempts the tread
And lets you down into despond.

Enough consistence to conform,
Enough form to yield to pressure,
Enough force to wink at a fraud.

Unbiassed between good and evil,
The slander's only what they're told,
The harm something they didn't mean—

They only breathe what's in the air,
They have certified-pure motives,
So pure as to be quite transparent.

They are immune. Are innocent.
They can never be convicted,
They have no record of convictions.

This poem really needs a chorus
Spoken in dialect by the damned
Who live like frogs and have learned quagtalk:

'On the one hand this, on the other hand that,
Having regard to, I heard for a fact,
What one would want to say about this is,
That's not my point, and where are we at.'

Because

My father and my mother never quarrelled.
They were united in a kind of love
As daily as the *Sydney Morning Herald*,
Rather than like the eagle or the dove.

I never saw them casually touch,
Or show a moment's joy in one another.
Why should this matter to me now so much?
I think it bore more hardly on my mother,

Who had more generous feelings to express.
My father had dammed up his Irish blood

Against all drinking praying fecklessness,
And stiffened into stone and creaking wood.

His lips would make a switching sound, as though
Spontaneous impulse must be kept at bay.
That it was mainly weakness I see now,
But then my feelings curled back in dismay.

Small things can pit the memory like a cyst:
Having seen other fathers greet their sons,
I put my childish face up to be kissed
After an absence. The rebuff still stuns

My blood. The poor man's curt embarrassment
At such a delicate proffer of affection
Cut like a saw. But home the lesson went:
My tenderness thenceforth escaped detection.

My mother sang *Because*, and *Annie Laurie*,
White Wings, and other songs; her voice was sweet.
I never gave enough, and I am sorry;
But we were all closed in the same defeat.

People do what they can; they were good people,
They cared for us and loved us. Once they stood
Tall in my childhood as the school, the steeple.
How can I judge without ingratitude?

Judgment is simply trying to reject
A part of what we are because it hurts.
The living cannot call the dead collect:
They won't accept the charge, and it reverts.

It's my own judgment day that I draw near,
Descending in the past, without a clue,
Down to that central deadness: the despair
Older than any hope I ever knew.

Kath Walker

We Are Going

For Grannie Coolwell

They came in to the little town
A semi-naked band subdued and silent,

All that remained of their tribe.
They came here to the place of their old bora ground
Where now the many white men hurry about like ants.
Notice of estate agent reads: 'Rubbish May Be Tipped Here'.
Now it half covers the traces of the old bora ring.
They sit and are confused, they cannot say their thoughts:
'We are as strangers here now, but the white tribe are the strangers.
We belong here, we are of the old ways.
We are the corroboree and the bora ground,
We are the old sacred ceremonies, the laws of the elders.
We are the wonder tales of Dream Time, the tribal legends told.
We are the past, the hunts and the laughing games, the wandering
    camp fires.
We are the lightning-bolt over Gaphembah Hill
Quick and terrible,
And the Thunderer after him, that loud fellow.
We are the quiet daybreak paling the dark lagoon.
We are the shadow-ghosts creeping back as the camp fires burn low.
We are nature and the past, all the old ways
Gone now and scattered.
The scrubs are gone, the hunting and the laughter.
The eagle is gone, the emu and the kangaroo are gone from this
    place.
The bora ring is gone.
The corroboree is gone.
And we are going.'

Aboriginal Women's Mourning Songs

North-eastern Arnhem Land

The blowflies buzz ...

Ah, the blowfly is whining there, its maggots are eating the flesh.
The blowflies buzz, their feet stray over the corpse ...
The buzzing goes on and on ...
Who is it, eating there, whose flesh are they eating? ...
Ah my daughter, come back here to me!
Ah, our daughter was taken ill—
You didn't sing for her, as a father should!
You are foolish and silly, you sing only to please the ears of women!

You like to lie close to a young girl, a virgin, and give her a child!
You will not stay in one place;
Here and there, all over the place, you go among the camps,
You go walking hither and thither, looking for sweethearts.
Ah, before it was here that you used to stay.
You should be ashamed to do that before all these strangers!
Presently I will take up a knife and cut you!
(B. says: 'This is all that I do: I get food to eat, and tobacco to
    smoke!')
No, you go to sit down beside some woman,
You sit close, close beside her ...
Ah, my lost, sick child—ah, the blowflies!
Soon I will hit that woman of yours, that Y.! She is rubbish,
    that woman of yours, her face is ugly, she smells like an
    evil spirit! Presently, when she is pregnant, I won't look
    after her! You, B., you, her husband, you indeed,
    all by yourself, you can help her in childbirth!

All you others, eat ...

Ah my daughter, my grandchild!
Ah, the snake with its tongue flickering, at Dagalbawei ...
Ah my daughter, ah, the mound of the snake!
Ah my grandchild! My grandchild!
At Bumbiwalwalyun, and far away, the snake scatters its young,
At Waidja and Dirmalangan, Ganal and Ngoiwul ...
My daughter, my grandchild! My daughter is sick and hungry!
All you others, you eat till your bellies burst!
You used to be jealous before, when your husband called her.
All you lot are alive still—ah, my daughter, my grandchild!
Ah, your father has cried and cried, while mucus flowed into his
    mouth!
My daughter, my husband! My daughter, sick and hungry!
Ah my daughter, my husband!
Presently your child will grow, and you won't be looking after him,
    because you will be dead! Presently other children will hit him,
    other women will not look after him properly...!
Ah, my daughter, my grandchild!

Translated by Catherine H. Berndt

Rosemary Dobson

Country Press

Under the dusty print of hobnailed boot,
Strewn on the floor the papers still assert
In ornamental gothic, swash italics
And bands of printer's flowers (traditional)
Mixed in a riot of typographic fancy,
This is the *Western Star*, the Farmer's Guide,
The Voice of Progress for the Nyngle District.
Page-proofs of double-spread with running headlines
Paper the walls, and sets of cigarette-cards
Where pouter-bosomed showgirls still display
The charms that dazzled in the nineteen hundreds.
Through gaping slats
Latticed with sun the ivy tendrils fall
Twining the disused platen thrust away
Under a pall of dust in nineteen-twenty.
Draw up a chair, sit down. Just shift the galleys.
You say you have a notice? There's no one dies
But what we know about it. Births, deaths and marriages,
Council reports, wool prices, river-heights,
The itinerant poem and the classified ads—
They all come homewards to the *Western Star*.
Joe's our type-setter. Meet Joe Burrell. Joe's
A promising lad—and Joe, near forty-seven,
Peers from a tennis-shade and, smiling vaguely,
Completes the headline for the Baptist Social.
The dance, the smoke-oh, and the children's picnic
Down by the river-flats beneath the willows—
They all come homewards and Joe sets them all,
Between the morning and the mid-day schooner.
Oh, *Western Star* that bringest all to fold,
The yarding sales, the champion shorthorn bull,
And Williams' pain-relieving liniment,
When I shall die
Set me up close against my fellow-men,
Cheer that cold column headed 'Deaths' with flowers,
Or mix me up with Births and Marriages;
Surround the tragic statement of my death
With euchre-drives and good-times-had-by-all
That, with these warm concomitants of life

Jostled and cheered, in lower-case italics
I shall go homewards in the *Western Star*.

The Edge

Three times to the world's end I went,
Three times returned as one who brings
Tidings of light beyond the dark
But voiceless stays, still marvelling.

After great pain I had great joy
Three times that never else I knew;
The last reflection of its light
Fades from the pupils of my eyes.

Webbed by the world again I walk
The mazy paths that women tread
Watchful lest any harm should come
To those who journeyed back with me.

But still, as Lazarus who was born
Again beyond the edge of death,
I see the world half otherwise
And tremble at its mysteries.

Folding the Sheets

You and I will fold the sheets
Advancing towards each other
From Burma, from Lapland,

From India where the sheets have been washed in the river
And pounded upon stones:
Together we will match the corners.

From China where women on either side of the river
Have washed their pale cloth in the White Stone Shallows
'Under the shining moon'.

We meet as though in the formal steps of a dance
To fold the sheets together, put them to air
In wind, in sun over bushes, or by the fire.

We stretch and pull from one side and then the other—
Your turn. Now mine.
We fold them and put them away until they are needed.

A wish for all people when they lie down in bed—
Smooth linen, cool cotton, the fragrance and stir of herbs
And the faint but perceptible scent of sweet clear water.

Colin Thiele

Tom Farley

Tom Farley, up to his knees in sheep
By the drafting yard, moves in a red fog
Of summer dust; moves, bent, in a rhythm deep
As the seasons, his hard-soft hands
Holding gentle conversation with his dog.

Tom Farley on his Mid-North run
Has a face as fresh and kindly as his sheep;
Wears an old felt hat with its brim full of sun,
Sees the waves of wool move as soothingly as sleep.

Tom Farley lives a life of moving sheep:
Sheep flowing down the slopes
In broad falls
Or unwinding slowly like slack ropes
From knots at dams;
Cataracts of sheep in flood down ledges
Leaping and bucking in angles and edges,
Tossing up like flotsam the horns of rams;
Sheep held in the hollows and valleys
In friendly lakes rippling gently in the sun
On Farley's run.

And Tom, sometimes caught in the rucking tide
Of backs, feels them break against him,
Carry him forward in their jostle and surge
Till, fingers crooked deep in wool, he wades wide
To the fence and at last stands free
Like a tired surfer plodding from the sea.

But Tom finds himself most deeply once a year
When the sheep-dog trials come to test his dog ...

Then, by riddled stump or fallen log
He sucks his pipe and—eyes alight,
Though ringed by the crows'-feet treading round their hollows—
Sums up the sheep and the brain of the dog that follows;

But when Tom and his noiseless shadow slip
On to the oval green where the renegade ewes
Fidget and shift, people pity the others' chances,
For these two are always surer, a little faster,
Fluid with the knowing talk of nods and glances—
A spiritual union of the dog and master.

Tom Farley and his dog, they say, will wipe
The field—so much at one in paddocks, yards and races
That folk would hardly be surprised
Some day to see them interchange their places,
See the dog stand up to fill his brier pipe,
And old Tom, dropping to the turf behind the flock,
Creep stealthily with feints and cunning graces,
And, nose to the ground, sink his teeth in a lagging hock.

Radiation Victim

Beneath your cooling coverlet you lie,
The unseen fire still burning in your flesh,
Yet all humanity may pass you by
Unheeded while you melt before its flame,
And the slim needles of its secret rays drive
Inwards to incinerate your name.
God, that we should see you slowly burn alive!

This is the stealthy modern way to die:
To take the passive metal in your grip
And unaware set all your hand on fire.
Walk down the street or work your innocent bench,
While the unfelt heat burns slowly to the bone
With flame that no man's artifice can quench.

A fine ghastliness this is to end our days:
An ancient incandescence fanned and freed
To leap the air invisibly until
Each mortal breast, ignited and ablaze,
Shrinks to its blackened ashes silently.
And a strange compassion has macabre birth
Now that the unseen fire may stalk and scorch
Its darting probe through the wide round Earth,
May thrust its flame against our cringing flesh
And make mankind its hideous secret torch.

Gwen Harwood

Homage to Ferd. Holthausen

At a street bookstall in Karlsruhe, my father
bought for my schoolboy son, then starting German,
Etymologisches Wörterbuch der Englischen Sprache
by Ferd. Holthausen, Professor of Kiel.
Lovely old binding, elegant type, good paper,
printed in Leipzig, 1917.
I like to think of Ferd. Holthausen sitting
with Skeat and Sweet and part of the New Oxford
(war having cut the final letters off)
working on his Büchlein (it's pocket sized)
transcribing words while Europe raged outside:
      Breviloquent, compagination, dittany,
      griskin, harmel, irrision, kilderkin, nimb,
      obnubilation, oleraceous, parpent—
O Holthausen, O Ferd.! O dear Professor!
Forgive me my papilionaceous mind.
Teach me to perlustrate my native language.
Let me be of your phratry. My pignoration,
see, is this smaragd, of porraceous hue.
Bless my tripudiation, stellify
my verses, Ferd., be ever at my scrutoire.

Death Has No Features of His Own

Death has no features of his own.
He'll take a young eye bathed in brightness
and the ranging cheekbones of a raddled queen.
Misery's cured by his appalling taste.
His house is without issue. He appears
garlanded with lovebirds, hearts and flowers.
Anything, everything.
                He'll wear my face and yours.
Not as we were, thank God. As we shall be
when we let go of the world, late ripe fruit falling.
What we are is beyond him utterly.

A Simple Story

A visiting conductor
   when I was seventeen,
took me back to his hotel room
   to cover the music scene.

I'd written a composition.
   Would wonders never cease—
here was a real musician
   prepared to hold my piece.

He spread my score on the counterpane
   with classic casualness,
and put one hand on the manuscript
   and the other down my dress.

It was hot as hell in the Windsor.
   I said I'd like a drink.
We talked across gin and grapefruit,
   and I heard the ice go clink

as I gazed at the lofty forehead
   of one who led the band,
and guessed at the hoarded sorrows
   no wife could understand.

I dreamed of a soaring passion
   as an egg might dream of flight,
while he read my crude sonata.
   If he'd said, 'That bar's not right,'

or, 'Have you thought of a coda?'
   or, 'Watch that first repeat,'
or, 'Modulate to the dominant,'
   he'd have had me at his feet.

But he shuffled it all together,
   and said, 'That's *lovely*, dear,'
as he put it down on the washstand
   in a way that made it clear

that I was no composer.
   And I being young and vain,
removed my lovely body
   from one who'd scorned my brain.

I swept off like Miss Virtue
   down dusty Roma Street,

and heard the goods trains whistle
  WHO? WHOOOOOO? in aching heat.

Max Harris

Message from a Cross

the figure stood a crucifix against the door
and we, just kids, watched the hard paw
laid on the joist, the heavy leaning
policeman saying, where's your maw and paw?
then we knew that something had occurred
and the raving tin piano knew.
the slow aspect of buttons stirred
us and the fatal terror of void grew
and grew and grew.

fetch Henry said the Cross and I ran
trembling to the outhouse and began
to tremor out the strange story of the man
and the Cross and what it meant.
he said, 'someone's dead' without intent
to pacify to smooth the body burden,
yet soon I sighed and the moment pent
in me relaxed, relaxed.

mad Derek had had another of his fits
down by the creek where he sits
cursing the birds, and smothered desperate
his eternal day in two inches of creek
water. They found him there meek
and sane, spreadeagled his weight
across a bough, a gumbough.

the weighty Cross, with caked knuckle joints
moves slowly from our vision and points
to the sun, a yellow daze, passive as loins
lying down the baked and timeless road
where often night had bent and showed
its claws streaking the gentle groins
and panting and panting.

Martin Buber in the Pub

My friends are borne to one another
By their lack of something to say;
The weight of inward thought is lifted
And they float to each other
Like paper darts: they offer the salt of themselves
Arab-like in hotels,
Humbler than they would have you believe.
Humanity is the smallest coin for tipping.
Allen relates a host of grandiose lies ...
These are the wafers of our religion.
Barnes is the butt of malice,
An unmysterious drinking of the blood ...
And the seas may boil outside. No doubt they do.
But we are in a silence of some sort,
Exchanging shells, which placed against the ear,
Occasionally echo the throbbing of a heart.

Nan McDonald

The Hatters

The hut in the bush of bark or rusty tin,
The feel of eyes watching, willing you to be gone:
Here lives a hatter. He has done with the world.
Whatever it was in the end he could not bear—
To look in the face of lecher and fool and see
Himself; the rub of the mask on bleeding skin;
The heavy yoke of God, daily put on,
To endure all things and give back love again—
He has chosen the bush, its simpler cruelty,
Its certain peace. I, too, could break the snare,
Take the hatter's path, say no to God and men....
Yet from such an end, good Lord, deliver me.

My grandfather, riding down Araluen way,
A young man then—it is eighty years and more
Since the rocks of those wild hillsides shone for him
In the yellow sun, and the singing river ran
Clear over nuggets of gold—passed carelessly
The humpy hidden in vines from the bright day
And a hatter fired at him from the dark of the door.

Solemn thought—at least, to me, you may laugh if you will—
That if his aim had been better I should not be.
More solemn, that in the end, between man and man,
There is no choice but this: to love or kill.
From the blood of my brother, Lord, deliver me.

Another lived in the sandhills, a sea-lulled hollow,
And raised a sign to ward off peering eyes:
'Beware of the lion.' Any trick was fair against them
But I think he believed it, had seen at morning there
On the rippled beach, through the fine-pricked tracery
Of crab and bird, strange tracks he dared not follow
Or at twilight, when the silver dune-grass sighs
Had seen the tawny sand that slept all day
Warm and quiet, rise up now, move stealthily
About his hut. Still he cries to me, 'Beware!
Beware the beast that lurks along this way!'
From the claws of madness, Lord, deliver me.

And in the mountains behind Jamberoo,
The bush dead still at noon, clouds hanging low,
I came on a hut, close barred, the windows darkened,
On its door one word: 'Silence!' And all around
A hush so deep no sound, it seemed, could be
Unwelcome—the shriek of a black cockatoo
Though it boded storm, the hungry cry of a crow,
Even human speech, so rare in that lost place.
I did not knock; I had no wish to see
One who desired a silence more profound.
What hand would have opened to me there? What face?
From the love of death, dear Lord, deliver me.

Burragorang

Coming to the farm that winter afternoon
I thought they had all died or gone away.
The river-oaks were keening, the wild blew cold
Down the long valley between mountain walls,
One with its cliffs sunward and blazing gold
And one in dark-blue shade. Late in the day
It was, late in the season. I remember
One yellow wattle danced and did not care
If it never flowered again; but the gate hung wide
And in the growing crop the weeds stood high
And at the house a pane was cracked, a door

Groaned to the wind, shifting on broken hinges.
Then a voice spoke, and someone moved inside.
That was what frightened me. They still lived there
If you could call it living. I had passed by
The churchyard where the slanting sunlight shone
On crosses and green graves of the old settlers
But the tongue of Death clamoured more loudly here
Saying, Let the thistles grow, there will be no harvest.
Let the house fall, for all this will be gone
And the waters over it, within a year.

Long ago, before the wars and the time of fear
My mother came to the valley, down the track
From the King's Tableland, a wild steep way.
They found the river running swift and clear
And crossed it, laughing, on a borrowed horse,
But for the rest they walked, sixty odd miles,
And none too long; they were young and friends together,
The mountains lifted up their hearts all day—
At morning blue through rising mist, at noon
Purple as grapes beyond the sun-bleached corn,
And deepening through the hours in fold on fold,
The wall of shadow and the wall of light,
Till the great crags stood black against the stars.
No dream troubled her sleep of what would be,
How the kind homesteads sheltering them by night,
Farms and farmers, before her children were old,
Wives, sons, cattle, would vanish utterly
As the tribes that earlier yet melted away
In dusk of river-oaks, with the songs they sang
And their dances, leaving a little ash and silence
About the sacred stones of Burragorang.

Today the wind blew up from Burragorang,
At its touch I felt my life shudder and stir,
The whole fine framework of things known and done
Slip from its centre like a broken door,
Seeing how the world could be no more than this:
Song failed and fire dead, the work begun
And left unfinished because it is no use,
A weed-grown crop that will not come to reaping,
Winter evening closing in, the end sure.
And then the stubborn flame leaps in my blood
To think how even now, above the cold
Wind-ruffled water there, the mountains rise
Casting their glory on the desolate flood

That has drowned all the good years, strong as of old,
High and more fair than any earthly city,
The walls of sapphire, the towers of burning gold.

Lex Banning

Epitaph for a Scientist

He saw the skull within the looping
beauty of schematic atoms;
he feared, perhaps too much, the cultured virus
emergent in the figured formulæ;
he could not, with complete detachment,
watch the purity of higher mathematics
turn viper, cobra, mamba, fer de lance;
he looked too often on the jet-plane's
deadly loveliness: and shot himself.
He was, you might say, killed by implication.

Apocalypse in Springtime

So I was in the city on this day:
and suddenly a darkness
came upon the city like night,
and it was night;
and all around me, and on either hand,
both above and below me,
there was—so it seemed—a dissolving
and a passing away.

And I listened with my ears, and heard
a great rushing
as the winds of the world left the earth,
and then there was silence,
and no sound, neither the roar of the city,
nor the voices of people,
nor the singing of birds, nor the crying
of any animal;
for the world that was audible had vanished
and passed away.

And I stretched forth both my hands,
but could touch nothing,

neither the buildings, nor the passers-by,
neither could I feel
the pavement underneath my feet,
nor the parts of my body;
for the world that was tangible had vanished
and passed away.

And I looked around and about me,
and could see nothing,
neither the heavens, nor the sea, nor the earth,
nor the waters under it;
for the world that was visible had vanished
and passed away.

In my nostrils there was a fleeting
fume of corruption,
and on my tongue a dying taste
of putrefaction,
and then these departed, and there was nothing;
for the world that was scent,
and the world that was savour had vanished
and passed away.

And all around me, and on either hand,
both above and below me,
there was nothing, and before me and behind;
for all of the fivefold
worlds of the world had vanished
and passed away.

And all my possessions of pride
had been taken from me,
and the wealth of my esteem stricken,
and the crown of my kingdom,
and all my human glory,
and I had nothing, and I was nothing;
for all things sensible had vanished
and passed away.

And I was alone in nothing,
and stood at the bar
of nothing, was accused by nothing,
and defended by nothing,
and nothing deliberated judgment
against me.

And the arbitrament of the judgment
was revealed to me.

Then the nothing faded into nothing,
and that into nothing,

and I was alone in a darkness like night,
but it was not night;
then the darkness faded into darkness,
and that into darkness,
and there was no light—but only
emptiness,
and a voice in the void lamenting
and dying away.

From the Native Cat Song Cycle
The Great Beam of the Milky Way

(Aranda people, Central Australia)

The great beam of the Milky Way
Sends out flashes of lightning incessantly
The great beam of the Milky Way
Casts a flickering fire glow over the sky forever.
The great beam of the Milky Way
Gleams and shines forever.
The great beam of the Milky Way
Burns bright crimson forever.
The great beam of the Milky Way
Trembles with deep desire forever.
The great beam of the Milky Way
Quivers with deep passion forever.
The great beam of the Milky Way
Trembles with unquenchable desire forever.
The great beam of the Milky Way
Draws all men to itself by their forelocks.
The great beam of the Milky Way
Unceasingly draws all men, wherever they may be.

The tnatantja pole rises into the air,—
The great beam of the Milky Way.
The kauaua pole rises into the air,—
The great beam of the Milky Way.
The great beam of the Milky Way
Strips itself bare like a plain.

'How the pole of the Milky Way is drawing me to itself—
How my own pole is drawing me to itself!'

'How the pole of the Milky Way is drawing me to itself—
From what a far country it is drawing me to itself!'
'Let the Milky Way be tied around with many bands;
Let the dweller in the earth-hollow be tied around with many
     bands!'
'The pole of the Milky Way has drawn me irresistibly—
The dweller in the earth-hollow has drawn me irresistibly.'

The great beam of the Milky Way,
The dweller in the earth-hollow, is trembling with desire forever.

The narrowing sea embraces it forever,—
Its swelling waves embrace it forever.
The sea, ever narrowing, forever embraces it,—
The great beam of the Milky Way.
Its embracing arms forever tremble about it,—
The great beam of the Milky Way.
Set in the bosom of the sea it stands,
Reverberating loudly without a pause.
Set in the bosom of the sea it stands,
Sea-flecked with drifts of foam.
In the bosom, in the sea it stands,
Casting a flickering fire glow over the sky forever.

Let them sit down around the pole of the Milky Way,
Let them sit down around the dweller in the earth-hollow.
Around the pole of the Milky Way let them sit down,
Around the dweller in the earth-hollow let them sit down.
In their camp-hollow let them present gifts to each other,—
Let them sort out their bullroarers!

Translated by T.G.H. Strehlow

Geoffrey Dutton
A Finished Gentleman

'In the distant desert you unexpectedly stumble on a finished
gentleman.' Captain George Grey,
Journals of Two Expeditions of Discovery

Under the white silence of the great gumtree avenue
My parents taught me to be an English gentleman,
And a thousand galahs rose like petals thrown at the sunset,
Swearing like the native Australians they are. Bastards! Bastards!

Yet no one more legitimate than I, whose ancestors
Planted the trees and houses here where no one had planted
Even a seed, or penned a sheep, or dammed a creek.
No style grows out of nothingness, droughts and scabby sheep
Teach patience but not manners, and so it was 1900,
And the second generation, and there was Grandfather, gleaming,
The Squire of Anlaby, with a steam-yacht, R.Y.S.,
Fourteen gardeners, and silver-gilt candlesticks for the church he
    was building.

And so with Oxford, rowing, and maybe the Diplomatic in view,
I grew among grass-seeds and dust-storms and later, in the scent
Of the distillery wafting across the Eton of Corio Bay,
Being expert at coping with visiting Governors and their intolerable
    A.D.C.'s,
And their ladies (though once I shot one of these in the bottom with
    an arrow),
Could tell a Holland and Holland from a Greener, English cloth
    from Australian,
Knew the Wars of the Roses but had scarcely heard of Eureka,
Could decline Omnis Gallia into any number of parts,
And after chanting 'Alpha Beta Gamma Delta,
Knock a lady down and belt her', learned to read
In Greek the speech of an Athenian lawyer in a dispute over drains,
Though I knew nothing of Bligh or Macarthur, Parkes or Deakin,
Could tell you the agonies of Xenophon, Livingstone, and someone
    up the Amazon,
But nothing of Sturt down the Murray, or Eyre across the Nullarbor,
Knew the *Revenge* and the *Golden Hind*, but not *Sirius* or the
    Endeavour.

And yet, in the coach-house I ran my finger over the acetylene
    lamps
Of my father's 1908 Talbot, first car driven across Australia,
Walked through the mulgas my mother had brought back from the
    Territory,
Grilled chops on gum-sticks, caught yabbies, had the slippery
    bumps
Of a rabbit's guts often in my hand, loved Australia passionately
As did my father and mother in between reading
The Illustrated London News, The Cornhill, Britannia and *Eve.*

And what did it give me, to be an Austroenglish gentleman?
A torment of comparative values, nothing here so old, so rare,
So fine. Trivial despairs at people who drank sweet wine,
Sat on Genoa velvet, walked in square-capped shoes,

Talked of nothing but marks, furlongs, overs, of dagoes and reffos,
Of long-hairs and sissies, the wisdom of the ordinary, decent bloke.

Well, as I look back, I was indeed a finished gentleman.
Twenty years to learn to be one, twenty years and more
To learn what Jack or Mick knew all the time, that here
It is we live, unless we pretend, or run away.

But hold it! The galahs are thicker than they ever were,
Four thousand marvellous sunset flowers tumbling
On to the shredded upper stalks of the great white trees.
Bastards! Bastards! they scream. Yes, Jack and Mick
Were ignorant bastards in another way. Maybe they could whittle
Myall stockwhip handles and ride straight home through the maze
Of mallee, and roll their own and recite all of 'The Sick Stockrider',
But this landscape was not cleared by such sweet simplicities alone,
And their bright axes would bounce off the rubbery jungle
Of ideas never thought necessary in this innocent country.
And, educated down, I still know the world's crooked hours are
    different
From the hands around me, raising schooners at closing time.

Burning Off

We let fire rip, we blacken the pale-gold acres,
But being farmers, we do it cautiously,
Sneaking first by the red clods of the firebreak
With our back-burn, cautiously watching it with water,
Drawing safe rings around our sacred trees.

Then inside the windward fence, mooed at by the neighbour's cows,
We drag the bouncing rake with its flaring straw bundle
And little wisps of flame snuggle into the stubble
Not yet revealing their true hunger. For fire
Is passionate of all plants, and becomes them,
Furious as creepers, sullen as thistles,
And sows its seed like bees on the wind.

Just now the flames run forward like children
In spurts and zigzags, not staying to argue
With the indomitable green of summer-loving weeds
Left standing proudly, horrible horehound, splendid artichoke.

This fire may be a child, but it does not tell its secrets,
How if it jumped the firebreak it would grow up a giant
Leaping from treetops, exploding the safest green.

For fire incorporates all the elements,
It makes air visible and angry,
It advances lashing like rain, there's a shield of shimmer
Before it streaming like a fish-shop window,
Its black clouds loom full as thunderstorms.

It flushes out earth's secrets, some of them terrible,
As once a black tomcat with its fur on fire
Sprang over two firebreaks and lit the neighbour's paddock.
Now a quail rockets lurchingly off
Pursued by a slanting goshawk,
And four shrewd whistling eagles hang high
Waiting for delicacies, grilled mouse or lizard.

It is all over, Earth exhausted sighs
In little volcanoes of smoking dung.
Fire seems to be a barren passion, uniting all,
Leaving nothing behind to fill the absence of all colour.

But watch the tractor going home across the blackness,
That instant trail the evidence of unharmed earth
Ready for rain, and the first, most vivid green
Springing electric from the paddock's night.

Fish Shop Windows

My favourite view of people
Is from behind a fish shop window.
They are thinking of something deeper
Than dollars. Up from below

Snapper tug at their dreams,
Their shells open like scallops,
And a groper in blue chasms
Haunts a cave in the reef rocks.

It is night-fishing in summer, and the whitebait
Stream like stars from the darkness
To the lamp, where the stab of the trident
Earths the spark of the garfish.

They remind me of a film, Russian,
Taken by a hidden camera
Beside a Leonardo, Mother
and Child; the love and wonder

Of a straight soldier with his bride.
The tears of a peasant woman,

And a girl with a baby, eyes wide
For herself and Mary in common.

How long are the lines hauled
By fisherman and Leonardo? ·
From the same black depths trawled,
Gemfish and grenadier,

Madonna and her baby,
Swim in those rapt faces,
The child of the sea's cradle,
Ichthyos, the sign of Jesus.

Dorothy Hewett

In Moncur Street

It's twenty years ago and more
since first I came to Moncur Street,
and lived with Aime and Alf among
the boarders on the second floor.

The stew was burnt, the budgie sang,
as Aime walked home the church-bells rang,
she banged the pots, ring-ding-a-ding,
she'd lost at Housie in the Spring.

But Sammy Smiles (that lovely man),
still visits her on Saturday,
Beat runs a book, and little Fay
whines in the stairwell every day
                    in Moncur Street
                    in Moncur Street.

Alf rose before the morning light,
and took a chopper in his hand;
he chopped and chopped in Oxford Street.
'Alf runs around without his head,
he's like a chook,' said Aime
                    and sighed
for Sammy Smiles (that lovely man),

and Sunny Corner where she played
at 'Ladies' in the willow's shade.
At sunset by the empty shops
they swapped their dusty acid drops:

who lounges in the crystal air,
but Sammy Smiles, with marcelled hair!

I woke up in the darkest night,
knew all the world had caught alight.
The surf was pounding in the weather,
and Moncur Street was mine forever.
The little bat upon the stair
came out and flapped: it wasn't there,

the snapshot album turned and turned,
the stew caught fire, the budgie burned,
the pensioners at drafts and dreams,
picked bugs between their trouser seams.

And Sammy Smiles (that lovely man!)
and Aime and Alf and little Fay,
and Beat and Bert and betting slips,
the man I loved, the child I bore,
have all gone under Bondi's hills,
and will return here nevermore,
                    in Moncur Street
                    in Moncur Street.

Alf starts up his steady snore,
'Them Bondi sandhills paved with gold,
I could've bought them for a song.'
The home brew bursts behind the door.
Aime lies upon her back and sighs:
'In Sunny Corner by the store
Sam kissed me once when I turned four.'

Dreams are deep and love is long:
she turns upon her other side.

Nancy Keesing

A Queer Thing

Wasn't this a queer thing? I stood with your mother
At mid-day in her hot, still, polished kitchen
Preparing a mountain of ordinary bread
And wholesome butter. Where can be more quiet
Than stifling Brisbane noon? I heard a tread
On the wooden stairs—a slow, deliberate climb.

'They're back early, and lunch not ready in time,'
I said. And she: 'It's my husband, ten years dead;
He often calls when all the house is empty.'
'But I am here.' 'You are not,' your mother said.

Reverie of a Mum

Here let me rest me feet!
The boys have gone to try
The shooting gallery, the girls
Are off to prospect for boys.
Here let me drop me bundle
Of bulging sample bags,
I was lucky to find this seat
In the shade, away from the noise.
We come on an èarly bus,
We seen the fruit and the jams,
The handicrafts and the flowers,
Bacon like marble, hams
Big as the side of a palace,
Wheels of golden cheese
Like off one of them olden chariots
From them spectacle films. And Jeez
The cakes done in royal icing!
There was one great galleon—clever!
All icing: sails, decks, ropes,
You could hardly credit. I never
Seen such a cake. It took me
Back to that Spanish Gob
Off the Yankee ship in the war years
And a lying, promising slob
He turned out. Now my eldest, Marie,
Her eyes are funny but,
As hot and black as that little goat's feet
And she's a stuck-up slut.
She's got ideas of the stage now
Since we let her stay on at school
And they chose her for Cleopatra
In that play they done by the pool
In Hyde Park there. It's queer,
You marry and you settle down
Like they say, and you never think
Of the boys who done you brown.
Jeez! When I think of me hair

With frangipanis, and a high
Pompadour style—I used to swing
As if I'd of owned the sky.
There was that night in the Dom.
(I'd tan my kids if they went
Where we used … war-time, but,)
And all around was the scent
Of gabardine coats and hair-oil
And frangipani in the night—
Whispers, rustling, and the giggles
When one Yank shinned up the light
And took out the bulb…. My God
But those boys knew what they wanted.
The whole world turned on velvet.
The sky came down and panted
Like a dog that's been running. Them fig-trees
Rattled that sky in their leaves.
Well, it isn't like that when you settle.
If my hubby knew! Funny though, I grieves
For them boys. Just sometimes. And the Vice Squad
Out on their surf-boat boots
Treading the Moreton Bay fig-leaves….
Fig-leaves! We up and we scoots
With my Spanish Yank having trouble,
It was funny giving coppers the slip,
The frangipani night laughed with us
As we dodged through the 'Loo to their ship.
We all took a sickie from the factory
When they sailed—'See youse again….'
Then the grey boys in jungle green come home.
And *that* was my castle in Spain.

Eric Rolls

Bamboo

I sing the quality of bamboo.
I cut a small cane and make a pipe to sing the quality of bamboo.
Bamboo is the comb in my hair.
Bamboo cut off my foreskin and pierced my nose.

I wore a toucan's wing-bone in my nose that time I hid in bamboo
And leapt from it to kill my first man.
I wrapped his head in banana leaves and bore it on a bamboo pole.

Bamboo stores the water I drink.
Bamboo made the spears I learnt to fish with.
Bamboo is the floor I stand on
Or a knife that will skin a cuscus.
Bamboo are the poisoned needles I push into the mud
So that an enemy treads himself to death.

Bamboo is the cage the foolish fish cannot swim out of
And the prop which holds open the snarc for the careless wallaby.
Bamboo is a platform for the dead.

Bamboo is all these things and more
Yet one man may carry a bundle of bamboo
As big as a log of pine which many men will strain under.

Bamboo are the rafters of the house I must soon build.
Bamboo are the anklets which Sauri wears on her right leg
And the bracelets which encase her left arm
From wrist to elbow.
Bamboo strings the cowrie shells which are part of her price
And bamboo will prod the five pigs I must drive to her father's
    house.

What is that which is round and hollow like bamboo?
It is as small as the pipe I play
Or as big as my water-carrier.
It is a water-carrier.
It bears two waters
And of one of these Sauri will drink so deeply
Her belly will swell rounder than a bundle of water-carriers.

But I sing of the quality of bamboo.

Rain Forest

It is difficult to keep sane in it.
Nothing is seen to move
Yet there is a noise of moving
And of closing in.
Water drips
And vines shift on trunks
Stealthily as garrotters.
One is grateful for sudden normal sounds—
The flapping of a goura pigeon
Or the braying of a bird of paradise.

The floor cannot be trusted.
The live root and the rotting log
Are covered with the same brown slime.
One must maintain faith
In the existence of the earth
Or lose the courage to walk.
Overhead is a blankness of green.
Leaves belong nowhere.
They have been spilled out of infinity
And hang as nebulous as fog.

Leeches draw attention to the lack of colour.
The thighs of the police-boys run with blood.
It is necessary to keep sane.
One might well open a vein
And decorate a bower for dying
With red rosettes.

Dog Fight

Inside
The wireless is irritable with static.
The relieving sig. turns down the volume
And strains to hear his call sign.

Outside
The relieved sig. is relieving himself.
He is trying to piss his full name in the dust.
He has been saving up for hours.
He has to concentrate to control the flow.

Overhead
Two Zeros come out of cloud.
They hope to beat the Lightnings to the take-off.

On the ground
The Lightnings are already rolling.
They have been forewarned.
The cloud was too far from the strip anyway.
One Zero turns and bolts.
The other climbs
To try to stop the Lightnings getting above him.

The sig. has finished his first Christian name neatly.
He takes two paces right and begins a capital W.

A morse signal offers an urgent weather report.
Two spotters jam each other in plain language

Reporting the Zeros
Which had already been reported.

The Lightnings are too fast for the Zero.
Only one goes in to attack.
It seems so easy:
There is a burst of smoke
And the Zero begins a slow spiral to ground.
It looks like a feather coming down.
You think about reaching up to catch it.

The sig. finds it harder near the end.
The pressure is dropping
And there is a T to be crossed.

The message about the Zeros
Has been relayed to Port Moresby
And the sig. has got down the coded weather report.
He is sending R for received.

There is another little burst of smoke
As the Zero hits the ground.
Two drops of urine
Make sufficient dent in the dust
To dot a final I.
A morse signal sounds the end of transmission.

W.N. Scott

Bundaberg Rum

God made the sugar cane grow where it's hot
and teetotal abstainers to grow where it's not.
Let the sin bosun warn of perdition to come,
we'll drink it and chance it, so bring on the rum.

Bundaberg rum, overproof rum,
will tan your insides and grow hair on your bum.
Let the blue ribbon beat on his old empty drum
or his waterlogged belly, we'll stick to our rum.

These are men who drink it, men indeed,
of the bushranging oldtime hairynecked breed.
They shave with their axes, they dress in old rags,
they feed on old boots, they sleep on old bags.

Dull care flies away when their voices resound
and the grass shrivels up when they spit on the ground.

When they finally die and are sunk in the clay
their bodies are pickled and never decay.
On the morning of Judgement, when the skies are rolled back
they'd stroll from their graves up the long golden track
and their voices will echo throughout Kingdom Come
as they toast the archangels in Bundaberg rum.

David Rowbotham

The Bus-stop on the Somme

Even if you are killed, you die.
My uncle, who survived the Somme,
Died waiting at a bus-stop, as though,
In the repeated boom
Of mud-wheeled guns, he had at last
Been accurately shelled,
Shattered by a deep unburied blast.
He died as though he had been killed.
Others at the bus-stop heard the boom.
It cannoned the act of living through
The trenches where we bury the Somme:
And the others waiting knew
The dead go on, don't stop at death
But go as my uncle did
That day on the accurate mud-wheeled earth,
When the shrapnel missed the others' head.

The Cliff

I remember the old joke,
Which isn't a joke now,
Of the drunk fallen at right-angles into the gutter.
Clinging with his finger-tips
To the edge, as to a cliff's edge,
He said to the passer-by,
'For Christsake help me up,
I can't hang on much longer.'
Laughter. Have another grog.
But life, not grog,
Tripped him into that illusion

With the boot of its reality.
You do not imagine cliffs unless there are cliffs.
You do not imagine death unless there is death.
Had I now been the passer-by
I would have helped him up
And turned away in horror at the rescue.
Had I been the drunk
I would have sat down at the edge of the cliff
And stared without a word of thanks,
Into the gutter.

Nebuchadnezzar's Kingdom-Come

Daniel in the lion's den
Confounded those who cast him in,
The priests and kings of Babylon
So like the beasts he prayed among.

The god of the land they stole him from
In Nebuchadnezzar's kingdom-come
Gave him mercy and release,
And undefiled he found his peace.

Now in the dens of Babylons
That lure or steal believing ones,
With tawny thoroughness the beasts
Spring as the prides of kings and priests.

For in the present kingdoms-come
The ancient gods are rendered dumb;
To be devoured is Daniel's doom,
And mauled angels stumble home.

Now prayer provokes the savagery
Which priests and kings in beasts set free
On captured innocence in the den,
Confounding deities, not men.

John Rowland

Canberra in April

Vast mild melancholy splendid
Day succeeds day in august chairmanship

Presiding over autumn. Poplars in valleys
Unwavering candleflames, balance over candid
Rough-linen fields, against a screen of hills

Sending invisible smokes from far below
To those majestic nostrils. A Tuscan landscape
On a larger scale; for olives eucalypts
In drifts and dots on hillheads, magpie and crow
For field-birds, light less intimate, long slopes stripped

Bare of vine or village, the human imprint
Scarcely apparent; distances immense
And glowing at the rim, as if the land
Were floating, like the round leaf of a water-plant
In a bright meniscus. Opposite, near at hand,

Outcrops of redbrick houses, northern trees
In costume, office-buildings
Like quartz-blocks flashing many-crystalled windows
Across the air. Oblivious, on their knees,
Of time and setting, admirals pick tomatoes

In their back gardens, hearty
Bankers exchange golf-scores, civil servants
Their after-office beers; the colony
Of diplomats prepares its cocktail parties
And politicians their escape to Melbourne.

This clean suburbia, house-proud but servantless
Is host to a multitude of children
Nightly conceived, born daily, riding bikes,
Requiring play-centres, schools and Progress
Associations: in cardigans and slacks

Their mothers polish kitchens, or in silk
White gloves and tight hats pour each other tea
In their best china, canvassing the merits
Of rival plumbers, grocers, Bega milk
And the cost of oil-fired heating or briquettes.

To every man his car, his wife's on Thursday
Plus one half-day she drops him at the office
(Air murmurous with typewriters) at eight-forty
To pick him up for lunch at home; one-thirty
Sees the streets gorged with his return to duty

And so the year revolves; files swell, are closed
And stored in basements, Parliaments adjourn
And reassemble, speeches are made and hooted.

Within the circle of the enfranchised
These invite those and are themselves invited,

At formal dinners, misprints of the *Times*
Compete with anecdotes of Rome or Paris
For after all, the capital is here.
The general populace sprays its roses, limes
Its vegetable patch and drinks its beer:

Golf at the weekend, gardening after five,
Indoor bowling, TV day and night
Lunchtime softball, shopping late on Friday—
As under glass the pattern of the hive
Swarms in its channels, purposeful and tidy,

Tempting romantics to dismay and spite,
Planners to satisfaction, both to heresy.
For everywhere, beyond the decent lawn
A visionary landscape wings the sight
And every child is rebel and unknown.

So long as daylight moon, night laced with stars
And luminous distance feed imagination
There's hope of strangeness to transcend, redeem
Purblind provincial comfort: summer fires
Under prodigious smokes, imperious storms,

A sense of the pale curving continent
That, though a cliché, may still work unseen
And, with its script of white-limbed trees, impart
A cure for habit, some beneficent
Simplicity or steadiness of heart.

Miidhu

War Dance

Tabi (occasional song) in Njamal, Pilbara region, North West Australia

I saw a band of warriors coming on
Parrying their shields
    and massing for attack.
I saw their headgear-sticks spreading
in wide array

When they rushed forward, and when surging back
I saw their emu feather tails sticking out behind them.

Translated by Georg von Brandenstein

Pudjipangu

Aeroplane

Tabi in Njamal

The ground drops back
Where the dust still whirls
Billowing from crusty Murgana strip.
Up and up the magician makes the slim body climb steadily.
Up and up twists the engine's song
Till the double wings are level in the windless sky.
Then the clever pilot tunes the engine down,
And aims quietly on high,
     It dwindles in the west.

Translated by Georg von Brandenstein

Smiler Narautjarri

The Witch Doctor's Magic Flight

Tabi in Ngarla

Out of the crowd, I have seen you travelling south of Pardoo,
High up and out of human sight,
In full regalia. Your outstretched arm bears the mystic torch,
Which is rope of twisted hair,
Beaming, sparkling far ahead,
Called the Murdinara with the gleaming point.
Clearly I see you there aloft,
Your halo burning around your crown.
So you travel, Parraruru.

Translated by Georg von Brandenstein

From the Dulngulg song cycle

Sunrise Sequence

Mudbara people, Wave Hill, Northern Territory

The day breaks—the first rays of the rising Sun, stretching her
    arms.
Daylight breaking, as the Sun rises to her feet.
Sun rising, scattering the darkness; lighting up the land ...
With disc shining, bringing daylight, as the birds whistle and call ...
People are moving about, talking, feeling the warmth.
Burning through the Gorge, she rises, walking westwards,
Wearing her waist-band of human hair.
She shines on the blossoming coolibah-tree, with its sprawling
    roots,
Its shady branches spreading ...

Translated by Ronald M. Berndt

Song Cycle of the Moon-Bone

Wonguri-Mandjigai people, north-eastern Arnhem Land

1

The people are making a camp of branches in that country at
    Arnhem Bay:
With the forked stick, the rail for the whole camp, the Mandjigai
    people are making it.
Branches and leaves are about the mouth of the hut: the middle is
    clear within.
They are thinking of rain, and of storing their clubs in case of a
    quarrel,
In the country of the Dugong, towards the wide clay-pans made by
    the Moonlight.
Thinking of rain, and of storing the fighting sticks.
They put up the rafters of arm-band-tree wood, put the branches on
    to the camp, at Arnhem Bay, in that place of the Dugong ...
And they block up the back of the hut with branches.
Carefully place the branches, for this is the camp of the Morning-
    Pigeon man,
And of the Middle-of-the-Camp man; of the Mangrove-Fish man;
    of two other head-men,

And of the Clay-pan man; of the Bayini-Anchor man, and of the
     Arnhem Bay country man;
Of the Whale man and of another head-man: of the Arnhem Bay
     Creek man;
Of the Scales-of-the-Rock-Cod man; of the Rock Cod man, and of
     the Place-of-the-Water man.

2

They are sitting about in the camp, among the branches, along the
     back of the camp:
Sitting along in lines in the camp, there in the shade of the paperbark
     trees:
Sitting along in a line, like the new white spreading clouds;
In the shade of the paperbarks, they are sitting resting like clouds.
People of the clouds, living there like the mist; like the mist sitting
     resting with arms on knees,
In here towards the shade, in this Place, in the shadow of paper-
     barks.
Sitting there in rows, those Wonguri-Mandjigai people, paperbarks
     along like a cloud.
Living on cycad-nut bread; sitting there with white-stained fingers,
Sitting in there resting, those people of the Sandfly clan ...
Sitting there like mist, at that place of the Dugong ... and of the
     Dugong's Entrails ...
Sitting resting there in the place of the Dugong ...
In that place of the Moonlight Clay Pans, and at the place of the
     Dugong ...
There at that Dugong place they are sitting all along.

3

Wake up from sleeping! Come, we go to see the clay pan, at the
     place of the Dugong ...
Walking along, stepping along, straightening up after resting:
Walking along, looking as we go down on to the clay pan.
Looking for lily plants as we go ... and looking for lily foliage ...
Circling around, searching towards the middle of the lily leaves to
     reach the rounded roots.
At that place of the Dugong ...
At that place of the Dugong's Tail ...
At that place of the Dugong; looking for food with stalks,
For lily foliage, and for the round-nut roots of the lily plant.

4

The birds saw the people walking along.
Crying, the white cockatoos flew over the clay pan of the Moon-
light;
From the place of the Dugong they flew, looking for lily-root food;
pushing the foliage down and eating the soft roots.
Crying, the birds flew down and along the clay pan, at that place of
the Dugong ...
Crying, flying down there along the clay pan ...
At the place of the Dugong, of the Tree-Limbs-Rubbing-Together,
and of the Evening Star.
Where the lily-root clay pan is ...
Where the cockatoos play, at that place of the Dugong ...
Flapping their wings they flew down, crying, 'We saw the people!'
There they are always living, those clans of the white cockatoo ...
And there is the Shag woman, and there her clan:
Birds, trampling the lily foliage, eating the soft round roots!

5

An animal track is running along: it is the track of the rat ...
Of the male rat, and the female rat, and the young that hang to her
teats as she runs,
The male rat hopping along, and the female rat, leaving paw-marks
as a sign ...
On the clay pans of the Dugong, and in the shade of the trees,
At the Dugong's place, and at the place of her Tail ...
Thus, they spread paw-mark messages all along their tracks,
In that place of the Evening Star, in the place of the Dugong ...
Among the lily plants and into the mist, into the Dugong place, and
into the place of her Entrails.
Backwards and forwards the rats run, always hopping along ...
Carrying swamp-grass for nesting, over the little tracks, leaving
their signs.
Backwards and forwards they run on the clay pan, around the place
of the Dugong.
Men saw their tracks at the Dugong's place, in the shade of the trees,
on the white clay;
Roads of the rats, paw-marks everywhere, running into the mist.
All around are their signs; and there men saw them down on the
clay pan, at the place of the Dugong.

6

A duck comes swooping down to the Moonlight clay pan, there at
    the place of the Dugong ...
From far away. 'I saw her flying over, in here at the clay pan ...'
Floating along, pushing the pool into ripples and preening her
    feathers.
'I carried these eggs from a long way off, from inland to Arnhem
    Bay ...'
Eggs, eggs, eggs; eggs she is carrying, swimming along.
She preens her feathers, and pulls at the lily foliage,
Drags at the lily leaves with her claws for food.
Swimming along, rippling the water among the lotus plants ...
Backwards and forwards: she pulls at the foliage, swimming along,
    floating and eating.
This bird is taking her food, the lotus food in the clay pan,
At the place of the Dugong there, at the place of the Dugong's
    Tail ...
Swimming along for food, floating, and rippling the water, there at
    the place of the Lilies.
Taking the lotus, the rounded roots and stalks of the lily; searching
    and eating there as she ripples the water.
'Because I have eggs, I give to my young the sound of the water.'
Splashing and preening herself, she ripples the water, among the
    lotus ...
Backwards and forwards, swimming along, rippling the water,
Floating along on the clay pan, at the place of the Dugong.

7

People were diving here at the place of the Dugong ...
Here they were digging all around, following up the lily stalks,
Digging into the mud for the rounded roots of the lily,
Digging them out at that place of the Dugong, and of the Evening
    Star,
Pushing aside the water while digging, and smearing themselves
    with mud ...
Piling up the mud as they dug, and washing the roots clean.
They saw arm after arm there digging: people thick like the mist ...
The Shag woman too was there, following up the lily stalks.
There they saw arm after arm of the Mandjigai Sandfly clan,
Following the stalks along, searching and digging for food:
Always there together, those Mandjigai Sandfly people.
They follow the stalks of the lotus and lily, looking for food.

The lilies that always grow there at the place of the Dugong ...
At that clay pan, at the place of the Dugong, at the place of the lilies.

8

Now the leech is swimming along ... It always lives there in the
    water ...
It takes hold of the leaves of the lily and pods of the lotus, and
    climbs up on to their stalks.
Swimming along and grasping hold of the leaves with its head ...
It always lives there in the water, and climbs up on to the people.
Always there, that leech, together with all its clan ...
Swimming along towards the trees, it climbs up and waits for
    people.
Hear it swimming along through the water, its head out ready to
    grasp us ...
Always living here and swimming along.
Because that leech is always there, for us, however it came there:
The leech that catches hold of those Mandjigai Sandfly people ...

9

The prawn is there, at the place of the Dugong, digging out mud
    with its claws ...
The hard-shelled prawn living there in the water, making soft little
    noises.
It burrows into the mud and casts it aside, among the lilies ...
Throwing aside the mud, with soft little noises ...
Digging out mud with its claws at the place of the Dugong, the place
    of the Dugong's Tail ...
Calling the bone bukalili, the catfish bukalili, the frog bukalili, the
    sacred tree bukalili ...
The prawn is burrowing, coming up, throwing aside the mud, and
    digging ...
Climbing up on to the lotus plants and on to their pods ...

Note: *bukalili* means sacred epithet, power name

10

Swimming along under the water, as bubbles rise to the surface, the
    tortoise moves in the swamp grass.
Swimming among the lily leaves and the grasses, catching them as
    she moves ...

Pushing them with her short arms. Her shell is marked with designs,
This tortoise carrying her young, in the clay pan, at the place of the
     Dugong ...
The short-armed Mararba tortoise, with special arm-bands, here at
     the place of the Dugong ...
Backwards and forwards she swims, the short-armed one of the
     Mararba, and the Dalwongu.
Carrying eggs about, in the clay pan, at the place of the Dugong ...
Her entrails twisting with eggs ...
Swimming along through the grass, and moving her patterned shell.
The tortoise with her young, and her special arm-bands,
Swimming along, moving her shell, with bubbles rising;
Throwing out her arms towards the place of the Dugong ...
This creature with the short arms, swimming and moving her shell;
This tortoise, swimming along with the drift of the water ...
Swimming with her short arms, at the place of the Dugong ...

11

Wild-grape vines are floating there in the billabong:
Their branches, joint by joint, spreading over the water.
Their branches move as they lie, backwards and forwards,
In the wind and the waves, at the Moonlight clay pan, at the place of
     the Dugong ...
Men see them lying there on the clay pan pool, in the shade of the
     paperbarks:
Their spreading limbs shift with the wind and the water:
Grape vines with their berries ...
Blown backwards and forwards as they lie, there at the place of the
     Dugong.
Always there, with their hanging grapes, in the clay pan of the
     Moonlight ...
Vine plants and roots and jointed limbs, with berry food, spreading
     over the water.

12

Now the New Moon is hanging, having cast away his bone:
Gradually he grows larger, taking on new bone and flesh.
Over there, far away, he has shed his bone: he shines on the place of
     the Lotus Root, and the place of the Dugong,
On the place of the Evening Star, of the Dugong's Tail, of the
     Moonlight clay pan ...
His old bone gone, now the New Moon grows larger;
Gradually growing, his new bone growing as well.

Over there, the horns of the old receding Moon bent down, sank
   into the place of the Dugong:
His horns were pointing towards the place of the Dugong.
Now the New Moon swells to fullness, his bone grown larger.
He looks on the water, hanging above it, at the place of the Lotus.
There he comes into sight, hanging above the sea, growing larger
   and older ...
There far away he has come back, hanging over the clans near
   Milingimbi ...
Hanging there in the sky, above those clans ...
'Now I'm becoming a big moon, slowly regaining my roundness' ...
In the far distance the horns of the Moon bend down, above
   Milingimbi,
Hanging a long way off, above Milingimbi Creek ...
Slowly the Moon Bone is growing, hanging there far away.
The bone is shining, the horns of the Moon bend down.
First the sickle Moon on the old Moon's shadow; slowly he grows,
And shining he hangs there at the place of the Evening Star ...
Then far away he goes sinking down, to lose his bone in the sea;
Diving towards the water, he sinks down out of sight.
The old Moon dies to grow new again, to rise up out of the sea.

13

Up and up soars the Evening Star, hanging there in the sky.
Men watch it, at the place of the Dugong and of the Clouds, and of
   the Evening Star.
A long way off, at the place of Mist, of Lilies and of the Dugong.
The Lotus, the Evening Star, hangs there on its long stalk, held by
   the Spirits.
It shines on that place of the Shade, on the Dugong place, and on to
   the Moonlight clay pan ...
The Evening Star is shining, back towards Milingimbi, and over the
   Wulamba people ...
Hanging there in the distance, towards the place of the Dugong,
The place of the Eggs, of the Tree-Limbs-Rubbing-Together, and of
   the Moonlight clay pan ...
Shining on its short stalk, the Evening Star, always there at the clay
   pan, at the place of the Dugong ...
There, far away, the long string hangs at the place of the Evening
   Star, the place of the Lilies.
Away there at Milingimbi ... at the place of the Full Moon,
Hanging above the head of that Wonguri tribesman:
The Evening Star goes down across the camp, among the white gum
   trees ...

Far away, in these places near Milingimbi ...
Goes down among the Ngurulwulu people, towards the camp and
    the gum trees,
At the place of the Crocodiles, and of the Evening Star, away
    towards Milingimbi ...
The Evening Star is going down, the Lotus Flower on its stalk ...
Going down among all those western clans ...
It brushes the heads of the uncircumcised people ...
Sinking down in the sky, that Evening Star, the Lotus ...
Shining on to the foreheads of all those head-men ...
On to the heads of all those Sandfly people ...
It sinks there into the place of the white gum trees, at Milingimbi.

Translated by Ronald M. Berndt

Francis Webb

End of the Picnic

When that humble-headed elder, the sea, gave his wide
Strenuous arm to a blasphemy, hauling the girth
And the sail and the black yard
Of unknown *Endeavour* towards this holy beach,
Heaven would be watching. And the two men. And the earth,
Immaculate, illuminant, out of reach.

It must break—on sacred water this swindle of a wave.
Thick canvas flogged the sticks. Hell lay hove-to.
Heaven did not move.
Two men stood safe: even when the prying, peering
Longboat, the devil's totem, cast off and grew,
No god shifted an inch to take a bearing.

It was Heaven-and-earth's jolting out of them shook the men.
It was uninitiate scurf and bone that fled.
Cook's column holds here.
Our ferry is homesick, whistling again and again;
But still I see how the myth of a daylight bled
Standing in ribbons, over our heads, for an hour.

Airliner

I am become a shell of delicate alleys
Stored with the bruit of the motors, resolute thunders

And unflagging dances of the nerves.
Beneath me the sad giant frescoes of the clouds:

Towerings and defiles through intense grey valleys,
Huge faces of kings, queens, castles—travelling cinders,
And monuments, and shrouds.
A fortress crammed with engines of warfare swerves

As we bank into it, and all the giant sad past
Clutches at me swimming through it: here
Is faith crumbling—here the engines of war
In sleek word and sad fresco of print,
Landscapes broken apart; and here at last
Is home all undulant, banners hanging drear
Or collapsing into chaos, burnt.
And now we are through, and now a barbarous shore

Grimaces in welcome, showing all its teeth
And now the elder sea all wrinkled with love
Sways tipsily up to us, and now the swing
Of the bridge; houses, islands, and many blue bushlands come.
Confine me in Pinchgut, bury me beneath
The bones of the old lag, analyse me above
The city lest I drunkenly sing
Of wattles, wars, childhoods, being at last home.

Wild Honey

Saboteur autumn has riddled the pampered folds
Of the sun; gum and willow whisper seditious things;
Servile leaves now kick and toss in revolution,
Wave bunting, die in operatic reds and golds;
And we, the drones, fated for the hundred stings,
Grope among chilly combs of self-contemplation
While the sun, on sufferance, from his palanquin
Offers creation one niggling lukewarm grin.

But today is Sports Day, not a shadow of doubt:
Scampering at the actual frosty feet
Of winter, under shavings of the pensioned blue,
We are the Spring. True, rain is about:
You mark old diggings along the arterial street
Of the temples, the stuttering eyeball, the residue
Of days spent nursing some drugged comatose pain,
Summer, autumn, winter the single sheet of rain.

And the sun is carted off; and a sudden shower:
Lines of lightning patrol the temples of the skies;

Drum, thunder, silence sing as one this day;
Our faces return to the one face of the flower
Sodden and harried by diehard disconsolate flies.
All seasons are crammed into pockets of the grey.
Joy, pain, desire, a moment ago set free,
Sag in pavilions of the grey finality.

Under rain, in atrophy, dare I watch this girl
Combing her hair before the grey broken mirror,
The golden sweetness trickling? Her eyes show
Awareness of my grey stare beyond the swirl
Of golden fronds: it is her due. And terror,
Rainlike, is all involved in the golden glow,
Playing diminuendo its dwarfish rôle
Between self-conscious fingers of the naked soul.

Down with the mind a moment, and let Eden
Be fullness without the prompted unnatural hunger,
Without the doomed shapely ersatz thought: see faith
As all such essential gestures, unforbidden,
Persisting through Fall and landslip; and see, stranger,
The overcoated concierge of death
As a toy for her gesture. See her hands like bees
Store golden combs among certified hollow trees.

Have the gates of death scrape open. Shall we meet
(Beyond the platoons of rainfall) a loftier hill
Hung with such delicate husbandries? Shall ascent
Be a travelling homeward, past the blue frosty feet
Of winter, past childhood, past the grey snake, the will?
Are gestures stars in sacred dishevelment,
The tiny, the pitiable, meaningless and rare
As a girl beleaguered by rain, and her yellow hair?

Vincent Buckley

Ghosts, Places, Stories, Questions

Ghosts, places, stories, questions:
the new life I demand of my bones.
Lights and darknesses about the hardening
mind. Beneath such questioning
I cling to the notion of the paradigm:
Troilus keeps his pale eyes even in the bronze-green
thickets of summer 1965.

There are myths living
even in our way of walking.
I sometimes think they look at me in the street,
'there's the man who came back from hell
with no Beatrice, and no hope of heaven';
or, with the touch of scholarship,
quantum mutatus ab illo,
discourteous, abrupt, with staring eyes,
hardly the same man.
Myths, certainly, but also
matters of sheer observation.
Life is a history of absences
and unprepared returns. Arcadia
cannot darken the shallow eyes.

And what was it at Thermopylae,
each watching his neighbour's bones
dissembling the death they had to pass through,
the Spartans thought, before they took their spears
and pressed their bodies to the brief defile?

The combing of hair soothed their hands,
but what rested their spirits, the three hundred
'picked men, of middle years, with living sons'
who oiled their bodies for battle as for the games?
There was surely
a revelation in those bodies, and the wind
carried their whispering to the watching hills
as the Persians came forward on their dead.

Where is the pride in losing
so predictably and so completely?
These have no relevance for me. Why then
do I think of them whenever
I tune my muscles for the strait of death?

Yes, and ghosts: how close to the marrow
can they come? At night I feel them
like drops of sweat running under the skin,
chill with myth; till I half expect my friends
('and at his coming the hair of their heads stood up')
to cry out, What is that inside you
that makes your shadow flicker on the grass?
Heatless and demanding presences,
I will endure you; but you shall not be my gods.
Arcadia cannot give you flesh; heaven
cannot make you more than spies of hell.

And what friends are they who, sweat-mastered
at the thunder-fanned and burning bush,
will walk more cautiously saying, Oh, that
is the God you belong to; that the woman.
Oh, that. When the bush turns to ashes
I still must touch my forehead to the ground,
because its radiance is in my body.

Gods are vulgar. So are journeys.
Ulysses sails to find a speck of blood
in the newly woven pattern; Orpheus
goes down to find mortality a blessing.
I walk beside these fires because I must,
in pain and trembling sometimes thanking God
for what they give me, the few poems
that are the holy spaces of my life.

Alan Riddell

At the Hammersmith Palais ...

the woman is using a handkerchief
to wipe the sweat from under her armpits.
She has just finished dancing a medley
of Latin-American numbers, and is as well known
in the home
for her
intolerance towards children
as
on the floor
for
the sustained violence of her terpsichorean expertise.

Grace Perry

Time of Turtles

One time
Columbus said this island and the seas
were full of tortoises
living rocks swimming in troughs of sun.

Always after recognition—annihilation—
the turtles have been gone two centuries.

For us it is not difficult
to imagine wind among almond trees
soft eggs buried in moonwhite sand
flotillas of greenbacks slicing faceless water
long days of old men grazing on sea grass
evening homecoming rituals within the reef
and those less fortunate
skimming up the dusk
striking the widemeshed flags
that change direction with each lurch of tide.
All night the struggle the chest tightening
and in the silver daylight not yet death
hauled up armoured in amber and gold
to hang like some condemned god by the arms
hot metal entering the hands the feet.
Out of their element
they were not offered the alternative
to suffocate facedown by their own weight.

We keep our mouths shut breathing infrequently
and unobserved squeeze tears from hopeless eyes.
Wedged like turtles we submit
upon our backs our heads on pillows.
Slowly we lose our seabright colours
and wait to die.

John Philip

Manly Ferry

The bridge is certainly the simplest answer,
with the lanes and the warehouses and the pubs
and the tramlines crouching behind the piers
like children playing hidey. But the ferry
is a spinster clad in green, timidly passing
the filthy ships lounging like doorway drunks
and dribbling rust and water from the scuppers.

Around the harbour, the white landlubber masts
and the fat old guns play sailors, and
the onlooker houses crane their necks.
On past the broken boxes and the vector

flight of gulls to where the little lighthouses
have donned their motley and their long noses
and wait for laughter and the children's pennies.

On past the thin sea-scarecrow buoys to where the cliffs
corniced by the waves leaping like their own dolphins,
support the green entablature of boys and dogs and grass.

Robin Gurr

Creation

God breathed,
and living man was given power
to scan, with perplexed rapture,
the completeness of creation:

and search into its mysteries,
and taste them,
and know them,
so they become a portion
of his living tissue,
glorifying it.

Of his own self he does nothing.
Nor does the Father do, for
already He has done.

R. F. Brissenden

Verandas

For Monique Delamotte

They don't build houses like that any more—not
With verandas the way they used to: wide verandas
Running round three sides of the place, with vines
Growing up the posts and along the eaves—passion-
fruit, grape, wistaria—and maiden-hair fern in pots,
And a water-bag slung from the roof in the shade with the water
Always cool and clean and tasting of canvas.

Comfortable worn cane chairs and shabby lounges,
Beds for the kids to sleep in, a ping-pong table,

A cage for the cockatoo the boys had caught
Twenty years ago by the creek, a box for the cat
And a blanket for the old blind dog to doze on—
There was room for everything and everybody,
And you lived out on the verandah through the summer.

That's where the talking happened—over a cup
Of tea with fresh sponge cake and scones, or a drink
(A beer for the men and a shandy for the girls)
On Sunday afternoons or warm dry evenings:
Do you remember, it always began, do you
Remember?—How it was Grandpa who forged the hook
They used to catch the biggest cod in the Lachlan—

And didn't we laugh when Nell in her English voice
Said: 'Hark at the rain!'—And who was the bloke that married
Great-aunt Edith and drove the coach from Bourke?
And weren't they working up Queensland way in that pub
Frank Gardiner ran, and nobody twigged who he was
Even though they called him the Darkie—and they never
Found it, did they, the gold: nobody found it.

And they never will—just like that reef at Wyalong:
Nothing but quartz and mullock. But the fishing
Was good in those days, Tom, they'd say: remember
The ducks, the way we'd watch them in their hundreds
Flying along the billabong at sunset?
You won't see that any more—they're all fished out,
The water-holes, and the mallee-fowl have gone.

And in the dark and under a rising moon
The yarning voices would drift and pause like a river
Eddying past the ears of the drowsing children
As they settled down in their beds and watched the possums
Playing high in the branches—and when they opened
Their eyes it would somehow always be morning with sunlight
Flooding level and bright along the veranda.

Ray Mathew

Seeing St. James's

Moving from the bus at the Loop it's possible suddenly
To stop and look up, and seeing St. James's (its spire

Go upwards, green before buildings, orbed and crossed
So truthfully that the sky's not roof but azure)
Suddenly to believe yourself standing in Moscow or some such
Imagined city of churches, and standing not lost.

You cross the road to examine the suddenness closely,
Though never believing the moment could hold itself longer,
And the cabs become silence-of-rubber agreeable monsters knelt
Politely to let you pass them (the one horn-clanger
Is part of the procession); they belong to the time. And you're not
Merely in Sunny Sydney, with Courtesy Week half-felt,

But some other place, stranger, among strangers, strangely;
The whole thing mysterious, different, momentary, tourist.
Yes! now you are tourist: you can distinguish the odd,
And the people don't touch you, you are not harassed
By them, you can take them as quietly as you would architecture
And see each in his turn: you can behave like God.

And just for that moment of sleight-of-hand acceptance clearly
You've been walking another planet; and if you were judged,
Why no one could hurt you,—not while you lived it. And,
Clearly, your self has been different, has not judged
Another: those whom you saw were those whom you saw and
So understood, not trying to understand.

Poem in Time of Winter

My head is unhappy,
My heart is like lead,
My chilblains are itchy,
I'd rather be dead.
My heart's like a horse-shoe,
And I never have luck,
But I don't give a damn,
I don't give a river,
I don't give a duck.

My girl's got a temper,
Her mother's a dog,
The pictures cost money,
She eats like a hog.
We ought to be kissing,
And I haven't the pluck,
But I don't give a damn,
I don't give a river,
I don't give a duck.

My friends are dying,
The happy are sad,
Are twisted with illness,
The good go mad.
I go to the church,
And they ask for the buck,
But I don't give a damn,
I don't give a river,
I don't give a duck.

The rain keeps raining,
The wet comes down,
It's so grey and horrible
To wait and drown
That I'd buy a car,
Or I'd thumb a truck—
But I don't give a damn,
I don't give a river,
I don't give a duck.

One Day

The sailor leaning on the rail thinks of home
As the boy leaning on the gate thinks of the sea,
For nothing that we have now in the mind
Is like what one day we will have to be.

And I that am your lover boy, your game,
Will one day hate and hurt you to be free,
For nothing that I have now as my self
Is like what one day I will have to be.

And all I have now as my very form
Will one day be as alien as that sea,
And the Australia that is now my heart
Will that day hold my heart away from me.

Bruce Beaver

Letters to Live Poets V

Three images of dying stick in my mind like morbid transfers
of the other side of life. First, a cow on my uncle's farm
had broken a leg calving. My uncle held a shot-gun to its poll

and fired both barrels. The dogs ran in to lick the blood welling from
the nostrils. We hauled the carcase behind a wooden sled to the burial ground,
a small island of dark trees centring a wide field.
On the way the top of the cow's head came loose and left a trail.
Heifers followed us and shrieked with eyes rolling at the blood.
We piled the heavy carcase high with old tyres and lit the pyre.
Sleeping and waking I saw the shattered head for many years to come.

The second incident occurred years later in a goods yard.
Near to a storage shed I came across a group of cats surrounding
such a scrawny bag of fur and bone it wasn't a bit funny.
This cat had eaten poisoned corn or a rat poisoned.
At first I'd thought it starving and had brought bacon from the galley.
The other cats moved back from me while I offered it the bacon.
It stretched out a claw at the meat, hooking it towards its mouth
then died before it bit. I watch the twitch of life pass up its spine
centre, then go out like a light snuffed. Its eyes had closed before
its life. Blinded. Starved with poison. The other cats began to move
away. I stood and looked and knew mortality like an old wound.

The third time clawed me in a room filled with smoke and proof-readers.
The air clanged with advertisements read aloud like crazy psalms.
A man was dying at his desk. His heart was broken and the kiss
of life rejected. As he died his fellow workers chanted on
and he was left with a handkerchief over his face where he lay dead
in his chair in a room full of the loud chanting of the living.
No one pleaded for silence while he remained or when he was gone stayed
their tongue. I read on then, knowing not a minute's silence will
the rest of us get. When they rang his ninety-year-old mother all she asked for
were his keys. Tomorrow we'll talk of life and sundry other things.

The Entertainer

The sand modeller always began by heaping the sand
into large and small mounds. From these he shaped
by patting and moulding with palms of hands and wooden paddle
the forms of single beings or groups of people and symbols.
A most unsubtle artist. All his themes were as obvious

and known as intimately to his audience as
a Greek tragedy or comedy to Attic
onlookers, almost participants. Most of his hungry-eyed watchers
were children—I was a child then and venerated his homely
skill—I speak of a time when there were still familial
arts: the orchestra of parents, sons and daughters;
the singing, acting and recitations at home or on visits
to uncles, aunts and cousins. My own parents were
participants in amateur theatricals.
One day as a small child I'd 'made up' myself as a clown
with white, red and blue greasepaint from their kit.
I'd forgotten what I'd done and went on an errand to
the nearest grocer to be met with much hilarity
and questioning. I'd fled in shame, empty handed.
The sand modeller's colours were as straightforward as my parents'
make-up kit—pink and white water colours for flesh,
brown and black for hair, blue and brown for eyes,
white, red and something like purple for robes in folds.
He applied painstakingly layer on layer of swiftly absorbed
colour on the already dampened surface
of, perhaps, Britannia with shield sword and lion
or dog, maybe, if it came out that way. Or if
it was during the Christmas holidays, a holy family
(the earthly one) of Joseph, Mary, Jesus complete
with crib (dark brown) a calf and a sheep (dark brown and grey)
and once with three crowned kings (two pink and white, one black).
As he modelled, adults and children would quietly gather,
the parents giving their children pennies to toss on to
the handkerchief he'd spread at the base of his inventions.
Once, and once only, a gang of brutes had pelted his art
with penny pieces harsh and hard-edged as bullets,
slicing into and through the forms and serene faces
(I saw later something like them in the frescoes
of Giotto), scattering sand and bleeding colours over
his tableaux. Quietly he'd set to repairing the damage
then he'd spoken briefly with his sympathizers—
the only time I ever heard him say a word
(his thanks for the safely tossed coins was underwritten).
He seemed surprised at such an unnecessary display
of vandalism. His innocence in face of such
premeditated anti-art—was he not
an outright challenge to the youths (and had I not
imagined the effect of a stone in the face of Joseph,
Jesus even, Mary perhaps)—his innocence
was almost unbelievable. It seemed he belonged

to a time when no child did such things, at least openly.
While I had only a year before tossed into the maw
of a Punch and Judy tent a gramophone arm and headpiece
found in a bin, (Was not Punch a homicidal
maniac?) and had fled behind a nearby pine
to watch the puppet master emerge, rubbing his head
and accusing the seated children, who all pointed towards me
as I fled into another time, another season.
So up to the years of war the sand modeller returned.
With each season the tableaux simpler, less worked over,
the colours paler as though his eyes only retained
the memoried intensity of hues. The cloth
covered ever more sparsely with scattered copper coins.
The last groupings vaguely patriotic and
given over to stilted studies of the Royal
Family. Quite safe from harm. The vandals had enlisted
or absconded. The entire length of beach was suddenly
strung with rolls of barbed wire rusting overnight,
the sea-wall topped by another barbed wire fence with iron
stanchions. Though all knew the Japanese guns would aim
beyond us for another twenty miles then range
back to pulverize us as an afterthought.
For several years I took to modelling ships in sand
with a friend between the barbed beach and the wired wall.
One of our friends was hospitalized with tetanus from
the wire. Then we had grown up suddenly and saw
the beach revert to the use of nominally pacific
bathers. Nobody noted the non-appearance of
the sand modeller. Nor did I before I began
to record the scenes of my childhood, then there came obliquely
the blank looks and wholly calm, coloured faces
of this and that grouping of his repertoire,
no larger than life yet agelessly impermanent
as the paradox itself, the brief and everlasting
human story written on the lapsing sands.

Peter Porter

Soliloquy at Potsdam

There are always the poor—
Getting themselves born in crowded houses,
Feeding on the parish, losing their teeth early

And learning to dodge blows, getting
Strong bodies—cases for the warped nut of the mind.
The masterful cat-o'-nine-tails, the merciful
Discipline of the hours of drill—better
Than being poor in crowded Europe, the swan-swept
Waters where the faces dredge for bread
And the soggy dead are robbed on their way to the grave.
I can hear it from this window, the musket-drill
On the barrack square. Later today I'll visit
The punishment block. Who else in Europe
Could take these verminous, clutching creatures
And break them into men? What of the shredded back
And the broken pelvis, when the side-drum sounds,
When the uniformed wave tilts and overwhelms
The cheese-trading burghers' world, the aldermanic
Principalities. The reformers sit at my table,
They talk well but they've never seen a battle
Or watched the formed brain in the flogged body
Marching to death on a bellyful of soup and orders.
There has to be misery so there can be discipline.
People will have to die because I cannot bear
Their clinging to life. Why are the best trumpeters
Always French? Watch the west, the watershed
Of revolution. Now back to Quantz. I like to think
That in an afternoon of three sonatas
A hundred regiments have marched more miles
Than lie between here and Vienna and not once
Has a man broken step. Who would be loved
If he could be feared and hated, yet still
Enjoy his lust, eat well and play the flute?

What I Have Written I Have Written

It is the little stone of unhappiness
which I keep with me. I had it as a child
and put it in a drawer. There came
a heap of paper to put beside it,
letters, poems, a brittle dust
of affection, sallowed by memory.

Aphorisms came. Not evil, but
the competition of two goods
brings you to the darkened room.
I gave the stone to a woman
and it glowed. I set my mind

to hydraulic work, lifting words
from their swamp. In the light from the stone
her face was bloated. When she died
the stone returned to me, a present
from reality. The two goods
were still contending. From wading pools
the children grew to darken
gardens with their shadows. Duty
is better than love, it suffers no betrayal.

Beginning again, I notice
I have less breath but the joining
is more golden. There is a long way to go,
among gardens and alarms,
after-dinner sleeps peopled by toads
and all the cries of childhood.
Someone comes to say my name
has been removed from the Honourable
Company of Scribes. Books in the room
turn their backs on me.

Old age will be the stone and me together.
I have become used to its weight
in my pocket and my brain.
To move it from lining to lining
like Beckett's tramp,
to modulate it to the major
or throw it at the public—
all is of no avail. But I'll add
to the songs of the stone. These words
I take from my religious instruction,
complete responsibility—
let them be entered in the record,
What I have written I have written.

On First Looking into Chapman's Hesiod

For 5p at a village fête I bought
Old Homer-Lucan who popped Keats's eyes,
Print smaller than the Book of Common Prayer
But Swinburne at the front, whose judgement is
Always immaculate. I'll never read a tenth
Of it in what life I have left to me
But I did look at *The Georgics*, as he calls
The Works and Days, and there I saw, not quite

The view from Darien but something strange
And balking—Australia, my own country
And its edgy managers—in the picture of
Euboean husbandry, terse family feuds
And the minds of gods tangential to the earth.

Like a Taree smallholder splitting logs
And philosophizing on his dangling billies,
The poet mixes hard agrarian instances
With sour sucks to his brother. Chapman, too,
That perpetual motion poetry machine,
Grinds up the classics like bone meal from
The abattoirs. And the same blunt patriotism,
A long-winded, emphatic, kelpie yapping
About our land, our time, our fate, our strange
And singular way of moons and showers, lakes
Filling oddly—yes, Australians are Boeotians,
Hard as headlands, and, to be fair, with days
As robust as the Scythian wind on stone.

To teach your grandmother to suck eggs
Is a textbook possibility in New South Wales
Or outside Ascra. And such a genealogy too!
The Age of Iron is here, but oh the memories
Of Gold—pioneers preaching to the stringybarks,
Boring the land to death with verses and with
Mental Homes. 'Care-flying ease' and 'Gift-
Devouring kings' become the Sonata of the Shotgun
And Europe's Entropy; for 'the axle-tree, the quern,
The hard, fate-fostered man' you choose among
The hand castrator, kerosene in honey tins
And mystic cattlemen: the Land of City States
Greets Australia in a farmer's gods.

Hesiod's father, caught in a miserable village,
Not helped by magic names like Helicon,
Sailed to improve his fortunes, and so did
All our fathers—in turn, their descendants
Lacked initiative, other than the doctors' daughters
Who tripped to England. Rough-nosed Hesiod
Was sure of his property to a slip-rail—
Had there been grants, he'd have farmed all
Summer and spent winter in Corinth
At the Creative Writing Class. Chapman, too,
Would vie with Steiner for the Pentecostal
Silver Tongue. Some of us feel at home nowhere,
Others in one generation fuse with the land.

I salute him then, the blunt old Greek whose way
Of life was as cunning as organic. His poet
Followers still make me feel déraciné
Within myself. One day they're on the campus,
The next in wide hats at a branding or
Sheep drenching, not actually performing
But looking the part and getting instances
For odes that bruise the blood. And history,
So interior a science it almost seems
Like true religion—who would have thought
Australia was the point of all that craft
Of politics in Europe? The apogee, it seems,
Is where your audience and its aspirations are.

'The colt, and mule, and horn-retorted steer'—
A good iambic line to paraphrase.
Long storms have blanched the million bones
Of the Aegean, and as many hurricanes
Will abrade the headstones of my native land:
Sparrows acclimatize but I still seek
The permanently upright city where
Speech is nature and plants conceive in pots,
Where one escapes from what one is and who
One was, where home is just a postmark
And country wisdom clings to calendars,
The opposite of a sunburned truth-teller's
World, haunted by precepts and the Pleiades.

R.A. Simpson

All Friends Together

A survey of present-day Australian poetry

Charles and Bruce, Geoff and Ron and Nancy
May publish books this year: some hope they won't.
Tom and Les, Robert, Nan and John—
We live our lives quietly using words
And write of dragons and birds: we are our critics.
Asia, of course, is waiting, but somewhere else.

Max and Rod and Les, and someone else,
Are writing well, and so are Charles and John.
Who would have thought they knew so many words.

Who would have thought this country had such critics.
Mary may come good some day—she won't,
Of course. And yet we may all hear from Nancy.

Nan and Don are better now than Nancy.
Robert, too, writes well for all the critics—
And did you see that latest thing by John?
Nothing queer—the 'queers' are somewhere else
Painting paintings. And all our poems won't
Be anything but normal. We know our words

And buy anthologies to read our words—
David, Robert, Ron and Alex and Nancy.
And did you choke upon that thing by John?
Wasps and grass, magpies and something else
Have often made us write: I'm sure they won't
Seem overdone; they always please the critics.

The critics know (of course, we are the critics)
The qualities of Max and Geoff and Nancy.
And so we carry on with Charles and John,
Tom and Alex, Robert, and someone else—
Big thoughts about a myth, and simple words.
Perhaps you think we'll stop, and yet we won't.

Sometimes I think we'll stop, and yet we won't—
John and David, Bruce and Ron and Nancy.
Robert and Les, Rod and someone else,
Who love the words of friends, and please the critics
With neat anthologies and simple words
Geoff and Max, Charles and Gwen and John.

Sometimes I think that Nancy, Don and John
And someone else are neither poets nor critics:
They won't like that. We only have our words.

Bruce Dawe

At Shagger's Funeral

At Shagger's funeral there wasn't much to say
That could be said
In front of his old mum—she frightened us, the way
She shook when the Reverend read
About the resurrection and the life, as if

The words meant something to her, shook, recoiled,
And sat there, stony, stiff
As Shagger, while the rest of us, well-oiled,
Tried hard to knuckle down to solemn facts,
Like the polished box in the chapel aisle
And the clasped professional sorrow, but the acts
Were locked inside us like a guilty smile
That caught up with us later, especially when
We went round to pick up his reclaimed Ford,
The old shag-wagon, and beat out the dust
From tetron cushions, poured
Oil in the hungry sump, flicked the forsaken
Kewpie doll on the dash-board,
Kicked hub-caps tubercular with rust.

The service closed with a prayer, and silence beat
Like a tongue in a closed mouth.
Of all the girls he'd loved or knocked or both,
Only Bev Whiteside showed—out in the street
She gripped her hand-bag, said, 'This is as far
As I'm going, boys, or any girl will go,
From now on.'

                        Later, standing about
The windy grave, hearing the currawongs shout
In the camphor-laurels, and his old lady cry
As if he'd really been a son and a half,
What could any of us say that wasn't a lie
Or that didn't end up in a laugh
At his expense—caught with his britches down
By death, whom he'd imagined out of town?

Suburban Lovers

Every morning they hold hands
on the fleet diesel that interprets them
like music on a roller-piano as they move
over the rhythmic rails. Her thoughts lie
kitten-curled in his while the slats of living
racket past them, back yards greying
with knowledge, embankments blazoned
with pig-face whose hardihood
be theirs, mantling with pugnacious flowers
stratas of clay, blank sandstone, sustaining them
against years' seepage, rain's intolerance.

Each evening they cross the line
while the boom-gate's slender arms constrain
the lines of waiting cars.
Stars now have flown up out of the east.
They halt at her gate. Next-door's children
scatter past, laughing. They smile. The moon,
calm as a seashore, raises its pale face.
Their hands dance in the breeze blowing
from a hundred perfumed gardens. On the cliff of kissing
they know this stillness come down upon them like a cone.
All day it has been suspended there, above their heads.

Elegy for Drowned Children

What does he do with them all, the old king:
Having such a shining haul of boys in his sure net,
How does he keep them happy, lead them to forget
The world above, the aching air, birds, spring?

Tender and solicitous must be his care
For these whom he takes down into his kingdom one by one
—Why else would they be taken out of the sweet sun,
Drowning towards him, water plaiting their hair?

Unless he loved them deeply how could he withstand
The voices of parents calling, calling like birds by the water's edge,
By swimming-pool, sand-bar, river-bank, rocky ledge,
The little heaps of clothes, the futures carefully planned?

Yet even an old acquisitive king must feel
Remorse poisoning his joy, since he allows
Particular boys each evening to arouse
From leaden-lidded sleep, softly to steal

Away to the whispering shore, there to plunge in,
And fluid as porpoises swim upward, upward through the dividing
Waters until, soon, each back home is striding
Over thresholds of welcome dream with wet and moonlit skin.

Evan Jones

Study in Blue

In his blue suit, an Oxford Standard Authors
Caught in his hand, I watch him passing by:

Nothing could be more sober, more discreet.
It's me O Lord—or rather, it is I.

A Dream

The train was going downwards very slowly
In a deep cutting; outside it was raining
Lightly, and I just could see the blur
Of heavy broken strata in the clay.
I was caught there, caught in the corridor
Trying to move, but it was desperate trying
Because it was so narrow and so crowded.
    Those people seemed to speak another language,
Standing with sullen faces or with stupid
Meaningless smiles, totally unresponsive
As I pushed through, shouting and elbowing.
    I knew the train was going down to Hell.

The Point

The point, I imagine, is
not to learn to expect
betrayal, self-deceit, lies
however thick they collect
in the cul-de-sac of one's days,
half-noticed, half-numbered, half-checked:
but rather to learn to praise
fidelity, trust and love
which in their modest ways
continue to be and move
(however mocked, however derided,
however difficult, indeed, to prove),
utterly undivided—
if inarticulate or mute,
still mortally decided.

Neither fashionable nor astute
this point to take to heart:
merely final and absolute:

without it no people, no life, no art.

Philip Martin

Tongues

The speaker is a woman whose husband has died after a long illness

Three days before he died the hospital called me:
He was unconscious, sinking. I went at once.
His face was closed, remote against the pillows.
I sat by the window. The leaves outside were moving.
Suddenly he began to speak. I thought
He was asking me for something, but before
I could cross the room I saw how fixed his eyes were,
And then realised: he was speaking verse,
But in a language neither of us knew.
Not English certainly, not German, and not Russian,
His family's language from the thirteenth century,
Though he had never learnt it.
                                        He continued
For a full minute, measured, authoritative.
I picked up the rhythm: four stresses to each line.
I recall only the opening words of one:
Alléndam tatsú ...
                              He seemed to be speaking
Past me, his eyes directed to the window,
Yet also to me. For thirty lines or more
He spoke, and then, as if the poem was finished,
Fell silent and lay back.
                                    Two hours after,
He spoke once more, in German, using my name.
His eyes were softened and again familiar.
We did not refer to the poem, then or later.
But though he was conscious almost until he died
He took no leave of me. And I think now
The poem was his taking-leave.
                                          His doctor,
Who speaks German fluently, believes
That what I heard was German, much distorted.
I am certain it was not: the voice was too
Distinct, unfaltering.
                                His father said,
'Ah yes. Of course I need not remind you, we
Are an old family. It was our forebears speaking.'

C.J. Koch

The Boy who Dreamed the Country Night

'Yes,' said the boy, 'first come the gum-tree crowds,
These are the first things you see, waving their spars
And black heads on the sky, to the meaningless stars.

'Yes,' said the boy, 'the stars have no meaning,
You must keep close to the ground.
And so let me hug the ground as I go:
The cold roads, led by the song of phone wires
        to the terrible countryside,
The road's cool stones, the poor pebbles, that
        prick my eyes with tears,
The nested lonely grass by the roadside, calling
        someone to make his bed there,
The lights of a suburb across the river—lost!
We are in the country.

 A mailbox, a track, a house;
Night roosts on the woodpile of the timid weatherboard
        farmhouse
Where an old man and his wife are sitting by the fire.
They stay by the fire, these old country people;
They never walk out where the secret trees wait;
Only the tender, dry grass has love in it,
And need not be feared. Sweet grass! Sweet to sleep there,
But who would ever dare, watched by the pitiless
        black-skinned trees,
And the land's cold eye?

'In the brown-smelling country bedroom,' said the boy,
'There is something old and dread; some sorrowing disease
The last century left, haunting dead flowers
Of the wallpaper here, whistling softly
In the washstand's fat white china jug.
But the country daughter doesn't seem to know of it,
Standing in her chaste white nightgown:
Her calm and cow-deep eyes look nowhere I can see,
And the dead years don't haunt her because she belongs to them;
Her long brown hair she brushes down before the wardrobe mirror
Is ancient hair; Grandma's hair, secret, let down only here.'

Shelly Beach

His bare feet warmed by the thick black dust,
His legs softly whipped by the tussock grass,
The boy came down to the inlet.
He was alone here and had never come before
To such a silent place.

In this forgotten ring of land
Sentineled with grey-gum corpses,
The dry grass was careless of its own soft death,
And the banks at the water's edge watched him sullenly;
They were ill with an illness that was very old.

The aboriginals had camped here, he was told,
The dead and gone Tasmanian dark men.
Now nothing moved but a heat-dance
On the miles of the opposite shore,
And the flat, timid water made the only sound,
Softly, very softly, licking the shells
Of the dead-white elbow of Shelly Beach.

His feet were guilty on the shells. The only smells
Were the smells of sickness:
Even the sun in the harsh, fringing grass
Made a yellow smell of decay.
And when an idiot sea-bird screeched across the bay
The boy believed the sound had made a curse,
Jarring on the piles of broken shells.

Vivian Smith

At an Exhibition of Historical Paintings, Hobart

The sadness in the human visage stares
out of these frames, out of these distant eyes;
the static bodies painted without love
that only lack of talent could disguise.

Those bland receding hills are too remote
where the quaint natives squat with awkward calm.
One carries a kangaroo like a worn toy,
his axe alert with emphasized alarm.

Those nearer woollen hills are now all streets;
even the water in the harbour's changed.
Much is alike and yet a slight precise
disparity seems intended and arranged—

as in that late pink terrace's façade.
How neat the houses look. How clean each brick.
One cannot say they look much older now,
but somehow more themselves, less accurate.

And see the pride in this expansive view:
churches, houses, farms, a prison tower;
a grand gesture like wide-open arms
showing the artist's trust, his clumsy power.

And this much later vision, grander still:
the main street sedate carriages unroll
towards the tentative, uncertain mountain:
a flow of lines the artist can't control—

the foreground nearly breaks out of its frame
the streets end so abruptly in the water …
But how some themes return. A whaling ship.
The last natives. Here that silent slaughter

is really not prefigured or avoided.
One merely sees a profile, a full face,
a body sitting stiffly in a chair:
the soon-forgotten absence of a race …

Album pieces: bowls of brown glazed fruit …
I'm drawn back yet again to those few studies
of native women whose long floral dresses
made them first aware of their own bodies.

History has made artists of all these
painters who lack energy and feature.
But how some gazes cling. Around the hall
the pathos of the past, the human creature.

Early Arrival: Sydney

Red cockatoo crests caught on coral-trees:
my Sydney emblems. Dragging the land in view
our ship hauls glass and concrete on its side
as gulls fly up and snatch and scream and glide
away on a sea smeared with a trace of blue.

The neons flicker and the skyline wakes.
The orange suburbs float through miles of calm;
a pastel-coloured terrace shades its slope.
While five gulls fight for nothing on a rope,
the breeze picks out a single listless palm.

The city's like a room far undersea
with locked arcades where shadow-waves subside.
Grey windows bend great cloud-shapes as they pass.
Beyond these tiles, tunnels, iron, glass,
the flat waters of green inlets ride
where all the folded yachts are chained away.

But here the huge hotels still sway in space
with the exactness of a foreign place.

Tasmania

Water colour country. Here the hills
rot like rugs beneath enormous skies
and all day long the shadows of the clouds
stain the paddocks with their running dyes.

In the small valleys and along the coast,
the land untamed between the scattered farms,
deconsecrated churches lose their paint
and failing pubs their fading coats of arms.

Beyond the beach the pine trees creak and moan,
in the long valley poplars in a row,
the hills breathing like a horse's flank
with grasses combed and clean of the last snow.

Fay Zwicky

Reckoning

Whom have We next? (His syntax is
perfect). This one is due for what
there is called joy.
                      I alone know
the span of her schooling.
Who else needs to know?
None but I, the Omnipotent.
Under my hat will I keep it
(vernacular master).

Her sullen

green fires will I spring
unburden her airs
allow time to pass
and in My pain's darkness
trample her glass.

Chris Wallace-Crabbe

The Secular

However you look at it,
The abundant secular,
How splendid it all appears
Shifting and coruscating
All over and everywhere,
All at once, repeatedly,
In little waves of motion
And stubbornly tangible.

Look, I grant all that you say:
Whoever the creator
He brutally botched the job,
But how tough his furniture
Really is made, piece by piece!
I jump on his solid stones
Or dance on these rustling fields
And hear the sap leap in trees
Already marked out for death.

Sporting the Plaid

Renowned as Black Geordie
my Arbroath grandfather
sprang fully armed from the same ten years

which threw up Hardy, James and Furphy:
no wonder I dote on their humour,
that scathing irony.

A burly snob, he hadn't a clue
what to do with his sepoys
till the Raj wiped out his commission

leaving him a helluva lot
of other irons in his furnace,
his friends reputedly Brunner & Mond,

César Franck, Anatole France
and Milan's grandiloquent 'Mr Green'
whose arias he continued to adore.

Blown to Australia, the old buck founded
a blague of Caledonian societies,
tatty diamond mines and a second family

with a blonde Highland schoolie from Cork,
spieling his impossible tales
of clan exploits

along the brown Jumna, on blue high seas,
in a Boxer Rising where
Crabbe's roughriders exerted

their mongoloid talents
ensuring the flood of opium
for a smoky god and fleshpink empire.

I suspect you of being a shit
but in stiff, perfect photographs
magnificent beyond belief

on the bridge between dandy and warlord.
The whisky fed your moustaches,
your children adoring you,

scared stiff, bloodthirsty, tribal.
When you were half-seas-over, roaring under the stars,
'I could break that cabhorse's neck

with one blow of the heel o' my hand',
you were all huff and puff, a bolt of plaid
woven out of dropped names.

The Shape-Changer

The first day he was travelling in Asia,
the next day he flew the flight of a wedge-tailed eagle,
the next day he was the gusting wind,
the next a bright campfire,
the next day he thought of St Kilda on those open, drifting,
    sleazy summer nights,
the next day he was a seal, big-eyed and sleeky-brown,

the next day the little cousin of Death
and the next a writhing snake
or an ancient painted clock with two pewter soldiers to
    strike the hours,
the next day he stood with all the workers, shoulder to shoulder,
the next day he grew like a tree, covered with sunlight,
the next he was black swimming off Elwood under the stars,
    many years ago,
the next day he was a yellowish lion
and the next the sandy, howling wind.
Being Proteus, he never dreamed at all.

David Malouf

The Year of the Foxes

When I was ten my mother, having sold
her old fox-fur (a ginger red bone-jawed
Magda Lupescu
of a fox that on her arm played
dead, cunningly dangled
a lean and tufted paw)

decided there was money to be made
from foxes, and bought via
the columns of the *Courier Mail* a whole
pack of them; they hung from penny hooks
in our panelled sitting-room, trailed from the backs
of chairs; and Brisbane ladies, rather
the worse for war, drove up in taxis wearing
a G.I. on their arm
and rang at our front door.

I slept across the hall, at night hearing
their thin cold cry. I dreamed the dangerous spark
of their eyes, brushes aflame
in our fur-hung, nomadic
tent in the suburbs, the dark fox-stink of them
cornered in their holes
and turning.

        Among my mother's show pieces—
Noritaki teacups, tall hock glasses
with stems like barley-sugar,
goldleaf *demitasses*—

the foxes, row upon row, thin-nosed, prick-eared,
dead.
      The cry of hounds
was lost behind mirror glass,
where ladies with silken snoods and finger-nails
of chinese laquer red
fastened a limp paw;
went down in their high heels
to the warm soft bitumen, wearing at throat
and elbow the rare spoils
of '44; old foxes, rusty red like dried-up wounds,
and a G.I. escort.

Guide to the Perplexed

As unpredictable as picnic weather, blue
eyes shine from the heads of perfect bullies,
angels turn away, the Golden Casket's drawn, for no
good reason a terminal illness is arrested. This
too a sort of gift—to be dealt thirteen
trumps, a full hand of masterpieces. Oil-fields
sleep for centuries under the camel
kingdoms. Horses are bred that carry algebra
north to solve the dreams of planet-watchers. Iron
weapons in the right hand, and a syntax
equal to the decisions that must be taken,
means more and faster highways, bigger
battles, further provinces to rule,
a land the delta floods and seed that makes
us more aggressive forebears. There is Justice
too of course; and solemnly we work
towards it. But luck comes undeserved as this world's
free and final grace. Though someone somewhere always
pays, we praise it, wishing at each season,
our friends, in life, in love, the lucky break.

Margaret Scott

Portrait of a Married Couple

Terentius Neo and wife. Their oval eyes
swim like a train of fish across the wall.
His, being upturned slightly at the corners,

seem a little uncertain of their course.
He's swarthy, heavy-featured, spruced up
with gleaming linen and laundered chin,
hair clipped short over nape and jug-handle ears,
like a boxer trying to breathe in a boiled shirt,
an upstart living down barbarian blood.
He's anxious and sullen,
his mouth unsure of how to keep a pose
and not much helped by the scroll he has to hold
gripped in his labourer's paw like a stick of bread.
But his wife is at home with her elegant little stylus
carefully pressed as though in thought to the lips.
Tablets, curls and toga are suitably modish.
Not vain so much as sure of what life owes her—
Terentius Neo must have been very rich.
But when Vesuvius blew its top
he would have blundered about
smashing in doors and heaving at fallen pillars.
She, outraged at such a disruption of her day,
would have packed all the jewels and accounts,
then sent, too late, for her litter.

Barry Humphries

('Edna Everage')

Edna's Hymn

Recitative:
When I get home from a day's shopping in a city street,
I pop on the kettle, though I'm nearly dropping on my feet—
Make a nice cup of tea.
Then I switch on my favourite channel,
It's the best time for me as I flick off my flyaway panel.
When I get home from a treat at a flesh-and-blood theatre—
If you call it a treat peering up and down each street for a meter—
I think of old songs and the memories they bring back,
While my thoughtful Norm helps me off with my left and right
     sling-back.
And I think of old songs from old shows as I powder my nose,
And I think of a dear old hymn that time will never dim for me
Before I met my Norm it was the only hymn for me.

Chorus:
All things bright and beautiful, all creatures great and small,
All things wise and wonderful, Australia has them all:
Our famous ballerinas, Joan Sutherland their star,
Our Hoover vacuum cleaners, our Cadbury's chocolate bar,
A cloth all Persil snowy for Austral picnic spread,
Where hums the humble blowie and beetroot stains the bread.

All things bright and beautiful—Pavlovas that we bake,
All things wise and wonderful—Australia takes the cake.
Our great big smiling beaches, the smell of thick Kwik Tan,
Our lovely juicy peaches that never blow the can,
Our gorgeous modern cities so famed throughout the earth,
The Paris end of Collins Street, the Melbourne end of Perth.

All things bright and beautiful—though cynics sneer and plot,
All things wise and wonderful—Australia's got the lot!
The Farex that we scrape off those wee Australian chins,
The phenol that we sprinkle inside our rubbish bins,
Our plate-glass picture windows, venetians open wide—
In the land where nothing happens, there's nothing much to hide.

All things bright and beautiful—
Our wonderful wealth of natural mineral resources.
All things wise and wonderful—
And our even more wonderful wealth of different brands of tomato
    sauces.

Coda:
Australia is a Saturday with races on the trannie;
Australia is the talcy smell of someone else's granny;
Australia is a kiddie with zinc cream on its nose;
Australia's voice is Melba's voice—it's also Normie Rowe's;
Australia's famous postage stamps are stuffed with flowers and
    fauna;
Australia is the Little Man who's open round the corner.
Australia is a sunburnt land of sand and surf and snow;
All ye who do not love her—ye know where ye can go.

Rodney Hall

Journey

The knife like a precious bond
quivering between his arm, my heart—

in the strangerface I read
dark hatreds personal as touch.

This is ritual, there's no disorder
all belongs. I might discover
how the human sacrifice could yearn
to accept the journey of his murder.

My shirt already snagged
on the waxy blade, frightened, courteous, I
turn to other passengers, lurching dolls
in the shuttered prison of a Cairo bus

and I'm reminded of a Queensland mission
potbellied elders nodding in the dust
victims of a sluggish death
the massacre by hand-out

I am not innocent. All the prolix
barbarism of my race
speaks in my bones my skin
my face. Independence proves a hoax.

How long can I expect this man
not to claim his due, or hope he won't be
liberated from his hard decision
by a sudden swerve or stab of brakes (me

dead for the sake of some dog's
hide or the saving of a ten pound
panelbeater's bill)? Spellbound I relax—
the knife steady, a precious bond.

Randolph Stow

The Ghost at Anlaby

For Geoffrey and Ninette Dutton

Now sulkies come haunting softwheeled down the
leaves; on the cool veranda, over
whisky, wistaria, gentlemen admire
antwaisted, hamsleeved, bellskirted ladies
crossing the lawns with fishtailed racquets
intent on tennis. Heart, unlearn your fire.

Forget now, forget. Below the willows
Tom Roberts squatters, George Lambert ladies,
whose boats and fancy made this dam a lake,
speak of, remember, no visitant stranger.
Once time was a sportsman, and I the quarry,
who now would sleep with death, for sleep's kind sake.

But O whose fingers, soft as wistaria,
played with my watch-chain, under the crabapples;
under the lilacs in October flower
whose fingers like lingering tendrils twined in
my hair, my beard? What phantom remembers
that wicked, warm, Edwardian midday hour?

Rosella-plumed sun, go quickly down on
my afternoon ghosts. Let purple night that
brings all lovers to their billiard-rooms descend.
Click of the balls. Among wraiths of cigar-smoke,
with rib-nudging stories I died before telling,
I shall go haunting in search of a friend, a friend.

My Wish for My Land

THE WOMAN:

My wish for my land is that ladies be beautiful,
that horses be spirited and gentlemen courteous
and all moustaches faultless.

My wish for my husband is that he read Tennyson.
My wish for my daughter is that she be interesting
and capture a million acres.

My wish for my sons is that they be chivalrous,
sun-tanned and tall, and that they bestow on me
perhaps a dozen grandsons.

My wish for my house is that linen be Irish
and tableware sterling, and that the piano
go never too long unplayed

My wish for myself is that I grow matronly,
straying in dove-grey silk through the roses
under the far far harking of the crows.

The Enemy

As well, maybe, that you cannot read our minds;
there are worse tools than swords and rifle-butts.

My enemy: my passion. At dead of night,
licking my wounds, I begin to think I love you.

Certainly none were ever so bound in love
as we are bound in hate: O my ideal!

One sight of you, and life grows meaningful.
One blow: new strength to every slave who watches;

one word: revived fidelity, fresh lust.
Time—weakness—absence—death can have no bearing.

You whom I serve, your perfect gentle knight,
can you divine that longed-for consummation?

Lover: I mean to take you like a sponge,
and wring your blood out on Hiroshima.

Sam Mitchell

Thunderstorm

Tabi in Njangumarda

After sundown the clouds start to burn,
A big one is bending low, stays and breaks up,
Then it rounds again and raises its forehead high.
On both ends sheet lightning shines.
In the middle where the first layer is gone,
You can see the flash, even inside your home.
Everything dissolves.
In the desert, wide-spread falls the cloudburst,
Drenching all the trees between the two sandhills.

Translated by Georg von Brandenstein

Thomas W. Shapcott

June Fugue

1.
Where shall we go? where shall we go?
—We shall go to the Museum
What shall we see? is there lots to see?
—We shall see rooms full of treasures
I want to see jewels and costumes
pharaohs and mummies
—We shall spend hours among relics
  We shall be able to look hard
  at the blackened wrists of mummies.

2.
Do you remember that June day we drove into the mountains
we sang together all the songs from *Salad Days* and *My Fair Lady?*
—Shall we sing those songs now? Remember them?
No I was thinking of the mountains   the walking track
through that patch of rainforest
—And when we reached the sunlight
      I picked you an everlasting daisy.
You were always bringing me things.

3.
Do you remember the images the children said
'Why don't trees have two legs?'
'Daddy look at the broken moon'
'Mummy come in come inside you'll get the dark all over you.'
Children are so unalike.
They all draw bodies of sticks and daisies and circles.

4.
Where is that human hand? where is the Egyptian Mummy?
I'm sick of stuffed birds like the cat brought in.
—It is a hand small as yours   but very dark
      dried out   a bundle of sticks
Where is it now show me   show me

5.
The attendants are bored   the children stop
and then laugh they move on   it is nothing
how shall I tell them the curse is true?

that out in the sunlight their shoulders are fingered
that already the things they bring in as Everlastings
have the smell of Museums   that once having drawn the circle
you will   get the dark all over you

The Litanies of Julia Pastrana (1832–1860)

The Lord's name be praised
for the health that keeps me performing my tasks each day
without faltering.
The Lord's name be praised
for my very tidy figure and the good strength of my spine to keep
me agile in dancing.
The Lord's name be hallowed
for the sharpness of my eyes and the excellent juices of my
digestion.
I am in debt to the Lord
for all things even my present employment—I who could have
withered on the dustheap of the high village am enabled to travel
to the curious and enquiring Capitals of Europe—
I am in debt to the Lord for all things
even my present expectations
for my Manager has made me a proposal of marriage. He loves
me for my own sake.
I am indebted to the Lord of all things
My body covered with hair that made me cringe in the dark from
the village stone-throwers has earned me true fortune and
undreamt of advantages,
my double row of teeth set in this bearded thick jaw that
frightened even myself as a child looking in the well with its cruel
reflections the Lord has made for me to be a wonder to the
learned physicians of London,
my wide thick nostrils that they called me ape-baby for in those
terrible village days are no more strange in the Lord's eye than the
immensely varied noses I see in the gaping audiences who are
compelled to suffer without any rewards,
The Lord's name be hallowed and praised.
for I have been instructed to consider all my born qualities as
accomplishments.
In my own tongue I sing a soft theme to the Lord,
In my own heart I dance with quietness—
not so loud that the sightseers will hear me; yet when I have a
new dress I remember its price and its prettiness, I hold myself
straight and proud—the Lord knows there is beauty in the long

black hair that covers my body. Let them see, let them stare. The
Lord knows that. He gives me pride in that. They pay their
pennies and I dance snappingly for their pennies and for the
money my Manager is keeping for me and for the Praise: the
praise I say, of the good Lord
the brother of understanding
who was himself many days in the desert and was jeered at and
has my heart in his dear keeping.

    II
Why do I dream in my lungs
high air and the mountain tightness?
I will never return there.
I had brothers led the chase and the hunt
has me still panting, awake with strained
unweeping eyes from my mattress of goosefeathers.
I had a father.
How the heart winces across years
how the smallest flower is remembered
the first blows.
The Lord trembled for me in those years.
High air of Mexico, still claimant over me.
These European sea coast cities burden themselves
sometimes it is like a feeling of
being within intestines,
sometimes it is like
cells, not an open cage.
But to move constantly
(I move protected by blinds and veils)
is the Lord's way, who travelled
and was also homeless.

    III
'The Ugliest Woman in the World'
dances for your patronage
and your curiosity,
you curious ones
you with pink faces and puffy eyes and hands stuffed
   into tight cloth purchased with broken mountains
you with sour mouths hiding bone-yellow teeth that have chewed
   upon the produce of a quarry of blind children
you with delicate complexions powdered from the estates
   of pork barons and blood-slimy dealers in villages

you festering citizens of the bulbous pendulous cities
    you breathers of discharged curses, brothers of god
    yea even brothers

IV

My red tinsel dress—will he tear roubles and banknotes into the
Volga managing my dowry—I told him I would adore I had such
spirits in me he was abashed then delighted he implored again—I
tell you he implored, God, and I had you, praise you, for the good
things in my body—how he liked me trim in red tinsel how he—is
it now—my child will be—like you, Lord, will be tall and fair and
with a good strong spine to walk upright—and without shadows
and veils—is it always like this, the pain is enlarging too widely—he
will be with shiny black hair and black eyes they can be my gift to
him and the dance and strut of a proud man—God the way my
father had a strut in the plaza—it is coming yet? how many hours
do you have cloth to mop me, all the hair on my body drags as never
before, all my body over the matted hair is heavy down, sodden—it
is to be, Lord, OPENING

V

THE MUMMIFIED APE WOMAN AND THE MUMMY
CHILD glassed, strung on a perch like a parrot, the child. How
grotesque! Look closer: how terribly real, not like a waxwork at all
but almost human. Lord!
Give thanks never to have
seen them
real
and alive
among
us.

Judith Rodriguez

New York Sonnet

to D.A., Sept. '75

New York has had it, newsmen all proclaim,
against which, who can save that mighty city?
New York is ruined—in moods, you'd say, still pretty
among her towers and rivers, her power and fame,
billions and wits and beauties; but her name!
They clean New York still, yet her subway's gritty;
New York gets more expensive—that's a pity;
New York is going bankrupt—that's a shame.

The midtown leaves have known one day of fall;
we, thirteen years, since meeting at that un-
promising dinner. Midtown's disreputable,
and off-the-record-strange, these fiddled months.
You send me to Museums; I smile up Madison's
bright miles, among crowds changingly beautiful.

Eskimo Occasion

I am in my Eskimo-hunting-song mood,
Aha!
The lawn is tundra   the car will not start
the sunlight is an avalanche   we are avalanche-struck at our
     breakfast
struck with sunlight through glass   me and my spoonfed daughters
out of this world in our kitchen.

I will sing the song of my daughter-hunting,
Oho!
The waves lay down   the ice grew strong
I sang the song   of dark water under ice
the song of winter fishing   the magic for seal rising
among the ancestor-masks.

I waited by water to dream new spirits,
Hoo!
The water spoke   the ice shouted
the sea opened   the sun made young shadows
they breathed my breathing   I took them from deep water
I brought them fur-warmed home.

I am dancing the years of the two great hunts,
Ya-hay!
It was I who waited   cold in the wind-break
I stamp like the bear   I call like the wind of the thaw
I leap like the sea spring-running.   My sunstruck daughters
    splutter
and chuckle and bang their spoons:

Mummy is singing at breakfast and dancing!
So big!

A Lifetime Devoted to Literature

In your twenties you knew with elegiac certainty
you would die young. Your father's heart attack
tallied, a verification.

Thirty was your worst year: the thirties fatal to genius,
and genius undeclared by the would-be oracles.
You gave thought to publication;

then a news item—friend dropped dead in the street—
co-eval, a get-up-and-go editorial
viceroy at thirty-four—

cheered you somehow. You planned aloud and in detail,
publishers ventured for you, reviews came your way
as you learned to joke and your hair thinned,

and several thromboses onward you inhabit unruffled
an active advisory presence: a sitter on Boards
preparing to live for ever.

Norman Talbot

Ballad of Old Women
& of how they
are constrained to simulate youth in
order to avoid shocking the young

Three old ladies in an apple tree
swinging their dimity legs,
eating one apple with a sharp fawn tooth
& a laugh could be heard for leagues.

One old girl in a swanny swing
whisking her toes in the summer,
showing the wrinkles behind her knees
& making the branches simmer.

Three skinny madams in bikini tags,
their midriffs carved like posts
with names that answer to the creaky hands
in their threefold persistent past.

A nice old lady with a nice young man
is plucking his hairs off his chest
to decide if to die & be beautiful
or live so lewdly chaste.

I love old ladies with a memorable twist
dancing to the back of the years—
only stopping en route for a hardwon kiss
& experienced stout like yours.

I love old women with their own age on
& snakes in their hair saying no—
a snakedancer only has to wriggle a bit
but a charmer has to know.

Graeme Hetherington

The Man from Changi

We pass the flayed carcass of a cow
Hung up by the roadside. Split and spread
It reminds you of hung drawn and quartered.
We try to trace it to an ancient source.

Procrustes measuring people to his bed?
Or was it those two catapulting trees?
Your search goes on. I'm years away,
A nine year old spell-bound on a couch

As I listen to my father's friend from Changi.
Sallow-skinned, thin as a rake and beady-eyed,
What he told to this day terrifies.
The time was mid-day. One of his mates

Had been tied, spread-eagled on the ground.
No heaving could dislodge the bowl of glass

Somehow secured to his glistening gut.
No blame lies with the rat for what it did.

Philip Hammial

Russians Breathing

Does the mouth refuse?
Does the head roll forward?
Is there something saves a life?
Is there an elaborate plot from youth onward?
Whose is the ultimate warble?
Which string should we pull?
Which face have we just had?
What would happen if all the lamps were at once?
What's this that reeks us over?
How much should we feign?
How soon is the Chinese future?
How many buy geese?
How can we fix the sky so it won't hurt?
Should something drip?

These teeth aren't correct.
Sleep now, pay later.
Two thousand buy, to save a face.
Don't be surprised if the score evens.
The fades are always quick.
It's love that reeks us over.
We'll be as pretty as we squeeze.
A lily learned is a star displayed.
Our lips will never synch.
We're only in it for the voice.
The cherishing hole is the consoling hole.
How we keep to a life is a living in itself.
Every winner runs to fat.
The mouth takes food.

Les A. Murray

Equanimity

Nests of golden porridge shattered in the silky-oak trees,
cobs and crusts of it, their glory box;
the jacarandas' open violet immensities
mirrored flat on the lawns,
weighted by sprinklers; birds, singly and in flocks
hopping over the suburb, eating, as birds do, in detail
and paying their peppercorns;
talk of 'the good life' tangles love with will
however; if we mention it, there is more to say:
the droughty light, for example, at telephone-wire
height above the carports, not the middle-ground
distilling news-photograph light of a smoggy Wednesday,
but that light of the north-west wind, hung on the sky
like the haze above cattleyards;
hungry mountain birds, too, drifting in for food, with the sound
of moist gullies about them, and the sound of the pinch-bar;
we must hear the profoundly unwished
garble of a neighbours' quarrel, and see repeatedly
the face we saw near the sportswear shop today
in which mouth-watering and tears couldn't be distinguished.

Fire-prone place-names apart
there is only love; there are no Arcadias.
Whatever its variants of meat-cuisine, worship, divorce,
human order has at heart
an equanimity. Quite different from inertia, it's a place
where the churchman's not defensive, the indignant aren't on the
    qui vive,
the loser has lost interest, the accountant is truant to remorse,
where the farmer has done enough struggling-to-survive
for one day, and the artist rests from theory—
where all are, in short, off the high comparative horse
of their identity.
Almost beneath notice, as attainable as gravity, it is
a continuous recovering moment. Pity the high madness
that misses it continually, ranging without rest between
assertion and unconsciousness,
the sort that makes hell seem a height of evolution.
Through the peace beneath effort
(even within effort: quiet air between the bars of our attention)

comes unpurchased lifelong plenishment;
Christ spoke to people most often on this level
especially when they chattered about kingship and the Romans;
all holiness speaks from it.

From the otherworld of action and media, this
interleaved continuing plane is hard to focus:
we are looking into the light—
it makes some smile, some grimace.
More natural to look at the birds about the street, their life
that is greedy, pinched, courageous and prudential
as any on these bricked tree-mingled miles of settlement,
to watch the unceasing on-off
grace that attends their nearly every movement,
the crimson parrot has it, alighting, tips, and recovers it,
the same grace moveless in the shapes of trees
and complex in ourselves and fellow walkers; we see it's indivisible
and scarcely willed. That it lights us from the incommensurable
we sometimes glimpse, from being trapped in the point
(bird minds and ours are so pointedly visual):
a field all foreground, and equally all background,
like a painting of equality. Of infinite detailed extent
like God's attention. Where nothing is diminished by perspective.

The Smell of Coal Smoke

John Brown, glowing far and down,
wartime Newcastle was a brown town,
handrolled cough and cardigan, rain on paving bricks,
big smoke to a four-year-old from the green sticks.
Train city, mother's city, coming on dark,
Japanese shell holes awesome in a park,
electric light and upstairs, encountered first that day,
sailors and funny ladies in Jerry's Fish Café.

It is always evening on those earliest trips,
raining through the tram wires where blue glare rips
across the gaze of wonderment and leaves thrilling tips.
The steelworks' vast roofed debris unrolling falls
of smoky stunning orange, its eye-hurting slump walls
mellow to lounge interiors, cut pile and curry-brown
with the Pears-Soap-smelling fire and a sense of ships
mourning to each other below in the town.

This was my mother's childhood and her difference,
her city-brisk relations who valued Sense

talking strike and colliery, engineering, fowls and war,
Brown's grit and miners breathing it, years before
as I sat near the fire, raptly touching coal,
its blockage, slick yet dusty, prisms massed and dense
in the iron scuttle, its hammered bulky roll
into the glaring grate to fracture and shoal,

its chips you couldn't draw with on the cement
made it a stone, tar crockery, different—
and I had three grandparents, while others had four:
where was my mother's father, never called Poor?
In his tie and his Vauxhall that had a boat bow
driving up the Coalfields, but where was he now?
Coal smoke as much as gum trees now had a tight scent
to summon deep brown evenings of the Japanese war,

to conjure gaslit pub yards, their razory frisson
and sense my dead grandfather, the Grafton Cornishman
rising through the night schools by the pressure in his chest
as his lungs creaked like mahogany with the grains of John Brown.
His city, mother's city, at its starriest
as swearing men with doctors' bags streamed by toward the docks
past the smoke-frothing wooden train that would take us home
    soon
with our day-old Henholme chickens peeping in their box.

Peter Steele

Marking Time

For days you find it one long zero hour,
   pen at the ready, helpless among
the bold irregulars of scholarship.
   They have the legs on you, claiming
that zebras are chiefly used to illustrate
   the letter Z, that the masculine
of dam is dash, that Adam's punishment
   lay in his keeping Eve, that St George
saved a little girl from a monstrous dragoon;
   a trapezium has become the thing
in the gymnasium, Socrates dies from taking
   an overdose of wedlock, heat
is transmitted by conviction. Given time,
   you'd fall them into squads to drill

backwards and forwards on the mind's bull-ring,
    like Graves with his exuberant soldiers,
but there's no time. They plunge into the night
    without memorial and without success
flailing at ignorance, sending back the word
    that the principal parts of the eye are the moat
and the beam, that we must aim at proper ghouls,
    that someone is condoning lust,
drugs, and a merry life.

J.S. Harry

Honesty-stones

The land between us
had grown so bare
the landscape so denuded—
all we had left was what we knew—
just the rocks and the shade they cast—
your eyes my eyes, across them.

We did not need to speak, to talk.
Everything was in the rocks.
It had been said before.

We could not live there.

Clive James

Johnny Weissmuller dead in Acapulco

Apart possibly from waving hello to the cliff-divers
Would the real Tarzan have ever touched Acapulco?
Not with a one-hundred-foot vine.
Jungle Jim maybe, but the Ape Man never.
They played a tape at his funeral
In the Valley of Light cemetery of how he had sounded
Almost fifty years back giving the pristine ape-call,
Which could only remind all present that in decline
He would wander distractedly in the garden
With his hands to his mouth and the unforgettable cry

Coming out like a croak—
This when he wasn't sitting in his swim-trunks
Beside the pool he couldn't enter without nurses.

Things had not been so bad before Mexico
But they were not great.
He was a greeter in Caesar's Palace like Joe Louis.
Sal, I want you should meet Johnny Weissmuller.
Johnny, Mr Sal Volatile is a friend of ours from Chicago.
With eighteen Tarzan movies behind him
Along with the five Olympic gold medals,
He had nothing in front except that irrepressible paunch
Which brought him down out of the tree house
To earth as Jungle Jim
So a safari suit could cover it up.
As Jungle Jim he wasn't just on salary,
He had a piece of the action,
But coming so late in the day it was not enough
And in Vegas only the smile was still intact.

As once it had all been intact, the Greek classic body
Unleashing the new-style front-up crawl like a baby
Lifting itself for the first time,
Going over the water almost as much as through it,
Curing itself of childhood polio
By making an aquaplane of its deep chest,
Each arm relaxing out of the water and stiffening into it,
The long legs kicking a trench that did not fill up
Until he came back on the next lap,
Invincible, easily breathing
The air in the spit-smooth, headlong, creek-around-a-rock trough
Carved by his features.

He had six wives like Henry VIII but don't laugh,
Because Henry VIII couldn't swim a stroke
And if you ever want to see a true king you should watch
    Weissmuller
In *Tarzan Escapes* cavorting underwater with Boy
In the clear river with networks of light on the shelving sand
Over which they fly weightless to hide from each other behind the
    log
While Jane wonders where they are.
You will wonder where you are too and be shy of the answer
Because it is Paradise.

When the crocodile made its inevitable entry into the clear river
Tarzan could always settle its hash with his bare hands

Or a knife at most,
But Jungle Jim usually had to shoot it
And later on he just never got to meet it face to face—
It was working for the Internal Revenue Service.

There was a chimpanzee at his funeral,
Which must have been someone's idea of a smart promotion,
And you might say dignity had fled,
But when Tarzan dropped from the tall tree and swam out of the
    splash
Like an otter with an outboard to save Boy from the waterfall
It looked like poetry to me,
And at home in the bath I would surface giving the ape-call.

Jan Owen

The Visitation

No angel has descended here;
only the Amish woman's hair
shines feather-soft beneath the wings
of her white cap whose ribbon clings,
looped in a Moebius strip of faith,
transparently against black cloth.
Shadows test the slanting light.
She leans a little to the right
so that our vision centres on
the sturdy limbs of her first-born.
Gently the small hands of the child,
resting on her own, are held
forward, an offering to our gaze.
We guess from her bewildered eyes
before we count the fingers spread
on her palms and, finding the caption, read:
*Six-fingered dwarfism: Amish boy
with Ellis-van Creveld syndrome.* Why
this should be, the woman's ceased to ask;
fulfilling her appointed task,
she reads from the Book, fastens her cap,
lifts the baby onto her lap.
A certain beauty lights them both—
this trust that shows us all the truth
hallows them brightly as any Raphael
Madonna and Child. Sad and still,

her look pierces the quick of now;
his searches stolidly past as though
toward a future taking shape
less ideally than her least hope.
The sins of the fathers pass us by this time
but touch us too: we have something to redeem.

Kate Llewellyn

Finished

There'll be no more
lying on your shoulder love
or listening for your car

there'll be no more
drinking on the verandah love
or eating roasted veal

there'll be no more
my legs around your neck love
and howling at the moon

there'll be no more
hits across my mouth love
and crawling on the floor

there'll be no more
smoking listening to you curse love
or smiling drinking more

there'll be no more
crying because you rage love
or dancing up your drive

there's no more
love love

Colonel

He rode a white horse
heading the Anzac Day parade
fought at Ladysmith
and Gallipoli

was 90
tall
and treated me
as his batman

helping him
down the hospital corridor
seemed holding rare archeology
by the elbow

I apologised for clumsiness
he said 'Never mind Sister
every beginning is difficult'
but he said it in Latin

his marriage of 60 years ended
when she died
he ran the funeral elegantly
with military style
and died a month later

Tjinapirrgarri

Emu Shot

Tabi in Ngarluma

At the undulating head he aims,
At the bobbing head, at the upper neck.
The shots whistle, hitting the river-stones.
The shots whistle, as it lies there riddled.
Feathers leap, hitting the river-stones.
Feathers leap, as it lies there riddled.
The emu chicks run to and fro
Coming back again and again.

Translated by Georg von Brandenstein

Gordon Mackay-Warna

Cattle Loading

Tabi in Njijapali

The wheels line up, pretty right, right:
Flush alongside the yardhouse,
And the truck waits ready.
Right-oh then, now the tray's level with the cattle-yard.
I look up and the cattle seem to float past,
I see forests of bullock-horns waving.

Translated by Georg von Brandenstein

Geoff Page

Grit

A doxology

I praise the country women
of my mother's generation
who bred, brought up and boasted
six Australians each—
the nearest doctor fifty miles
on a road cut off by flood;
the women who by wordless men
were courted away from typewriters
and taught themselves to drive—
I praise their style
in the gravel corners.
I praise the snakes they broke in two
and the switch of wire they kept in a cupboard.
I praise what they keep and what they lose—
the long road in to the abattoirs,
the stare which cures
a stockman of shooting swans.
I praise the prints, the wide straw brims
they wore out to the clothes line;
I praise each oily crow that watched them.
I praise the tilting weather—

the dry creeks and the steady floods
and the few good weeks between.
I praise each column in the ledger
they kept up late by mosquito and lamp-light;
the temerity of the banker
reining them in at last—or trying;
the machinations for chequered paddocks
swung on the children's names;
the companies just one step ahead;
the tax clerk, in his way, also.
I praise each one of their six children
discovering in turn
the river in its tempers
the rapids and the river trees;
the children who grew up to horse sweat
and those who made it to the city.
I praise the stringy maxims
that served instead of prayers;
also the day that each child found
a slogan not enough,
surprising themselves in a camera flash
and bringing no extra paddocks.
I praise the boast of country women:
they could have been a wife
to any of a dozen men
and damn well made it work.
I praise what I have seen
to be much more than this.
I praise their politics of leather;
the ideologies in a line of cattle;
the minds that would not
stoop to whisky.
I praise their scorn
for the city of options, the scholars
in their turning chairs and air-conditioned theories.
I praise also that moment
when they headed off in tears—
the car in a toolshed failing to start,
a bootfull of fencing wire.
I praise the forty years
when they did not. I praise
each day and evening of their lives—
that hard abundance year by year
mapped in a single word.

Inscription at Villers-Bretonneux

The dead at Villers-Bretonneux
rise gently on a slope towards
the sky. The land is trim—skylines

of ploughed earth and steeples; unfallen
rain still hanging in the air;
confusion smoothed away

and everything put back—the village
too (red brick/white sills) in nineteen
twenty, unchanged since. Headstones

speak a dry consensus. Just one
breaks free: 'Lives Lost, Hearts Broken—
And For What?'. I think of the woman

and those she saddened by insisting—
the Melbourne clerk
who must have let it through.

Premeditations

'Family of Four/Shot Dead'

With a pull-through and the .22
on the back step as the moon
breaks over the stockade barn

the afternoon
is trembling in his fingers:

the banker's shallow eyes
the barman's face a net of blood
the gate still scraping in the dirt
the dog stretched tight
in half-wit welcome.

Somewhere behind him
straight through timber
cracked plates are going
back to shelves
well past resentment now.
Four cups shiver on their hooks
and soap-raw palms on faded cotton
defer the small reward
of tea.

And at the table
two slight girls with lunar faces
are one day more
grown used to silences
fatigue and long division
brought back thirty miles by bus
on gravel they turn through
even in dreams.

Out in the house paddock
the shadows of harrows
are merging with the earth
as if it weren't already
mortgaged to the wind.
Fingers ply more smoothly now
the flannel cloth and pull-through—
and the moon has gone completely.

Inside behind him
three iron beds
are passive and accepting

as they will be again
when only the dog
will wake on its chain to morning.

Geoffrey Lehmann

Pope Alexander VI

It's good, my child, you often wash your hair
So it retains its gold—my favourite colour.
Your soft young lobe pierced by a golden ear-ring.
I feel so old.
           On seaside holidays
I stand at dusk upon a crumbling headland
And watch water drag across a reef edge.
                        But ah! tonight
The Tiber will throw back the steady blaze
Of lights around the Vatican.
Flutes and bass-viols will sound across the waters,
Men fully clothed will jump with drunken laughter
And soak the coolness in, then climb out dripping.

I shall throw nuts to harlots dancing naked
So they will bend deliciously to eat them.

Rome is the great test of your faith,
Imperial city built upon a sewer.
The drowsy gold eyes of a gilded virgin,
Gold flaking off from gold and underneath
Plaster deteriorating into dust.
And clever men have seen her and despaired.
Wise men expecting nothing have survived.

Men laugh at priestly arrogance.
Bear in mind that my lips though they absolve
A thousand souls may yet themselves be damned.
Supreme hierarchy and democracy,
And I the head of this great organism,
Not a dead logical system but a being
Sordid and stupid yet magnificent,
A mother to all men.

Listen to my angelic choirs, augmented
To drown the ribald shrieks from my suite.
In the midst of pillow fights suddenly we hear
The majestic swelling of the *Dies Irae*.
Only the corrupt can be truly humble.

A bible smeared with arsenic—sodomy
In vestries, bribery in basilicas,
Garlic-rank congregations, all these are
The dirty vestments of the Holy Spirit.

Though I may burn,
Remember my polluted hands
Are a link in the apostolic line,
And that I am God's glory manifested.

Gently Lucrezia, do not bite.

Night Flower

Sussex Street sleeps in mists of nickel moonlight
And echoes ghostly music, but the sound
Inside is crushing, voices, drums, stars jerked
From electric guitars, and swaying, shaking bodies:
Young, beautiful and cruel my friends are dancing.
Night in your cold vase hold this crumbling flower,
Stung smiles, dark corridors where bodies push

To a white stately room of bare feet stamping
A gritty floor, figures dissolving in shadows,
The dance, this great, sad, bitter swaying thing
Which burns and moves and kisses us with salt.

A Poem for Maurice O'Shea

It is wine-harvest, summer, the year's heart.
At night the vines bend on their wires, old sheds
Of whitewashed galvanized iron bake in the moon,
And Maurice's cats sidle in the wind.

'Gypsum takes away harshness...clarify
With albumen....' Love failed and has become
A vineyard, carbon dioxide in dark vats
Which prickles when you thrust your arm in wine.

But through the vineyards a ghost woman walks,
Whose failure honed his art, sharpened that nose,
That long thin delicate nose which peers and sniffs
Into a long-necked glass, then passes on.

The moonlit water-tank gobbles, rumbling briefly.
A possum thumps upon the roof but Maurice
In hock-pale light is sitting at a desk
Writing in vine-scrawl of the wine he loves,

Myopic eyes given a quizzical look
By thick-lensed, rimless, gold-framed spectacles,
And always ready for a laugh, whisking
Up culinary marvels on a kerosene stove,

And once a bandicoot cooked in red wine
Greeted by ignorant cries of 'Bravo Maurice!
A champion dish!' as bits of bandicoot
Exquisitely dissolved in portly stomachs.

'I do not like machines. We use the hand-press....'
Men grunt and push a handle slowly turning
Upon a metal thread, and the great press
Squeezes the grapes till Maurice calls, 'Enough!'

Feeling inside his chest (which cancer eats
Like secret phylloxera through his body)
The texture, substance, weight of grapes, that moment
The first juice breaks and floods—and it's just right.

But wine is more than art, or the fine mind
Sniffing at mathematical purities,

Or testing acidity levels in a lab,
Wine is a man inside a darkened cask,

Hunched in that primal gloom, scouring out filth,
The terror as he crawls in through the bung-hole,
Or when they haul him by his helpless arms
From that claustrophobic hole back to the world.

Wine is an ancient Catholic God, whose sun
Beats on Pokolbin earth, demanding faith,
And also works, the hand, weary from turning
The soil and dropping grapes in metal buckets.

And wine is also wisdom, which announces
As Maurice does, we should drink common wine
As well, for too much fine wine spoils the palate.
And he is quiet and shy behind his fame.

In khaki shirt and shorts, with battered hat
Maurice at vintage time stumps through his vineyard,
Dust on his forehead, sweat beneath his arms,
Retires inside the whitewashed galvanized shack

And sits and smokes, drinking a cup of coffee
Poured from an elegant metal percolator,
A taste rare then, but student days in France
And his French mother gave him a Gallic flair.

He smokes. Ah yes! But don't smoke near the cellars!
He'll cut your arm off if you smoke near there!
Those purple bubbles, maroon foam must breathe only
From polished concrete vats, cool stone, good oak.

Now Maurice sits tonight alone and humble
In summer's heart and gets up from his desk,
And pours some red, savouring it like a baby.
Night and wine, his face wavering on the glass.

Pambardu

Windmill At Mandanthanunguna

Tabi in Jindjiparndi

Where the pipe ends he had fixed the long trough—
Where the pipe ends in the early dawn a dead man stood up,

Coming around on the edge with a clang up to the wheel head.

'Tjeerarringarra,' says the pumping rod, it's the windmill tail
That turns in the wind, up on the edge with a clang,

                                          the wheel head,

It pulls a bunch of gadgets in the metal casing,
Pulls what is wheeling the pump wheel to work.
What gleams in its centre

                    pushing the shining rod into the ground?

Translated by Georg von Brandenstein

Andrew Taylor

The Beast with Two Backs

Only the clouds were new
scenario out of the best pens
(all of them) and the setting
straight Manet

But the clouds
newly born of the sewage farm
the water treatment section of the steel mill
the heavy hydrogen plant etc.
found those first
fumbles of adultery
novel enough to rain on

at least they *came*

while the orchestra in the pit
well it was an old tune on
new instruments

and as we drove back through rain
only we we said
would attempt the moon in a deluge

After the flood we had our memories
beasts coupled in the cabin of a car
nothing was changed and nothing was the same

Nigel Roberts

After / the Moratorium Reading

the marie antoinette / slice
of cake / was
awarded to—
who ever said
after this reading / let's
get it on / at Michael's place / I heard
that guy
from Canberra's got
some farout
vietnamese
shit.

The Gull's Flight

The gull's flight
is low
flat
& hard

they go
to sea
to the edge
where the day's fire
is lit

they go
as shiftworkers
to the dawn.

Alan Alexander

The Gathering Place

Albany in a time of khaki.
Anzacs in the Sound.
'Post it for me, nipper.'—

Transports and escorts
Brought into the harbour
To be coaled at the deepwater
Two by two.

Archdeacon Louth
With his white handkerchief
A fluttering signal
In a lucky street.

I have eyes on a sunny morning.
The brave convoy in single file
Steaming past Breaksea and Michaelmas.

For Raftery

(Last of the wandering Gaelic versemakers)

Blind poet, fiddler, Raftery,
Such a scarecrow sweetness, wailful charm
You surely spread in the villages
Amongst the gawking girls, the crones
Tied to a half-door, dropping harm,

And the men having a drop with you,
Folk of the west you knew and sung
Who spared you bread and pence, and kept
Your words with them till the scholar caught
The Galway rains along your tongue,

And saw your ragged coat of truth,
The bright sun in the passing show,
Mary Hynes the village girl,
Born in darkness, your love of loves,
Rinsing her beauty at cockcrow,

Chiding and gracious about the house,
Stirring the fire, washing delph,
Proud and not a little afraid
Of the poet whose selfish trade it was
To keep no beauty to himself.

Julian Croft

D-Zug

Right from the ambiguous start
when in the wrench and snatch of coupling
the child called out
'the station's moving and we are standing still,'

I'd never known which track my heart
was on, the up express, all stations down,
or where to get out
if the station's moving and we are standing still;

I wasn't sure if the crumpled face floating
backward, mirror or window, was my own
or yours, or to shout
it's the next train moving, I'm standing still,

but tonight, expressed down rival tracks
through air-conditioned night, I saw an orange globe
of warmth burn past, then out,
and I was moving, you were standing still.

Greenhalgh's Pub

Hot, humid, the smell of sewage
here on the Bund. Moons flash from wave to wave,
the Whangpo juggles glaciers and tides.

I could be Greenhalgh himself
strolling down Blood Alley
to see a family of knife throwers

in my pocket a contract
for the famous dog woman of Hefei,
a partnership for Sian's siamese twins.

The canvas flap draws back in Bourke
and Bugilbone, at Pallamallawa they gasp,
that's nothing they say in Jackadgery

half the O'Briens are like that,
and that's the ones they let out...
But I'm not Greenhalgh, I'm a looker-on.

Along the walls of his pub photographs
I grew up with: giants, dwarves, jugglers,
three-legged men and rip-van-winkle-women.

1923, 1930, a great year '33,
opium and the pox filled the Bund
with frights enough for Billy's Creek

and people desperate to learn
what no self-respecting kelpie would.
And now I stand in the Bund myself

watching from within those photographs
and remembering Saturday afternoons
drunk and disgusting amid the race calls

planning the next rape or petty theft
bragging about the latest atrocity,
all of us freaks with the price of our own admission:

here on the Whangpo where the new moon rises
I know Greenhalgh's pub has left its mark:
I can't walk tall in the gutters of China.

Graffiti

She worked in the newsagent, redhaired
face narrow as a terrace, glassed in eyes,
nose like an awning, her name was Alice

she'd sidle in taking even less space that way
cutting through the steam of the espresso machine
looking for Alec, who wasn't looking for her.

But he'd follow her, round the corner into the lane
against the wall. They'd come back pale and unchanged
she'd sit there with nothing to say until

she'd been ignored an hour and then she'd
get up, turn sideways and disappear—
at least front on against the bricks she was seen.

Sun a mirra yelled the kids outside
the headlines changed but Alice came out each day
the oldfashioned broadsheet up against the wall.

Then Alec needed money for a hunting bow
scoring with stationary targets was not enough
Go on, he said, go down the shop she'll have

her bankbook with her. I went, you'd think
a southerly was blowing, the glassed-in front
shut up, the awnings down, she didn't say a word
then like I was the landlord she handed me the book.
Off to the bank and the book slid squarely down the chute
ding went the bell just like a fair bull at the show.

I waited, they called the names, the *Artemis* passed
down the harbour, then I realised I didn't know her name
had no idea at all. Alice, money, body, soul, without a name.

I'd thought, well hell she knows what she's doing
I'm not getting any why should I etc
her pride, face, the few quid that she'd saved

all here, and I'd no idea what to do:
I lied, said that she'd taken ill her sister
sent me down to get the money for a taxi home

I didn't know her name: they paid without demur
and so did I to Alec and even took back the book.
He never went hunting didn't buy a bow

but spent the money getting drunk—I helped him;
now here I should make the joke about Cupid's dart,
the hunter hunted, and Diana's revenge

but I can't make it, it didn't happen, and my memory's partial
I'm neither sun nor mirror, history nor art,
I followed, watched, was acolyte at the rites

then found when I turned round to look
there was too much of me on the wall
I couldn't bend the bow or pay the price.

Allen Afterman

Their Thoughts Cling to Everything
They See on the Way

Now, to tense stillness as the door is slammed

Talk around them, someone is praying, someone is joking
    To the bad breath sifting through their nostrils

Being shoved, smothered, someone is forcing them down
    To their own curse subsiding

Their child's shape moving under their chest
    They cling
to the feel of fluff in her hair tickling their cheek

To the stifling odour, vomit is wetting their fingers
    To their mother's porch wreathed with climbing rose vines
and beds of yellow narcissi

To their bowels moving, pissing
To maybe they're not dying, maybe the others only faint
    They cling
to a photograph of Roosevelt sitting with Stalin

To coughing, to scorching in the throat
    To their lungs sticking, they can't open their lungs

The expression of the kapo coaxing them in

To exist dear God please help me

To the roughness of the cement rubbing their palms

Van Diemen's Land

In this land vague malevolence
hung upon the skin, olive grey, a gas...
Evil in the lungs, humming in the nostrils, flies;
world no one wanted to live in,
an open pit—
chained thieves peopled the camps of new Ararat.
Sadism was twisted into the root

and snuff for floggin's—
for the militia ladies, rum for amnesia,
boys for the laddies.
Fleisch und Blut.

Eucalyptus too hard to cut, nothing sharper than a shell,
no animal of service, one edible fern,
one fungus.
Land without a fruit-bearing tree,
as though Truth were exiled and the Lie remained.

Here women would carry on their teats
small black skulls;
last of the race, the scourged Eve—
Truganini, would die in a boarding-house.

This old, bloodied island,
with their dark shadows swept off the shore and the movement
in the bush—
there is the smell of Poland
despite the sea breeze and the sheep dung.
Parklands root in mass graves,
the bush is like a derelict house...
Farmland is lush—
flushed, deep, dark, maroon.

You who dreamed of an Australia
del Espiritu Santo, of the Holy Spirit—
this was the South, which is reversed;
the lost, fallen continent...

Weep for those who wandered through their garden,
who conceived with terror in their hearts,
for those we tore to pieces—

Pietà

I leave it for you to say why it is
that every moment we are awake we do not weep?
How is it we walk the streets
and do not fall on our knees before anyone
who is still beautiful, or who is ugly?
I think of those pyramids in sealed chambers;
of those sealed in ghettos
who ate the arms of their children, dead in frozen urine.
Would you picture this with me?

How is it we are able to forget them;
that we dare to have other than those children?

I think of the mute, black children
their mothers held by the scruff of the neck
for the minutes it took...

Why is it
we do not memorize each name, every word whispered,
the texture of the ground, the colour of the clouds,
the executioner's gestures...

Why is it that every moment we are awake we do not weep?

Jennifer Rankin

The Sea and other stories

First there was the island
knocked off the cliff into the sea.
Next came the impact and the storms.
Now there are five sailors and a boat breaking up.

Beneath these great granite cliffs
the sea is oiled in blackness.
Not even the moon eases itself into this thick night.
Five sleeping sailors and a course hard set.

They enter the ring of the island.
Their boat is taking its head.
They enter the leering shadow of cliff
whose cap of thin grass, wind-whipped

hugs to itself a small skull of earth
gripping down out of the air.
Beneath the boat this shadow is mirrored.
Black reef of heavy weed juts into the sea.

Five men are asleep caressed in the jaw of the earth.
They lie, white-skinned, between such smiling teeth.
And now there is the rending! the tearing of wood!
the bending of black sea and sky!

The oiling of screams and their slivering out
the rushing and filling
the slow sounding-up of new space.

Great granite cliffs tilt
their shadow against the sky.
They tease the men.

And two of the sailors are lumps of white body
sleep-torn and floating face down on the water.

Still the storm beats and circles the island.
Still the cliffs beckon and tilt.
Two bodies free and drifting are part of storm's landscape
drifting and floating free
for the fish-hawk, the transforming, the mouthing of the sea.
Then the moon slides through.
On jagged reefs three sailors are being smashed

soundlessly their tongues struggle for the cliffs.
Each sailor bleeds his body into the sea.

The moon is linking the island to the cliffs.
Sliding over the sea it pulls at the tide and the men.
Three sailors turn inside their bodies, inside the storm.
Reaching out they touch the moon
fingers clawing at glistening rock.

With each wave they are lifted and dropped
lifting and dropping, rising and falling,
the moon, the tide and the storm.

Their fingers have broken
their soft flesh has drowned
they are leaving their skin in the sea.

．　．　．　．

I am watching three sailors climbing the cliff.
For three weeks they have climbed.
I have with me a deck-chair and sunglasses.
I watch from a niche in the cliff.

The sailors appear to be bleeding.
They have great holes in their hearts.
They appear to be climbing within a circular storm.
I see the lightning splitting their limbs
only their sinews cling to the cliff.

One small thin figure reaches the top.
On the rocks below my brother is searching for oysters.
He prizes them off with his strong pen-knife.

Three men now sway on the grass of the cliff-top.
I adjust my binoculars, phase for long-range.
On the rocks below my brother is opening a body.

Into a dawn mist the sailors shiver and stumble
I have made a tape of their moaning.
Now they are crawling away from the sea.

A great cloud of birds lifts off the land
I return to my watch
slowly it circles the cliff,
timing again the long climb up.

Three naked sailors, pale as sea-water
float now over grass.
They shadow the night, follow it in beyond horizons.

．　．　．　．

On the heavy door of a winter farmhouse
two sailors are pounding.
A third watches in silence.
He is carrying the cliff in his hands.

They wait and the door does not open.

Two sailors beat again at the door.
The door does not open.

Two sailors turn to the cliff.
They wrest it away from their mate.
They rush at the door.
They ram the door with the cliff.

And the door swells for one moment and is bending
rising and falling, lifting and dropping,
the door for one moment and the cliff it is bending
the sea and the sailors
watching and lying in deckchairs
prizing with knives, carrying cliffs,
struggling with moonrise and storms.
The door swells and is sucked away.

Inside the house an old couple are huddled in bed.
They dream of a storm that smashes their door.
They dream of a cliff and the sea.
They dream of three men who sit at their table
bleeding and naked
They dream of two bodies
bleeding and naked
They dream of the sea.

They huddle and dream.

And my brother is signalling from his marine rock platform.
He points at a storm that is encircling the island.

The old couple stare at the cliff in their house
its shadow is tilting their night.
They wait for the rending, the tearing, the smashing
they lie in their great floating bed.

And now they are drowning face down in the sheets
and now they are drowning again
always the men who remind in their kitchen
always the cliff and the breaking of wood

rising and falling, lifting and dropping
an old couple facing the sea.

I watch from my deck chair. My brother is calling.
Three sailors are climbing the cliff.

Public Corroboree Songs

Nunggubuyu people, south-eastern Arnhem Land

Koel (Rainbird) and effigy

holding the feathered dancing string
koel, koel and string/koel, string/koel
it sneaks up to us, string/koel
it stalks, cries out, string/koel, 'give it to me'
koel, string/koel, koel, string
it talks with a voice from on top
from the jungle fig tree, calling to each other, string/koel
string/koel, string/koel—they throw the feathered
   dancing string back and forth
I heard their voice

Goanna

goanna chases grasshopper
it looks around stretching up its neck, goanna
goanna, goanna
it shuts the entrance to its nest with sand
   it cleans itself, it cleans itself, goanna
goanna, goanna
goanna, thin one
with claws, twisting its body, goanna
it looks for grasshopper, goanna, thin one

Flood Water

running downhill, spilling over, searching and spilling
ever increasing, gathering sticks, enlarging
flood water, flood water
it flows out, flood water, flood water
it has gathered up sticks, flood water, flood water
the flood water takes itself to the brackish water
   [to the sea]
flood water, flood water

Mission Work-Boat

reaching out into the sea, passing the waves its exhaust smoking
rigging has been taken up, the whole boat vibrates, the engine
    tapping
everything they tie down with rope, exhaust smoking
reaching out through the sea, pushing a way through the sea
the propeller makes bubbles in the water, the engine the sound of
    bubbling
everything they tie down with ropes

Translated by Mungayana Nundhirribala

R.R. Davidson

The Gravy Train

I lived for many years in the bush—far out—and I starved for lack
    of rain
Till I slipped the yoke that had kept me broke and caught the Gravy
    Train;
Now the bridle may rot on the stockyard rail, the shovel in the
    drain,
And the crowbar rust in the yellow dust, or ever I work again.

The ringers shall strive with the starving stock, but I will not be
    there—
I'd rather the pub than the gidyea scrub; and I'll weep in my icy
    beer
When I think of the years I left behind, of the futile fruitless fight
To wrest a home from the stubborn loam, before I saw the light.

We are 'the backbone of the land', the politicians say.
There's plenty of sweat and a ton of debt—but bloody little pay;
There's flood and fire and dust and drought, tears and an overdraft,
A wornout wife and a wasted life, rewarding all the graft.

So I've got a job with the Council mob and I live in a house rent
    free,
And I drive from the bar in a Council car, when I go home to tea.
The cattle may die by the dried-up dam or perish on the plain,
The bank may sweat about the debt—I'm on the Gravy Train.

Roger McDonald

1915

Up they go, yawning,
the crack of knuckles dropped
to smooth the heaving
in their legs, while some,
ashamed, split bile
between their teeth,
and hum to drown their stomachs.

Others touch their lips
on splintered wood
to reach for home—
'a bloke's a mug'
thinks one (who sees
a ringbarked hill)
another hisses drily
(leaping burrs).

All dreaming,
when the whistle
splits the pea, as up
they scramble, pockets fat
with Champion Flake
in battered tins,
and letters wadded thick
from Mum (who says
'always keep
some warm clothes on . . .')

Up from slits in dirt
they rise, and here they stop.
A cold long light swings over.

Hard like ice
it cracks their shins—
they feel a drill and mallet
climb their bones, then cold
then warmth as blood spills out from pockets,
chests, and mouths.
No mother comes to help, although
a metal voice is whining
'boys, relax', as one
by one they totter to their knees.

The Blizzard

A man blew away.

His clothes gulped wind like sails.
He rotated—his burberry capped with ice
gripping, gripping, gripping
each faint revolution.

Now he's under the liquid ice
which never sets hard, but is
churned to a vast granita.

This was late summer, when all animal life
headed north, leaving a riddle:
'In what respect is the penguin
in other than dress
like man?'

'When she lays an egg
in this terrible wind
and puts a stone on top—
for the effort breaks

your heart, watching.'

M-----n, the meteorologist, posed this
re-entering the hut, his face clamped hard with ice
like a sculpted pie,
one eye and his mouth
and the words an abstraction of pain.

I too went out in the blizzard
at midnight, in weather twenty-five below,
when down the wind
a bird shrieked gliding at head-height,
beak and eyes and white-pinioned trunk
a heartbeat, straining.

I dreamed of that wind-rider
later, back in the hut, where the temperature sputtered
seven above freezing . . .
warmed by coal, in my fur sack, I thought
no, the bird was never the blown man coming back
but could have been.
                              Later that year during sledging
I saw how death and thoughts like this
glided together, and to be brave
was to be persistently

dull, if you could,
in the face of such beauty,
and I was glad for reciting Robert W. Service
at our celebration dinners—
though at the end, at the very end,
all polar hands die under gas lamps
in lifting fog, the scrape of leaves at a window,
and a full scoop of anthracite
red in the grate.

When the blown man suddenly froze
I thought of that.

Here the driven snow will polish rusted chains in a week
and rub aluminium saucepans thin.
It blew the gust-meter down
at two hundred miles an hour (estimated)
howling with open mouth
until the sky parted and God looked down
with a cold deep face.

Apis mellifica

In a dreamlike fall, the long
spoon in the honey-jar descends—a bubble going

down, he thinks, a silver bell.
He stands there a while,

humming, twisting the spoon
slowly from side to side. (The moon

drops from an amber-coloured cloud,
on the horizon a metal sphere rides

heavily over water, hunting the crushed ocean floor.)
Fifteen pounds of honey in the tall jar—

nectar, the fall of pollen, bees in the Yellow Box tree
filling that flowery head once a year

with a huge thought, all of it here.
Now the spoon climbs up as though something

is spoken by light
and shade in their alternating

vowels of movement, and held—as though what the tree
thought

was taken away and stored,

deepened, like an old colour, and understood.

Craig Powell

Nativity

What gifts shall we bring in worship
to the cold child half-asleep?
no cattle moan by his manger
no star shines for hope

The Innocents die in the ditches
One hand under his head
his mother suckles a victim
who will not be wine or bread

but a saviour   human   terrible
whose bones wince for the day
we hang our brutish weakness
in his body   on a tree

All is suffered   the infant
cringes   begins to wail ..
stone-eyed   the mother of Judas
watches as we kneel

Nicholas Hasluck

Islands

Islands which have
never existed
have made their way
on to maps nonetheless.

And having done so
have held their place,
quite respectably,
sometimes for centuries.

Voyages of undiscovery, deep
into the charted wastes,

were then required
to move them off.

The Auroras, for instance.
Beneath Cape Horn.
Sighted first in 1762
and confirmed by
Captain Manuel de Oyarvido
thirty years later.

But since the voyage of
someone whose name
escapes me, on a date
I can't quite remember—
they are now known
not to exist.

Cartographers—hands high
in the frail rigging of
latitudes and longitudes—
wiped them out, reluctantly.

And so, some mariners,
who pushed beyond the pale,
forfeit the names they left
in lonely seas.

Remember them.
Respect their enterprise.
It takes a certain
kind of boldness
to have seen such
islands first of all.

In the mind's atlas,
footnotes, like broken rules,
are not without importance.

Who found America?

Those canny trawlers,
absent for months,
fishing the depths,
must have been somewhere
with their sealed lips.

From *Rottnest Island*

V
Christmas Day. 1696.
Came to the Southland.
Drew back. Approached
an island five leagues
from the main shore,
bays and rocky outcrops.
Waited four days.

Gloves for the oarsmen;
extra rations in the boats
going ashore. Arrived at
early light; glad to be
over the reef, touching land.
Anchored safely. De Vlamingh
to his own tent. Then, night.

Birds floating to our hands.
Surmounted some low hills.
A clover leaf of lakes at
the centre, mostly brine.

Walked northwards. Lizards,
reptiles. A rat-like creature
hunching its back; droppings
like loathsome birds' eggs.
Spiky bracken. Limestone.
No signs of habitation.

Returned to the ship after
three days. The Southland
hazy in the morning sun.
Set sail ...

VI
All day the bicycles come and go
from General Store to bungalow.

From bungalow to Bakery and back
to get the makings for a midday snack.

At night, again, like carefree ships,
the bikes drift past on random trips.

Down to the Tearooms beneath the stars,
a younger brother on the handlebars.

To visit the pub; friends, perhaps.
Jokes about fishing; afternoon naps.

A hand of cards and a quiet beer.
The days cycle past, year by year.

Cycling back to the bungalow,
we can see the mainland lights aglow.

Out there, way out, that luminous shelf,
the haze of light and the city itself.

John Tranter

The Great Artist Reconsiders the Homeric Simile

He looks back over the last metaphor
and his eyes shift their focus, his gaze weakly
taking in the litter on the desk and then
the blurred garden, its order and composition:
bare trees, a path strewn with leaves,
a distant figure dawdling at the gate—
light dazzles the window-pane with brilliant
diamonds of dew—he sighs, and drops his pen.
As when a detective in the spring has found
a junk-struck hippy crouching in her pad
at the dead end of Desolation Alley, and
has faked the evidence and booked her, soon
her man returning giftless from his rounds
sees the flat empty and his girl-friend gone;
at that he freaks out, and checks his stride
and with short uneasy steps circles the block,
with smothered groans repeating her name; but she
lies on the cell floor, overdosed,
a heap of bright rags—never again
will those disco mirrors catch her image
floating by, nor the bathroom echo her
withdrawal screams—as that poor addict
hides in horror till the heat cools off,
nor knows his loss, so Matthew Arnold brooded
on his failing similes. His cup of tea
grew cold as he stared out at the Autumn
leaves; a change of air was what he needed,

a holiday at Dover, or Torquay ...
and as he mused, the lounger at the gate—
the Future—turned his back, and walked away.

Lufthansa

Flying up a valley in the Alps where the rock
rushes past like a broken diorama
I'm struck by an acute feeling of precision—
the way the wing-tips flex, just a little
as the German crew adjust the tilt of the sky and
bank us all into a minor course correction
while the turbo-props gulp at the mist
with their old-fashioned thirsty thunder—or
you notice how the hostess, perfecting a smile
as she offers you a dozen drinks, enacts what is
almost a craft: Technical Drawing, for example,
a subject where desire and function, in the hands
of a Dürer, can force a thousand fine ink lines
to bite into the doubts of an epoch, spelling
Humanism. Those ice reefs repeat the motto
whispered by the snow-drifts on the north side
of the woods and model villages: the sun
has a favourite leaning, and the Nordic flaw
is a glow alcohol can fan into a flame.
And what is this truth that holds the grey
shaking metal whole while we believe in it?
The radar keeps its sweeping intermittent promises
speaking metaphysics on the phosphor screen;
our faith is sad and practical, and leads back
to our bodies, to the smile behind the drink
trolley and her white knuckles as the plane drops
a hundred feet. The sun slanting through a porthole
blitzes the ice-blocks in my glass of lemonade
and splinters light across the cabin ceiling.
No, two drinks—one for me, one for Katharina
sleeping somewhere—suddenly the Captain
lifts us up and over the final wall
explaining roads, a town, a distant lake
as a dictionary of shelter—sleeping elsewhere
under a night sky growing bright with stars.

David Foster

From *The Fleeing Atalanta*

98

Alchemists say the Stone turns lead to gold
This is true
Chemists say lead cannot be turned to gold
This is true
Lead has never been turned to gold
No one who found the Stone used it
To turn lead to gold

I myself found the Stone
For a brief time, and in that time
I wished, but did not wish to turn lead to gold
I asked to be ridded of my greatest problem
The lust that had ruined me as a man
To my surprise, my lust was not
Abolished but fulfilled:
The hardest irony of all

104

Seeking heat men become cold, and look for meaning
And know instinctively where to find it
Choose what they seek in brothels and public bars
Where the Stone lies hidden in the sewer.
See Christ's life as a parable
Of the search for the Stone, revealed
And arrogated from the many by the few. Who spent his time
Seeking among publicans and sinners those who sought wives
And communion with God through wine
Who knew instinctively where to look.
And we had better look until we are tired of looking too, though
Our instincts seem to fail. Better cold
Than neither hot nor cold
Better cold than lukewarm.
In a well-executed death
Christ died as an eponym
For birth-giving death, arousing
The annoyance of the lukewarm, while the heavens
Fertilised the earth. The cold which receives the heat
As when the earth receives rain

Is greatly rewarded, being
Desperate for heat.
Heat which is so hot it does not make lukewarm
But infinitely hot, the increment being so great.
Christ spoke in parables of vineyards and marriage feasts
And said, let them receive it
Who are able to receive it.
Those who contend with the heat, and lose
Are better than those who do not contend
Let no one abstain except he who receives
For he who withholds without receiving is least acceptable of all
Only those who can see can see who is blind
Men look for meaning, but they do not find it without the help of
    God
Who in defiance of instinct seeks whom He chooses:
Who says the antithesis of I seek without finding is not I find what
    I seek
But I seek what I find

109

Don't give everything
How many times have you heard them say
Don't give everything
You would think that they
Had given everything and lost, but hardly
A thing could be further from the truth.
They lost because they did not give everything
They thought that they had nothing to give
But everything is nothing till it is given
To someone else, then it becomes something.
Beyond a certain threshold to give is to acquire, and we
Should not care that others have universally failed
When it is so obvious to us why: I say
The laws of nature are functioning perfectly:
The threshold will extend us till we die

Robert Adamson

Dead Horse Bay

Quick hands on spinning ropes
at dawn, blood rising
to the jumping cords.

Ice-pack over bad burns
and cat fish venom.
Rock salt against gut-slime.

A southerly blowing up
on the full tide, nets
in mud and mesh-gutting snags.

The bread tasting
like kero-sponge, crazed gulls
crashing into the stern.

Mullet at three cents a pound
by the time sun hits
the bar of the Angler's Rest.

Get drunk enough to keep at it,
clean the gear for tonight
and another bash.

Remember that night in 68
How we killed 'em
right through the month?

Couldn't have gone wrong—
so thick you could've
walked over the water.

When the bream are running
like that, nothing can touch you
everything seems to matter,

you don't want 'em to stop
and you can't slow down
and you can't imagine.

Gumaitj People

Arnhem Land

Songs from the Goulburn Island Song Cycle

Song 10

The bird saw the young Burara girls, twisting their strings, making
    string figures.
Watching with head poised, the bird cries ...

The pigeon saw the young Gunwinggu girls, twisting their
    strings ...
With head poised, saw their hands moving, saw the blood as they
    moved their heels.
The pigeon watches them, flapping its wings and calling out as it
    sees the blood.
The cry goes out to Blue Mud Bay, among the new paperbark
    shoots ...
The cry of the bird goes over to Goulburn Island ...
Perched on the topmost leaves of the cabbage palm ...
Clasping the cabbage palm with its claws ...
Crying out as it sees the blood.
It saw them twisting their strings, moving the string-patterns—
    young girls of the Gunwinggu tribe ...

Song 11

They saw the young girls twisting their strings, Goulburn Island
    men and men from the Woolen River:
Young girls of the western clans, twisting their breast girdles among
    the cabbage palm foliage ...
Stealthily creeping, the men grasp the cabbage tree leaves to search
    for their sweethearts.
Stealthily moving, they bend down to hide with their lovers among
    the foliage ...
With penis erect, those Goulburn Island men, from the young girls'
    swaying buttocks ...
They are always there, at the wide expanse of water ...
Always there, at the billabong edged with bamboo.
Feeling the urge for play, as they saw the young girls of the western
    clans,
Saw the young girls hiding themselves, twisting the strings ...
Girls twisting their breast girdles, making string figures: and men
    with erect penes,
Goulburn Island men, as the young girls sway their buttocks.

Song 12

They seize the young girls of the western tribes, with their swaying
    buttocks—those Goulburn Island men ...
Young girls squealing in pain, from the long penis ...
Girls of the western clans, desiring pleasure, pushed on to their
    backs among the cabbage palm foliage ...
Lying down, copulating—always there, moving their buttocks ...
Men of Goulburn Island, with long penes ...

Seizing the beautiful young girls, of the western tribes ...
They are always there at that billabong edged with bamboo ...
Hear the sound of their buttocks, the men from Goulburn Island
    moving their penes ...
For these are beautiful girls, of the western tribes ...
And the penis becomes erect, as their buttocks move ...
They are always there at the place of Standing Clouds, of the rising
    western clouds,
Pushed on to their backs, lying down among the cabbage palm
    foliage ...

Song 13

Ejaculating into their vaginas—young girls of the western tribes.
Ejaculating semen, into the young Burara girls ...
Those Goulburn Island men, with their long penes;
Semen flowing from them into the young girls ...
For they are always there, moving their buttocks.
They are always there, at the wide expanse of water ...
Ejaculating, among the cabbage palm foliage:
They cry out, those young girls of the Nagara tribe ...
He ejaculates semen for her, among the cabbage palm foliage ...
Ejaculating for the young girls of the western clans ...
From the long penes of men from Goulburn Island ...
They are always there at the open expanse of water, at the sea-eagle
    nest ...
Ejaculating semen, for the young girls ...
Into the young girls of the western tribes ...
For they are ours—it is for this that they make string figures ... [the
    men say]
Thus we ejaculate for her—into the young girl's vagina.
Semen, among the cabbage palm foliage ...
Thus we push her over, among the foliage;
We ejaculate semen into their vaginas—young girls of the western
    tribes ...
Ejaculating semen, into the young Burara girls ...
For they move their buttocks, those people from Goulburn Island.

Translated by Ronald M. Berndt

Robert Gray

Flames and Dangling Wire

On a highway over the marshland.
Off to one side, the smoke of different fires in a row,
like fingers spread and dragged to smudge:
it is an always-burning dump.

Behind us, the city
driven like stakes into the earth.
A waterbird lifts above this silt
as a turtle moves on the Galapagos shore.

We turn off down a gravel road,
approaching the dump. All the air wobbles
in some cheap mirror.
There is a fog over the hot sun.

Now the distant buildings are stencilled in the smoke.
And we come to a landscape of tin cans,
of cars like skulls,
that is rolling in its sand dune shapes.

Among these vast grey plastic sheets of heat,
shadowy figures
who seem engaged in identifying the dead—
they are the attendants, in overalls and goggles,

forking over rubbish on the dampened fires.
A sour smoke
is hauled out everywhere,
thin, like rope. And there are others moving—scavengers.

As in hell the devils
might pick about amongst our souls, for vestiges
of appetite
with which to stimulate themselves,

so these figures
seem to be wandering, disconsolate, with an eternity
for turning up
some peculiar sensation.

We get out and move around, also.
The smell is huge,
blasting the mouth dry:
the tons of rotten newspaper, and great cuds of cloth …

And standing where I see the mirage of the city
I realize I am in the future.
This is how it shall be after men have gone.
It will be made of things that worked.

A labourer hoists an unidentifiable mulch
on his fork, throws it in the flame:
something flaps
like the rag held up in 'The Raft of the Medusa'.

Another, approached through the smoke;
and for a moment he could seem that demon of the long barge pole.
—It is a man, wiping his eyes.
Someone who worked here would have to weep,

and so we speak. The rims beneath his eyes are wet
as an oyster, and red.
Knowing all that he does about us,
how can he avoid a hatred of men?

Going on, I notice an old radio, that spills
its dangling wire—
and I realize how somewhere the voices it received
are still travelling,

skidding away, riddled, around the arc of the universe;
and with them, the horse-laughs, and the Chopin
which was the sound of the curtains lifting,
one time, to a coast of light.

Curriculum Vitae

1

Once, playing cricket, beneath a toast-dry hill,
I heard the bat crack, but watched a moment longer
a swallow, racing lightly, just above the ground. I was impressed by
    the way
the bird skimmed, fast as a cricket ball.
It was decided for me, within that instant,
where my interests lay.

And the trajectories at dusk of random moths and lone decisive
    swallow
will often still preoccupy me, until dew occludes the air.

2

I can remember there were swallows that used to sew together
the bars of a cattle yard.
I would be sitting in morning sunlight
on the top rail, to feel its polished surface
beneath my hands.
A silvery, weathered log with the sheen of thistle's flax.

3

A cow was in the stocks with the calm expression of a Quaker;
and my father stretched his fingers,
a pianist seated on a chopping block. He bent his forehead to an
    instrument
like something out of Heath Robinson—
a dangling bagpipes, big as a piano,
that was played by tugging at organ stops.
The cow began to loosen its milk: its tits were disgorged,
the size and colour of small carrots;
and milk was flourished in the bucket, two skewer-thin daggers
sharpened on each other underhand.
Then, as the bucket filled, there would be the sound of a tap running
into deep suds at the end of a bath.
Finally, the calf was let in to have its turn,
and this sounded like a workman building-up a big lather between
    his hands.

The concrete in those bails was shattered, but lay together
as though a platform of river stones; and water ran there constantly
from a hose, breaking up and bearing off
the hot lava of any cow-pats. That water was delicate and closely-
    branched—
a long weed fluttering, on such a breezy morning.

4

There were big dents of cloud-shadow on the blue-forested
    mountain;
and far off, across
the paddocks, through midday heat, the fluttering silk scarf
of a light purple range.
Our mountain was the kite, and those in the distance, its tail,
through all the heat-wavering days.

And many broken, dead trees had been left standing about,
like stone ruins: pillars that held out the remnants

of cloisters and fine stonework,
with rubble beneath them. But the air was so clear; so uncrowded
with any past—
arbitrary corridors, unpeopled, through the air.
Room for the mind to travel on and on.
I used to have to stop, often, to stand there, in that immense
    amphitheatre
of silence and light.

5

I remember watching our three or four geese let loose and rushing,
with their heads beating sideways like metronomes,
towards a dam where the mountain-top hung;
and when they entered the water, that mountain's image came apart
suddenly, the way a cabbage falls into coleslaw.
Everything was changed, as easily as that.

6

Since then, I have been, for instance, in Petticoat Lane—pushing by
through narrow, stacked alleys,
among the tons of rotting garbage for sale,
and have seen the really poor.
Those people seemed just dangling paper dolls, threaded onto
a genetic string—
the genes of poverty, starch, lack of sun,
and stunted, hopeless spirit everywhere. Their crossed eyes, warts,
twisted faces, snaggle teeth,
drunkenness were Dickens still, in '70 something,
again in '82.—People in greasy rags, on crutches, weeding wet butts
from the gutter, wild-eyed,
spiky-haired, foul-muttering.
The women were shaped like slapped-together piles of clay. They
    scrabbled
amongst junk, scratching themselves viciously,
shouting and oblivious ...

What is such an evil, but the continuing effect
of Capital's Stalinism?
Enclosure, as John Clare has said, lets not a thing remain.

And then, an hour later, in the West End I found
how much worse I thought the fleshy,
askance, meringue-coloured, prissy-lipped upperclass face—so
    sleek

in its obliviousness.
People go rotten with culture, also.

7

Another time, in Washington, when my girlfriend had gone
to see someone,
and while I was sitting at an upstairs window, I watched the bald
    man
who lived next door, after he'd argued once more
with his wife, come out to stand alone,
also, in their backyard—round as a pebble, in his singlet,
but nowhere near so hard.
He was standing with chin sunk,
holding the garden hose—a narrowed stream
he felt around with
closely, like a blind man's cane.
It disturbed me to see him like that—and then, as I started to
    consider myself,
I saw that I was walking
in those silver paddocks, again,
which as a kid I'd known.

8

Or, travelling alone in Europe once, and staying in a provincial city,
indolent and homesick of an afternoon,
I turned, as ever, to the museum.
In such a mood, however, the masterpiece will often no longer
    serve:
it seems too strenuous and too elevated;
it belongs in a world too far beyond one's own.
From experience, one has learned at these times to follow that
    arrow, *Ecole française*
XIXe siècle. There, on an attic floor,
unnoticed by the attendant, a newspaper crumpled
over his boots, or along the deserted outer corridors,
before tall windows, in the light from which
many of them are cancelled,
hang one's faithful mediocrities—in sympathy with whom
one had thought to be borne through until dinnertime.
Armand Guillaumin, Léon Cogniet, Jules Dupré, Félix Ziem:
no artistic claims can be made for these. Their sluggish or
    bituminous pigment,
greasy sheen, and craquelure,

their failures, so complex and sad, have earned them
'an undisturbed repose'.
And yet, even these harmless,
unassuming, and forgotten, as I glanced among them, on this
   occasion,
were forgotten
by their one idle, arbitrary re-creator,
and the landscapes that came far more vividly before my eyes
were all memories.

9

Into my mind there has always come, when travelling,
images of the twisted Hawkesbury bush
crackling in the heat, and scattering its bark and twigs about,
white sunlight flicked
thickly on the frothy surges
and troughs of its greenery; and within those forests,
great pools of deep fern, afloat
beneath a sandstone rock-lip; and of the Platonic blueness
of the sky; and recollections of Coledale and Thirroul
on their clifftops, where sea-spray
blows among the pines and eucalypts; and, most of all, of those
   forests,
cool, light-flouncing, with white female limbs,
and the yeasted green pastures,
where my mind first opened, like a bubble from a glass-blower's
   tube,
and shone, reflecting
things as they are—
there, where I have felt, anxiously, I would find them
a while longer,
after passing Kempsey, once more, on the Mail train of an early
   morning.

Mark O'Connor

Turtles Hatching

Waiting for weeks till the last one is ready to run, they

break through to twilight: the life-race is on.
Winds and oceans that call give no order but one:
'Downhill, fast; when you hit water, swim.' Last

will be picked; so will first. One in a hundred survives.
So they break sand & run, downhill as if cursed. (Seagulls
halloo joy, ghost-crabs skitter out.) They are high-revving toys,

each wound for his chance. The course is uncertain,
ten sandy yards to cool foam, or half of a low-tide mile
over pits and castles of rock-crab, every hole an abyss,

every cross-ridge a death-lane; unable to stop,
indifferent whether scrambling in sand, scrabbling in slime,
or sculling deluded through sand-pools to beaches of death.

Caught in cracks they push hard down the crab's throat,
still punting on while life lasts, in search of the dark
and lovely reef water, the splash in the in-walled ear.

Their limbs have no setting but *go*. Friendly and clean,
with their leathery touch in the palm, likeable as a dry
handshake, a childish pleasure to handle, determined

as cats; this driving downhill force that will reach,
tourist, twice the mass of your coffin, yet weigh,
till it comes ashore, not a gram.

Tweaks the heart, though, to see them seek fate in a crab-hole.
I pulled one out once, wedged and still struggling
down, dropped it with a jerk—a great horny claw

like a parrot's beak had crushed the midsection, sheared
off the head, and behind moved the armoured tarantula legs
of a hairy scuttler with lobe-stalked eyes.

In pity I gathered a living brother, hiked it over the rock-flat
(fighting on in my hand) while its brethren, obedient,
filed along moonless crevices, sating ambuscades of queued up
    crabs,

laid it down on a rock slope, a foot from the water. It flopped
on straight for its freedom, tripped over a two-inch ledge—
fell and rocked on its back. (A crab darted out, saw my shadow,
    back

sidled to shadow.) It squirmed and righted itself, hurried
on (since Nature has taught them to fear no predator
but time, no approach will deflect them), found the slight wash of

a ripple and lost half its weight; then re-stranded, pressed on, met
the incoming surf of a wavelet, capsized, scrambled up, then
plugged on, hit new surf and breasted it well; turned its

flippers to sculling, still floating, too light to submerge;
spiralled a clumsy provocative line, spinnering out
to the moon, lucky with absent sharks and gentle water.

Slipping in, as it left, the shadow, a thousand times larger,
of a parent come shoreward to lay; two ends of the earthbound
process linked in the incomprehensible meeting of kin.

As the small shadow pedalled and bobbed, the great one wavered
    and slid.
For a second the greater obscured the lesser, than as surely
slid on; and the lesser was gone.

Fire

The oldest human fossil;
my castles those the stone age saw.
I am man's comforter, tiger-fence,
and my own master. Burning the past
I give cold sand, clean ash.
I am wisdom's father, technology's
mother, the first safe nest on ground;
Heraclitan flux made visible; round me
familiar grunts first made a family's meaning.

Still I burn with hot indifference; follow
who feeds me best. And my best servants
died before speech was baked in clay.

The Sun-Hunters

In old stories the jungle was busy
breeding monsters to attack
your intrepid explorers. Peccaries, pythons,
piranhas, and giant wife-seizing apes—
the rank green bubbled with them.
You used your 10 cartridges a day.

Today we know rainforest
is too busy to feel men passing through.
(Pity the Spanish conquistadors
marching for months in full armor!)
Mammals in a jungle are harmless hangers-on,
though the forest *is* magic,
and 20 years will turn

the farmer's pink elapsed porker
into Labrador-sized black foraging swine.
The jolly green game of strangle-my-neighbour
leaves little time for pointless assaults
on inedible bipeds—the real prize
in a jungle is not white flesh
but a place in the sun.

The bright spot that illumines the floor
from 9.30 to 10 most mornings
is some sapling's hope
of becoming a tree.
From above you see only the glorious
Upper Circle, not the slums beneath.
Even parasitic festoons seem gay,
those tons of creeper riding
on strangled boughs. But this is like
judging a country by its brochure.
Rain-forest is envy visible
and justified, in its dog-shade-dog world.
A blue quandong, emerging, shows
no sign of the struggle that brought it up
past the death of a thousand siblings
through a blanket of shade the height
of two dozen men on each other's shoulders.

Down below is the gloom of green knives.
Where cedar seeds patter to ground
a thicket of embryos starts the long climb.
Creepers fling lassoos, wrestle them
down to the soil like roped calves.
Promising thrusts to the canopy
are torn up by pigs,
blasted by a half-dozen caterpillars.
(A blue Ulysses floats on up
from the sapling it has doomed.)
The stillness is of impending death:
of wrestlers waiting for neckbones to crack.
The name of this pattern is Balance of Scarceness:
the rarer the tree, the scarcer what eats it—
ichneumon eats caterpillar, eats tree, eats light...

The strangler-fig sends out cathedral flanks,
vast in its leafless underworld, composing
a Gothic hall of arc-and-secant roots
round the plundered trunks.

Creepers lace all against the storm—
corruption making itself indispensable—till
guy-ropes hold up a miles-square tent,
the poles all slightly suspect.
Master of all is old Python-trunk himself
the giant Aristolochia.
Follow him, and you re-live history. Here
he began, spiralling up sheer
through thirty dark metres;
that Indian rope-trick speaks
of a host-tree, rotted and gone,
whose dimensions show
in the oak-thick swaying coil
like lathe-turnings run to fat.
There, near the river, he surged into light,
then roamed for a decade over the mangroves
before he returned to the jungle.
Here a side-stem has touched soil
and sent out suckers. Fed
from rhizomes below, they twine like smooth cords
leafless until they reach the light.
Some, missing their hold at the canopy,
dangle the giddy way down, to rub
on the earth before rising afresh.
Others have twined their hopes
up a cycloned-off stump that ends bare
half way to the sun—
around it the stems mat and dangle
stranded on a rotting trapeze.

Here his main-stalk straddled a dying white-cedar
and fifty years later fell down in spirals
that hang like the bowels of a gutted pig.
For five years he tried to save himself
festooning the underbrush with coils of flute-edged wood,
till here, down on his luck he sprawls,
waist-thick where a sapling snapped.
He rubs on the ground, striking roots, then rises sheer
as a bell-pull, the rope of a cathedral bell,
up into the light to smother a hectare.

Hal Colebatch

On the Death of Ludwig Erhard

If he had only been a more inspiring Leader,
and fired his vision till it touched the skies!
If he had but done one really high mass-murder,
it is probable some legend would arise.

If but he had believed the Superman emergent,
and seen himself as proof of that belief,
it is certain that his death would leave some Faithful
with a desolating sense of loss and grief.

If he had expressed some vaster dialectic,
or incarnation of some General Will,
if he had had the grace to be a Tragic Hero
whose dreams were shattered, we would praise him still.

If he had known himself possessed of Truth,
and those who disagreed as vermin to be slain,
he would be remembered as at least a great idealist,
as some have been, and some will be again.

But since he was a fat and kindly man,
who humbly cleared ruins, and successfully applied
prosaic knowledge for mere human happiness,
one assumes the poets' songs will be denied.

One Tourist's Cologne

Two eyes, the cathedral's spires look black
and baleful over the bridge. My old Ford van
struggles over high concrete. A middle-aged gentleman
directs me: Dünnewald, the little camping spot
in a few hectares of wood. At night I try
to imagine wolves. My first German forest.
Dwarf-delvings here? In the swimming-pool children play.
'Mützen für die Kleinen', a lady tells me there.
Quite right. They need their little bathing caps.
People give directions. Young and old
go out of their way to help. I try to understand.
Faint factory smoke in the air. The good burghers of Cologne
take their evening walks by the Rhine.
It is not easy to find

a real camping-place in this country, to find anything of The Wild.
At the cathedral fat men in scarlet
hold out their money boxes Für den Dom.
Six hundred years to build. They say a young architect
lost his soul to the devil over it. But it was finished in the end.
What did he dream of? Viewed from the ground close by
it is power, sheer size, a mountain of dark stone.
Further away something else—
the architect's skyward vision. Would it change
if the stone were white and new?
Bonn is nearby. Is this the core
of Germany today? What a lot of work
for some great architect! Will this country ever
dream of a future? Who may guess
what romanticism leads to? It must be the least of crimes
to play it safe, to play it safe.
Where is the soul here? Where the new blueprints?
'Boredom', another architect wrote,
'is the one hellish torture the poet forgot to describe.'
We have the Lorelei, and Dünnewald, white rhine-boats, suited
   Turks,
tourists für den Dom, and other payments made.
This is the boredom of what? There are bodies of opposite sexes,
intense inner lives, I suppose, for those equipped.
Respectability, respectability. Who dares sneer
at a country where people are not tortured?
To wish more? And further? How can we have both?
The razor's edge stands tall in so many airs.
The ultimate bourgeois city? Our van can barely crawl through
the quaint medieval streets, where every house is new.

Rhyll McMaster

Tanks

Travelling,
where darkness hauls the world
back underground,
we pass a solid water tank;
squatting on wooden stumps
its corrugations gleam the dull combusting silver
of elephant hide.

Summer nights breed tanks
and a belief that the moon
was made from a tank smashed into sky passage,
empty and dank, corroded by lichens.

In hollows behind outhouses
or back of a wall of pepper trees, tanks
are sleeping, stirring.
They expand, become nervous and rough
and, grinning with iron dimples
begin to move out to the edge of town
to wait for the lorry to Places Unknown.

Mutton Bird Man

'Come girlies and fellas, as quick as you can
this mutton bird oil will give you a shine,
a real humdinger—see the bird on front?
Here's a free try for the first in line.'
At his post on Main Beach, the sun spat on his tan,
treacle and boot polish rubbed into wood—
Mahogany Man in a white tennis hat.

'There's a brave girlie, now just stand still
while I rub it down here and over the hill!
See her skin glisten? She'll be brown as a bun,'
said the prancing old spruiker, his calves like hams
as his muscles in motion played darts with the sun.

'It's a Surfers Paradise, but hell for the girl
with flesh like white pudding; come give it a whirl.
For ten shillings and sixpence you'll shine like silk
you'll be sweet and brown as a rum and milk.'

I wonder what happened to the Mutton Bird Man
who smacked birds on the head with a great big stick?
In the gloom of the evening on the Mutton Bird isle
those birds would gather without much style
with their stumpy wings and fatty breasts
digging burrows on the sandhills' crests ...

Sleep little birdies, I'm sure he's gone
to that Great Big Beach where justice is done,
stumping the dunes on his withered pegs,
surrounded by 'girlies' no longer fresh,
their skin like the frills on overfried eggs.

Peter Kocan

Cows

Cows graze across the hill,
Measuring the day
As their shadows tell
Irrelevant time. Their gait is half-way
Between moving and standing still.

The sun is gentle on the green
Of their meadow, their mouths deep
In its heavy warmth.
A watcher could fall asleep
Into the depth
Of that untroubled scene.

From each dewdrop morning
To every day's end
They follow the cycle
Of the rhythm of the world turning
In its season. A miracle
Of normalcy is a cow's mind.

Beyond thought's prickling fever
They dwell in the grace
Of their own true concerns,
And in that place
Know they will live forever
With butterflies around their horns.

An Inmate

That quiet man with the hoe is a beast
Of rape, or arson, or murder. In him
Lies embodied a huge evil, affirmed
And diagnosed; a guilt, documented
In all of the appropriate sources.

His infamy has died to a bean patch
In this place for the Criminally Insane
And the long years in which to ponder
Every ageing twinge of a routine
Prefiguring the coffin's tedium.

This man has been severed like a cancer
From the flesh of the world. Now speak, Justice,
And explain why it seems always, beyond
The last tangled skein of cause and effect,
One finds only the victims of victims!

Yet, this Spring day, as he tends the bean rows
The wind grants him full measure of sweet scent;
The sun does not quibble to warm him;
Nor do small birds see him as anything
But a familiar part of their scene.

For there is a scheme of things much greater
Than any he could be banished from:
One whose only law is that Time enact
Both decay and renewal equally,
Keeping no record and bearing no grudge.

And if, somehow, he could simply enter
To that earth-deep empathy, even he
—Poor inmate plotting a ritual
Of knotted sheets for his midnight hour—
Might find a sense of worth, a part to play.

The Mutineer's Ballad

The paleness of hunger
Had put such beauty on.
My darling sighed as softly
As a little swan.

Softly she sighed and settled
As I sat by the bed,
Wishing she'd be ugly
And hearty instead.

Some need fine carriages
And emeralds and silk.
My swan needed just a crumb
And a sip of milk.

I promised I'd not leave her long
And ran to beg a penny.
The people went to and fro
But none gave any.

They flung me their red curses,
The blue coins of their eyes,

But never a brown penny
For what a penny buys.

I swore to my darling
I'd not leave her long,
And would have kept my promise
But for the press-gang.

O it was a madman
They took from the shore!
But I grew sane directly
Aboard a man-o'-war.

For the sails' colour
Is pallid as the swan,
And the wind in the rigging
Sighs on and on.

Tomorrow from the yardarm
I'll return to her
With gold of sunrise gathered
High in the air.

Gary Catalano

The Jews Speak in Heaven

We stood at the edge
of the gouged pit

and looked down
into history. With all

those unbroken clods
at its edge

it looked like
a tin-can, hastily

torn open.
As we listened

to new metal
slipping into

the greased bolts
how could we

reproach the sky
when it showed us

no Jehovah? There
—there was the warmth

of known
stretchmarked flesh

and there, too,
the strains of a

familiar tune
ringing

in our heads. Soon it became
so loud

our ears
even bled.

Australia

I breathe the air of another country
when I walk among these people.
How terrible it is!

Generations have yearned for the new life
and it comes to this!
What will hold them upright

when their dreams are repossessed
and sold again at a discount?
But give me the smell of used nails

rusting in tins, and the dreams
that were swaddled in hessian.
I want the scene before it changed—

the blackberry-choked creeks,
the roads going nowhere, the shyness
of youth. Let me see again

the glitter of galvanized iron,
the scatter of farms and chicken-sheds,
and pictures like this:

in an afternoon of its own
a tortoise makes its slow way
across a road of blue metal and tar.

It pulls in its head at the sound
of an approaching car, whose driver stops,
gets out, then moves it into the tall grass

at the side of the road,
where a creek has begun to unthread itself
from a soak, and etch its straggly line

across the adjoining paddock,
whose wall of trees closes off the scene
from all the other countries in the world.

Martin Johnston

In Memoriam

A painting would have been the best way to get things over
but my father's old Winsor & Newtons still sit in their tin box
unused for three years except for when I painted
a shoddy flamboyant number on our front door.
They have hardened and cracked like introverted poets.

Coloured inks will soak through the best bond paper
in a soft fuzz of amoebas, a sunset blur
of fruit-coloured clouds, a weak ambiguous vision.
I could never use chalk or charcoal.
The poem must stalk on its own thin mantis legs.

We become, in any case, too attached to colour.
Graphite and lignite, slate and marble
that make cliff-faces, monuments, holes in the ground
have a greater permanence in their crumbling way
but aren't what we like to look at

or not in themselves. Ever since we learned about emblems
and correspondences, we have mirrored ourselves in the sea
and the rock; and the subtle shadowed faces
of our friends and rivals, as the light changes, reflect
the obliquities of our shadows, our syntax, our blood.

O'Hara, Berryman, Seferis, Pound
have a lot in common. Not only are they all dead poets
but they make up a metrically perfect line
running on iambic sleepers to whatever personal
ameliorations I think, for me, they're good for.

And that's the way the game goes. Reading the Saturday papers
and the cultured magazines, I find my nightmares visited
by a terrible vision of contemporaries writing elegies
notebooked and rainslicked at the graveside
or serial as Magritte's windows or Dunne's time

in a recession of identical rooms.
Whether there is particular grief in the deaths of poets
is a question that much engages us,
that we answer always in the affirmative,
a priori, because it's very useful to us to do so.

Pale watercolour lovers in the pastel sun
we can rape and chomp our friends' corpses at midnight,
hunch and sidle in the morgue, our eyes
a tracery of red veins in the Gothick crypt, and the tourist
maps show Transylvania's regular trains, its ordered roads.

Because it does come down to rape, this invasion
of one's substance by that of another
without connivance. And not the strongest or fiercest
can fight it, but must lie back and open
up to the slime and spawn.

Death and rebirth myths are made by poets, and no wonder:
one Dransfield can feed dozens of us for a month,
a Webb for years. And they're fair game, we can plead continuance,
no poet ever died a poet: as the salt muck filled Shelley
the empyrean gave way to the nibbling fish and the cold.

I should have hauled out the oils and tried to do a townscape
after all, a grey square with stoas and colonnades
toothed with eroding busts, their long shadows staining
each other and the foreshortened watchers'
death-watch beetle-scuttle across clattering bleached stone.

For the fan of letters opens and shuts and the wind blows
errant zig-zags of light and night through the phrases,
chops, remoulds, effaces. Theologians
have always found dismembered cannibals tough.
The whole thing becomes too tight, which is not at all

what's needed, whatever sensualists may say.
Too like Zen archery, too painful somewhere around
what used to be called the heart. The parataxis
of time and light could have flowed around and through
these dead and living poets and myself.

That would have been a pretty nonsense. Instead the flicker-
flicker of a zoetrope. In this peepshow world
all styles come down to punctuation. O Mayakovsky,
Buckmaster, all of you, they're circumventing Euclid.
They knew that parallel lines in curved space meet

eventually, somewhere: in the black hole between spaces,
the full stop with no sentence on either side,
between the moving magic-lantern slides.
Not that you wouldn't have gone there yourselves willingly:
where the blood pours out the dead come to the feast.

Dennis Haskell

The Call

A stilled room to which I am called
by an unknown voice, not knowing,
because of its great stillness,
that it calls from my son's sleep.
In the bush nothing stirs. For once
no breeze grabs hold of the curtains.
Sunk back into his body the voice quietens.
I shift his legs, twisted in the sheets,
grateful that this sudden nightmare
has crept back into its own beginnings.
In his sleep I can hold his arms or arrange his breathing
without objection,
his will gone, sleep
like the end of an illness.

How we look for meaning in such actions,
as if God's voice called from the centre of our sleep,
but there is nothing: only a silence so complete
love itself might become a sickness.
What we inherit from the bush is a need for voices:
myself calling to my son in his recurrent silence.

So I listen again for his voice, or someone's: nothing
but silence come on us as it eventually must
and the need for sound greater than the need for any thing.
'God' is a word sunk deep in the blood, signifying
the certainty
silence will one day flood our arteries,
the hope for some voice, come
prowling through our sleep.

Over the tips of the trees, out across the face of the ocean,
nothing moves.
It is a humid January night with no breeze.
His body is in my hands.

Michael Dransfield

That Which We Call a Rose

Black greyed into white a nightmare of bicycling
over childhood roads harried peaceless
tomorrow came a mirage packed in hypodermic
the city we lived in then was not of your making
it was built by sculptors in the narcotic rooms of Stanley St
we solved time an error in judgement
it was stolen by the bosses and marketed as the eight hour day

Waking under a bridge in Canberra to chill scrawl
seeing the designs we had painted on its concrete like gnawed fresco
Venice with merchants feasting while Cimabue sank deeper into
                                        cobweb
as the huns approached in skin boats
back in the world Ric and George on the morgue-lists of morning
one dead of hunger the other of overdose their ideals precluded them
from the Great Society they are with the angels now

I dreamt of satori a sudden crystal wherein civilisation was seen
more truly than with cameras but it was your world not ours
yours is a glut of martyrs money and carbon monoxide
I dreamt of next week perhaps then we would eat again
                                        sleep in a house again
perhaps we would wake to find humanity where at present
freedom is obsolete and honour a heresy. Innocently
I dreamt that madness passes like a dream.

Fix

It is waking in the night,
after the theatres and before the milkman,
alerted by some signal from the golden drug tapeworm
that eats yr flesh and drinks yr peace;
you reach for a needle and busy yrself
preparing the utopia substance in a blackened
spoon held in candle flame

by now yr thumb and finger are leathery
being so often burned this way—
it hurts much less than withdrawal and the hand
is needed for little else now anyway.
Then cordon off the arm with a belt,
probe for a vein, send the dream-transfusion out
on a voyage among your body machinery. Hits you like sleep—
sweet, illusory, fast, with a semblance of forever.
For a while the fires die down in you,
until you die down in the fires.
Once you have become a drug addict
you will never want to be anything else.

Pioneer Lane

Erskineville. The sun came round a corner,
and saw, and went. The sun's habitual corner.
Nothing unusual. The air they breathe
rolls out obscenely from the factory chimneys.
Old age. Just that. No more. And an appraisal
of work-years wasting in these sunless narrows
of terrace-streets which close themselves away,
rejecting newness like the baby stifled
by Leagues Club widows and the warm indifference
of public bars, and traffic loud and poisonous.
Day is so stale; sit in the sun; let it
warm away your questions. Things seem better
in the sun, even when you are old,
as old as these—or so we think—or almost.
Their retribution comes beyond the grave.
Not savage or pretentiously hostile,
they'll gather round, these veterans of Lone Pine
and Villers-Bret. and Passchendaele and Ypres,
a circle close with friendship; and there'll be
no pension-degradation; they'll be free,
these pioneers who made Australia
and fought to keep it, time on bitter time,
a place they could grow old in, never thinking
they'd be despised for even that senescence.
They think I know, of those who stayed behind
in the warm ridges of Gallipoli,
or Flanders mud. A cigarette-smoke circle,
two coins tossed high into the endless year,
falling to choruses of 'Jesus Christ'.

Marion Alexopoulos

Night Flight

Passengers afloat on many thousand feet
of air.
We hiss like a wind pipe,
tunnel through the night
sheathed in our grey jet.
There are a few lights for readers
propped over satin pages,
others in dental postures
deep in mucousy sleep.
Engines hum to airborne babies.
Outside the wide mouth of blue-black
opens, air-greedy, star-toothed.
My forehead against the glass
caught between worlds,
he comes flying up to touch me.
A hand bridges altitude;
a voice says, 'I am coming with you.'
A dead man swims
beyond the fuselage.

Richard Tipping

Men at Work

jack hammer! brain chiseller! come out!
abandon your fortress of warning signs
& surrender! you are surrounded
by an evergrowing angry mob
of ears! even oldwar veterans
poke their tongues out at you
like medals! urchins mock your prattle
by lighting squibs! dogs bark! even dada
was never so unkind! you are making the street
shudder with your furious
staccato farts! boatloads of earmuffs
will not suffice! trench digger! you are outcast
like embarrassing pyjamas! go back to dental school
where you belong!

Mangoes

For Robyn Ravlich

mangoes are not cigarettes
mangoes are fleshy skinful passionate fruits
mangoes are hungry to be sucked
mangoes are glad to be stuck in the teeth
mangoes like slush & kissing

mangoes are not filter tipped
mangoes are idiosyncratic seasonal seducers
mangoes are worse than adams apple
mangoes are what parents & parliaments warn against
mangoes like making rude noises

mangoes are not extra mild
mangoes are greedy delicious tongueteasers
mangoes are violently soft
mangoes are fibrous intestinal lovebites
mangoes like beginning once again

mangoes are not cigarettes
mangoes are tangible sensual intelligence
mangoes are debauched antisocialites
mangoes are a positive good in the world
mangoes like poetry

Susan Hampton

The Crafty Butcher

It's a real old-fashioned butcher's shop
with carcasses on hooks, watch your shoulder,
and sawdust on the floor.
The boy's arms are red-streaked:
he's had his hands inside a cow.
His face has soft white hairs, and while he
tenderly wraps my meat I watch the boss at work.
He reaches to a whole leg on a hook
and slick, neat as an eye in the future,
there's a fingerhold: he tugs the muscle
and begins his craft.

He knows exactly where to put the knife in
and the angle and depth of the cut, and
there's the big knuckle of the knee
and a glistening white thighbone.
A few drops of blood hit the floor,
and away comes the round steak. I reach down
and feel the running muscle
at the back of my thigh, solid as the cow's
which is now hung by the fingerhold
on an empty hook. Don't wince, this
is the craft of the butcher. Look at his face,
those cheekbones, he's perfectly calm
and good at his job.

Then there's just the leg bone with that
glowing knuckle white as the lack of pain
after death, and clean as a finishing line.

The Fire Station's Delight

The fire station's delight
is the energy of sudden arrival
this red love that burns through cities
and sets whole buildings awash.
There are no fires today: in the station
near the deli, the men concentrate on the
Jarlsberg, brie, blue castello, roll-mops,
cottage cheese, Latvian black bread, olives,
the dry white wine. One of the men
has hung a bird cage at the window
of the lunch room.

Now one fireman, leaning back and
patting his flannel shirt, looks out at
The Alternative Grass Centre, the new shop
across the road. The owner's cat
is walking across the display of
All Purpose Super-grass Carpet Turf.
The cat has the appearance of a tiger
because the display is a miniature
garden scene. There is an oblong
swimming pool, as long as the cat
which stretches out on the synthetic turf
beside it. Reclining on a banana chair
is a doll dressed in a bikini and
sunglasses. On the grass beside her is a
miniature bottle of Bio-therm.

Behind the firemen, coming down
from the upstairs room, is one
of their wives, carrying a tray of
just baked strudel. She accuses them
of not making the coffee, and they laugh,
pointing to the display in the window
across the road. She waits for the traffic
to pass, and looks intently at the cat
and the doll. 'The cat looks like a tiger,'
she says, 'doesn't it.'

Just then the phone rings, the bell goes wild,
there is a rush for serge and brass buttons,
huge boots are pulled on and the men leap away,
the town is burning somewhere.

Alan Gould

Ice

(Cromdale, 1892)

To windward midnight glowed, iridium sheen
as though Antarctica was raiding northward—
colossal silent submarine migration.

No one spoke. By dawn the sea was astral,
dazzling planets moving over opal;
our further skyline was an unclasped necklace.

It was the edge of world, yet when the wharfs
bulked like icebergs by the khaki Thames
I knew no image that was nearer home.

For some it shone, hypnotic as cocaine,
and others prone to say 'here angels hatch'
were lulled to watchfulness. The place was ours

and made our deaths a richer, harder burden.
By noon the ship was through, a spore, a vessel.

Galaxies

Hamburg: the clock hands move upon their star.
A liner glides along the Elbe, its lights

move through the city's lights, a galaxy
passing in silence through a galaxy.

My girl's behind me on the bed. She smokes
and minutes tick. Her time is waiting for
a time to end, a time to start. As mine is.
We are the flowers of our lineage,

were sinuous, bluff-mannered in the wine room
with all our company at like pursuits,
transactions that the liquor tantalised,
that led into this silence and this calm.

Yes, here I took myself, yes here was taken.
And here she chose to lie and here was lain.
Our choices and our fates, we house them both
like galaxies that pass through one another.

The liner's disappeared behind the docklands:
my girl is getting dressed again behind me.
I'll close the curtain on this night sky's map,
step out into the dark I know knows me.

Pearls

Tonight our heaven is an estuary
in which from some Egyptian balcony
a mocking queen has tossed her million pearls.

There's full-moon nights when sea and sky are halves
of one dark mollusc in the island legend
where wave enfolds with moon and genders pearls.

It is at night that heaven spends with freedom,
when we invent our sprees of spending frenzy
in hot Madras among the tents of pearls,

our fingers stringing moons of rose and milk
for working girls in Melbourne or New York ...
mere images to find the gist of pearls.

Our gestures are to match it, heaven's glut.
There's Cleopatra dropping that huge pearl
in stinging vinegar and drinking it,

and, stepping from her crust of stones and pearls,
that lavish Roman, Lollia Paulina—
voluptuaries each, each blind in this,

to snatch the pearl beneath the show of pearls.
I'm mindful also of that Japanese
drawing up his cages on a jetty

in 1905, who'd sown for seven years
seed-pearls that the plankton ate, at last
farming the itch that clothes a throat in pearls,

farming the fluky irritant that dives
deep into the oyster's mantle, globing
slowly, cyst-pearl or blister-pearl,

baroque, mellizas, torneadas, gem
with debris at its centre, moon that sweat
will yellow, never pearl without the show of pearl.

Mere images, concretions round a notion
for making time vivacious and unheeding
as a throat illumined once by pearls.

Let daybreak move behind us like a hand
and lightly brush away this heaven's pearls,
this trade-wind idleness between two harbours.

Jamie Grant

An Auditor Thinks about Female Nature

I have climbed all the way to the summit
of each of those dome-smooth alps, to rest

in whispers of mountain breeze, one hand
braced on the cairn, circled with smaller stones...

The geometric centre of the prairie
is a shallow well which doesn't have

a function. The legends of that place
refer to a giant vine—the roughness

of its bark, the texture of hemp or of cork—
connecting the well to a sky which teemed

perpetual nourishment. Lie down there
and listen to the ground: eons away,

the lava-shifts, the gnash of plates—faint sounds
scratch the ear drum, like the censored thunder

when someone lifts up furniture, in rooms
behind your wall. Sparse transparent grass blades.

The table land's waste spaces ...　The City
is located at the junction of two

highways: its suburbs spreading outwards
are shaped into a fan. All my commerce

centres on the harbour. When the vessels
go there, they soon unload their cargo, their

hard prows nudging into a salt-slick wharf.
Sometimes the storms upstream can dye the river

scarlet—the colour of house bricks, of sandstone...
On the other side of the mountains, there

is said to be another city. Rumours
of its influence have reached the provinces

where pragmatism rules our way of thinking.
Its produce, they say, is called Art. I tried,

once, to imagine the form of its gaudy
turrets, the ornamental ponds, the groves

of statuary; but the room inside
my head remained unfurnished, its walls as blank

as the lined sheets in life's stern ledger book.

Planes Landing

White metal tubes contain
whole villages: they descend
this steel-white mist, their noise
dazzling to lanes and chimneypots
like a memory of light.

Our hotel's top floor hides in fog
that spreads
across the country like an icecap.
Through double glass windows
we watch the jets subside

onto pale nets of cobweb hedges,
their slanting tails go down
behind skeleton elms
that hang round the village roofs
like television masts.

Where the hedges intersect
are small vacant fields,
their water green vague as holes
in a fishnet, colours leached
into spider-thick cloud.

We discover we're both thinking
about the crowd of strangers
all gazing straight ahead
down a tunnel of chairs. That's also
the tunnel of self. Their belts click

tight. Sloping down the aisle
discreet as a hostess, sticky
as cobwebs, the same thought nets
each separate mind. Each passenger
imagining death,

muzak spreading like ice.

Jennifer Maiden

The Mother-in-law of the Marquis de Sade

To sit people on gas-stove jets,
to plug them into light-sockets,
to prod with sparklers, stand
them barefoot in buckets of dry ice:
            I remember I devised
all these things in the bored
South Africa of childhood,
            the shrill
Brazil that still entrances
the clean children next door
when sometimes as I work
I leave my mind ajar
to overhear their play—unless
their mother hears as well
& threatens them with pain.

            When I was at home
there were jonquils beside the front path
& that word had lonely incision.
            When I was five
all my heroines were 'Jonquil':

now she lingers on, a kind
           of libidinous, sweet
'Shakespeare' but more explicitly
literate & camp. More than most
I always dreamt of princesses & torture,
but dreaded all the fiery
masks of punishment.

I have read that once in the Terror
the Marquis was appointed Magistrate
& none of the felons, not even
his mother-in-law, with whom
he had feuded for life, went to death.
With his books this made his ruin
double in the minds of government.

John Forbes

Malta

The sky was carpeted with Italian flak. Crump!
It explodes in the war comic. 'Stone the crows'
We think 'That was close'. Closer than we think
They sing 'If ever a wiz there was it's that
Wonderful wizard of Oz' or 'Circuits & bumps & loops
Laddie & how to get out of a spin'. Maria Schneider
Says: 'Tu es cet homme'. I loop the loop. 'Wizard
Prang, Red Leader!' exclaims the Wing Commander
'Want a beer?' All this helps the war along. We
Fight the Hearts & Minds campaign. For instance,
'My heart throbs inside a sandbagged blast-pen
But a lousy dumbness holds my tongue. It's a matter
Of mind over matter, my head avoiding the matter
Cradled in the space between your tits.' I'm not
But the aircrew are trained for this. They kept
Australia free. That is, up to scratch—not
Spectacular, but par for the course ('The sky was
Carpeted ...' etc.) I hope you can see this. It's
A picture of my father who almost flew a bomber.
Up close he looks like me—both cocky, a cigarette
Balanced on the edge of the intense inane. This comic
Is called 'Torpedoes Running'. Then later, over
Malta in a terminal spin, I throw away the rule book
& bring her in. Then a terrific Italian raid begins.

Up, Up, Home & Away

For Ranald Allen, Linn Cameron, Landon Watts
& Jenny Redford returning from Bali

Man Rapes 25 in fight
For Life & by then you
know it's time to go
       tropical skiing

Tho' the stunned haircuts
glooped in the passport
photos on arriving our
       thirst went South

Do you know Bob Hope? His
quips from the movie stoked
our days in the equable
       climate of Bali

We never knew such relief!
Flying over the Timor Sea
all we did was breathe &
       the food wishes

you were here, re-learning
how to loll & let the intense
inane clarify your skull. Crazed?
       You bet we were

But what's the damage to
a manual suntan & the
highs of sleep abuse?
       Remember our song

'Glue me to the reef again'?
How glad we were to let
others do their thinking
       for us. And now,

'in the pink' & happy blue
as the sunset glows & ends
like the Wasted Daze
       Dance Orchestra's

Special Number Grande Finale
we add water to the Acme
Instant Sydney, arrive home
       & have a party!

Angel

not serious about drugs
and into the sky that's
open like a face and
when night arrives the
smiling starts we being
our own stars as the days
pass in their cars and
the stereo fills with mud
we don't care   we walk
in the rhythm of a face
that's awake in the air
and I'd like to kiss you
but you've just washed
your hair. the night goes
on and we do too until
like pills dissolving
turn a glass of water
blue it's dawn and we
go to sleep we dream
like crazy and get rich
and go away.

Philip Salom

The Well

Strange and slow work: they dug in turn
a deepening well through the yellow pug,
peeling the thick clay from crow-bars
and picks; roped the full bucket up.

My father and a hired man, shoulders
at the concrete liners that cased the earth
and inched down in the gullet of work.

The tarpaulin above, white,
to billow and gulp the air
down to the man moving in the clay.

Winter

The day was close, overcast like a grey belly
pressing against my skin. Already
the stink of penny-royal
in the swamp. Our new dog
pounded through the shallows
sooling himself at imagined animals,
flinging showers from his silver-bluish coat.
Or seeing the dark among the trees
would return from this uncertainty,
stare at me with his strange blue eyes.
Then barked at belligerent crows
scattering on tree tops, their torn wings,
black fingers prodding the grey.

I kept to the track, the dark clay
patched with cinders, imprint
of tractor tyres like wintering fossils.
Past the sodden paper-barks,
rotting leaves spilling from crevices,
dodder vines tangling in the branches.

To where the brown, flooded river
leant on our bridge. I saw like pain
the dog run too suddenly to the slimy edge
slide on this greasy jaw of the river—
and was gone, gulped under,
dragged beneath the bridge by driftwood
smooth, crooked as severed limbs.

I groped in the froth along the edge,
kneeling on all fours, my eyes pounding
at the grey-green slime on the boards.
Felt the distended belly of the river
bump under the bridge;
claw marks deep in the wood.

The World of Dreams

The world of dreams
is no salvation
no-one lives in it
except the mad
who are sane there.
It is our half-life

by which we balance
and is replaced
by art and memory
against all better judgement.

It is wiser than us
but has no manners
it's as modern
as modern poetry
and always has been
it's as ancient
as cave paintings
and always will be.
You can fly in dreams
enter minds and bodies
more than mere technique
dreams speak in images
that are as obstinate
as they are strange
more dramatic than logic
thought is linear
dream's holistic
direct and yet oblique
as foreign films.

When it speaks
we are reminded
language is wakefulness
dubbed onto our actions,
as crude, simplistic
as white subtitles
amidst the colour.
When it's all over
it's what you saw
that you remember.

It seems the dying
take notice of their dreams
whereas the living
do more controlling
one is wisdom
one is ulterior motive
both are thrilling.
Dreams have common subjects
his and her illicit skins
bodies caught in images

each is electric
murdering or at peace.
Even an old boot if dreamt
is Ibsen's gun upon the wall.
You go to sleep exhausted
you can wake up drained
two lives a day.
It's every part of us
Tao, wheel, rose, cross,
every pagan urging as well.
Dreams save us from
the world   the world
saves us from our dreams.

Andrew Sant

Homage to the Canal People

Steered straight into this century I see narrowboats
loaded with coal, cheese, vats of vinegar trailing
a hard century behind them along
the polluted Grand Union, yet their cabins are bright
as their paintings of roses and castles
entering Oxford or Chester, a vivid variation
on a theme bleak and slow
as three-miles-an-hour journeys for boatmen
with more rain than sun
working into their faces.
It's pride that brightened them, and acceptance
that heaven's easy chair was far off as the dandies
composing themselves to ignore their progress through towns
like the arrival of gypsies,
cloth caps pulled down against
complacency. So they denied them a privilege—
their cabin doors closed tight
on china, brasswork and lace
fine as webs slung
across the just-after-dawn hedges, yet
those cabins were no larger than a gentleman's pantry.

Long damp days scattering moorhens
from the pounds, then a staircase of locks,
instinctive manoeuvrings through gushes of water,

hard hands straining on ropes
to steady a full seventy foot boat—
I imagine eyes also twisted
like knots between man and wife
till a good pint could loose them,
could knock over incidents like skittles and
with a brutal laugh set them up again;
that's canal pub community
a sharing of feelings, an abandonment
with gossip flying so fast it was prophetic
the boats outside moored with the children
like all relevant history, in the shadow
of the Swan, or the Bird in Hand.

Soundwaves

Selecting a loose vibration from the taut air
and threading it through the wired network
into an infectious signal, the stylish receiver—

translating that which has remained latent,
an invisible vast shimmer of potential
that it required aerial genius to unravel,

becoming apparent, now, when I press
a red button and suddenly a full-scale
illusory orchestra, releasing a score,

has assembled beside me, ushering
in a Beethoven symphony, the mind dreaming its composure,
its glitter, many cellos and polished violins

traversing the continent, peak to peak, a relayed signal.
The sound is transmitted only so far:
the weak transistors, in passenger cabins

of liners bucking across the Atlantic
are flawed, ejected from the system
like spent cartridges, until

the unseen peaks of the Indies
are identified, through static, with a jangling
of American music, all ears cocked, intent

as when the first report was relayed
back from the moon, bounced into kitchens, living rooms—
these immaterial islands all

pace, sound and imagined geographies.
So much is unseen. Here, this far
south, beneath a darkened mountain in Tasmania,

the northern cities' stations, at night, compete
for airspace, fade in and out, like several Mardi Gras,
the radio's occasional brash visitors.

I'll tune in as finely as possible
to the rapid fire of news, the hyperactive
music as if, suddenly, I'm travelling

in a car at high speed where the mind
is a curious receiver, exposed, intent
on that which is always about to be revealed.

Peter Goldsworthy

Act Six

Act six begins
when the curtain falls,
the corpses awake,
the daggers are cleaned.

Act six
is Juliet in the supermarket,
Mr Macbeth on the 8.15.

In act six
Hamlet sucks a tranquilliser,
Romeo washes up

and death
is gentle and anonymous—
Lear's respirator
switched discreetly off.

After Babel

I read once of a valley
where men and women
spoke a different tongue.

I know that any uncooked theory
can find its tribe
—but this might just be true.

For us there are three languages
—yours, mine, and the English between,
a wall of noises.

At times our children interpret,
or music connects our moods.
There are also monosyllables,

the deeper grammar of fucking,
a language too subjective
for nouns.

But even after conjugation
the tense is still the same
—present imperfect.

We take our mouths from each other.
We carry away our tongues,
and the separate dictionaries of our heads.

Conal Fitzpatrick

Discovering Lasseter

I am reading a diary at night
and watching the city:
it is granite crawling with millipedes of light.

Lasseter's diary . . . .
the words, . . *created in heaven* . .
the city sits tethered like Jason's incendiary Fleece.

My looking on the city
is like Lasseter gazing at *his* find:
he who became truly antipodean

when drunken with thirst, he lay on his back in the desert
and   breathless   mapped out the endless reef
of the night sky.

Robert Harris

Sydney

A radio grovels from over the fence.
Sorrow, demography, wars pour forth—
inertia and thrilling causes
one could almost cry for.

Above all, song. But songs that are
like blanks for coin and buy complaint.
My one truth's to be that it wants me base.
When they got rid of the gallows

our fathers wanted a godless world.
Emptiest day—secular sandstone
innocent blocks to build with,
tendernesses so acute they would

turn wakings violet. That was the prize,
the earth restored. An ideal carnival
ignored on each side of a window.
Now, if a beauty offered her trust

corruption would probably pour from my mouth.
They'd all home in Hosts of advising
harpies, zealous incorruptible sons.
And I have cursed myself, fool I am

for swiftly rippling lights below
a favourite nightmare. Come, we need thy eye,
they sing, come with us we will let
dawn in ! Spare us who do not wish again

to hear that huge crabs ate *Emden*'s wounded,
that failure in the soul comes of desire.
The clouds are forgiven for having fumbled lightning
as I sing this in darkness.

Isaiah by Kerosene Lantern Light

This voice an older friend has kept
to patronise the single name he swears by
saying aha, aha to me.

The heresy hunter, sifting these lines
another shrieks through serapax and heroin
that we have a 'culture'.

These are the very same who shall wait
for plainer faces after they've glutted on beauty,
a mild people back from the dead

shall speak the doors down '
to the last hullo reaching the last crooked hutch
in forest or forest-like deeps of the town.

These who teach with the fingers and answer
with laughter, with anger, shall be in derision
and the waiting long, and the blue and white days

like a grave in a senseless universe.
I believe this wick and this open book
in the light's oval, and I disbelieve

everything this generation has told me.

John Foulcher

Wars of Imperialism

From 66 to 70 A.D. Rome and Palestine tore
Jerusalem—in history it's small, strong only to the Jews
who lost, living since then in tents.

Yet I think we should see more in this:
things ended when their Temple fell. Like a honeycomb,
cells progressively damp and alone, the great home
of God was peeled; brick by brick,
places more holy exposed to the light, the Romans marched,
spiralling in. And when light came
to the last place, the centre, He must have left...

Did they know what they set free then?
Something was there,
changing to light from ages of nothing—
scorching the known world, ripping the new world.

After the Flood

The motor stops, the boat thuds mud—the river's bed
at the limit of the farm.
Now grass pricks the air again,

its light coat of mud sizzling into dust
under our feet—even the trees are flexed in grey.

The house is the same, though, except for the stain
tied like a ribbon around the walls—
the door grips, bursts, and in the quiet light
it all seems as we left it.
Then the mud
larded over everything, the smell, and the cupboards
cracked and tossed across the room...

After hours of discovery, all that's left
is to begin. In the shade below the river-level windows,
we dig caves.
It is tedious, heavy work;
the yard piles
like an auction sale, chairs and tables drying,
the feather juice of mattresses.

In the shed, books huddle on the rafters, dry
by two inches. Only my childhood Bible,
coloured in the borders, was caught
in the water—Joshua, Moses, Christ and the Pharisees
swirl in crayon rainbows. The sun blooms them
now, though the pages are brittle with dirt.

Philip Mead

From a Republican Grave:
Daniel Henry Deniehy. 1828–1865.

Who are they now? since the Bathurst ground
    first went to warm me, run
to my hole with a murderous black and
    all those godless Chinee,
sleeping roundly, God's compost.
    There were those who thought that
I was one who always hesitates
    at what he loves, but when it loves
back, embraces it too much, as if
    I was there for the moment.
Not so, I knew myself to have
    a heart like the falcon's stoop,
and ready to build in a tower like the rook,
    if given some sort of chance;

if building then were not so much a matter
        of grasping in the name of God,
God who is so masteringly off-hand
        with any human vision.
Holy Mother, I had some of your control,
        stumbling, dying in the arms of surcease.
I couldn't turn and face the hunter,
        that's that. How many do?...
But who walks down Castlereagh Street now,
        walking with the times, as if today
were simply a matter of how and next?
        Who are they now? carrying themselves
from Faction-rooms to Monsignor,
        with a fat hand in a mauve glove.
Does my voice, the one true faithful gift
        I had, I'm sure, still carry
some small echo across the way there..?
        Well then politics was never
the kind of place where every man could
        believe and trust in what his
father would have hoped he was, or where
        one man, left alone
in his room could hold himself like
        a malacca cane, straight,
not for the world. All that I ever wanted
        was to lie down and feel
that I had gone some way towards that
        symmetry in life I knew
was there, that a sort of retribution
        could lie in the hand of a friend,
not so far away, not to think
        I would cast less of my own
shadow when the sun came round again;
        to lie back and know that I
had filled the cup a little instead of having
        poured it out for someone
I never knew: and more than anything
        to dream, silent as the hero
shut between the pages, that high on
        the back of the ranges and
ringing from the absolute centre
        of the forest, that gentlest
bird of all is breathing life into
        her heart's bell,
for myself more than anyone.

The Man and the Tree

For David Campbell

I felt the season changing in the yard today
    along the wooden fence and in the leaves.
    The almond is always first to break in flower
    and everything it has it gives.

There was a man standing underneath in innocence,
    whose place was there, whose face
    was hurt with years like the branches.
    He was saying what the tree was saying:
    this is your sign of mutability and joy.

Make your speech from what is living, here.
    Work to know the word that's damp
    underneath like a stone, the word
    that harvests in the sun, the half-word
    she turns in her sleep to say.

Make your sentence lead the life you lead,
    and when it comes, there will be art
    to choose the simplest word of all.

The almond tree in spring is brave,
    all it says is honour life
    and take the new growth as chance.

Look how the passion in the moving of the season
    loosens conversation in the heart.

Be with us as a bearing tree, in flower
    growing in the world, now that
    all you made has let the winter in.

Andrew Lansdown

Two Men

There are two men.

A man on the ground
is tossing bricks
to another on the scaffolding.

He swings each weight
in both hands
down to his knees
and up in a single movement.

How the bricks float up
to the catcher's hands!
like bubbles lifting
through the water
from the bottom of an aquarium.

Mercy

Across the footpath (tidy
as Euclid's brain
bar the rude little daisy
bold between two slabs)
the hose
follows itself   and

coming suddenly upon its end
throws a tantrum
before a regiment of roses.

                                                But

back along its torso,
in the middle of the path,
a pin-prick spray
sets the daisy dancing.

Behind the Veil

How often my grandparents allude to death, now.
The simplest plans and preparations for the new year
They preface and conclude: *If we're still here.*
Age, bodily decrepitude will not allow
Illusion. Before death, all things somehow
Become transient and grave. Joy and regret
Marry each other at the altar of memory. Who can forget
Our mortality? Even youths and social visionaries will bow.

For all this, my grandparents are at peace, hoping for the face
Of Christ our Saviour. Death will degrade:
Even for the redeemed, this peppercorn must be paid.
But He is the resurrection: they are sure of His power and grace.

Still, they are lonely in the shadow of death.
Oh for His face! hidden by the veil of each breath!

Kevin Hart

The Members of the Orchestra

Walk onto the dark stage dressed for a funeral
or a wedding and we, the anxious ones, quieten
as we wait to discover which it will be tonight:

they sit or stand before thin books written
in a foreign script, more alien than Chinese,
but its secret contents will be revealed now

as at the reading of a dead relation's will,
for the last member has entered, slightly late
as befits his honour, like a famous lecturer

with a new theory and a pointer to make it clear.
Alas, he too cannot talk except in the language
of the deaf and dumb, but as he waves his hands

the members of the orchestra commence their act
of complicated ventriloquism, each making
his instrument speak our long-forgotten native tongue.

Now one violin reaches above the rest, rehearsing
the articulate sorrow of things in this world
where we have suddenly woken to find a music

as curious as the relation between an object
and its name. We are taken by the hand and led
through the old darkness that separates us

from things in themselves, through the soft fold
of evening that keeps two days apart. And now
each instrument tells its story in details

that become the whole, the entire forest contained
within a leaf: the orchestra is quickly building
a city of living air about us where we can live

and know our selves at last, for we have given up
our selves, as at our wedding or our funeral,
to take on something new, something that was always there.

The Horizon

Whenever you take a step
I am with you leading you meeting your eyes
I am here at dawn watching
the old priest hurrying to Mass
ready to greet him with my gift of blood.

How easily I shed the clothing
you try to give me
you who cannot bear to see me as I truly am
your trees mountains buildings I have no time for them.

I was here
before the stone received its hardness,
this entire world could not even be conceived
before the thought of me.

You comfort yourselves,
you say I am only a line never reached
that I do not exist as you do
but none of this is true:
you see only the top line of my head
beneath that I have the world
with all its fields sun moonlight and rain.

You who hate departures,
you who forever try to shut me out
listen to me:
whenever you think of death
whenever you enter the room of someone gone from you
I will be peering through the window
I will catch you
even though my net has only one string
you have no use for mirrors
who lie to you until it is too late
look at me and see the only truth
your past what you are now
all your future sorrows and your only blessing.

Flemington Racecourse

The racehorses assemble at the starting barrier
in all the finery of a medieval pageant, the jockeys
in silks like figures from a tarot pack, the bookies

in leather and tweeds standing beside their boards
each confident that the future has been controlled;
and everyone, except the dissembling birds, is still

concentrating on a frisky tail, a flashing red light.
They go, against the clock, leaving the shouting crowd
in noiseless elegance, the jockeys with heads bent

and bottoms raised like cyclists in the Tour de France.
The electronic timer divides time into its hairs
as the horses break ground, continually printing

the earth with emblems of good fortune, all leaning
towards the fence, bunched up and fighting, until
two suddenly break free from the pack and only the timer

is beating them, each number something impulsive
and longed-for, like life continuing after death.
Thousands have come to watch, forgetting cars, yet

at the turn nothing can be seen, there is only
the sound of a storm approaching, streamlining
on the straight into the particulars of faces

straining to be the first to get the future over with.
Only the timer is heartless now, and the manic voice
of the commentator, like a loud typewriter, crams

each new second with more words than ever before.
Our eyes will tell us so much more, how one horse
now leaves the others easily, like a fresh runner

just handed a baton, how it pushes through the air
as though the final run were straight downhill.
The future has fooled the past, and joined its ranks—

it's autumn with paper leaves, and even the brilliant,
evil mind of the timer stops as the horses slow down,
their ordeal over now, and all of time before them.

Philip Hodgins

Self-Pity

Is not one of the seven deadly sins
although it gets more use since
that unsuspecting day when euphemisms

dropped their masks and the message was
WORDS CAN KILL.
Now the thought of never growing old
is with me all the time. I'm like the traveller
on the kerb in a strange city, gaping—
'My dreams!
I only put them down for a minute!'

Resting in the library was double-edged.
A close reading of the modernist big names
showed up themes of self-pity
and I, cheated by myself, could
write poems only in the first person singular—
This is serious and this is what it's like.
But happiness has been serendipity. It
happened in the ambulance on the way back
from celltrifuge. I sat up like a child
and smiled at dying young, at all
love's awfulness.

Making Hay

In rectangular vertigo the balepress
gives prodigious birth.
From conception to delivery
takes less than a minute.
Humming down slow rows
of lucerne and paspalum it chews grass,
snakeskins, thistles, feathers, anything.
By midday it can do no more.
The paddock is a maze of compression
soon to be unravelled
by hay carters starting at the edges.
Shirtless in cowskin chaps and gloves
they perform their complex dance
with eighty-pound bales
on an earthquaking load that shoves
a slackchained,
bouncing, banging, balesucking escalator
down bays of the marvellous smell
of cut grass.
When the dance is done,
easing to the monolith, they sit
with cigarettes on what they've made.

After the hay has been restacked
they take a big tyre tube
to the swimming hole and muddy the water
worse than cattle,
slushing after the slippery tube.
With one stye eye and sleek
black skin it is the nearest thing
to a leviathan in this billabong.

Linda Molony

Cat Washing

Deliberate as scrimshaw
                    but with the speed of ease
Her tongue lancets over
                    the right shoulder
                                    gleaning
Granules of
            dust and dried blood
                            rasping
The tense heads of fleas
                    electrons lying low
                                    listening
To their heaven of
                catquills
                    dampen down

In a rhythmic thatching.

Every so often
            a tooth
                    scythes through

Richard Allen

Epitaph for the Western Intelligentsia

what we come round to
in the end
is that all our thinking
has brought us nowhere

that the trail-blazing journey
has ended where it began
that thought is at best
a protection against further thought

that the heathens we sought to save
the masses to educate
need neither our salvation
nor our education

that we therefore
serve no particular purpose
perform no particular function
have no particular place to go

& we roll to the ground
& we cry out like children
& we bark like dogs
& we learn to wag our tails

ACKNOWLEDGEMENTS

We wish to thank the copyright-holders for permission to use the following material:

Robert Adamson: 'Dead Horse Bay' from *Selected Poems*, Angus & Robertson. Allen Afterman: 'Their Thoughts Cling to Everything They See on the Way', 'Van Diemen's Land', 'Pietà' from *Purple Adam*, Angus & Robertson. Alan Alexander: 'The Gathering Place' from *Scarpdancer*; 'For Raftery' from *In the Sun's Eye*, both Fremantle Arts Centre Press. Marion Alexopolous: 'Night Flight' from *The Younger Australian Poets*, Hale & Iremonger. Richard Allen: 'Epitaph for the Western Intelligentsia' from *Poetry Australia*, South Head Press. Ethel Anderson: 'Afternoon in the Garden' from *Sunday At Yarralumla: A Symphony*, Angus & Robertson, 1947. Joan Aronsten: 'Ad Infinitum' from *Poetry Australia*, South Head Press. Dorothy Auchterlonie: 'The Tree', Angus & Robertson. Bruce Beaver: 'Letters to Live Poets V', 'The Entertainer' from *Selected Poems*, Angus & Robertson. John Blight: 'The Coral Reef' from *My Beachcombing Days*; 'Mangrove' from *A Beachcomber's Diary*; 'Oyster-Eaters' from *Selected Poems*, Angus & Robertson. Robert Bray: 'The Execution of Madame du Barry' from *Poems 1961–1971*, Jacaranda Press, 1972. Robert Brissenden: 'Verandahs', © R.F. & R.L. Brissenden. Vincent Buckley: 'Ghosts, Places, Stories, Questions', from *Selected Poems*, Angus & Robertson. David Campbell: 'Song for the Cattle', 'Hear the Bird of Day' from *Selected Poems*; 'Duchesses' from *The Man in the Honeysuckle*, Angus & Robertson. Gary Catalano: 'The Jews Speak in Heaven', Hale & Iremonger; 'Australia' first published *The Age Monthly Review*. Hal Colebatch: 'On the Death of Ludwig Erhard', 'One Tourist's Cologne' from *Outer Charting*, Angus & Robertson. Julian Croft: 'D-Zug', 'Greenhalgh's Pub', 'Graffiti' from *Breakfast in Shanghai*, Angus & Robertson. Bruce Dawe: 'At Shagger's Funeral', 'Suburban Lovers', 'Elegy For Drowned Children' from *Condolences of the Season*, Longman Cheshire, 1971. C.J. Dennis: 'The Traveller' from *Selected Verse of C.J. Dennis*, Angus & Robertson. Djalparmiwi: 'The blowflies buzz ...' from 'Expressions of Grief among Aboriginal Women' by Catherine H. Berndt, in *Oceania*, 1950, vol. XX, no. 4, pp. 319–22. Djurberaui: 'All you others, eat ...' from 'Expressions of Grief among Aboriginal Women' by Catherine H. Berndt, in *Oceania*, 1950, vol. XX, no. 4, pp. 310–12. Rosemary Dobson: 'Country Press', 'The Edge' from *Selected Poems*, Angus & Robertson; 'Folding the Sheets', Hale & Iremonger. Michael Dransfield: 'That Which We Call a Rose', 'Fix' both from *Streets of The Long Voyage*, University of Queensland Press, 1974; 'Pioneer Lane' from *Voyage of Solitude*, University of Queensland Press, 1978. Geoffrey Dutton: 'Fish Shop Windows' from *Selective Affinities*, Angus & Robertson; 'A Finished Gentleman', 'Burning Off' © Geoffrey Dutton. Louis Esson: 'The Shearer's Wife'. Robert D. FitzGerald: 'Copernicus', 'Grace Before Meat', 'The Wind at Your Door' from *Forty*

Years' Poems, Angus & Robertson. Conal Fitzpatrick: 'Discovering Lasseter' from *Wollongong Poems*, Hale & Iremonger, 1984. John Forbes: 'Up, Up, Home and Away' from *Tropical Skiing*, Angus & Robertson, 1976; 'Malta' from *Poetry Australia*, South Head Press, 1977. David Foster: 'From The Fleeing Atalanta: Poems 98, 104, 109'. John Foulcher: 'Wars of Imperialism', 'After the Flood' from *Light Pressure*, Angus & Robertson. Mary Fullerton ('E'): 'A Man's a Sliding Mood' from *The Wonder and the Apple*; 'Unit', 'Poetry' from *Moles Do So Little With Their Privacy*, Angus & Robertson. Mary Gilmore: 'The Little Shoes That Died', 'The Saturday Tub', 'The Harvesters' from *The Passionate Heart and Other Poems*, Angus & Robertson. Peter Goldsworthy: 'Act Six', 'After Babel' from *Readings From Ecclesiastes*, Angus & Robertson. Alan Gould: 'Ice' from *Astral Sea*; 'Galaxies', 'Pearls' from *The Pausing of the Hours*, Angus & Robertson. Jamie Grant: 'An Auditor Thinks About Female Nature', 'Planes Landing' from *The Refinery*, Angus & Robertson. Robert Gray: 'Flames and Dangling Wire' from *Grass Script*; 'Curriculum Vitae' from *The Skylight*, Angus & Robertson. Rodney Hall: 'Journey' from *A Soapbox Omnibus*, University of Queensland Press, 1973. Philip Hammial: 'Russians Breathing' from *Swarm*, Island Press, 1979. Susan Hampton: 'The Crafty Butcher', 'The Fire Station's Delight'. W.E. Harney: 'West of Alice' from *Content to Lie in the Sun*. Charles Harpur: 'A Basket of Summer Fruit', 'Wellington', 'A Flight of Wild Ducks' from *The Poetical Works of Charles Harpur* edited by Elizabeth Perkins, 1984. Max Harris: 'Message from a Cross', 'Martin Buber in the Pub'. Robert Harris: 'Isaiah By Kerosene Lantern Light' from *The Clouds Passes Over*, Angus & Robertson; 'Sydney', Senor Press. J.S. Harry: 'Honesty-stones' from *The Deer Under The Skin*, University of Queensland Press. Kevin Hart: 'The Members of the Orchestra', 'Flemington Racecourse' from *Your Shadow*; 'The Horizon' from *The Lines of the Hand*, Angus & Robertson. William Hart-Smith: 'Boomerang', 'Golden Pheasant', 'The Inca Tupac Upanqui' from *Selected Poems 1936–1984*, Angus & Robertson. Gwen Harwood: 'Homage to Ferd. Holthausen', 'Death Has No Features of His Own', 'A Simple Story' from *The Lion's Bride*, Angus & Robertson. Dennis Haskell: 'The Call' from *Listening At Night*, Angus & Robertson. Percy Haslam: Aboriginal songs from the 1850s 'Kilaben Bay Song' (Awabakel), 'Women's rondo' (Awabakel), 'The Tongue-Pointing Songs' (Kamilaroi); 'The drunk man' (Wolaroi) from tribal and language research of Mr Percy Haslam, MA, Convocation Scholar at University of Newcastle. Nicholas Hasluck: 'Islands', 'From Rottnest Island' both Freshwater Bay Press. Charles W. Hayward: 'King George V' originally published in the *Bulletin*. Graeme Hetherington: 'The Man from Changi', South Head Press. Dorothy Hewett: 'In Moncur Street' from *Rapunzel in Surburbia*, Prism Books. A.D. Hope: 'A Blason', 'Faustus' from *Collected Poems 1930–1970*; 'Parabola' from *A Late Picking*, Angus & Robertson. Barry Humphries (Edna Everage): 'Edna's Hymn' from *The All-Time Favourite Australian Song Book*, Angus & Robertson. Martin Johnston: 'In Memoriam' from *Surfer's Paradise*, University of Queensland Press. Evan Jones: 'Study in Blue', 'A Dream', 'The Point'. Nancy Keesing: 'Reverie of a Mum' from *Showground Sketchbook*, Angus & Robertson; 'A Queer Thing' © Nancy Keesing. Peter Kocan: 'Cows' from *Armistice*; 'The Mutineer's Ballad', from

Freedom to Breathe, Angus & Robertson; 'An Inmate' from *The Other Side of the Fence*, University of Queensland Press, 1975. C.J. Koch: 'Shelly Beach' first published *Jindyworoback Anthology*, 1952; 'The Boy Who Dreamed the Country Night', from the *Bulletin*, May 1954. Eve Langley: 'This Year, Before It Ends', Angus & Robertson. Andrew Lansdown: 'Two Men', 'Mercy', 'Behind the Veil' from *Counterpoise*, Angus & Robertson. Joyce Lee: 'My Father's Country', South Head Press; 'Firebell For Peace'. Geoffrey Lehmann: 'Pope Alexander VI', 'Poem for Maurice O'Shea' from *Selected Poems*; 'Night Flower' from *A Voyage of Lions*, Angus & Robertson. Francis Letters: 'The Inglorious Milton', permission courtesy Kathleen Letters. Jack Lindsay: 'Question Time', 'Angry Dusk', 'To my father Norman alone in the Blue Mountains'. Kate Llewellyn: 'Finished', 'Colonel'. Robert Lowe: 'Songs of the Squatters, I & II' from *Poetry Australia*, Cook Bicentennial issue, 1970, South Head Press. James McAuley: 'Terra Australis', 'Liberal or Innocent by Definition', 'Because' from *Collected Poems*, Angus & Robertson. Hugh McCrae: 'The Mimshi Maiden' from *The Best Poems of Hugh McCrae*, Angus & Robertson. Ronald McCuaig: 'Betty by the Sea', 'Recitative', 'Au tombeau de mon père' from *The Ballad of Bloodthirsty Bessie*, Angus & Robertson. Nan McDonald: 'The Hatters', 'Burragorang' from *Selected Poems*, Angus & Robertson. Robert McDonald: 'The Blizzard', 'Apis mellifica'; '1915' from *Airship*, University of Queensland Press, 1975. Rhyll McMaster: 'Tanks' from *The Brineshrimp*, University of Queensland Press, 1972; 'Mutton Bird Man'. Frederick Macartney: 'Kyrielle: Party Politics' from *Selected Poems of Frederick T. Macartney*, Angus & Robertson. Dorothea Mackellar: 'Arms and the Woman', 'Fancy Dress', both permission courtesy Curtis Brown (Aust.) Pty Ltd. Kenneth Mackenzie: 'Shall then another', 'Table-birds', 'Caesura' from *The Poems of Kenneth Mackenzie*, Angus & Robertson. Francis MacNamara ('Frank the Poet'): 'A petition from the chain gang at Newcastle ...', 'For the Company underground' from *Frank the Poet*, John Meredith & Rex Whalan (Red Rooster Press). Jennifer Maiden: 'The mother-in-law of the Marquis de Sade' from *Birthstones*, Angus & Robertson. David Malouf: 'Guide to the Perplexed' from *Selected Poems*, Angus & Robertson; 'The Year of the Foxes'. John Manifold: 'Fife Tune', 'Makhno's Philosophers' from *OP. 8 Poems 1961–69*, University of Queensland Press, 1971. David Martin: 'Dreams in German' from *Meanjin Quarterly*. Philip Martin: 'Tongues' from *A Bone Flute*, Australian National University Press. Ray Mathew: 'Seeing St James's', 'Poem in Time of Winter', 'One Day', Angus & Robertson. Philip Mead: 'From a Republican Grave', Angus & Robertson; 'The Man and the Tree' from *The River is in The South*, University of Queensland Press, 1984. E.G. Moll: 'The Bush Speaks', 'Clearing for the Plough', 'Beware the Cuckoo' from *Poems*, Angus & Robertson. Linda Molony: 'Cat Washing' previously published in *Quadrant*, September 1983. Les A. Murray: 'Equanimity', 'The Smell of Coal Smoke' from *The People's Otherworld*, Angus & Robertson. Smiler Narautjarri: 'Sunrise Sequence' from *The First Australians* by R.M. and C.H. Berndt, Ure Smith, Sydney, 1952: p. 15; 'Song Cycle of the Moon-Bone' from 'A Wonguri-Mandjigai song cycle of the Moon-Bone' by Ronald M. Berndt, in *Oceania*, 1948, vol. XIX, no. 1, pp. 16–50. John Shaw Neilson: 'To the Red Lory', 'May', 'Schoolgirls Hastening' from *The Poems of Shaw Neilson*, Angus &

Robertson. John O'Brien: 'The Field of the Cloth of Gold' from *The Parish of St Mel's*, Angus & Robertson. Mark O'Connor: 'The Sun-Hunters'; 'Turtles Hatching', 'Fire' from *The Eating Tree*, Angus & Robertson. Bernard O'Dowd: 'Cupid', Lothian Pty Ltd. Geoff Page: 'Grit' from *Cassandra Paddocks*; 'Premeditations' from *Clairvoyant in Autumn*, Angus & Robertson; 'Inscription at Villers-Bretonneux', Makar Press. Vance Palmer: 'The Snake', 'The Farmer Remembers the Somme', reproduced by permission of the Estate of Vance Palmer. A.B. Paterson: 'The Travelling Post Office', 'Father Riley's Horse', 'Old Australian Ways' from *The Collected Verse of A.B. Paterson*, reprinted with the permission of Angus & Robertson Publishers, © Retusa Pty Ltd. Grace Perry: 'Time of Turtles', South Head Press. Hal Porter: 'Four Winds', 'In a Bed-sitter', 'Hobart Town, Van Diemen's Land' from *Elijah's Ravens: Poems of Hal Porter*, Angus & Robertson. Peter Porter: 'Soliloquy at Potsdam', 'What I Have Written I Have Written', 'On First Looking into Chapman's Hesiod', from *Peter Porter Collected Poems*, Oxford University Press, 1983. Craig Powell: 'Nativity', South Head Press. Public Corroboree Songs, Nuggubyu, South East Arnhem land: 'Koel (Rainbird) and effigy', 'Goanna', 'Flood Water', 'Mission Work Boat' from D.C. Biernoff, *The Nature of Song in South-Eastern Arnhem Land*, Musicology IV, 1974. Jennifer Rankin: 'The Sea and other stories', South Head Press. Elizabeth Riddell: 'Wakeful in the Township', 'Suburban Song', 'The Letter' from *Forbears*, Angus & Robertson. Nigel Roberts: 'The Gull's Flight' from Steps for Astaire, Hale & Iremonger, 1983; 'After/The Moratorium Reading'. Roland Robinson: Aboriginal Oral Traditions 'Mapooram' (related by Fred Biggs), 'The Star-Tribes' (related by Fred Biggs), 'The Two Sisters' (related by Manoowa), 'The Platypus' (related by Dick Donnelly), 'Captain Cook' (related by Percy Mumbella), from *Altjeringa*, A.W. & A.H. Reed Pty Ltd. Roland Robinson: 'Deep Well', 'The Cradle' both from *Deep Well*, Edwards & Shaw; 'The Creek' from *Poet's Choice*, Island Press, 1976. Judith Rodriguez: 'Eskimo Occasion', 'A Lifetime Devoted to Literature' from *Waterlife*, University of Queensland Press, 1976; 'New York Sonnet'. Eric Rolls: 'Bamboo', 'Dog Fight' and 'Rain Forest' all from *The Green Mosaic: Memoirs of New Guinea*, Thomas Nelson, 1977; permission courtesy Curtis Brown (Aust.) Pty Ltd. David Rowbotham: 'Nebuchadnezzar's Kingdom-Come' from *The Pen of Feathers*, Angus & Robertson, 1971; 'Bus-stop on the Somme', 'The Cliff' from *Selected Poems*, University of Queensland Press, 1975. John Rowland: 'Canberra in April' from *The Feast of Ancestors*, Angus & Robertson. Philip Salom: 'The Well', 'Winter' from *The Silent Piano*, Fremantle Arts Centre Press, 1980; 'The World of Dreams'. Andrew Sant: 'Homage to the Canal People', from *The Caught Sky*; 'Sound waves' from *The Flower Industry*, Angus & Robertson. Margaret Scott: 'Portrait of a Married Couple' from *Visited*, Angus & Robertson. W.N. Scott: 'Bundaberg Rum'. Thomas Shapcott: 'June Fugue' from *Shabbytown Calandar*, University of Queensland Press, 1975; 'The Litanies of Julie Pastranma from *Selected Poems*, University of Queensland Press, 1981. R.A. Simpson: 'All Friends Together' from *Selected Poems*, University of Queensland Press, 1981. Kenneth Slessor: 'A Bushranger', 'Metempsychosis', 'Five Bells' from *Selected Poems*, Angus & Robertson. Vivian Smith: 'At an Exhibition of Historical Paintings, Hobart', 'Early

Arrival: Sydney', 'Tasmania' from *Tide Country*, Angus & Robertson. Peter Steele: 'Marking Time' from *Word from Lilliput*, Hawthorn Press, Melbourne, 1973. Douglas Stewart: 'Leopard Skin', 'A Country Song', 'Terra Australis' from *Selected Poems*, Angus & Robertson. Harold Stewart: 'The Sage in Unison', Angus & Robertson. Randolph Stow: 'The Ghost at Anlaby', 'My Wish For My Land', 'The Enemy' from *Selected Poems—A Counterfeit Silence*, Angus & Robertson. Norman Talbot: 'Ballad of Old Women' from *Poems for a Female Universe*, South Head Press, 1978. Andrew Taylor: 'The Beast with Two Backs' from *The Cat's Chin and Ears: A Bestiary*, poets of the Month Series, 1976. Colin Thiele: 'Tom Farley', 'Radiation Victim' both from *Selection Verse*, Rigby, 1970. Richard Tipping: 'Men At Work', 'Mangoes' from *Domestic Hardcore*, University of Queensland Press, 1975. John Tranter: 'The Great Artist Reconsiders the Homeric Simile', 'Lufthansa'. Brian Vrepont: 'The Bomber', Angus & Robertson. Kath Walker: 'We are Going' from *My People*, Jacaranda Wiley Ltd. Chris Wallace-Crabbe: 'Sporting the Plaid', 'The Secular', 'The Shape-Changer', Angus & Robertson. Francis Webb: 'The End of the Picnic', 'Airliner', 'Wild Honey' from *Collected Poems*, Angus & Robertson. Frank Wilmot ('Furnley Maurice'): 'Echoes of Wheels ...', 'Whenever I Have ...', 'The Victoria Markets Recollected in Tranquility' from *Poems by Furney Maurice*, Lothian, 1944. Sam Woolagoodjah: 'Lalai' (Dreamtime), from *Poetry Australia*, South Head Press. Judith Wright: 'Nigger's Leap, New England', 'Legend', 'Wings' from *Judith Wright's Collected Poems 1942–1970*, Angus & Robertson. Fay Zwicky: 'Reckoning' from *Kaddish & Other Poems*, University of Queensland Press.

Details for the acknowledgements are as supplied by copyright-holders. Every efforts has been made to trace the original source of all material contained in this book. Where the attempt has been unsuccessful the editor and publisher would be pleased to hear from the author/publisher concerned, to rectify any omission.

INDEX OF FIRST LINES

A bloke I know came rolling home as shickered as he could be, 87
A corrugated iron shack. One room, 174
A frail and tenuous mist lingers on baffled and intricate branches, 110
A Gentle Annie, willow wind, the West, 169
A man blew away, 318
A mob of dressing-tables is grazing, 199
A painting would have been the best way to get things over, 347
A radio grovels from over the fence, 369
A stilled room to which I am called, 349
A trickle of sand on the grave's edge, 195
A visiting conductor, 215
Across the footpath (tidy, 374
Act six begins, 367
Adieu, the years are a broken song, 110
After sundown the clouds start to burn, 280
Ah my daughter, my grandchild, 209
Ah, the blowfly is whining there, its maggots are eating the flesh, 208
Albany in a time of khaki, 305
Alchemists say the Stone turns lead to gold, 325
All day long, at Scott's or Menzies', I await the gorging crowd, 59
Apart possibly from waving hello to the cliff-divers, 292
Ardent in love and cold in charity, 86
As I rode in to Burrumbeet, 95
As night was falling slowly on city, town and bush, 83
As unpredictable as picnic weather, blue, 275
As well, maybe, that you cannot read our minds, 280
At a street bookstall in Karlsruhe, my father, 214
At Shagger's funeral there wasn't much to say, 263
At the full face of the forest lies our little town, 93
At the undulating head he aims, 296

Back in *tachanka* days, when Red and Green, 202
Barks the melancholy dog, 163
Because his soup was cold, he needs must sulk, 131
Before the glare o'dawn I rise, 98
Behold! wood into bird and bird to wood again, 165
Beneath your cooling coverlet you lie, 213
Between great coloured vanes the butterflies, 197
Beware the cuckoo, though she bring, 137
Black greyed into white a nightmare of bicycling, 350
Blind poet, fiddler, Raftery, 306
Bright, consuming Spirit. No power on earth so great as Thee, 94
By channels of coolness the echoes are calling, 50

Captain Quiros and Mr William Lane, 191
Charles and Bruce, Geoff and Ron and Nancy, 262
Christmas Day. 1696, 322
Come all you gallant poachers, that ramble void of care, 15
Come all you Lachlan men, and a sorrowful tale I'll tell, 55

Come all young girls, both far and near, and listen unto me, 17
'Come girlies and fellas, as quick as you can, 342
Coming to the farm that winter afternoon, 218
Cook admired the native courage, made, 183
Cows graze across the hill, 343
Crunching their food in their mouths, —, 179
Cut yer name across me backbone, 16

Daniel in the lion's den, 235
Death has no features of his own, 214
Deliberate as scrimshaw, 379
Dick Briggs a wealthy farmer's son, 42
Djanbun's the platypus. He was a man one time, 178
Does the mouth refuse?, 288
Don't give everything, 326
Down in the South, by the waste without sail on it—, 51
Down the red stock route, 198
Dreaming I sat by the fire last night, 69
Dreamtime, 1

Echoes of wheels and singing lashes, 101
Ecstatic thought's the thing, 87
Ela! Ngorokan-ta killi-bin-bin katan, 36
Endless lanes sunken in the clay, 109
England's poor who wanderers be, 34
Erskineville. The sun came round a corner, 351
Even if you are killed, you die, 234
Every morning they hold hands, 264
Every wild she-bird has nest and mate in the warm April weather, 58

Far up the River—hark! 'tis the loud shock, 33
Fear it has faded and the night, 93
Fire in the heavens, and fire along the hills, 91
First see those ample melons—brindles o'er, 31
First there was the island, 312
Flying up a valley in the Alps where the rock, 324
For days you find it one long zero hour, 291
For 5p at a village fête I bought, 260
From 66 to 70 A.D. Rome and Palestine tore, 370
Ghosts, places, stories, questions, 248
Give me a harsh land to wring music from, 167
Go out and camp somewhere. You're lying down, 175
goanna chases grasshopper, 315
God breathed, 252
God made the sugar cane grow where it's hot, 233
God our fathers formerly knew, 131
Golden Pheasant. Mating Pair, 165
Great captain if you will! great Duke! great Slave!, 32

Had Life remained one whole, 86
Hail South Australia! blessed clime, 16
Hamburg: the clock hands move upon their star, 355
He came over to London and straight away strode, 122
He did his duty both by peers and peasants, 77
He looks back over the last metaphor, 323

He rode a white horse, 295
He saw the skull within the looping, 220
He watched them as they walked towards the tree, 201
Hear, the bird of day, 199
Her drooping flowers dabble upon, 159
Here let me rest me feet!, 229
His bare feet warmed by the thick black dust, 269
holding the feathered dancing string, 315
Hot, humid, the smell of sewage, 307
How often my grandparents allude to death, now, 374
How will our unborn children scoff at us, 57
However you look at it, 272

I am a gentle Anarchist, 56
I am at Deep Well where the spirit trees, 173
I am become a shell of delicate alleys, 246
I am in my Eskimo-hunting-song mood, 285
I am reading a diary at night, 368
I breathe the air of another country, 346
I can close my eyes one heartbeat, 185
I felt the season changing in the yard today, 373
I had heard the bird's name, and searched with intent, 194
I have climbed all the way to the summit, 357
I killed a snake this morning in the grass, 115
I lay face-downward on the grass, 78
I leave it for you to say why it is, 311
I lived for many years in the bush—far out—and I starved for lack of rain, 316
I praise the country women, 297
I read once of a valley, 367
I remember the old joke, 234
I rose from daylong desk at last, 130
I said to my companion, this is walking, 137
I saw a band of warriors coming on, 237
I saw its periscope in the tide, 194
I sing the quality of bamboo, 230
I take my pen in hand, 164
I went on Friday afternoons, 160
I will be your lover, 135
If he had only been a more inspiring Leader, 340
If you want a game to tame you and to take your measure in, 99
I'm a broken-hearted miner, who loves his cup to drain, 49
I'm like all lovers, wanting love to be, 120
In a dreamlike fall, the long, 319
In a hollow of the forest, 108
In from the fields they come, 68
In his blue suit, an Oxford Standard Authors, 265
In old stories the jungle was busy, 337
In rectangular vertigo the balepress, 378
In the baroque style of coral, India, 193
In the multitude of counsellors, 118
In this land vague malevolence, 310
In your twenties you knew with elegiac certainty, 286
Inside, 232
Is not one of the seven deadly sins, 377
Islands which have, 320

It is difficult to keep sane in it, 231
It is the little stone of unhappiness, 259
It is waking in the night, 350
It is wine-harvest, summer, the year's heart, 302
It's a real old-fashioned butcher's shop, 353
It's good, my child, you often wash your hair, 300
It's twenty years ago and more, 227
I've come back all skin and bone, 39
I've dropped me swag in many camps, 112

jack hammer! brainchiseller! come out!, 352
Jackey Jackey gallops on a horse like a swallow, 140
Jemmy Ball, a lucky digger, 46
John Brown, glowing far and down, 290
John Gilbert was a bushranger, 53

Kangaroo, Kangaroo!, 6
Keen as the blade of the guillotine, grey as its steel, 172
Kelly on a mountain, 150

Laying the pen aside, when he had signed, 154
Let us sing of Federation, 67
Life is in the rice-field, wealth in the wheat—, 145
Look, among the boughs. Those stars are men, 176
Lust's too genteel to let the weather in, 170

Man Rapes 25 in fight, 361
mangoes are not cigarettes, 353
Mike Howe's head with frozen frown, 171
Moving from the bus at the Loop it's possible suddenly, 253
My ancestor was called on to go out—, 147
My father and my mother never quarrelled, 206
My favourite view of people, 226
My foundling, my fondling, my frolic first-footer, 153
My friends are borne to one another, 217
My head is unhappy, 254
My wish for my land is that ladies be beautiful, 279

Nests of golden porridge shattered in the silky-oak trees, 289
New York has had it, newsmen all proclaim, 285
Nga ba ya! Ah, it is so!, 37
Ngandu-nga? Who comes?, 38
No angel has descended here, 294
North of our science, east of the hashish dream, 135
not serious about drugs, 362
Now all the dogs with folded paws, 163
Now sulkies come haunting softwheeled down the, 278
Now, to tense stillness as the door is slammed, 309

O! farewell, my country—my kindred—my lover, 11
O this weather! this weather!, 8
O, where were we before time was, 133
O wistful eyes that haunt the gloom of sleep, 92
Oh, hark the dogs are barking, love, 48
Oh, he was a handsome trotter, and he couldn't be completer, 65

Oh, tell me why you make the school, 119
Oh, the hireling sun in a slipshod way, 99
Oh, who has not heard of the Wooyeo Ball, 64
On a highway over the marshland, 330
On the Island of the Spirits of the Dead, 176
Once, playing cricket, beneath a toast-dry hill, 331
One morning in spring, 202
One time, 250
Only the clouds were new, 304
Out of the crowd, I have seen you travelling south of Pardoo, 238
Out on the board the old shearer stands, 122

Passengers afloat on many thousand feet, 352
Peter broke the ragged branch to push his nostrils closer, 151
Publika-or wiri thea Public house screaming, 38
Put the sun a thought below his prime, 111

Quick hands on spinning ropes, 326

reaching out into the sea, passing the waves its exhaust smoking, 316
Red cockatoo crests caught on coral-trees, 270
Red is the down which is covering me, 180
Renowned as Black Geordie, 272
Right from the ambiguous start, 307
Round the island of Zipangu, 96
running downhill, spilling over, searching and spilling, 315

Saboteur autumn has riddled the pampered folds, 247
Schute, Bell, Badgery, Lumby, 190
Scrape the bottom of the hole: gather up the stuff!, 77
See them sprawl with earth for bed, 139
See those resplendent creatures, as they glide, 57
Seeking heat men become cold, and look for meaning, 325
Selecting a loose vibration from the taut air, 366
Seven pairs of leopard-skin underpants, 189
Shall then another do what I have done—, 187
She smiled behind a lawny cloud, 117
She worked in the newsagent, redhaired, 308
Shyly the silver-hatted mushrooms make, 92
Since I've been in this colony I've written many a song, 41
So I was in the city on this day, 220
Sometimes at night when the heart stumbles and stops, 189
Sometimes I wish that I were Helen-fair, 121
Splinters of the sky.   In the air they float, 181
Steered straight into this century I see narrowboats, 365
Strange and slow work: they dug in turn, 362
Suddenly to become John Benbow, walking down William Street, 141
Sussex Street sleeps in mists of nickel moonlight, 301
Sweet silence after bells!, 91

Terentius Neo and wife. Their oval eyes, 275
That quiet man with the hoe is a beast, 343
The bird saw the young Burara girls, twisting their strings, making string figures, 327
The blacksmith's boy went out with a rifle, 196
The bridge is certainly the simplest answer, 251

The cock that crowed this dawn up, heard, 145
The Commissioner bet me a pony—I won, 30
The Currency Lads may fill their glasses, 18
The day breaks—the first rays of the rising Sun, stretching her arms, 239
The day was close, overcast like a grey belly, 363
The dead at Villers-Bretonneux, 299
The eastward spurs tip backward from the sun, 195
The farmer's son is good and mad, 160
the figure stood a crucifix against the door, 216
The fire station's delight, 354
The first day he was travelling in Asia, 273
The great beam of the Milky Way, 222
The ground drops back, 238
The gull's flight, 305
The gum has no shade, 28
The hut in the bush of bark or rusty tin, 217
The Inca Tupac Upanqui, 166
The knife like a precious bond, 277
The land between us, 292
The London lights are far abeam, 73
The Lord's name be praised, 282
the marie antoinette / slice, 305
The match-bark of the younger dog sets fire to, 188
The motor stops, the boat thuds mud—the river's bed, 370
The oldest human fossil, 337
The paleness of hunger, 344
The people are making a camp of branches in that country at Arnhem Bay, 239
The point, I imagine, is, 266
The preacher quoted, and the cranks, 66
The racehorses assemble at the starting barrier, 376
The ringneck parrots, in scattered flocks,—, 183
The roving breezes come and go, the reed beds sweep and sway, 70
The sadness in the human visage stares, 269
The sailor leaning on the rail thinks of home, 255
The sand modeller always began by heaping the sand, 256
The shadow of morality drifts over the trenches, 323
The sky was carpeted with Italian flak. Crump!, 360
The springtime it brings on the shearing, 55
The Sun sank in the thunderous sky of the town, 114
The train was going downwards very slowly, 266
The war to end them all, 186
The wheels line up, pretty right, right, 297
The Woman at the Washtub, 61
the woman is using a handkerchief, 250
The world of dreams, 363
The young girl dancing lifts her face, 114
There are always the poor—, 258
There are two men, 373
There is a place in distant seas, 7
There once was a bull named the Duke of Buccleuch, 63
There'll be no more, 295
There's a class of men (and women) who are always on their guard—, 82
There's a trade you all know well, 168
There's an ordinary woman whom the English call 'the Queen', 79
These are the little shoes that died, 68

They came in to the little town, 207
They don't build houses like that any more—not, 252
They said there was a woman in the hills, 123
This is the solid-looking quagmire, 206
This is where the People take tea—, 132
This voice an older friend has kept, 369
This year, before it ends, holds out time as a weight to us, 157
Though on the day your hard blue eyes met mine, 116
Though the waters, wind-stirred and red-glowing, 183
Though you in your hermitage, 140
Three days before he died the hospital called me, 267
Three images of dying stick in my mind like morbid transfers, 255
Three old ladies in an apple tree, 286
Three times to the world's end I went, 211
Through tranquil years they watched the changes, 136
Time that is moved by little fidget wheels, 142
To get recruits for Pain, I use, 75
To sit people on gas-stove jets, 359
To windward midnight glowed, iridium sheen, 355
Tom Farley, up to his knees in sheep, 212
Tonight our heaven is an estuary, 356
Travelling, 341
Tungeei, that was her native name, 179
'Twas said of Greece two thousand years ago, 14
'Twas the horse thief, Andy Regan, that was hunted like a dog, 71
Two eyes, the cathedral's spires look black, 340

Undated dreams: the sea of Heringsdorf, 200
Under the dusty print of hobnailed boot, 210
Under the white silence of the great gumtree avenue, 223
Unto the Person Kind there came, 60
Up they go, yawning, 317

Vast mild melancholy splendid, 235
Voyage within you, on the fabled ocean, 205

Waiting for weeks till the last one is ready to run, they, 335
Walk onto the dark stage dressed for a funeral, 375
Wasn't this a queer thing? I stood with your mother, 228
Water colour country. Here the hills, 271
We are travelling west of Alice Springs, and Sam is at the wheel, 134
We had many problems set us when Coolgardie was a camp, 85
We let fire rip, we blacken the pale-gold acres, 225
We pass the flayed carcass of a cow, 287
We shipped him at the Sandwich Isles, 88
We stood at the edge, 345
What does he do with them all, the old king, 265
What gifts shall we bring in worship, 320
What if I do go armed? she said, 116
what we come round to, 380
When a disciple asked of Lu Chü how, 204
When Christ from Heaven comes down straightway, 22
When I get home from a day's shopping in a city street, 276
When I was but thirteen or so, 113
When I was still a child, 121

When I was ten my mother, having sold, 274
When maize stands more than ten feet high, 12
When shearing comes, lay down your drums, 38
When that humble-headed elder, the sea, gave his wide, 246
When the census is taken, of course, 45
When you wear a cloudy collar and a shirt that isn't white, 81
Whenever I have, in all humility, moved, 102
Whenever you take a step, 376
Where shall we go? where shall we go?, 281
Where the pipe ends he had fixed the long trough—, 303
White creek sand!, 182
White metal tubes contain, 358
Who are they now? since the Bathurst ground, 371
'Who made God, daddy?', 138
Whom have We next? (His syntax is, 271
Will they never fade or pass!, 115
Winds are bleak, stars are bright, 102
With a pint of flour and a sheet of bark, 14
With a pull-through and the .22, 299
With reverence and submission due, 19
Within his office, smiling, 63

Year after year the princess lies asleep, 155
'Yes,' said the boy, 'first come the gum-tree crowds, 268
You and I will fold the sheets, 211
You are one of those clear cold creeks, 175
You exquisite girl, dressed absurdly deliciously artificially, 157
You prisoners of New South Wales, 23
You see the smoke at Kapunda, 95

INDEX OF AUTHORS AND TITLES

Aboriginal Oral Traditions, 175–9
Aboriginal Songs, Central Australian, 179–83
Aboriginal Women's Mourning Songs, 208–9
Act Six, 367
Ad Infinitum, 195
Adamson, Robert, 326–7
Aeroplane, 238
After Babel, 367
After the Flood, 370
After / the Moratorium Reading, 305
Afterman, Allen, 309–11
Afternoon in the Garden, 111
Airliner, 246
Alexander, Alan, 305–6
Alexopoulos, Marion, 352
All Friends Together, 262
All you others, eat …, 209
Allen, Richard, 380
Anderson, Ethel, 111
Angel, 362
Angry Dusk, 139
Apis mellifica, 319
Apocalypse in Springtime, 220
Aranda Native Cat Song Cycle, 222–3
Arms and the Woman, 116
Aronsten, Joan, 195
At an Exhibition of Historical Paintings, Hobart, 269
At Shagger's Funeral, 263
At the Hammersmith Palais …, 250
Au tombeau de mon père, 160
Auchterlonie, Dorothy, 201–2
Auditor Thinks about Female Nature, An, 357
Australia, 346
Awabakal songs, 36–7

Bad Break!, A, 66
Ballad of Old Women, 286
Bamboo, 230
Banks of the Condamine, The, 48
Banning, Lex, 220–2
Barrier, The, 78
Basket of Summer Fruit, A, 31
Bastard from the Bush, The, 83
Beast with Two Backs, The, 304
Beaver, Bruce, 225–8

Because, 206
Behind the Veil, 374
Bell-birds, 50
Betty by the Sea, 159
Beware the Cuckoo, 137
Beyond Kerguelen, 51
Blason, A, 153
Blight, John, 193–4
Blizzard, The, 318
blowflies buzz …, The, 208
Boake, Barcroft, 77–8
Bomber, The, 108
Boomerang, 165
Boy who Dreamed the Country Night, The, 268
Brabazon, Francis, 137–8
Brady, E.J., 88–91
Bray, J.J., 172–3
Brennan, Christopher, 91–2
Brereton, J. Le Gay, 92
Brissenden, R.F., 252–3
Brother Eagles, The, 181
Buckley, Vincent, 248–50
Bundaberg Rum, 233
Burning Off, 225
Burragorang, 218
Bush Speaks, The, 135
Bushranger, A, 140
Bus-stop on the Somme, The, 234

Caesura, 189
Call, The, 349
Cambridge, Ada, 57–9
Campbell, David, 198–200
Canberra in April, 235
Captain Cook, 179
Cat Washing, 379
Catalano, Gary, 345–7
Cattle Loading, 297
Clarke, Marcus, 59–60
Clearing for the Plough, 136
Click go the Shears, 122
Cliff, The, 234
Colebatch, Hal, 340–1
Colonel, 295
Colonial Nomenclature, 14
Convicts' Rum Song, The, 16
Convict's Tour to Hell, A, 23
Copernicus, 145

Coral Reef, The, 193
Country Press, 210
Country Song, A, 190
Cows, 343
Coxon, William W. (?), 41–2
Cradle, The, 174
Crafty Butcher, The, 353
Creation, 252
Creek, The, 175
Croft, Julian, 307–9
Cupid, 75
Curriculum Vitae, 331

Daley, Victor, 60–3
Dancer, The, 114
Davidson, R.R., 316
Davies, Arthur, 151–3
Dawe, Bruce, 263–5
Dead Horse Bay, 326
Death Has No Features of His Own,
214
Deep Well, 173
Dennis, C.J., 95–6
Detsinyi, Ludwig, 200–1
Devaney, James, 130
Dick Briggs from Australia, 42
Digger's Song, The, 77
Diggins-oh, The, 39
Dinky di, 122
Discovering Lasseter, 368
Dobson, Rosemary, 210–12
Dog Fight, 232
Dove, The, 63
Dransfield, Michael, 350–1
Dream, A, 266
Dreams in German, 200
drunk man, The, 38
'Dryblower', 85–6
Duchesses, 199
Duke of Buccleuch, The, 63
Dulngulg Song Cycle, 239
Dunn, Max, 133–4
Dutton, Geoffrey, 223–7
Dyson, Will, 99–101
D-Zug, 307

'E', 86–7
Early Arrival: Sydney, 270
Echoes of wheels ..., 101
Edge, The, 211
Edna's Hymn, 276
Elegy For Drowned Children, 265
Emu Shot, 296
End of the Picnic, 246
Enemy, The, 280

English Queen, The, 79
Entertainer, The, 256
Epitaph for a Scientist, 220
Epitaph for the Western Intelligentsia,
380
Equanimity, 289
Eskimo Occasion, 285
Esson, Louis, 98
'Everage, Edna', 276–7
Execution of Madame du Barry, The,
172
Exile of Erin, The, 11

Fancy Dress, 117
Fashion, 57
Farmer Remembers the Somme, The,
115
Father Riley's Horse, 71
Faustus, 154
Federation, 67
Female Transport, The, 17
Field, Barron, 6–7
Field of the Cloth of Gold, The, 99
Fife Tune, 202
Finished, 295
Finished Gentleman, A, 223
Finnin, Mary, 150
Fire, 337
Fire in the heavens, 91
Fire Station's Delight, The, 354
Firebell for Peace, 186
Fish Shop Windows, 226
FitzGerald, Robert D., 145–50
Fitzpatrick, Conal, 368
Five Bells, 142
Fix, 350
Flames and Dangling Wire, 330
Flash Colonial Barman, The, 41
Flight of Wild Ducks, A, 33
Flood Water, 315
Fleeing Atalanta: Poems 98, 104, 109,
From The, 325
Flemington Racecourse, 376
Folding the Sheets, 211
For Raftery, 306
For the Company underground, 22
Forbes, John, 360–2
Foster, David, 325–6
Foulcher, John, 370–1
Four Winds, 169
From a Republican Grave, 371
From Rottnest Island, 322
(From the diary of an Australian
soldier), 110
Fullerton, Mary, 86–7
Future Verdict, The, 57

Galaxies, 355
Garchooka, the Cockatoo, 183
Gathering Place, The, 305
Gellert, Leon, 131
Gentle Anarchist, The, 56
Ghost at Anlaby, The, 278
Ghosts, Places, Stories, Questions, 248
Gilmore, Mary, 68–9
Goanna, 315
Golden Pheasant, 165
Goldsworthy, Peter, 367–8
Goodge, W.T., 65–7
Gould, Alan, 355–7
Grace Before Meat, 145
Graffiti, 308
Grano, Paul L., 131–3
Grant, Jamie, 357–9
Gravy Train, The, 316
Gray, Robert, 330–5
Great Artist Reconsiders the Homeric
    Simile, The, 323
Great Beam of the Milky Way, The, 222
Great South Land, From The, 183
Greenhalgh's Pub, 307
Grit, 297
Guide to the Perplexed, 275
Gull's Flight, The, 305
Gumaitj People, 327–9
Gurr, Robin, 252

Hail South Australia!, 16
Hall, Rodney, 277–8
Hammial, Philip, 288
Hampton, Susan, 353–5
Harford, Lesbia, 120–1
Harney, W.E., 134–5
Harpur, Charles, 31–4
Harris, Max, 216–17
Harris, Robert, 369–70
Harry, J.S., 292
Hart, Kevin, 375–7
Hartigan, P.J., 99
Hart-Smith, William, 165–7
Harvesters, The, 68
Harwood, Gwen, 214–16
Haskell, Dennis, 349–50
Hasluck, Nicholas, 320–3
Hatters, The, 217
Hayward, Charles W., 77
Headlined in Heaven, 131
Hear the Bird of Day, 199
Heritage, 116
Hetherington, Graeme, 287–8
Hewett, Dorothy, 227–8
Hey, Boys! Up Go We!, 12

Hobart Town, Van Diemen's Land, 171
Hodgins, Philip, 377–9
Hollow at Ilbalintja Soak, The, 182
Homage to Ferd. Holthausen, 214
Homage to the Canal People, 365
Honesty-stones, 292
Hooton, Harry, 157–9
Hope, A.D., 153–7
Horizon, The, 376
Hot Day in Sydney, A, 8
House-Mates, 131
How We Drove the Trotter, 65
Humphries, Barry, 276–7

Ice, 355
In a Bed-sitter, 170
In a Chain-store Cafeteria, 132
In Memoriam, 347
In Moncur Street, 227
Inca Tupac Upanqui, The, 166
Ingamells, Rex, 183–5
Inglorious Milton, The, 135
Inmate, An, 343
Inscription at Villers-Bretonneux, 299
Isaiah By Kerosene Lantern Light, 369
Islands, 320

James, Clive, 292–4
Jews Speak in Heaven, The, 345
John Gilbert was a Bushranger, 53
Johnny Weissmuller dead in Acapulco,
    292
Johnston, Martin, 347–9
Jones, Evan, 265–6
Journey, 277
June Fugue, 281

Kamilaroi songs, 38
Kangaroo, The, 6
Kangaroos, 179
Keesing, Nancy, 228–30
Kendall, Henry, 50–3
Kilaben Bay song, 36
King George V, 77
Kocan, Peter, 343–5
Koch, C.J., 268–9
Koel (Rainbird) and effigy, 315
Kyrielle: Party Politics, 118

Lalai (Dreamtime), 1
Lang, John Dunmore, 14–15
Langley, Eve, 157
Lansdown, Andrew, 373–5
Lass in the Female Factory, The, 18
Lavater, Louis, 78

Lawson, Henry, 79–83
Leaves, 110
Lee, Joyce, 185–6
Legend, 196
Lehmann, Geoffrey, 300–3
Leopard Skin, 189
Letter, The, 164
Letters, Francis, 135
Letters to Live Poets V, 255
Liberal or Innocent by Definition, 206
Lifetime Devoted to Literature, A, 286
Limejuice Tub, The, 13
Lindsay, Jack, 138–40
Litanies of Julia Pastrana (1832–1860),
    The, 282
Little Shoes that Died, The, 68
Llewellyn, Kate, 295–6
Lowe, Robert, 28–31
Lufthansa, 324

Macartney, Frederick, 118–19
McAuley, James, 205–7
McCrae, Hugh, 96–8
McCuaig, Ronald, 159–62
McDonald, Nan, 217–20
McDonald, Roger, 317–20
McGuire, Jack (?), 55
Mackay-Warna, Gordon, 297
Mackellar, Dorothea, 116–17
Mackenzie, Kenneth, 187–9
McMaster, Rhyll, 341–2
MacNamara, Francis, 19–28
Maiden, Jennifer, 359–60
Makhno's Philosophers, 202
Making Hay, 378
Malouf, David, 274–5
Malta, 360
Man and the Tree, The, 373
Man from Changi, The, 287
Man from Strathbogie, The, 150
Mangoes, 353
Mangrove, 194
Manifold, John, 202–4
Manly Ferry, 251
Manning, Frederic, 109–10
Man's a Sliding Mood, A, 86
Mapooram, 175
Marking time, 291
Marriage, 114
Martin, David, 200–1
Martin, Philip, 267
Martin Buber in the Pub, 217
Mathew, Ray, 253–5
Matthews, Harley, 123–30
'Maurice, Furnley', 101–8

May, 92
Mead, Philip, 371–3
Members of the Orchestra, The, 375
Men at Work, 352
Men who Come Behind, The, 82
Mercy, 374
Message from a Cross, 216
Metempsychosis, 141
Miidhu, 237–8
Mimshi Maiden, The, 96
Mission Work Boat, 316
Mitchell, Sam, 280
Moggy's Wedding, 46
Moll, E.G., 135–7
Molony, Linda, 379
Mother Doorstep, 60
Mother-in-law of the Marquis de Sade,
    The, 359
Mudie, Ian, 167
Murphy, E.G., 85–6
Murray, Les A., 289–91
Mutineer's Ballad, The, 344
Mutton Bird Man, 342
My Father's Country, 185
My Wish for My Land, 279

Narautjarri, Smiler, 238
Narranyeri people, 95
Nativity, 320
Nebuchadnezzar's Kingdom-Come, 235
Neilson, John Shaw, 92–4
New York Sonnet, 285
Ngunaitponi, 94–5
Nigger's Leap, New England, 195
Night Flight, 352
Night Flower, 301
1915, 317
Nunggubuyu People, 315–16

O, where were we before time was, 133
'O' Brien, John', 99
O'Conner, Mark, 335–9
O'Dowd, Bernard, 75–7
Old Australian Ways, 73
On First Looking into Chapman's
    Hesiod, 260
On the Death of Ludwig Erhard, 340
One Day, 255
One Tourist's Cologne, 340
Our Coming Countrymen, 34
Overbury, E.J., 55–6
Overlander, The, 168
Owen, Jan, 294–5
Oyster-Eaters, The, 194

Page, Geoff, 297–300
Palmer, Vance, 115–16
Pambardu, 303–4
Parabola, 155
Parkes, Henry, 34–6
Paterson, Andrew Barton, 70–5
Pearls, 356
Perry, Grace, 250–1
petition from the chain gang, A, 19
Phelp, J.A., 63–4
Philip, John, 251–2
Pietà, 311
Pioneer Lane, 351
Planes Landing, 358
Platypus, The, 178
Poem for Maurice O'Shea, A, 302
Poem in Time of Winter, 254
Poems: XIV, XXII, LXIX, 120
Poetry, 87
Point, The, 266
Pope Alexander VI, 300
Porter, Hal, 169–72
Porter, Peter, 258–62
Portrait of a Married Couple, 275
Powell, Craig, 320
Premeditations, 299
Pudjipangu, 238

Queer Thing, A, 228
Question Time, 138

Radiation Victim, 213
Rain Forest, 231
Rankin, Jennifer, 312–15
Recitative, 160
Reckoning, 271
Retrospection, 119
Reverie of a Mum, 229
Riddell, Alan, 250
Riddell, Elizabeth, 163–5
Ringneck Parrots, 183
Roberts, Nigel, 305
Robinson, Roland, 173–5
Rodriguez, Judith, 285–6
Rolls, Eric, 230–3
Romance, 113
Rowbotham, David, 234–5
Rowland, John, 235–7
Russians Breathing, 288

Sage in Unison, The, 204
Salom, Philip, 362–5
Sant, Andrew, 365–7
Saturday Tub, The, 69
Schoolgirls Hastening, 93

Scott, Margaret, 275–6
Scott, W.N., 233–4
Sea and other stories, The, 312
Search, The, 112
Secular, The, 272
Seeing St. James's, 253
Self-pity, 377
Shall then another, 187
Shapcott, Thomas W., 281–4
Shape-Changer, The, 273
Shaw, Charles, 112–13
Shaw, Dunstan, 119–20
Shearer's Wife, The, 98
Shelly Beach, 269
Shickered As He Could Be , 87
Simple Story, A, 215
Simpson, R.A., 262–3
Slessor, Kenneth, 140–5
Smell of Coal Smoke, The, 290
Smith, Vivian, 269–71
Smiths, The, 85
Snake, The, 115
Soliloquy at Potsdam, 258
Song Cycle of the Moon-bone, 239
Song for the Cattle, 198
Song of Hungarrda, The, 94
Song of the Progenitor-Hero Anakotar-
    inja, 180
Song: The Railway Train, 95
Songs from the Goulburn Island Song
    Cycle, 327
Songs of the Squatters, I and II, 28
Sound waves, 366
Sporting the Plaid, 272
Springtime it Brings On the Shearing,
    The, 55
Star-Tribes, The, 176
Steele, Peter, 291–2
Stephens, James Brunton, 56–7
Stewart, Douglas, 189–93
Stewart, Harold, 204–5
Stow, Randolph, 278–80
Streets of Forbes, The, 55
Stringybark Cockatoo, The, 49
Study in Blue, 265
Suburban Lovers, 264
Suburban Song, 163
Sun-Hunters, The, 337
Sunrise Sequence, 239
Sweet Disorder in the Dress, A, 157
Sweet silence after bells!, 91
Sydney, 369

Table-birds, 188
Taking the Census, 45

Talbot, Norman, 286–7
Tanks, 341
Tasmania, 271
Taylor, Andrew, 304
Terra Australis, 191–3
That Which We Call a Rose, 350
Thatcher, Charles R., 42–7
Their Thoughts Cling to Everything they See on the Way, 309
There is a Place in Distant Seas, 7
Thiele, Colin, 212–13
This Land, 167
This Year, Before It Ends, 157
Thunderstorm, 280
Time of Turtles, 250
Tipping, Richard, 352–3
Tjinapirrgarri, 296
To my father Norman alone in the Blue Mountains, 140
To the Red Lory, 93
Tom Farley, 212
Tongues, 267
Tranter, John, 323–4
Traveller, The, 95
Travelling Post Office, The, 70
Tree, The, 201
Trenches, The, 109
Trubridge, B.A., 108–9
Trucker, The, 99
Turner, W.J., 113–14
Turtles Hatching, 335
Two Men, 373
Two Sisters, The, 176
Two tongue-pointing (satirical) songs, 38

Unaipon, David, 94–5
Unborn, 92
Unit, 86
Up, Up, Home & Away, 361

Van Diemen's Land, 15, 310
Verandahs, 252
Victoria Market, 137
Victoria Markets Recollected in Tran-
quillity, The, 102
Virgin Martyr, The, 58
Vision, 130
Visitation, The, 294
'Vrepont, Brian', 108–9

Wail of the Waiter, The, 59
Wakeful in the Township, 163
Walker, Kath, 207–8
Wallace-Crabbe, Chris, 272–4
War Dance, 237
Wars of Imperialism, 370
We Are Going, 207
Webb, Francis, 246–8
Well, The, 362
Wellington, 32
West of Alice, 134
West Paddocks, 151
Whaler's Pig, The, 88
Whaler's Rhyme, 38
What I Have Written I Have Written, 259
Whately, Richard, 7–8
When Your Pants Begin to Go, 81
Whenever I have …, 102
Wild Honey, 247
Wilmot, Frank, 101–8
Wind At Your Door, The, 147
Windmill at Mandanthanunguna, 303
Wings, 197
Winter, 363
Witch Doctor's Magic Flight, The, 238
Wolaroi song, 38
Woman at the Washtub, The, 61
Women are not Gentlemen, 123
Women's rondo, 37
Wonguri-Mandjigai People, 239-46
Woolagoodjah, Sam, 1–5
Wooyeo Ball, The, 64
World of Dreams, The, 363
Wright, Judith, 195–8

Year of the Foxes, The, 274

Zwicky, Fay, 271–2